ADOLESCENT GIRLS IN CRISIS

ADOLESCENT GIRLS IN CRISIS

Intervention and Hope

Martha B. Straus

W. W. Norton & Company
New York • London

For information about permission to
reproduce selections from this book, write to
Permissions, W. W. Norton & Company, Inc.,
500 Fifth Avenue, New York, NY 10110

Manufacturing by: Haddon Craftsmen
Production Manager: Leeann Graham

Library of Congress Cataloging-in-Publication Data

Straus, Martha B., 1956–
  Adolescent girls in crisis : intervention and hope / Martha B. Straus. — 1st ed.
    p. ; cm.
"A Norton professional book."
Includes bibliographical references and index.
ISBN 978-0-393-70447-1 (hardcover)
1. Adolescent psychotherapy. 2. Teenage girls — Mental health. 3. Teenage
girls — Psychology I. Title
[DNLM: 1. Mental Disorders—therapy. 2. Adolescent Development. 3. Ado-
lescent Psychology. 4. Adolescent. WS 463 S912a 2007]

RJ503.S79 2007
616.89'140835–dc22   2007011544

ISBN 13: 978-0-393-70447-1

W. W. Norton & Company, Inc., 500 Fifth Avenue, New York, N.Y. 10110
www.wwnorton.com

W. W. Norton & Company Ltd., Castle House,
75/76 Wells St., London W1T 3QT
1 2 3 4 5 6 7 8 9 0

To my parents, Betty and Nathan Straus,
for always believing that the wildest fillies could
become the best horses.

CONTENTS

Acknowledgments

This is a book about adolescent girls. Thus it is fitting that my first acknowledgment goes to those teens I know and love the best, Lizzy and
Molly Straus, the two shining, albeit occasionally challenging and hum-
bling, exemplars in my life.

Deepest gratitude also goes to:

Peter, my beloved shy carpenter, who designed and built us a beautiful place to work, live, and be happy, who endured my irritating inability
to write and listen at the same time, and who believed, even through the
defeating and bleak Vermont winter, that I could finish this project;

My parents, Betty and Nathan, siblings, Andi, and Joey, and my cousins,
Billy and Lynne, for still being immutable in their love;

Beloved women friends down the road, over the highway and across
the country, with their straight talk and raucous laughter;

The bright and supremely competent Jenna Forrider, research assistant extraordinaire;

My wonderful editors at Norton, Susan Munro, former editor and ger-
minator of the idea for this book, and Deborah Malmud, eternally patient,
smart, and supportive;

And to all the adolescent girls and their families I have had the pleasure to treat over the years, for believing that I could help them—and showing me the way.

This preface is written from the trenches. It is quiet here because it is a Saturday morning, and my primary combatants are both still asleep, having stayed up late watching *Wedding Crashers* for the 27th time. They curled up together in Lizzy's bed, with her laptop perched between them. It was a cozy sight, but their easy intimacy belies years of intense warfare between them. Lizzy once told her TV-watching, gum-snapping, Oreo-consuming little sister that she was, "everything that's wrong with America." For her part, Molly attempted to Elmer's glue Lizzy's door shut, and then gave a horrible shag haircut to Lizzy's door beads. These stories are amusing memories from back in the distant reaches of time, BT (Before Teenager). During this BT era, I was a confident, even smug, parent and therapist, eternally patient, generally optimistic. Even though the girls fought with each other and caused sisterly misery on a grand scale, I had strategies abounding for regaining the peace, and the arguments with me were pretty tolerable—as I probably inaccurately recall now.

Then imperceptibly, they entered this next life stage, and my expertise began to ooze from me like perspiration. I had been an angry and confused adolescent girl back in the day, so I simply (and incorrectly) assumed that most anything they went through would be like looking in the mirror for me. I suppose like many of us who came of age in the 1960s and 1970s, I figured I had pretty much invented adolescent alienation and risk-taking. I would recognize all the signs and symptoms; I'd know what to do. Plus, I reasoned, I was a trained professional. People paid big bucks to hear me speak, to seek my counsel. I had logged the hours. I had the answers, so bring on adolescent girlhood.

To say that the past few years have taught me humility is a glaring understatement. Words like *shame*, *despair*, and *fury* sadly fit better. Many times, when my kids have gotten in serious trouble, have made hideously bad choices, have slammed doors and sobbed in their beds, have raged at me (and me at them), shredding the fine veneer of family life even further, my self-assurance has leaked out some more. I fantasize sometimes that if I were found out, the impersonation police would come and cart me away for pretending to be an "expert" on adolescent girls when I was so patently a rank amateur. (Please note as well that *expert* has mutated to "expert" and even "so-called expert" during the past five years.)

Also, I hadn't anticipated that the new closeness between my teenaged kids would often be exclusive, that I'd be dismissed to the Old Team so abruptly. Turns out I even had unfounded confidence in my coolness, my years following Dylan and the Dead notwithstanding.

But throughout the period of AT, I've made some discoveries that are a little transformative, too. I find myself listening differently to parent-clients as they discuss the jams they are in with their girls. While I think I'm actually hoping they'll give me good suggestions sometimes, I'm also less quick to judge, and much more sympathetic. I know that if these problems had easy solutions clients would have figured them out without me.

I like to think that I've also become an easier friend. Parents of other teens I knew socially have always shared their worry stories with me, but in recent years I take some solace and strength in their misery, too, realizing that we are all groping along together, finding our collective way. The sharing fortifies all of us. We've all driven a few hours with adolescents, wanting to say something but the music is too throbbing, or the silence too loud.

And I've also rediscovered what I think I knew all along, that the steady hum of love and connection has to continue into the teen years, even growing louder at times to drown out all the other competing sounds. The hum is the small but vital vibration of family life. It is in the back-to-school supplies shopping in the fall, and late-night snacks after homework in the winter. It's in pancakes for breakfast and tea for a cold, listening to music they love, and occasional wild family meals with table manners that require overlooking so, unchastised, they'll stay just a little longer.

Inevitably, we lose the hum as busy lives and preoccupations overtake us. What's more important though is our determination to retune when we stop and can't find the resonance. With adolescent girls, as with all people, this conscious repair makes us stronger and deepens our intimacy. I'm not as relentlessly optimistic as I once was but I still know how to hold hope in the hum.

As my adolescents wake up, and bleary-eyed come to find me, sprawling on the couch and each other, my day begins again. The conflicts and misunderstandings of yesterday are mostly forgiven or forgotten. We reconnect and move ahead yet another time. Being on the front line like this has surely humbled me (and has made it harder to write this book), but it gives me a different kind of hope, too. Helping adolescent girls in crisis is about fixing broken connections with them. It's as deceptively simple as that.

So while I think what you're about to read will be valuable and useful, I feel compelled to tell you this up front: Even though we have to keep trying (and that's really what matters ultimately), no one really knows what to do all the time, not even the so-called experts. If you don't believe me, ask my adolescent girls.

ADOLESCENT GIRLS IN CRISIS

Too many adolescent girls are in a crisis of rage and despair. By the thousands, they disappear through starvation, carve indecipherable messages onto their arms, hide weeping in their rooms, run far from home, try to die, join gangs, get pregnant, forget who they are with alcohol and drugs, and sign off on their futures by dropping out of school. They feel unsafe, unknown, and unloved. Their experience isn't like anything we can imagine from our own teen years; the risks they face are far greater than ever before.

Adolescent Girls in Crisis describes how to reach the kids behind these frightening behaviors, the struggling families and systems coming to their aid, and the culture of violence that is trying to devastate them. This book, written for counselors and therapists, will also help parents with the toughest decisions they'll ever have to make: when to get more involved, when to back off, when to hospitalize, how to just sit nearby and listen.

Lots of adults are worrying about adolescent girls; programs, interventions, and experts abound, ready to help. Parents pore over *Reviving Ophelia* (Pipher, 1994) trying to figure out what is happening to their beloved daughters. And therapists *are* making a difference for the girls and families we treat. But for every success we may have with a troubled girl, there are many others to take her place, with stories that sound even harder and sadder. Why?

The reasons are complicated and compelling: Interventions are weak and fragmented; institutions are overwhelmed, with inadequate resources; the gap between the rich and poor is growing; the stakes have gotten higher; normal adolescent experimentation has become deadly. There is no more innocence; kids are living cynically, taking their cues from adults about what's valuable and who's not; parents, busy with their own lives and working too hard, are ignorant or helpless; families and communities don't care for their own the way they need to. Schools are overcrowded and alienating; violence in society, especially violence against girls, has become too toxic to withstand, and permeates the media, the Internet, and the streets; advertising contributes to unprecedented feelings of self-loathing and neediness. These girls think they have no future; too many of the jobs in the changing world are impossibly high-tech or numbingly dead-end. The backlash against feminism is severe; misogyny is at an all-time high; it's time to worry about boys instead. The list of explanations is long; we seem to have a good grasp of the problem. And our increasing awareness and understanding still helps girls—if just one at a time. All this knowledge and concern has seemingly had little impact on the collective distress of adolescent girls.

Further, the response of adults is not entirely compassionate. *Adolescent Girls in Crisis* is also written to "set the record straight." It counters the marginalization of adolescent girls in the popular press and consciousness with better information and real strategies to help. The distorted and despairing depictions that lead to hand wringing and hopelessness require critical analysis. Are girls really meaner than boys now and sexually out of control? Are they more violent, disengaged, and purposeless? Too much of what we read in the news suggests a kind of thinly veiled hostility toward and fear of girls, disguised as concern. But the result of such news is to sensationalize, excite, estrange, and ultimately diminish adolescent girls. It limits the discourse about them to pieces of girl, and to extremes of either our prurient obsession with their sexuality, or our paternalistic need to contain them. This book is written to help make girls whole again.

The lower and fragmenting expectations that adults have for some girls also make it harder for them to hold onto their own sense of purpose and future as they grow. Many are cultivating instead a rage that can take a while for us to see. Segregated from adult contact by choice and culture, they become suspicious of us and what we have to offer. Most often, girls, unlike boys, retreat, harming themselves, not others. Parents may notice the absence, but chalk it up to the mysteries of female adolescence. Or they'll ask what's wrong. But daughters will keep them out while secretly wishing for more questions, and more attention. Sometimes, parents give up too soon, taking a shut door at face value.

If they confide in anyone, depressed and anxious girls confide mostly in friends. Or they'll finally find their way to school guidance counselors and teachers, sobbing that they have tried to kill themselves, they may be pregnant, they're vomiting every meal, that they're being harassed or abused. Some girls figure out how to tell their parents how miserable they feel, some leave notes or even poems around hoping adults will read them. The path is often tortuous, and usually it takes a while before they do tell, or we do notice. But what do we do next? *Adolescent Girls in Crisis* answers this question.

It appears that many girls have also fully entered territory that used to be the province of boys. They're smoking and drinking, they're getting arrested, they're homeless and on the run—most of them right in believing that the streets are safer than their homes have been. They're out of the mainstream in large numbers. Girls, it seems, are doing all the rages—and outrages.

Still, these girls are communicating, reaching out, craving contact, hoping. We have to listen harder, respond more quickly, guide them more surely. We need to help them take on a culture that insists upon winners and losers, cheerleaders and geeks, predators and victims, Madonnas and whores, privilege and disadvantage. It takes courage and resilience to get through the adolescent passage into responsible adulthood. Their rage and despair contain the seeds of powerful hope. In fact, it's the passion of these girls that makes therapy, and healing, possible. Here's how.

Adolescent Girls in Crisis is divided into two sections. Although both parts have intervention in mind, the first provides the background and developmental theory that informs good practice. It is written within a developmental–relational–systemic framework, exploring the roles of the individual, family, community, and culture upon adolescent girl development. This section begins by entering the secret lives of adolescent girls (information obtained both from 25 years of practice, life, supervision, and the research literature), and discussing how development gets nipped in the bud for so many as they succumb to intolerable pressure from family, community, and society. The rage they experience is mirrored and amplified by a culture of violence against women, and institutions that encourage girls to vanish just as they are beginning to show up. In too many ways, girls are fighting a kind of war (seemingly, at times, against themselves) in which their very survival is at issue.

This section also considers the importance of attachment and belonging for girls, and the loss of vital connections that adolescence brings for so many. Here, *Adolescent Girls in Crisis* argues, girls become increasingly disengaged from home, school, purposeful work, and community involvement exactly at the developmental point when they need even more meaningful contacts than ever before in their lives. In fact, for girls, a sense of isolation usually leads directly to considerable distress. And because their identity is so fused with relationships, without a measure of social success somewhere, despair drips in steadily, like a leaky faucet. This section concludes with a critical analysis of the social policies that keep girls disconnected and disenfranchised.

Adolescent Girls in Crisis's second section takes on identification, diagnosis, and treatment of many of the troubled and troubling behaviors, what to look for before there's a crisis (and when a crisis has begun), what to worry about, and, most of all, what to do. A transtheoretical model, rooted in developmental, relational, and systemic paradigms is proposed. The 10 principles of good practice that underlie this work are largely adaptable to more specific theories and techniques. The all-important first meetings are described in detail, with special attention devoted to calming the systems, getting the adolescent engaged in the solution, finding strengths to build on, and creating a reasonable plan of action. Through empathy and respect, with concern for both the adolescent and her family, we can make thoughtful decisions about what's most important to start working on.

This section explores interventions: therapies for adolescent girls that are best suited to different disorders and problems, medications that can help (in a chapter written by Robert Racusin, MD, a child psychiatrist), and out-of-home options including hospitalization and alternative programs. Filled with concrete strategies and also informed by research and clinical experience, these chapters provide guidelines for making solid and compassionate treatment decisions during frightening and volatile times. Finally, *Adolescent Girls in Crisis* briefly looks ahead, considering the hopeful future for adolescent girls in their journey to become strong and confident women.

Giles Corey and the Dance of the Seven Veils

It was me there
Under those planks and stones.
Some round and smooth as children
Others smearing coal on my belly.

The grain of the wood was of course
Simple, northerly,
More like a river than anything else
That chases itself into the sea.

And when I will drift
Like a bathroom door after a hurricane
My skin will soak up all the salt
And I will collect a shell around me
Like a mayfly.

When I am an oyster
(my only fears gulls and late tides)
I promise to be a surer shoe,
More like my own scapula, a wing
Rough as regiment
And twice as lonely.

I will leap as if to fly
(though, if you remember,
I will be only half an angel)

And this wanting will grow to pearl in my guts.
I too will go, if like Salome
I may be pressed to death,
in my mother's garden
By soldiers' shields (surely an early planting
Yields an early bloom)
For desiring.

—*Elizabeth B. Straus*

I
The Culture of Rage
and Despair

CHAPTER ONE

THE SECRET LIVES
OF TEENAGE GIRLS

Delia is 15. Her parents say she's always been a great kid. They're recently divorced and they both work full time. They don't really speak to each other, but they are caring parents. Delia has a little brother with special needs; they give him the attention he requires, and she's always been very understanding about that. She helps him, too. Delia's been getting bad grades in school this year even though she had selected classes that weren't challenging for her. She's not participating in any extracurricular activities because she didn't make the varsity soccer team, and spends most of her free time at home and in her room. Delia's been feeling overwhelmed and depressed for several months, but she didn't tell anyone about it. She doesn't want to worry her parents so she tells her mother she's fine, she has friends, she's just not that motivated in school right now. And girls "chat" on the Internet so it's been hard for either of her parents to glean much from the silent telephone about Delia's social problems. Delia does go to occasional parties. Indeed, two nights before we met, she went to a little gathering where she got alcohol poisoning and almost died. Her mother was completely shocked and rightfully terrified. She called for an appointment saying she didn't know that Delia was so unhappy, and she didn't believe Delia had ever consumed alcohol before. Therapy became an opportunity for Delia and her parents to get to know each other again.

Like Delia, too many teenage girls have become strangers among us. Maybe parents, teachers, therapists, and other adults who care are too inattentive, or maybe we can't resist the cultural riptide that is pulling our girls away. Perhaps we believe the darkness of this adolescent tunnel is just a journey they'll get through on their own anyway, as so many of us did before them. Maybe our reactions are the best we can muster, so we have to just trust that we're doing a good enough job intervening and helping.

And it's true: the vast majority of these girls will, with a little luck, emerge on the adult side by their late 20s, a little bruised and lonely perhaps, but whole enough. Some will make it into therapists' offices then, and wonder, how was it possible that no one saw, that no one tried to help, that no one seemed to know what to do? In hindsight anyway, their suffering was obvious enough.

Often, our responses aren't even adequate. We can do better by girls. Whatever the causes (and it matters what they are), the loss is theirs and ours. It's deeply personal, explicitly cultural, unarguably societal. Now so many are furious, and they'll do anything, no matter how wild or self-destructive, to get us back (even if it means getting back at us). There's hope in the anger; they're doing what they must to get our attention, to be noticed, held, and guided through the passage. They're not giving up.

And that rage is exactly the fuel we need. When we reach out to them with a hopeful intensity that matches their despair, the synergy we'll create could heat a small Vermont town for the winter. In disconnection from adults, and from purpose, we lost them. In relationship and participation we'll come to know them again. The crisis of adolescent girls belies a failure of sensible social policy, overwhelmed institutions, and the hollow excesses of commerce. But like politics, all adolescence is local. Girls become resilient one at a time, and their healing occurs in families, in schools, and in communities.

Maybe someone, usually a parent, once knew them in glorious, intimate detail. When they were born, if they were lucky, an adult who cared knew when they ate and slept, the length of their eyelashes and fingernails, what made them smile, startle, and screech. A vigilant caretaker could be certain of where they were, each minute. In the wrong location? They were simply lifted up and moved somewhere else. Adult knowledge was powerful and made kids safe—and parents confident.

In all other life experiences, we know more as time goes on. With children, sometimes it seems, we can only know less. They take their first steps, symbolically, away from our arms. Parental attunement at its best is oscillating and full of disconnections.

And it doesn't help that privacy in the Western world comes quickly—too quickly. When they begin school, even preschool, suddenly, girls have secret lives. Things happen during their days that parents will never know about, no matter how vigilant they are, how many questions they ask, how intimate they remain in other ways. Sadly, contemporary parents aren't usually that attentive. Busy with adult lives—work, relationships, chores—providing kids with teams and activities, encouraging their friendships, getting dinner on the table, and bills paid, parents seldom spend all that much time with their children, even when they're young enough to still have bedtimes.

Maybe Delia's parents shouldn't have been so surprised when they realized their daughter was depressed and binge drinking. But it is common that girls lead mysterious lives: they have friends their parents have never met, are listening to bands they've never heard of (and maybe even more astonishingly, to those geriatric groups from the '60s), are using designer drugs unknown a couple of decades ago, are starving and binging, crying themselves to sleep, and carving incomprehensible messages into their arms. Parents, and the rest of the adults who might be responsible for these children, may hardly have had a clue, even though in retrospect, such clues are usually strewn about like dirty laundry.

Conversation with adolescent girls sometimes seems like intergalactic travel, and because we don't know what else to do, the most tenacious adults among us keep speaking English and adhering to our familiar customs, with predictably mixed results. We practice that humorous definition of insanity: We do the same thing repeatedly, each time expecting a new outcome. And we probably are a little off-kilter, finding ourselves in bewilderingly alien territory. We were adolescents once; how could it be so different?

Sometimes, adults nearby may have glimmers of the child they knew; a moment of enthusiasm, a poignant vulnerability, unveiled neediness. Parents may be at home, waiting for them, trying to get them to eat, to sleep, to shower, to talk, and their daughters don't seem to notice or care. But a common complaint among girls is that their parents are "never there." They want to share a few details late, when most adults can't keep their eyes open, and are hurt when they learn they didn't hear of plans to eat at Aunt Sally's. On their birthday, they may expect the same kind of chocolate cake with green frosting they had when they were 8, and into emerging adulthood insist on sitting in "their" chair at the dinner table. They have a few stuffed animals they won't part with that they'll take to college or their own apartment with them one day. Even if they flinch or duck when caring adults want to hug them, they may be devastated that such contact has diminished.

As has probably been the case for hundreds of years, teenage girls can be so exasperating. They express bitter resentment—even raising the possibility that adults might be ruining their lives—when needs aren't met instantly upon request. There are times when seemingly every limit imposed by parents' leads to a fight, or silent fury. Favors done yesterday are forgotten; they want to know what have you done for me today? They weep, they sulk, and they rant. They "borrow" without asking, and express insufficient remorse when they damage or lose the item. They feel things deeply.

The new angle on this old and familiar story is the anger. They're mad at themselves, their families, and their communities. Many are furious about living entrapped in a culture that seemingly offers them so many choices but insists that they kill so much time with concerns about how they look and behave. Just at the moment in life when they have the skills and experience to begin to really take a stand, they feel compelled to shrink and disappear. Thank goodness some of them are enraged.

When we can stand out of the line of fire, we see that this very passion is what makes adolescent girls so compelling and remarkable. And, as we try to know them again, we may also find that they don't have to be strangers. Theirs is a language we can learn. We must first be willing to take the time, and to summon up our best adult selves.

A Day in the Life

We make many assumptions about teenage girls, most of them inaccurate. Adults—parents, researchers, teachers, therapists, people who care about these kids—know remarkably little about how they spend their days, think about their lives, plan their futures, feel about themselves and others. We base our often-erroneous impressions on our memories—of our own teen years, of those little girls we used to know so well—and on our teenagers' most overt behaviors.

But the differences are disorienting, like visiting a city we once lived in with a transformed downtown. Our references to the past offer only little guidance. And teenage girls often act in such confusing ways that we frequently don't know whether to approach or withdraw, to talk or be silent, to do or to wait, to try again, or to give up. A map of the town helps us to familiarize ourselves with streets we really ought to recognize.

How Teenaged Girls Spend Their Time

Teenaged girls spend, on average, about half of their waking hours at school and working. Surprisingly, they spend less than 10% of their time with friends outside of school (Schneider & Stevenson, 1999). Contrary to common belief, adolescent girls are alone much more than they are with friends.

When they are with their peers, girls report a higher sense of self-esteem, and feel happier, more powerful, and more motivated than when alone (Schneider & Stevenson, 1999). When teens are together, they tend to spend around a quarter of their time socializing—hanging out or partying; another quarter on maintaining their appearance, eating and moving from place-to-place; slightly less than a quarter on homework; and about 10% on hobbies and exercise. They devote the remaining 15% to watching television and playing games.

Girls gab as much as they always have, and a primary enduring topic of conversation is relationships—their own and those of others'. They also discuss their parents quite a bit. As Mary Pipher (1994) notes, "Adolescents claim not to hear their parents, but with their friends they discuss endlessly all parental attitudes. With amazing acuity, they sense nuances, doubt, shades of ambiguity, discrepancy, and hypocrisy" (p. 24). The peer culture is also more compelling, pervasive, and unguided than in the past. In the absence of sufficient adult involvement, the peer group becomes a mixed blessing because it supports girls while seldom raising expectations for behavior. For many, the social group comes to offer values at the lowest common denominator—but it beats being alone.

And teenage girls are alone 20% of their waking hours—more than twice as much time as they spend with friends. Alienation is such a key element of despair for adolescent girls, and so the extent and meaning of their solitude is noteworthy. This percentage translates to about 3½ hours each day. Time spent alone increases as students progress from middle school through high school; 12th graders spend close to 50% more time alone than 6th graders (Schneider & Stevenson, 1999).

Teenaged girls are mostly alone, even during the few waking hours of their day when other family members are also home—and conscious. On average, they are conversing with parents (when talking is the primary activity) less than 45 minutes a week (Hofferth, 2001; R. Putnam, 2000). The research on communication suggests that, consequently, many adolescents feel inadequately connected to their parents and families (Doherty & Carlson, 2002). Once they don't need adults to meet as many physical and instrumental needs, the opportunities for interaction may diminish rapidly. During most of this "family time," in the evenings and on the weekends, teens are in their rooms: on the phone, listening to music, on the computer, or otherwise engaged. And their parents are similarly preoccupied with the tasks of their own lives.

The family supper is also history: there has been a 33% decrease over the past three decades in families who say they have dinner regularly (R. Putnam, 2000). In the typical American household, (including those with younger kids) the average number of dinners eaten together is three per week; the average length of dinner is 20 minutes (Wylie, 1997). Teenage girls are skipping supper, grabbing fast food, or something out of the fridge, and retreating back to their rooms. Even factoring in a generous allotment of peer socialization, family time, and the occasional shared meal, many teenage girls are virtually alone upward of six hours a day.

The more adolescent girls are alone, the less likely it is that they use their solitude productively, or with real pleasure. They spend considerable time "killing time" watching TV (about 21 hours a week, on average) and movies, talking on the phone, playing on the computer and Internet, and attending to their appearance and possessions. And it isn't hard, in most schools, to get by with precious little homework. Teenaged girls are spending less than 15% of their free time completing school assignments (Schneider & Stevenson, 1999).

Girls who are alone more than 3½ hours a day are more likely than those who are rarely alone to watch television and sleep, and as may be evident, are less likely to participate in sports and other extracurricular activities. Adults may look at this loafing schedule and turn deep shades of envy-green. Many of us feel as though we haven't had three free hours since we were adolescents. But too much solitude can be stressful. Teenagers report having lower self-esteem, being less happy, enjoying what they are doing less, and feeling less active when they are alone (Csikszentmihalyi, 1997).

Over the preteen and teen years, too much alone-time is also associated with early involvement with sex, drugs, alcohol, and the legal system (Office of Juvenile Justice and Delinquency Prevention, 1999). It isn't surprising that unsupervised time after school is most commonly when teenagers have sexual intercourse, and most juvenile crimes are committed. Children who start to take care of themselves after school at 8 or 9 years of age are twice as likely as kids with adults around them to get into premature sex, illegal substances, and delinquent activity.

Although it is likely that they have extra hours to do homework, as a group, teens who have more free time also do less well academically. Studies show that nearly 8 in 10 teens (79%) who engage in after-school activities are "A" and "B" students but only half (52%) of adolescents who do not participate in after-school activities earn these high marks. The adolescent who participates in no other activities is also five times as likely (15 versus 3%) to be a "D" student, and three times more likely to skip classes and use drugs (Afterschool Alliance, 2004). Too much time alone is associated with a range of emotional, educational, and behavioral problems for girls, even if they seem to want it, or say they prefer it.

How Teenage Girls Feel

Popular culture appears designed to keep adolescent girls fretting over the dullest possible topics, reinforcing a worldview that barely extends beyond the bathroom scale, the lunchroom table, and the local mall. Developmentally, many girls are susceptible to this limited and limiting range because they tend to think concretely and egocentrically anyway. The pressure to conform is reinforced by parents, teachers, and peers who, even in this modern era, still adhere to the deadly notion that good girls are meek and respectful. Teenage girls are outwardly and reflexively obedient to the expectations of adults and peers, and to the edicts of fashion and advertising, but at an often devastating personal cost.

Stressed Good Girls

Throughout their lives, girls of all races and classes have to face the restricting and polarizing ways that we talk about being male or female. With the onset of adolescence and the development of more abstract reasoning abilities, many girls gain a new awareness about what the dominant culture has to say about gender roles (Brown & Gilligan, 1992). These messages are reinforced, about 3,000 times a day, by advertising (Kilbourne, 1999). Girls feel deeply the pressure to be either one or the other: pure or sexual, passive or active, feeling or thinking, selfless or selfish, good or bad—in essence the same old dichotomy: feminine or masculine.

The choices that girls make are often informed by this extreme way of thinking. Girls who resist loudly during this period of social conformity, may find themselves outcasts from the "popular" groups. Their resistance creates both adult and peer anxiety not only because they are disrupting conventional sex role socialization, but because they are disturbing the prevailing polarized construction of social reality (Haste, 1994).

But many girls are protesting, not just those who are confrontational and vocal. A growing body of exciting research describes adolescent girls' frustration and anger at the impossibility of bringing their rich and varied life experiences into relationship with such a narrow social construction (Brown, 1998, 2003; Brown & Gilligan, 1992; Fine, 1992; Haste, 1994; Rogers, 1993). In more subtle but persistent ways, they're refusing to fit easily into the one-dimensional category, "female." These young protesters have been driven underground. And as Brown (1998) has noted, they often struggle with what to do next:

> At early adolescence girls seemed to see the patriarchal framework for the first time and name its effect on their lives: they would have to narrow their feelings and modulate their voices if they were to make a smooth transition into the dominant culture. Strong feelings like anger would push people away; full use of their bodies and their brains would make people uncomfortable. (p. x)

To respond to this new awareness, girls behave in a variety of ways, some of them quite self-destructive. This gender-based stress crosses race and class lines. In its most simple and obvious form, even the most articulate and entitled girls struggle with the same old oppression: popularity (as defined by whether high-status boys like them) via a desperate slavery to appearance and artifice, even if it betrays the girl's core sense of self. And with such pretense as a goal, the chances for disappointment and self-loathing are virtually guaranteed. Those who resist entirely face ostracism; those who concede face loss. Accommodating to the stress of these rigid gender roles, therefore, leads to a near-universal experience of sadness shared by even the most furious and defiant girl.

Sadness

As girls make the transition through adolescence, they invariably sustain losses in order to fit in. No matter how loud the protest, it's usual to find genuine sorrow below the surface. These losses include, for example, the loss of voice that Brown (1998) describes, the narrowing of desires and expectations, capitulation to conventional notions of femininity, and the loss of childhood itself. Girls lose the authentic connections they once had with parents and friends, and a simple body that they can be in charge of. They lose the nurture of unsexualized hugging and cuddling. They lose the supportive familiarity of local elementary schools to the chaos and anonymity of regional middle and high schools. They lose confidence, and ambition, and wonder.

Not surprisingly, the theme of loss is recurrent in therapy with adolescent girls. Though we don't always think of it this way, treatment of adolescent girls is in some part, grief work. Of all the losses they typically endure, however, perhaps none is more harmful to development than being cut off from the vital connection they've had to their true feelings, especially anger.

Anger

By the time they reach adolescence, girls learn that anger is a complicated emotion for people, but especially for women. They are under extreme pressure to split off their anger and will be rewarded socially when they do. Younger girls seem more resilient in part because they know why they're mad and can say so. By contrast, teenaged girls, especially those from the white middle class, "learn what to say, how to speak, what to feel and think, if they want to be the right kind of girl, if they want to be listened to, accepted, rewarded, included" (Brown, 1998, p. 12). Good girls don't get mad: conventional femininity and anger are subversive of each other.

In a myriad of subtle and overt ways, girls get the message that they aren't supposed to be angry. Given how passionately they feel most of the time, and the range of injustices and losses they experience, they pay a mighty toll for even trying to give up their anger. Later, though maybe not until they become adult women, they often find they've turned their rage into depression. Jean Baker Miller (1976) has suggested that girls and women learn that this transformation of anger into (a more socially acceptable) depression ensures they won't be ostracized from the group that they depend upon for their survival and well-being. Girls usually do whatever they have to so they can stay connected with people.

Many girls don't realize that their anger has been changed over until they grow into depressed adults. But the connection between suppressed anger and depression is widely accepted. In one depression workbook for women for example, readers are asked to look back at how their anger was met when they were younger, and fill out this checklist (Frankel, 1992, pp. 21–22):

1. I was sent to my room until I cooled off.
2. I was told that nice girls don't get angry.
3. I was ignored.
4. I was punished (physically, verbally, or lost some privilege).
5. I was threatened with religious implications (e.g., not going to heaven or God wouldn't like it).
6. I was told to turn the other cheek.
7. I was made fun of, laughed at, or my anger became a family joke.
8. I had love, and affection withheld from me.
9. I was told my anger wasn't justified.
10. I was told anger wasn't ladylike.
11. I was treated as if I were out of control.
12. I was told that I was weak or somehow less of a person for being angry.
13. I was treated as if I had committed a sin.
14. I was told it was a flaw in my character (e.g., "You're just like your father.")
15. I was told I was ugly or in some other way physically unappealing.

This is a compelling list on its own, to be sure. And when girls stop expressing anger directly, they are not merely losing touch with feelings. Along with this loss of expression comes the loss of a capacity to locate the source of their pain and thus to do something about it. Many adults who ask adolescent girls about feelings are amazed to hear how little internal connection there seems to be between experience and this emotion. When girls can be angry, they can also be reassured that they are worth such powerful feelings—there is someone in there worth being mad about.

Anger serves an additional purpose because it can also connect people who are enduring similar injustice. Although depression doesn't actively alienate others the way that rage might, ironically, it is ultimately more isolating and private. Without anger, girls also lose the impetus to act against any inequity done to them—and we don't need to send any more silenced women out into the world. Down the line, too, if we take away girls' anger, then we also take away the foundation for women's political resistance (Brown, 1998; Fine, 1992). Such methodology sounds more like the treatment of girls and women in less-democratic countries, but sadly describes too much of U.S. cultural silencing as well.

In a climate that forbids or overly regulates the expression of angry feelings, attendant frustration and fear often lead to aggression. Not surprisingly then, girls express a good deal of aggression, though it is likely to become increasingly indirect after it peaks at around age 11. Our limited tolerance for such aggression in middle-school aged girls is belied by our animalistic descriptions of their "cattiness" and "bitchiness." But the meanness is legendary; such may be the consequence of anger ignored, deferred, and buried.

Indirect Aggression

Adolescent girls often become expert at indirect aggression, defined by researchers as "a type of behavior in which the perpetrator attempts to inflict pain in such a manner that she makes it seem as though there has been no intention at all. Accordingly, she is more likely to avoid counteraggression and if possible to remain unidentified" (Bjorkqvist, Lagerspetz, & Kaukiainen, 1992, p. 117). Girls express indirect aggression in two ways: toward others, and toward themselves.

Oddly, most people don't see this behavior in girls as problematic, and we are generally willing to write it off by more-or-less accepting it as a kind of fact, that "girls will be girls." We don't consider it to be a maladaptive response to narrow and oppressive expectations for femininity. Instead, when we compare the indirect aggression of girls to boys slugging each other at recess, we reframe it as a sign of girls' greater emotional and psychological maturity, a consequence of increased social intelligence and better self-control.

But indirectness leads to confusion. Girls may smile, cry, or stare blankly when they're really furious. At other times, they may express anger to conceal problems (for example, saying they hate their teacher instead of admitting they don't understand the assignment). Such indirectness then has a huge effect on our ability to respond authentically and directly to girls' feelings. Worse, over time, girls have increasing difficulty identifying their angry feelings in the first place.

Relational Aggression

A growing body of research describes the ways in which adolescent girls express indirect aggression in their relationships (e.g., Brown, 2003; Crick & Nelson, 2002; Eder, 1990; Merten, 1997; Remillard & Lamb, 2005; Rys & Bear, 1997; Underwood, 2003). "Relational aggression" has been defined as a form of aggression "characterized by the threat of withdrawal of affiliation for the purposes of controlling the behavior of others" (Rys & Bear, p. 89). A variety of studies crossing race and class have found that girls use teasing, gossip, and meanness as a substitute for unacceptable direct expression of feelings and more open competition among them.

Notably, when relational aggression is included in assessments of aggression, gender differences disappear, and boys are no more likely than girls to be aggressive (Conway, 2005; Crick & Rose, 2000). Early on, prior to age 4, there are no differences in aggressive expression between boys and girls, but through the elementary school years, boys do engage in more physically aggressive and destructive behavior than do girls (Keenan & Shaw, 1997). Boys' early aggressive behavior predicts subsequent antisocial behavior. By contrast, girls who are aggressive in the early years are, by adolescence, twice as likely as boys to have internalizing problems, such as depression and anxiety. This rate applies to every subsequent age group except the elderly (Nolen-Hoeksema, 1994).

There is a growing body of evidence to suggest that relational aggression can also be as concerning as direct aggression because it is associated with significant psychological difficulties later on (Conway, 2005; Zahn-Waxler, Klimes-Dougan, & Slattery, 2000). Of course, the comparison is limited to the suffering of the aggressors; the direct violence of boys against others certainly carries the potential for greater physical harm and lethality. Still, while the reasons for this are not entirely clear, girls who engage in relational aggression are themselves at comparable risk.

Some researchers suggest that teases, insults, and verbal cruelty all appear to serve a common and necessary function for girls (Merten, 1997). These forms of relational aggression may help girls define their social groups, support one another, protect themselves from male ridicule, and distance themselves from dominant gender roles—all the while avoiding direct expression of anger and overt competition. In this analysis, relational aggression makes some sense.

How else can angry girls maintain popularity in the face of relentless expectations to be super nice? Girls who aren't all "sugar and spice" risk being called "stuck up"—and worse. Girls who express rage directly are shunned and sanctioned. But through meanness girls are able to provide an enlightening "discourse about hierarchical position, popularity, and invulnerability" (Merten, 1997, p. 188). The cattiness of girls can be functional: through it they socialize others into group behavior and norms, practice self-defense strategies, and solidify their group relationships. Relational aggression has its casualties, but may be more of a creative response to limited gender options than we usually see it to be.

Self-Aggression

Aggression against the self is another way in which girl anger goes underground during the middle- and high-school years. Indeed, self-aggression is a most serious problem for teenage girls. Beyond relational aggression, we have ample support for the contention that compared with boys of the same age, adolescent girls are taking it out on themselves. They are more *stressed* (Brooks-Gunn, 1991; Cohen-Sandler, 2005); are more likely to be *depressed* (Gore & Colten, 1991; Nolen-Hoeksema, 1994; Waller et al., 2006); suffer from all varieties of *eating disorders*, including obesity (Maine, 2000; Shroff & Thompson, 2006) experience greater *distress over their looks* (Brumberg, 1997; Peterson, Ellenberg, & Crossan, 2003); *attempt suicide* more frequently (The Commonwealth Fund, 1999; Molina & Duarte, 2006); and *self-mutilate* at significantly higher rates (Rodham, Hawton, & Evans, 2005; Smith, Cox, & Saradjian, 1999; van der Kolk, Perry, & Herman, 1991). The indirect expression of anger is connected to a host of other developmental problems faced by girls.

So when anger is unexpressed, girls often turn it into the more socially acceptable but patently self-destructive forms of communication. Symptoms then become a kind of code to break, or a metaphor for these unspoken emotions. Unable to communicate directly, these girls only provide concerned adults with clues that we need to trace, like detectives, back to the source. We'll need to ask, for example:

- Who else is the adolescent angry at? Why?
- Who else is angry at the adolescent? Why?
- How is this particular behavior the most effective communication at this time?
- In what other ways has she attempted to communicate her distress and what was the response?

- When did she start being angry, and what happened when she first expressed it?
- What changed in her life to make her angry?
- What other feelings are being enacted (fear, sorrow, confusion, despair)?
- What response does she say she'd like to have from others?
- What realistically is going to happen? How effective is the communication? Will she need to escalate, change symptoms, suffer more, before people respond sufficiently?

Self-aggression is seldom the first or only way that angry, frustrated girls spread the word that they are mad, but, sadly, it is usually the most potent means for them to get the support and attention they seek.

Other Feelings and Passions

Teenage girls are infinitely more ambivalent and complicated than so much attention to self-aggression might suggest. It is important not to label or marginalize the girls who struggle; indeed they are also trying to develop coherent identities, to take on adult roles, and to integrate an emerging sexuality into their sense of self, just like the girls who seem to be doing better. In fact, they are often one and the same youngster, at different points in time.

And those who attempt suicide, drop out of school, get depressed, engage in high-risk sexual activity, use food self-destructively, self-mutilate, and contend with a pervasive sense of worthlessness may be our best teachers about what girls need from adults. When we listen past the symptom, we invariably learn that a sad and angry girl hasn't had a safe opportunity to explore or experience her own possibility or potency in the world around her.

We also get to travel across a fertile landscape in which contradiction is made human. No one can accuse adolescent girls of a foolish consistency.

Contradictions

Therapists typically make ample room in discussions for acknowledging girls' feelings and experiences. But we sometimes get drawn into taking on the other half of the ambivalence that they feel. Before responding to girls, we might consider the exact flip side of their statements, and all the variations in between, and try to get them to embrace the whole mess of possibilities. This way we'll help them move from a world in which experiences are black *or* white, to understanding that they can be both black and white — and all the shades of gray. This acceptance of complexity and contradiction comes slowly over the course of adolescence. It can be painful to feel so uneven, so different each morning, perhaps, especially in a culture that likes to reduce experiences to produce quick, decisive, and clear evaluations.

Grand Confidence and Relentless Self-Doubt

Typically, though, the surge in development over the course of adolescence is accompanied by some contradictory beliefs. On the one hand, for example, teenaged girls often overestimate what they are capable of, believe they can judge both their abilities and the intentions of others with remarkable accuracy, and believe (whether or not it is so) that they are more adept than their parents at a great number of things. They can navigate their way around the Internet with greater agility than most of us — and are then similarly certain that in some obscure Internet "chat room" they can tell whether someone is a predatory adult or a relatively benign 14-year-old boy.

On the other hand, though, they are frequently consumed by paralyzing feelings of inadequacy, ugliness, indecisiveness, and impotence. They feel the expectations bar has suddenly gone up many notches higher than they can leap; they're exposed and sensitive to microscopic injustices, the social landscape is a minefield.

This inherently conflicting set of self-beliefs leads girls to some peculiar ways of behaving. At times they seem expansive and grandiose, brimming with confidence and possibility, while at others, they cave in despair. It's important to remember that both ways of being in the world are real for them, both kinds of voices need to be heard, both can come from the same girl.

Being a Good Girl with Bad Feelings

Another set of conflicts adolescent girls must make sense of is how to be "good" — that traditional and stultifying compliance and agreeability — in the face of genuine passion and confusion that is not "good" at all. Anger, though a big component, is only one of the problems. All of the feelings that can't be spoken are included: jealousy, sexuality, sadness, embarrassment, irritation, insecurity, loneliness, greed, disappointment, boredom, upset, stress, devastation, guilt, and any other bad ones.

Girls get trapped inside this logic trap for three reasons. First, because they feel so sensitive, they are more reluctant to open themselves to ridicule or humiliation. Admitting to "bad" feelings leaves them exposed, and vulnerable. This, of course, leads to increased isolation because they are then unknown by others around them who only see the "good" feelings.

Second, they don't know how to resolve so many contradictions in emotional content. They want behavior to be consistent and genuine and, especially younger adolescents, don't fully grasp the notion that good people can and will do bad things. Lacking a broad sense of self to work with, they have trouble, developmentally, in comprehending that all these different experiences could be authentic. Thus they become unnerved when they feel something so intensely that is exactly the opposite of what they previously felt, and felt deeply. They expect one Truth and contend with a dizzying array of truths. So, wanting it to be one or the other, they don't know whether they are good or bad, or will continue to feel good or bad, about a great many things.

Finally, and perhaps most importantly, the socialization process cuts girls off from expressing their genuine feelings. Instead, they learn to say what they're supposed to say, careful not to be hurtful or rude. As Carol Gilligan and colleagues note, the choice for girls is whether to speak one's own truth or stay connected to others (Gilligan, Rogers, & Tolman, 1991). Girls learn by early adolescence that they're supposed to be friendly, passive, compliant, and gentle. And they learn that when their feelings do not correspond to these behaviors, they should keep these feelings to themselves.

Feminine Achievement

Adolescent girls receive contradictory messages about school achievement, too. An interesting minority of white privileged "Alpha girls" (Kindlon, 2006) are making some confident, high-achieving waves; many studies similarly conclude that, overall, girls are now more academically successful than they have been in the past and many are doing better than their male counterparts. Still, this is only a part of the story for girls in school. Most girls are still working hard to conceal their intelligence just as they have in past generations. They're often so successful at this that they even convince themselves, too. Additionally, the very qualities that teachers prefer in students—manners, obedience, compliance, orderliness, and cleanliness—are typical girl qualities. Yet girls who meet these criteria will actually get less attention than their rowdier peers (DeZolt & Henning-Stout, 1999). And when adults reinforce such qualities, we further encourage girls to become less assertive and direct.

By middle school, when there is an enormous increase in the pressure for social success, too often girls feel they must choose between a desired peer group and academic excellence. Popular girls are willing to hide their capabilities in public in order to retain their perceived social standing, which will be hampered by too many flashy grades and too much ambition. Here smart girls go underground some more. They know that what matters is not whether you are smart, but whether you are in tune with the social cues. Girls who stay under the teachers' radar by getting "C's" and keeping out of trouble, can oblige everyone, except their authentic selves.

Being Reliant and Defiant

A 1990s parenting guide has the humorous and revealing title: *Get Out of My Life but First Could You Drive Me and Cheryl to the Mall* (Wolf, 1992). This sentiment aptly sums up the reliant–defiant logic. Adolescent girls are masters of this seemingly contradictory way of operating in the world. On the one hand, they may need many of the same supports of money, time, and effort that they've always had—perhaps more if they want rides to get places and will only wear name-brand clothing. Even with part-time jobs, girls will require financial help to buy things they need; even the most independent 15-year-old needs a hand remembering her doctor's appointments. Parents of highly autonomous girls still act as auxiliary alarm clocks and ports-in-a-storm. Even estranged girls usually still have the advantages of room and board, or "three hots and a cot" as the saying goes. As hard as it is for some girls (and parents!) to accept, it now takes about 25 (or more) years for most humans to learn to fully function independently and competently. Evolution and the high-tech economy have combined to make humans take a longer time to stand on their own feet.

All the same, though, adolescent girls are also seeking ways to get power over their own lives, to disconnect from their child selves, and eventually to forge adult connections with their parents. Often, too, the defiance is in exact proportion to how weak and dependent a girl feels. Confident girls can afford to rebel less; they feel they have more control of their lives. Resistance to adult supremacy, however ill conceived to our eyes, is fundamentally about becoming "their own person." Oppositional behavior serves to redefine the lines of control and domination in a culture that can be quite punishing to girls who act against authority. It's a delicate balance between reliance and defiance though: Too much of either extreme usually leads to more rather than less adult control.

We also give girls a mixed message about how reliant they should be. We tell them we want them to become competent and independent. At the same time, they've been saturated through the years with a compelling fantasy (the point of many fairy tales) that someone will come along to take care of them. Astonishing numbers of girls still plan on marrying a rich man. And many girls really do believe and expect that someone should take care of them. In fact, they're right to assume that they are entitled to some support until they leave home.

Reliance has its practical limits over the long haul though. Unprecedented numbers of women are living alone—widowed, divorced, never married—and raising children on their own, so even if someone "should" care for them, it isn't happening as often, or for as long anymore. And even during their adolescence, we need our girls to function with less adult guidance than we may have had at that age. In reality, we rely on them, too. We may also unwittingly contribute to the mixed messages they are trying to sort through. We tell them: you can look and act like an adult but be home by nine; be assertive but don't talk back; think for yourself but do what I say. It's confusing for us all.

Hurry Up and Wait

Adolescent girls lose track of time. They often seem unattached to the way it passes on watches and calendars. They're busy attending to now, to deadlines and plans, to what's happening in their hearts and minds. They're proceeding on the NTKB ("need-to-know-basis"). A prosaic reference to hours and days bears little resemblance to this racing and halting of a girl's internal clock. Like T.S. Eliot's Prufrock, we may have measured out our lives with coffee spoons but girls are dreamily stirring their first cups. Many young adolescents have only been able to tell time for a few years. They don't have enough hours under their belt to know how long an hour feels (perhaps, though, only therapists really know this).

This discrepancy can be very frustrating and upsetting for us all. On the one hand, time can travel so slowly for a teenage girl that sitting through a dull class, being grounded for a week, or having to wait three weeks for the dance is almost intolerable. On the other hand, time can pass so quickly that she'll forget to call when she says she will, or miss the due date for a term paper. Adults tend to write this time warp off as histrionics, self-involvement, and poor planning. But we miss out on understanding a developmental reality when we unempathically impose our old sense of time on them.

Being Unique and Fitting In

I remember meeting for the first time with Melanie, a girl who was part of the large "freak" group in her school. She had hair in colors of the rainbow, wore ripped jeans and a tie-dyed shirt, and her backpack was covered with signs of everlasting loyalty to the memory of Jerry Garcia. To me, she looked like every other kid in her crowd (and a lot of kids from my old crowd, too). I'd probably passed her in the halls of her school many times, without really noticing her. But she told me, right off, that being different was extremely important to her. She waved her hand from head to toe, to emphasize the point, so I would be sure to understand what she meant: she wanted me to *see* the ways in which she was unique, her own person.

And I knew this seeing was my job (though a little reminder never hurts). Finding her way into a group with a strong physical identity, Melanie had established herself at once as different (from the preps, jocks, goths, and so on) and the same (a freak). She had a compelling and vital agenda to be part of a group. At the same time, and more importantly, she wanted me to acknowledge her as an individual and not just dismiss her as another freak. The contradictions between these needs create profound tension for girls. It's hard to shape both an individual persona and a group identity, to both stand out and fit in, all at once.

Piercing the Silence

Tattoos and piercings, too, describe a fascinating if contradictory set of beliefs. In many ways, of course, they're just new expressions of a new generation. "Teenagers" have been busily creating their own culture, set distinctly apart from adult stuffiness since the end of World War II

(Palladino, 1996). In fact, those of us who came of age in the 1960s and 1970s believed we had turned adolescent rebellion into an art form. But our own profound counterculture experiences, suffused as they were with a vision of the world we wanted to create, are inadequate to prepare us for the pervasive underlying feeling of pessimism and hopelessness described by too many of the adolescents we live and work with. And we seem to see it most in the kids who are marking up their bodies—at least they stand out most.

Maybe we can't fully comprehend the way adolescents today are drowning in a sea of objects. For the middle class, anyway, cars, phones, pagers, CD players, iPods, computers, brand-name clothes, and bedroom TV's are altogether common. Some of today's adolescents may not have connections and purpose, but they have *things*. This is sad because relationships with things are ultimately unsatisfying; they surely cannot help adolescent girls feel safe and connected.

Such alienation from meaning and purpose feeds on an adolescent's passion for living in the present. And in this vein, tattoos, piercings, brandings, and other body art appear also to represent a ceremony of individual expression and a present time in life, when thinking about the future is beside the point if it's even possible to consider at all. As Gaines (1991) concludes:

> They seem convinced there's no point in trying, that maybe this is all there is. So they get high, they party on, they tattoo and pierce their bodies in a celebration of the moment. They try one last time to stand out in a crowd, hoping to be heard once before it's all over. (p. 202)

Many of these adornments are in-your-face, too, although most girls deny that's the point (and there are often many more adornments we don't see). The conscious, stated functions are aesthetics, "I like the way it looks"; autonomy, "It's my body and I can do what I want to it"; and authentic identity, "I don't care what people think, this is an expression of my true self." Seen this way, tattooing and body piercing may be highly individualistic and transitory juvenile acts, delightfully repugnant to adults, (and so perhaps lacking the dissolute despair that Gaines describes).

But on the other hand, piercing and tattooing are also about the inverse: belonging and permanence. In a culture where teenagers are viewed mostly as faceless consumers, the tattoo or piercing is another way to be part of an identifiable group, with similar values and concerns. A tattoo or piercing is also a transitional object an adolescent can take along into the future, bridging her evolving identity into adulthood. In a life without certainty, or rituals of passage, where flux and skepticism are defining principles, a tattoo is immutable, a stand for something, a forever sign.

Tattoos and piercings may serve all the same functions of all the other trends and fads teenagers have spawned over the past few generations — identity formation, group affiliation, helping to define and present the external self. But it is the irreversibility of body art that gives it this magnetic appeal for adolescent girls. Such permanence may speak to their longing for a future beneath their terror and despair about how to have one.

Why Worry?

Teenage girls are navigating a dangerous world. They are less protected than was the case earlier in their lives; the culture is hurting them, and they are hurting themselves. It is impossible to count the ways, the number of girls. Many large-scale studies have concluded that about 25 to 30% of all adolescents have quite significant psychological problems (Achenbach & Howell, 1993; The Commonwealth Fund, 1999; Dryfoos, 1990; Waller et al., 2006). Dryfoos's compelling data, supported by subsequent surveys, suggest that one in four adolescents are at risk for problems so severe they have little chance of becoming responsible adults. They are not learning the skills necessary to participate in the educational system or to make the transition into the labor force. They cannot become responsible parents because they have limited experience in family life and lack resources to raise their own children.

And these national surveys tell only part of the story. Clinical data from a broad variety of sources also suggest that adolescents are evincing more problems and greater severity of distress than was true of earlier generations (Garbarino, 2006; Pipher, 1994; Straus, 1994; Taffel, 2005). In surveys using a broader definition of emotional disturbance than employed by epidemiological approaches, closer to half of all adolescent girls were found to be in notable emotional turmoil (Carnegie Council on Adolescent Development, 1995; The Commonwealth Fund, 1999; Elmen & Offer, 1993). Studies that cast a wider net to include those adolescents who are not getting clinical treatment but are having considerable difficulties "getting through" their adolescent years, indicate what parents, teachers, and therapists know: many girls are suffering.

Of course these data also mean that better than half of adolescent girls get through the teenage years intact. Some, particularly those from the white middle class, are as successful or more so than their male peers. Although this book isn't about them, plenty of girls are having a pretty smooth ride. And though adolescence lasts a longer time than ever before, it's still a small portion of a whole life. By the end of high school, many of the girls who have struggled also emerge in one piece. We have to expect a certain amount of suffering and doubt as an inevitable part of life, after all. The greater awareness that accompanies adolescence insures some pain; how could it not? At the same time as we delve into the problems, we must not lose sight of reasons to be hopeful: sources of pride, competence, success, motivation, and self-esteem for the girls we treat. We must find ways to admire and delight in the strength and possibilities for the girls who seem most lost, frightened, and despairing.

Still, too many girls are in too much pain. We need to worry because millions of girls are not coping even reasonably well with the biological, cognitive, social, and emotional changes that are a part of adolescence, are not relating well to their families and peers, and are not realizing the dreams we had for them. And, most of all, we need to worry because too many girls are not dreaming their own dreams anymore.

Chapter 1: Thoughts for Intervention

- When a girl acts out, can you see the hope in it? What do you imagine she's hoping adults will do to intervene?
- Is there a developmental point in a girl's life that you can describe where she changed from being known by adults to being unknown? What was happening then—for her and in her environment? How did she manage to go underground?
- Ask girls how they spend their free time, how much they are alone, how they feel about it, what they do with it. Find out how much more they're alone now, and why. Help them do more with their time, adding more meaning and interests to it.

- Promote shades-of-gray thinking. Note the passion in the strong opinions, encourage more inclusive reasoning, respect the process of mastering strong emotions, offer reassurance: "I can see that this has really upset you, and we will come up with a plan to help you feel better about it."
- Ask girls what they feel they have lost and left behind, as they became teens. Look for the sadness beneath the more defiant or confused presentation. Find out when they became aware of the losses and how they have coped.
- Ask about anger—what makes her mad, where it registers in her body, how she expresses it, how people respond to her when she expresses it? If she doesn't express anger directly, what is the toll it takes on her and on relationships? What is the role of anger in her life?
- Ask the girl about relational aggression, what she thinks she does with it, how it makes her feel. Brainstorm about other ways to communicate, ask whether there are girls who are not engaging in it, and the benefits as well as the problems with it.
- Make a sociogram with the girl of her complex network of friendships. Find out how girls are treating one another in her social circle.
- Ask girls about their dreams, and how their dreams have changed over their lives. Note how realistic or magical these aspirations are, and always encourage the vision of a competent future self.

CHAPTER TWO

THE ADOLESCENT PASSAGE

Laura is 17, and she's had a lot of momentum going into her senior year. Her grades have been good, she doesn't use drugs, and she's a starter on the varsity basketball team. She holds a part-time job at a local clothing store and has earned the respect of her employers. She has a large extended family in the area, and relationships among members are strong. Laura's best friends are a stable group of girls she's known and played sports with her whole life. Indeed, up until now, she's practically been the poster child for a smooth transition through adolescence.

But through this fall, with the pressures of senior year—college applications, repeated standardized testing, thoughts about leaving home, tougher classes, added responsibilities on the team, juggling work with everything else she's doing—Laura has begun to falter. She's gotten caught cutting classes, and is in trouble with her coach for harassing younger teammates. She's missing school deadlines, and blowing off college applications. She wants to quit work because she feels too overwhelmed to keep up. Laura requested therapy for herself when her parents confronted her about her change in attitude and behavior. She noted in the first session: "I'm just never really happy anymore, and even when I feel okay, I know it won't last."

When an adolescent girl struggles with her life, we commonly ask about a transition: Was there a time before things got hard, and what was it like? Did the problems arrive gradually or suddenly? What kinds of changes made things more difficult for her? How does she think she got derailed? How do others see her and the problem now? How did they view her before? With 20–20 hindsight, could anyone have seen it coming? Why all the rage?

The questions imply an (often accurate) assumption that we could have taken before and after pictures: of the girl before the challenges of adolescence and after it hit. For Laura, we were able to identify specific stressors, but for many girls the picture requires closer scrutiny to become clear. Thus it is important to understand what this developmental period does to and for girls and the many ways they can lose traction as they travel toward adulthood.

The History of Adolescent Girls: From Person to Consumer

Not so long ago, teenage girls as we know them today didn't even exist. The distinct period of development we call adolescence appears to have emerged in the United States in the late 19th century, as Americans made the transition from living on farms and in small towns to working in industries and living in cities. Early in the 20th century, the evolution from childhood to adulthood became more ambiguous and prolonged, and adolescence was invented. In a short period of time, three major social policy changes served to create institutional support for this developmental interlude: the juvenile justice system was separated from adult procedures, high-school attendance became compulsory, and legislation preventing child labor was passed. As industrialization narrowed the labor market, childhood was extended also to exclude adolescents from competing with adults for jobs.

Although the impact of all of these changes was initially greater for boys—girls were still mostly in training to become wives and mothers— this period defines an irrevocable cultural shift that affected everyone. But these turn-of-the last century solutions need some fine-tuning (if not a complete overhaul): consider, for example, the overcrowded juvenile courts, rehabilitation and detention facilities, high-school dropout and illiteracy rates, and lack of decent jobs for adolescents ready and needing to work.

While adolescents emerged at the turn of the last century, "teenagers" as a distinct consumer group evolved out of the post-World War II period. In the more prosperous postwar economy, teenagers proved to have the time and disposition to try out new products, and the inclination and ability to spend freely. Postwar teenagers, with money to spare, had different expectations about their rights and responsibilities; no longer adhering to the idea they should be seen and not heard. As Palladino (1996) notes:

> In the days before Pearl Harbor, adult marketers had naturally assumed that their job was to tell teenagers who they were and what they wanted to buy. Ten years later, they would be asking teenagers to speak for themselves and presenting the younger generation as bona fide consumers with a right to spend their own (and their parents') money as they pleased. (p. 102)

The creation of a class of people called "teenagers" is not just a change in semantics, but really a shift in perspective, driven almost entirely by the marketplace. Adolescents, once valued for what they could produce and offer to families and communities, have come to be viewed almost entirely as consumers, buying and using but contributing little or nothing. Once adolescents shared substantially in their parents' work; now they may only know vaguely what their parents really do for a living. Their possible economic contribution—filling the dead-end, dead-brain service jobs—is mostly valuable because these jobs provide them with more money to spend.

The evolution from person/adolescent to consumer/teenager has had dramatic and deleterious effects both on the way adults view teenage girls, and more importantly, on how they see themselves. Over the latter part of the 20th century, girls unwittingly became participants in their own objectification. They appeared to be willing subjects in the transition from person to target group; from having problems that could be solved by people to those remedied by lotions, cigarettes, and sneakers. It is no coincidence that girls are obsessing about their bodies as never before while the diet industry alone grosses over $36 billion a year (Kilbourne, 1999). And concerned adults are doing little to protect girls from this deluge of consumerism. As Joan Brumberg, author of *The Body Project: An Intimate History of American Girls* (1997) describes:

> Contemporary girls are in trouble because we are experiencing a mismatch between biology and culture. At this moment in our history, young women develop physically earlier than ever before, but they do so within a society that does not protect or nurture them in ways that were once a hallmark of American life. Instead

of supporting our early-maturing girls, or offering them some special relief or protection from the unrelenting self-scrutiny that
the marketplace and modern media both thrive on, contemporary
culture exacerbates normal adolescent self-consciousness, and encourages precocious sexuality. Too often popular culture and peer
groups, rather than parents or other responsible adults, call the
cadence in contemporary teenage life. (p. 197)

The insidious and cynical lessons of commerce have been shattering to
teenage girls, particularly because their major impact is felt at a time in development when girls desperately crave connection and meaning, and
find it less available. Girls come to trust their relationships with products
more than with humans, to believe that they'll get intimacy, respect, and
excitement from things and not from people. Seen through this lens, the
history of adolescent girls becomes a saga of alienation: first from meaningful participation in the life of the family and later from authentic human connection to others and to themselves.

Emerging Adulthood

The turn of this century has been witness to another developmental shift,
further prolonging the period of time for transition between childhood
and adulthood. Emerging adulthood (Arnett, 2000) appears to be a phenomenon of converging demographic, social, economic, and developmental factors unique to this point in our history. It characterizes the late
teens and early 20s (ages 18–25 or so) as a time of flux and exploration of
possibilities; a unique developmental phase with its own psychological
tasks and functions. The popular press has coined the terms *adultolescents*
and *twixters* to describe the same age group. Emerging adulthood as a
newly defined period of life seems to be a real phenomenon of the 21st
century in many industrialized countries. Emerging adults also appear to
identify easily with these descriptions of their transitional lives, with so
little about the future established for certain.

One of the fascinating aspects of emerging adulthood is the potential
extended developmental moratorium it defines, at least for middle class
Americans. Emerging adults explore life possibilities ahead of them, and
"gradually arrive at more enduring choices in love, work, and worldviews"
(Arnett, 2000, p. 479). This phase of life stands, paradoxically, alongside
the multitude of developmental pressures faced by younger adolescents.

Society needs children who can take care of themselves. Our expectations for adolescent independent functioning are monumental. But then the need seems to change midstream, back in the other direction. We push for these girls to be self-reliant, but then don't have a social structure that can foster their transition to independence for many more years.

We now have more adults than places for adults. The demographics—people living longer, baby boomers having reproduced at high rates, delayed retirement, inadequate social policies, and an economy that no longer generates widespread opportunity—together these mean that the prospects for independent young adulthood are quite dismal. An economically and emotionally secure future is more distant than it was a generation ago.

Since the 1970s, labor market conditions have changed substantially in terms of education and experience needed, occupational and industrial mix of jobs, and geographic location of jobs. Younger, less experienced, less educated, less skilled workers have increasingly less favorable positions in the labor market. And the cost of education is astronomical; the average person leaves college with $18,900 in student loans, compared with $9,000 for 1992 graduates (Draut & Silva, 2004). Indeed, the economics of emerging adulthood are quite stark. In one large-scale study of 18 to 34-year-olds, one in five said they significantly changed their career plans because of student loans and credit card debt, nearly 40% delayed buying a home, and 20% reported their debt burden caused them to delay starting a family (Draut, 2006).

A changing economy is a big part of the reason for emerging adulthood, but it is really only one piece of the explanation. Economic instability is seemingly connected to romantic uncertainty; the median age of marriage for women in 1970 was 21; now it's 25 years. Age of first childbirth follows a similar delayed pattern (U.S. Bureau of the Census, 1997). Along with economic forces that keep adolescents living with their parents (or returning to the nest after some time away), and the later ages of marriage, Arnett (2004) suggests that longer and more available education, the advent of reliable birth control and smaller families, and the cultural acceptance of premarital sexuality and cohabitation, all further contribute to the period of emerging adulthood.

Notably, these changes suggest many developmental benefits for girls. Foremost may be added the opportunity to develop a coherent sense of self and interests before entering and settling into long-term adult roles—which still for most will mean taking care of children and partners while working a lot of hours outside the home. And evolution (along with modern science) has given us a gift of extended development throughout the long course of life; our Western desire to rush through stages limits the opportunity for healthy growth. If girls struggle in adolescence, it is perhaps reassuring to know that they still have the years of emerging adulthood ahead in which to sort out identity issues before the full onslaught of adult expectations is upon them.

Developmental Tasks

We speak about adolescence as though it were a monolithic event, something that happens at once with the onset of puberty, and ceases with a 20th birthday. In reality though, puberty is only a single aspect of the stage, and chronological age provides just one small source of information. Before they can function as adults, teenagers undergo remarkable alterations in physical, cognitive, brain, social, and emotional development. Though it may seem excessive, with emerging adulthood in the mix, the period between childhood proper (ending at about 10 or 11 years of age) and adulthood (beginning at about 28 or so), the transitional time can be just about 20 years long! When we consider our expectations for young adolescents, we should also remember that they have many years ahead to master adolescent tasks.

For the sake of simplification, and at the risk of overgeneralization, it seems that the period of time we call adolescence for girls can be divided roughly into three phases: earlier adolescence (11–15 more or less), is marked by the onset of puberty, entry into middle school, shifting cognitive and social abilities, and increased emotionality and egocentrism; later adolescence (somewhere around 16–20) is defined by an increasing ability to reason abstractly, expectations for leaving high school, greater independence, and changes in legal status; and emerging adulthood (19–25 or so) is identified as above by exploration and integration of identity and possibilities in love, work, and worldview.

With so many changes and so much time, it shouldn't surprise us that most girls develop unevenly. For example, some girls who are very bright and cognitively advanced are also very immature and emotionally delayed. Some who are physically mature are socially awkward. Some girls have enormous discrepancies in development while others seem more all-of-a-piece. Some look like they're handling the transitions and challenges and then, like Laura, suddenly crumble; others stumble along but develop slowly but surely.

And although significant variability is expected, we still need to know something about the "normal range" in adolescent development. We will be marking out a broad and varied territory, without the goal of limiting or labeling girls who are struggling, but rather to assess their relative strengths and weaknesses. We want to know what tasks of adolescence they've managed, and, based on what we know about typical trajectories, what sorts of challenges remain.

Most importantly, we can be more effective in guiding and supporting a girl if we can keep in mind some comparative developmental information. We use this knowledge to contrast chronological and developmental ages, maintaining a more dynamic understanding of how she is functioning at a particular moment in time. It is useful to remember that most aspects of development follow a reasonably predictable course. Thus our expectations and concerns are specific to the girl and her particular circumstances, and also general, informed by how she is proceeding along these developmental trajectories.

Physical Development

Much of the rage and distress faced by adolescent girls is connected in some way to the rapid physical changes they must accommodate in a culture where standards for female beauty resemble the bony shape of an adolescent boy. This adjustment is compounded by the fact that American girls today start menstruating about two years earlier than did young women at the turn of the 20th century; it isn't abnormal to see some signs of maturation in girls as young as 8 or 9 years old. Girls are often entering puberty before they have the emotional, cognitive, and social skills to cope with it.

The normal range for menstruation is now between 10.5 and 15.5 years, though girls rarely menstruate before reaching 100 pounds (and often stop when they drop below this weight while dieting excessively). Starting somewhere around age 10, girls begin to grow rapidly; an average of 3.2 inches a year. This is accompanied also by a spurt in weight gain, mostly in the form of fat added to their hips and thighs (as contrasted with the addition of muscle in boys).

But the averages tell only part of the story: by age 8, 48% of African-American girls and 15% of white girls show some signs of puberty

(Kaplowitz & Oberfield, 1999). Some scientists believe that earlier puberty in girls is associated with the addition of hormones to food and hair products, and being overweight, since fat cells manufacture leptin, a hormone that might contribute to early maturation (Kaplowitz & Oberfield, 1999; Zuckerman, 1999).

Early puberty puts young girls at risk for sexual behavior, and for the predatory interest of older males. Secondary sex characteristics and surges in hormones focus girls' attention on their attraction to others and their own sexual attractiveness. Girls are now engaging in sexual activity at earlier ages than a generation ago and are having their first sexual experience at ages and rates comparable to those of boys. Many girls are also having sex with older boys and young men rather than with boys of their own age. Further, girls who have sex for the first time before age 16 report more frequently that their first sexual encounter was unwanted than do girls who were older when they first had intercourse (Commonwealth Fund, 1999).

With puberty, girls become more concerned with how women are "supposed" to behave at the same time that others, especially males, start reacting to them in markedly gendered ways. Parents of young adolescent girls also tend to become more reactive to appearances; for example, they may comment on how a daughter's clothes fit, or how her hair looks. The rules for behavior are, somewhat suddenly, based upon physical appearance more than interests, abilities, or other standards.

One result of these converging influences is to make girls more anxious about themselves as evidenced by increased depression, lower self-esteem, more dissatisfaction with their bodies, and diminished academic achievement (Galambos, Almeida, & Petersen, 1990; Shroff & Thompson, 2006). Such concerns frequently lead girls to revert to the security of stricter gender norms. The onset of puberty leads to more sexualized and more stereotypical behavior even for younger girls. They try to do what is expected of them and these new bodies, but the contradictions and mixed messages are entirely confusing. With puberty, girls are denigrated and idealized (i.e., the madonna–whore or good girl–slut dichotomy that still prevails); protected and abused; included in adult discussions and sent to their rooms; encouraged and discriminated against; noticed and silenced; and exactly at the moment in development when they get bigger and stronger, they get the message they should be smaller and more delicate — or at least to take up less space. There are many good reasons so few of us would like to be 12 years old again.

In recent years, premenstrual syndrome (PMS) has been assigned greater validity as a problem associated with menses in adolescence. Up through the 1980s, PMS was a joke—the reason why women shouldn't run for higher office, or a myth that supposedly gave women the chance to rant and rave without consequences. In reality, many adolescent girls experience some of the symptoms of PMS, and it helps them to know that there is a biological–hormonal reason for the changes they're experiencing, which include: increased acne, bloating and weight gain associated with water-retention, breast tenderness, lower-back and pelvic pain, depression, irritability, and increased anxiety. Girls who suffer from PMS appreciate some encouragement to take it easy on themselves for a few days until the symptoms abate.

Puberty also influences the natural circadian rhythms of sleep; the onset of puberty means that girls will tend to stay awake later and want to sleep later in the morning. If these girls are not properly supervised to go to bed early, because they need to wake up for school, they'll tend to be sleep-deprived. This in turn will hurt their ability to concentrate and learn in school. Sleep-deprived girls are also less able to consider the long-term implications of their actions, and are more vulnerable to peer pressure. Fatigue in adolescent girls is associated with family conflict, fights at school, and chronic irritability (Zuckerman, 1999). These problems of sleep deprivation, commonly associated with adolescence, are of particular concern for girls who enter puberty before the teen years.

Cognitive Development

Cognitive changes in adolescence are also rapid and remarkable, with important implications for therapy strategies and expectations. Still, most early and midadolescent girls remain very concrete in their reasoning ability; in Piagetian terms, they are not yet capable of formal operational thought, although they are well past the age of 12 when he predicted it would begin to develop (Piaget, 1954). The lags in cognitive development stand in stark contrast to the relatively fast pace of physical changes, often leading to astonishing discrepancies between the maturity of body and mind in teenage girls.

The implications of concrete reasoning abilities can be seen in many areas of development. Young adolescent girls live egocentrically, in the present, and struggle to anticipate any consequences they have not experienced repeatedly. They tend not to take into consideration all available information, and jump to conclusions based upon immediate, visceral experiences. For example, they may decide that someone hates them because she didn't look at them in the hall. They tend to think categorically, in black and white, giving little attention to exceptions. People are good or bad, friends or enemies. They will overgeneralize wildly. For example, they'll believe that they're the only ones with a curfew because they know someone who doesn't have one, or that when one friend doesn't call as planned, they have no friends. Young adolescent girls overestimate their abilities, and in turn, denigrate the knowledge and experience of parents. Early in adolescence, most girls have difficulty really seeing any perspective other than their own.

Child psychologist David Elkind (1967) also described two additional features of the self-conscious reasoning of early adolescents: the personal fable and the imaginary audience. The personal fable refers to the adolescent's belief that she is unique and that no one has ever had the same feelings or thoughts. Some girls think no one "could possibly understand" how they feel, for example. The imaginary audience refers to the belief that other people are just as preoccupied with the adolescent's appearance and behavior as she is, and this is reflected in the girl's public self-consciousness. It also extends to exquisite embarrassment about parents; girls think everyone is noticing how their mother dresses or chews, for example.

Concrete reasoning in an adolescent girl also tends to coincide with more highly emotional reasoning. Pipher (1994) has described the concrete and emotional aspect of girls' thinking in this way:

> If you feel something is true, it must be true. If a teenager feels like a nerd, she is a nerd. If she feels her parents are unfair, they are unfair. If she feels she will be invited to homecoming, then she will be invited. There is a limited ability to sort facts from feelings. Thinking is still magical in the sense that thinking something makes it so. (p. 60)

Girls think in extreme and chaotic ways partly because their reasoning is so imbued with feelings. Compared to the more logical and abstract abilities of later adolescence, the distorted logic of a young adolescent can sound ridiculous to adult ears. And even as a girl develops the ability to generate alternatives, she may feel flooded by so many possibilities, and be unable to determine the most compelling logic of a particular course of action.

Sometimes, the girl in early- to midadolescence loses sight of the most practical solution to a problem and comes up with some tangential or irrelevant alternative. For example, she may be able to come up with 10 reasons why her parents should allow her to go to the movies with some friends, and then tell them they'll be ruining her social life if they say "no" (not the best reason). Thus, even after girls can come up with more possibilities, this doesn't ensure better logic — in fact they may even seem more confused for a time.

Concrete reasoning also leads younger adolescents to feel and act in more fragmented ways. An increased striving for a unified self-definition during adolescence is an important developmental shift. During the late elementary and middle-school years, for example, girls may be aware that they act differently in various situations, but don't have a unifying experience of themselves that would lead to an organized self-system. It's difficult for a girl to know what we mean when we tell her to "be herself" until she develops a more integrated sense of who she is.

In one study of this "self-system," Bernstein (1980) asked 10-, 15-, and 20-year-olds to list the ways they act with different people and to put these statements together in a unifying statement about themselves. The researcher noted clear age-related trends. Ten-year-olds simply repeated past statements about themselves. Fifteen-year-olds were able to recognize that their actions were sometimes discrepant or contradictory, and often referred to feeling like "two different people." However, 20-year-olds were able to provide broad statements about themselves, recognizing the discrepancies in their actions, but organizing them into a network of complex and interconnected intentions, with an underlying unifying principle.

As girls develop, adolescent reasoning becomes more abstract, and concepts like justice, honesty, and loyalty take on new meaning. The simple black and white emotional reasoning of early adolescence gives way to gray expanses of uncertainty, ambiguity, and debate — for both boys and girls. But mature thought in girls is much more related to their level of interpersonal reasoning, supporting the idea that girls develop a more relational self than boys do (e.g., Gilligan, 1982).

For adolescent girls, the whole process of thinking more deeply becomes burdensome at points, particularly where it involves making decisions that stir anxiety, or feel traumatic. Some girls deal with ambiguity and ambivalence by making sudden, impulsive decisions. Sometimes the indecision shows up as procrastination and postponement. Some girls succumb to the temptation to shut down and avoid the hard work of making sense out of difficult and complicated experiences. Sometimes they stop thinking for themselves altogether with a mindless loyalty to junk culture, or a cultish adherence to a group or idea. Girls can be overwhelmed by their new awareness of the complexity of their lives, and may try to reduce the whole mess by only thinking about drugs, food, or sex. By reducing and distorting reality, they are able to focus on a single, tangible problem that seems a whole lot easier than taking on the tangled skein of ideas and experiences.

When we speak with girls about their thinking—about themselves, others, and the world—we need to keep in mind the developmental presses and limitations they may have. They may not be able to reason in a logical and abstract way simply because they have not reached the point in their cognitive growth where this is possible.

And cognitive change through adolescence is not only marked by this gradual stepwise transition from concrete to abstract reasoning. Much more dramatically, it really describes an entire perceptual shift that transforms consciousness from a child's way of knowing to an adult's awareness. This process is sweeping and complex. It can be challenging, for them and for us, as they explore the expanding edges of how they think and perceive. So to have a productive conversation with adolescent girls, we need to be aware of how they reason about themselves, their relationships, and the world. We must meet them in that style of thinking, and build from there.

Brain Development

The ascendance of neuroscience has opened a window into the mysteries of adolescent behavior that is very much worth looking through. In earlier times, explanations for erratic behavior featured hormones, and struggles with individuation; the rapid and dramatic changes in adolescent brains offer further insight into their emotional ways.

During adolescence, the brain is not just developing, it is actually going through a profound remodeling, ultimately becoming richer, more complex, and more efficient. The prefrontal cortex, often referred to as the "CEO," or executive of the brain, is one of the last areas of the brain to fully mature.

A child's brain produces a large number of neural connections in the prefrontal cortex just before puberty—connections that diminish almost by half over the course of adolescence through a "use it or lose it" pruning

(Weinberger, Elvevag, & Giedd, 2005). Through this process, the brain becomes leaner and more efficient. Thus, over the course of the teen years, it is possible, with adult support developing the new hardwiring, to see significant progress in such skills as setting priorities, organizing plans and ideas, forming strategies, controlling impulses, and allocating attention, all resulting from the gradual reconstruction of the prefrontal cortex. At the same time these executive functions of the brain are developing, the limbic system, which is tied to strong emotion, is already fully active and reactive (Siegel, 1999; Strauch, 2003).

This "pruning" of cortical synapses is normal, but quite drastic. It means that we cannot expect young adolescent girls to be reflective and in control of their impulses. That old expression "going limbic," used to describe someone's emotional reactivity, is more neurologically accurate for adolescents than we might have imagined.

The extent of pruning and specific circuits pruned is determined by experiences and genes, and is perhaps intensified by excessive amounts of stress (Siegel, 1999). Thus, for example, adolescents who are traumatized may have even more synaptic pruning, further impeding their ability to think systematically and logically. Such structural changes appear also to be accompanied by a shift in the balance of neurochemicals, particularly dopamine, in the adolescent brain (Spear, 2000).

Research on brain chemistry is noteworthy because recent studies have concluded that together these brain differences also appear to make adolescents particularly vulnerable to risk-taking, addiction, and mental illness (Chambers, Taylor, & Potenza, 2003; Spear, 2000). Some neuroscientists are now saying that the prefrontal cortex is not fully reorganized and developed until the late 20s; some conclude that "it's possible that the frontal lobe only starts maturing at age 17 to 19" (Yurgelun-Todd, 1998). Interestingly, this description of neurological delay coincides with the developmental period of emerging adulthood. The cultural transition to adulthood merges precisely with the time the brain is finishing up its major reconstruction project. By the late 20s, the emerging adult is ready to take hold—presumably with a cortex that is capable of handling the job ahead.

Executive Functioning

As follows logically from this discussion of the transforming prefrontal cortex in adolescents, the development of mature executive functioning (EF) also proceeds unevenly and over time. Our demands on the EF of adolescent girls lead to so much anxiety, frustration, anger, and disappointment that it is worth considering their developing executive skills when deciding how much external structure and support they will need to solve problems and make safe decisions.

Most researchers in EF agree that the term is an umbrella construct for a collection of interrelated functions that are responsible for purposeful, goal-directed, problem-solving behavior. A useful metaphor for conceptualizing their general purpose is the orchestra: the component "instruments" of the orchestra are the "basic" domain-specific cognitive functions (e.g., language, perception, memory) while the conductor serves as the directing system — making intentional decisions regarding the final output of the music and recruiting the necessary components for reaching the intended goal. Thus, the executive functions are defined as the control or self-regulatory processes that organize and direct all cognitive activity, emotional response, and overt behavior. In cognitive and educational psychology, the executive functions are described in terms of metacognition, the domain-general functions that serve an oversight role.

Specific subdomains that make up executive control include the abilities to: initiate behavior, inhibit competing actions or stimuli, select relevant task goals, plan and organize a means to solve complex problems, shift problem-solving strategies flexibly when necessary, and monitor and evaluate behavior. The working memory capacity to hold information actively "online" in the service of problem solving is also described within this domain of functioning (Pennington, Bennetto, McAleer, & Roberts, 1996). Finally, the executive functions are not exclusive to cognition; emotional control is also relevant to effective problem-solving activity and is likely to be a fundamental aspect required for effective metacognitive functioning (Racusin, Maerlender, Sengupta, Isquith, & Straus, 2005).

We can tailor our intervention strategies and remediation efforts accordingly when we have a sense of a girl's developing EF. If a girl has trouble planning and organizing, or responds impulsively, or has difficulty with transitions, for example, we need to be sure she is even capable of these executive skills. Our demands for competent and independent behavior so often exceed the EF of adolescents; interventions can help develop these functions, but a girl may have lags in one or many of them when she first comes into treatment.

The implications of adolescent brain research are clear: adults must be more present to support and guide teens than they may otherwise believe. As researcher Daniel Weinberger (2001) of the National Institutes of Health has said, "Parents provide their children with a land-lease prefrontal cortex during all those years that it takes to grow one, particularly when the inner urges for impulsive action intensify" (p. 3). We now have a much better idea about why adolescent brains have so much trouble with organization and long term planning, and are particularly susceptible to getting derailed along the way. We must always keep in mind that only adults are capable of thinking like adults.

Social Development

As children move from egocentrism to more capable perspective taking, their relationships with both peers and adults will deepen and vary. Forming and maintaining a satisfying social life is not just what adolescents *seem* to be doing much of the time; it is also a central developmental task.

Relationships with Peers

Teenagers who have close friendships and are accepted by peers typically are higher in self-esteem, more socially skilled, and more academically successful (Berndt & Savin-Williams, 1993; Pakaslahti, Karjalainen, & Keltikangas-Jaervinen, 2002). Studies have indicated that friendships satisfy adolescents' desires for intimacy and greatly enhance their interpersonal skills, sensitivity, and understanding (Laursen, 1993; Thomas & Daubman, 2001). As a corollary, adolescents who lack supportive friendships or who are rejected by many of their peers show poor psychological, social, and academic adjustment (Doll, 1996; Hussong, 2000).

Longitudinal studies have even demonstrated a significant relationship between how well adolescents get along with their peers and how well adjusted they are as adults. Teenagers who have difficulties finding and maintaining friends are more likely as adults to be unemployed, aggressive, or have poor mental health (Doll, 1996; Laursen & Mooney, 2005). Though it seems to be getting harder all the time, girls must develop a complex set of social skills over the course of adolescence or they are at significantly increased risk of emotional and behavioral problems throughout the rest of their lives.

The rules and expectations for peer socialization change quite dramatically between elementary school and middle school, and then again in high school. These shifts appear to correspond with individual and group development and the varieties of institutional support. As students progress through the grades, classes, and schools generally get bigger and structurally more complex; larger numbers of adults come into contact

with students for shorter amounts of time, and adult monitoring and structuring of a student's day decreases rather dramatically. These gradual differences have major consequences for the nature and quality of teenaged-
girl friendships.

White, middle-class girls have smaller and more fluid friendship
groups than a generation or two ago. This change appears to stem largely
from the regionalization of the junior high and high schools that draw students from many different neighborhoods. Some girls have friends whom
they only see in school, with little opportunity to socialize elsewhere.
Blacks are more likely than whites to have a network of neighborhood
friends with whom they have contact outside of school (e.g., Clark & Ayers,
1991; Dubois & Hirsch, 1990). However, it is harder now for adolescent
girls of all races to find safe places in common to "hang-out" when not in
school, which limits opportunities for socialization in significant ways.

Some researchers also note that it is also more unusual for girls now to
have tight, closed peer groups in school and they are more apt to move
from one group to another every few weeks or months. While girls may
have a "best friend," the intimate connection is unlikely to endure over
the span of years. In one national study, girls in 10th grade were asked to
name everyone in their peer group. They named an average of 11 girls.
Two years later, they named an average of 9 girls, three-quarters of these
friends weren't on the original list (Schneider & Stevenson, 1999).

The social group, at least for white middle-class girls, is more fluid
now for several reasons. Girls have many more opportunities in the larger
schools, and state that they select groups based upon evolving interests—
sports, theater, or music, for example. They also change crowds because of
conflicts within a group that can't be resolved. With so many people to
choose from, girls don't seem to need to work it out as much as they might
have to in a smaller setting. While not all schools have such identifiable
cliques, girls may switch groups to stand out in some clearer way, becoming, for example, cheerleaders, nerds, goths, headbangers, jocks, preps,
druggies, gangbangers, homies, rednecks, and so on. Wide curricular
choices in large schools make it difficult for students to be in the same
classes with the same group of people, and variable schedules may make
it difficult for them to eat lunch with friends or even acquaintances.

While most girls, especially in junior high, identify a "popular" group,
this identity appears also to become more fluid and of less consequence
through high school, based mostly in economic advantage. In the typical
middle school, the "popular" girls are still frequently the more economi-

cally privileged and attractive. Perhaps not surprisingly, they tend to be middle class, wear name-brand clothing, and are considered by their peers to have more boys interested in them (Wiseman, 2002).

The consequences of unpopularity can be devastating. In schools where basic rules of competition mean some must fail and some must be marginalized, unpopularity is also significant. In this vein, Evans and Eder (1993) describe a "cycle of isolation" in white middle school girls who are highly visible "due to perceived deficiencies in the very areas of deepest normative concern: appearance, mental maturity, and gender identification" (p. 164). Once a student was viewed negatively in any one of these areas, other disparaging characteristics were assigned by classmates, most often in the form of "negative sexual labeling"—such as being called a "slut" or a "faggot" (Evans & Eder, 1993, p. 165). In the absence of adult intervention, and expectations to the contrary, the rigid definitions for popularity can draw deep lines between those who fit in and those who will be excluded.

In the American middle school, anyway, concern with popularity—and lack of it—is still serious business. The social isolation of individual girls is fostered in schools where sexist and homophobic behavior goes unnoticed or unpunished. The high level of social anxiety common to middle school girls is perpetuated through "school policies and practices that promote social visibility and social hierarchy among students" (Evans & Eder, 1993, p. 168). Girls who see themselves as outcasts from the "popular" crowd sometimes figure out how to band together (Brown, 1998), but more often they become extremely isolated. This marginalization of some girls increases their risk for depression and other problems manifold (Waller et al., 2006).

Issues of popularity may be less clear-cut for high school girls. Some research has concluded that three-quarters of high-school students report they are at least "somewhat popular," though only 10% consider themselves "very popular" (Schneider & Stevenson, 1999). Thankfully, the cruel judgments and harsh influences of the peer group decline somewhat over adolescence—most high-school seniors state they are significantly less motivated or upset by group pressure than junior-high school kids (Steinberg, Brown, & Dornbusch, 1997). But this lack of influence may additionally be attributed to relatively weak ties within peer groups and with others in high school.

Peer influence is also connected closely to the decreasing levels of trust and increasing feelings of competition in these social relationships.

Thus, the levels of influence and trust decrease concurrently. For example, in a longitudinal study of ethnically diverse urban poor and working class adolescents, Way and colleagues (Way, 1996; Way & Robinson, 2003) found that both the boys and the girls spoke increasingly about not trusting their same-sex peers as they went through high school. In their freshman year, 40% of the adolescents in Way's study spoke about not trusting their peers. By their junior year, however, 87% spoke about not trusting their peers. In addition, 75% of the boys and 33% of the girls spoke about not having any close friends as a consequence of not trusting their peers. Instead of becoming more intimate over the course of high school, both low-income boys and girls (though especially boys) became more isolated and alienated from their classmates.

These findings seem to be of equal concern for white middle-class girls, though the relevant research focuses more on competition and rivalry among them. In one study, for example, Duff (1996) found that 95% of white high-school girls reported competition as an issue in their friendships, compared with 38% of girls of color. In addition, 81% of white girls reported jealousy as an issue in their close friendships with other girls, compared with 31% of the girls of color.

The research on friendships, taken as a whole, suggests that many girls, across races and classes, and even those with a best friend, or a couple of close acquaintances, do feel more disconnected from classmates these days. This lack of connection can lead to mistrust, loneliness, and aimlessness. As the peer group shifts, the adolescent girl must reestablish herself anew. And like someone practicing the same passage of music repeatedly, she doesn't get experience playing the whole piece—with all the depth and nuance that having more sustained and intimate relationships can bring.

Relationships With Adults

Current research on girls' social development postulates that, rather than simply moving away from parental and other adult relationships, girls appear to respond to a developmental press for meaningful connectedness, especially with adult women—mothers, friends, teachers, and counselors (Apter, 1990; Brown & Gilligan, 1992; Debold, Brown, Weseen & Brookins, 1999; Orenstein, 1994; Pipher, 1994). Although there is relatively less research on girls' relationships with their fathers and mentoring men, a growing body of evidence supports the significant benefits for development in these relationships, too (Apter, 1993; McHale, Kim,

Whiteman, & Crouter, 2004; Snarey, 1993). Girls need to have many adult models in order to grow through adolescence. Parents and other adults together form the stable foundation for a developing social identity; they cannot be phased out as friendships are ostensibly phased in. Peers may take up more time in adolescence but we are off base culturally and developmentally if we then infer that this means it is time to sideline the adults.

Moreover, rather than establishing a false dichotomy between autonomy and affiliation, contemporary theory holds that girls want both, even at the same time. As Fishel (1999) has suggested, ". . . separation and connection can occur in tandem . . . parent–child fighting can be a sign of wanting to be known better" (p. 263). Fights are perhaps a way that girls stay close and assert distance all at once. Adolescent girls are, of course, moving along, from relative dependence to relative self-reliance. But the goal of all the struggles in relationships, as Apter's hallmark (1990) study concludes, is to find a new way of relating, not to leave entirely. Apter found that girls wanted to be engaged in vibrant, searching, and challenging relationships, and were miserable when their mothers withdrew from the fray. And while some conflict is inevitable, as adolescents get ready to take off, it only seems like the defining principle. In fact, for girls clashing can be another way of being in relationship with a trusted adult. From this larger vantage point, such discord, unsettling though it may be, is just one more aspect of these evolving intimate relationships.

Taken together with the serious consequences of social isolation for girls, the importance of sustained connections with both peers and adults must be underscored. And the task is not merely to be able to make friends, and get along with adults (though these are laudable and necessary skills, too). But rather, over the course of adolescence, girls need to learn how to nourish and deepen their connections, to be empathic without losing themselves in compassion, to be mindful of others, to be intentional in relationships, and to make amends when there is a rupture in a friendship. These are complex tasks, one and all, difficult for many adults, too.

Emotional Development

As brain research has suggested, young adolescent emotions are, in many ways, still immature, and their emotional growth also typically lags significantly behind their physical development. Their emotions are unmodulated by experience and, with the limbic system at full throttle, tend to be extreme and volatile. If excited, girls are apt to react disproportionately to an event. They can be overcome by joy as well as rage. Because their feelings are unstable, the attendant behaviors can be erratic, too. Interestingly, a growing body of research suggests that the experience, expression, and regulation of emotions follow a predictable developmental timeline. Shirk and Russell (1996) have a detailed review of these data.

We need to gauge how well a girl manages her internal experiences in light of important data describing the many complicated steps involved. We may accurately attribute mood swings and inarticulate emoting to hormones, willfulness, and pruning in the brain. But at the same time we are probably seeing a girl who simply does not yet have the necessary skills; she might not be developmentally capable of using language to mediate and regulate powerful feelings.

Emotional Experience

We want adolescent girls to be able to identify their feelings and describe them with words. This is, of course, the main focus of adult therapy, and we believe such a skill to be one of the hallmarks of emotional maturity. Setting aside for the moment the compelling evidence provided by Brown (1998), that girls lose this ability under a cultural press to be nice, this is still a significant developmental task for all.

Emotional experience is made up of a complex network of interrelated abilities, each with its own developmental course. The first task is the recognition and identification of feelings. As they mature, girls are supposed to become increasingly capable of sorting out subtle differences in emotions. This ability, in turn, is closely connected to the development of a more sophisticated and nuanced vocabulary that can be applied to the feelings. Older girls' emotional inferences also become more accurate and they move from simple labeling—glad, sad, mad, bad, scared—to more specific emotions like proud, ashamed, grateful, bewildered, and relieved. But the process is more difficult than merely labeling emotions; it also entails an ability to grasp the meaning of emotional experiences. For example, a girl who is upset and has homework she forgot about may believe she is mad because her parents are badgering her, or because she is stressed about a tough deadline. These explanations suggest quite different meanings for a strong feeling. Young adolescents externalize blame quite freely; this makes it harder for them to take responsibility. At the same time, matching explanations to emotional experiences can also be developmentally challenging.

Adolescent girls may struggle emotionally because they may not recognize their feelings, they may not be able to put them into words, and they may not be able to understand the meaning of these emotions. But their emotional experience is even more complicated because they are frequently contending with many concurrent and conflicting feelings. An extreme but clear example of this is with abused girls who may feel love, sadness, fear, and rage, among other potent emotions, often all at once. By 10 years of age, only some girls can even comprehend that they can have two incompatible emotions, and even then only if the two emotions are evoked by different situations (Shirk & Russell, 1996). For example, they can be thrilled about taking an airplane and scared about being away from home. Only with formal operations, in mid- to late-adolescence, can most girls understand that contradictory emotions may be directed toward the same event. For example, it takes a long time, developmentally, before girls can know, at once, that they are relieved that their parents won't let them go to an unsupervised party; embarrassed that their friends may think poorly of them; and angry that they are being controlled this way. Younger adolescents tend to be just mad in this situation, and that's because they don't have the developmental ability to grasp the complexity of these feelings.

Emotional Expression

The way that adolescent girls express their feelings is often of concern to adults. They may act out distressed feelings, harm themselves, or conceal it all behind a smile, but something seems awry in the communication. Girls don't have much permission to be angry, it is true, but they could also be unable or unwilling to delve into their dark worlds because they don't know how. As with all other kinds of development, useful emotional expression is a skill set that children and adolescents acquire over time.

The research literature on the development of emotional expression concludes consistently that most children and young adolescents do not want to talk about negative feelings. But they may be increasingly adept and empathic when the emotions in question are not their own. Given a hypothetical person or situation, or the old "I have a friend with this problem" frame, some girls demonstrate more ability than when attempting to talk about their own situations. An adolescent girl's expression of feelings may be greater when her own pain or confusion isn't the central concern.

Emotional expression is also difficult for many girls because they live so much in the present, and we want them to talk about events of the remote and not-so-remote past. In a typical adolescent life, last weekend seems so long ago. They may be full of feelings now; the upheaval of the past may feel of little consequence in the present. Girls may have the developmental ability to recognize the enduring nature of feelings, but not the capacity to rearrange experiences, bring the past onto the screen in Technicolor; filing away the exciting and challenging present for a time.

Our quest for direct emotional expression is worthwhile, but hard for many reasons. When we ask about feelings and girls smile and say "fine," or shrug and say "I don't know," they're often telling a kind of truth. They're not necessarily being defensive or resistant as we sometimes may imagine. Especially when girls come from homes and communities where "talking about feelings" is taboo, or culturally atypical, this line of inquiry may seem as confusing as the New York City subway system is to an outsider. For some adolescents, the possibility of an emotional meltdown—becoming so overwhelmed by raw feeling that they can't make sense of it—is also great. And then they won't be able to think coherently about feelings anyway, as anyone who has sat with a raging or sobbing teenager knows.

We want girls to be more fully expressive, and more authentic in their descriptions of how they feel. This is perhaps one of psychotherapy's greatest gifts to them. But we can't expect either a nuanced vocabulary or an affective range when we begin our work. The naming of real feelings is a tremendous accomplishment for girls. The comforting words the late Fred Rogers offered about hard conversations with children do ring true: "If it's mentionable, it's manageable." But for many, this is a developmental goal rather than a prerequisite for therapy.

Emotional Regulation

Adolescent girls often have difficulty regulating their emotional worlds. They have temper tantrums, cry when someone looks at them "the wrong way," pick fights over trivial matters, and laugh so hard they fall out of their chairs. In fact, most disorders of childhood and adolescence seem to involve a problem with emotional regulation (Cicchetti, & Rogosh, 2002; Cole, Michel, & O'Donnell, 1994; Dahl, 2001; Shirk & Russell, 1996), so it is noteworthy that this aspect of emotional development also follows a timeline of its own.

Over the years, children become increasingly competent at both modulating their emotional experience (beyond the all-or-none method of preschool emoting) and controlling the expression of actions. Infants and young children rely to a great extent upon the support of adults to help them regulate their emotions; strong attachments are the cornerstones of this developing capacity. The secure and upset toddler comes to expect that a caring adult will kiss her bumps and bruises, and hold or remove her from the scene when she loses control.

As these children get older, they are expected to take on the tasks of calming and regulating themselves. For example, most school-age children are capable of feeling very angry without becoming violent. Emotionally attached children additionally develop a kind of "dimmer switch" that enables them to react in proportion to the intensity of experiences. With this internal regulation, their reactions should be different if they break a shoelace or fail a test or lose a beloved dog.

By adolescence, though, problems with emotional regulation are compounded by brain renovations, the influx of pubertal and stress hormones, increased external expectations for emotional control (based on adult fantasies about adolescent competence), and dramatically decreased adult intervention. This is not (to say the least) a winning combination of events for emotionally regulated behavior.

In reality, girls often become more dysregulated than they were in the past, and are more like preschoolers in their all-or-none management of their internal states—in the most extreme cases, they may either seem out of control, or completely shut down. And girls with an early history of losses and broken attachments may never have developed the capacity to self-regulate in the first place. Others need to find out where external limits are because they are not actually capable of providing their own. The emotionality may serve the same function as in infancy—to get someone to hold them, if only metaphorically. Over the course of adolescence, most girls can develop both better defenses and new skills to aid them in modulating powerful feelings. However, until they improve in self-soothing and problem solving, it is incumbent upon caring adults to help them stay in control.

Are There Normal Adolescents Out There?

Even when an adolescent girl acts like an adolescent girl, concerned people still wonder whether her behavior is normal? There seem to be some fairly invariant aspects of adolescent behavior that still can cause us to worry and feel confused. And because neither children nor adults usually act this way, we are easily bewildered and disoriented.

There are many ways to define normal, which include: the absence of pathology; a utopian state; a statistical average; and systemically. The systems model emphasizes a view of normality as the result of an individual's ability to change and adapt as part of a social system that also fluctuates over time. In this view, adjustment and disturbance are examined longitudinally, looking at interactions between the person and the social system (Elmen & Offer, 1993).

The systems perspective is useful here because it highlights the difficulty and complexity of defining normality for adolescents as a group. Adolescent behavior is contextual, based upon individual developmental and interpersonal information, and we can only look at what's normal for one teenager at a time. We need to take into consideration what external forces are operating, too, at a given point in time, and in a given environment. No generalizations extend across all races, cultures, and classes, family structures, and personal histories. Tracking physical, cognitive, social, and emotional development is more like looking at a variety of growth curves, with each girl progressing along her own paths. As Elmen and Offer (1993) note, "Perhaps more than at any other time during the life span, one individual at adolescence is as unique in his or her normality as another is unique in his or her disturbance" (p. 12). When we ask whether a particular behavior is normal, we need to know more about an adolescent, and about her context, too, and then we can make a decision—keeping in mind we may need to revise it sometime later. When someone asks us whether a particular behavior is normal, the first answer is usually, "Tell me more."

Describing Girls

For many girls, childhood is very brief, and getting briefer all the time. Consequently, the extended period we now call adolescence generally refers to the years between ages 10 and 19, when girls are somewhere between 5th and 12th grades in school. Since girls mature physically and emotionally more rapidly than boys, and from a younger age participate more eagerly in teen culture, they lose childhood more quickly. By the time they graduate from high school, nearly one in three adolescent girls will experience significant symptoms of depression, anxiety, or eating disorders, a rate approximately twice the rate for boys (Commonwealth Fund, 1999). It is important to underscore though that this statistic describes both a percentage of girls about whom there is concern and a minority of girls. Thus any consideration of the many stresses and problems faced by girls needs to be balanced by acknowledgment of the strength and resilience that most girls also exhibit.

There are more than 18.7 million adolescent girls in the United States (U.S. Bureau of the Census, 1997). One in five of them live in a family with income at or below the poverty line. More than one in four (26%) are in single-parent homes, more than half (54%) of which are poor (Annie E. Casey Foundation, 2006).

While the proportion of the American population ages 10 to 19 is expected to decline in the future as the boomers reach ripe old age, the proportion of minority adolescents (Hispanic, black, Asian American, native Hawaiian, and American Indian/Alaskan Native) is expected to increase, from approximately 34% of the total population in 1998 to 45% in 2020, to 56% in 2050 (Day, 1996).

The Vulnerability of Girls

Adolescent girls are particularly vulnerable to certain health and mental health problems. One in five high-school girls (19%) describes her health as fair or poor, and one in four report a failure to get medical care they felt they needed (Commonwealth Fund, 1999). Although these data suggest good overall health among adolescent girls, significant minorities are coping with chronic disease or disabling conditions, which require continuing medical attention.

Insulin dependent diabetes mellitus, which affects 1 out of 800 adolescents, and has a peak onset of 10 to 14, is more common among girls than boys. Thyroid gland disorders, which also often begin in adolescence, occur nine times more often among girls than boys. Other chronic conditions found with frequency in girls include acne, juvenile rheumatoid arthritis, scoliosis, urinary tract infections, and migraine. Childhood asthma affects girls and boys at similar rates, but girls are less likely to outgrow it, which puts them at risk for later development of pulmonary disease (McArney, Kreipe, Orr, & Comerci, 1992).

Sexually Transmitted Diseases

Adolescent girls have the highest rates of sexually transmitted diseases, except for HIV/AIDS, of any age group of women or men, and their infections typically result in more severe complications. Gonorrhea, a reportable disease, affects five times as many girls as boys between the ages of 10 and 14, and twice as many girls between 15 and 19. Adolescent girls also have the highest rates of chlamydia, a common cause of pelvic inflammatory disease sometimes resulting in sterility (Litt, 1997).

HIV/AIDS continues to pose a growing threat to adolescent girls, particularly those belonging to minority groups. Although the number of people diagnosed with AIDS in the United States each year has decreased by more than 50% over the past two decades, the proportion of AIDS cases among girls and women (13 years of age and older) increased in this same period, from 7% in 1985 to 27% in 2005 (Centers for Disease Control, 2005). Of particular concern is the finding that, in the 13 to 19 age group, girls comprise over half (51%) of reported HIV cases, the vast majority infected through sexual contact. Racial and ethnic minorities represent most of these new cases. Between 2001 and 2005, an estimated 83% of girls and women newly diagnosed with HIV/AIDS in the United States were African American or Hispanic (Centers for Disease Control, 2005).

Pregnancy

About one million teenage girls get pregnant every year in America; one-third voluntarily terminates the pregnancy, one out of seven miscarries, and approximately half give birth. The teenage birth rate has been declining since 1960, despite media hype to the contrary. Nonetheless, pregnancy and birth rates for teenage girls in America are higher than in most Western developed countries. Also, compared to 1960, a substantially greater share of today's more than 500,000 teenage births are to girls who are not married. Native American girls have the highest birth rates and Asian American girls the lowest. The birthrate for unmarried black girls has declined for each of the last several years. However, the birth rate for black and Hispanic teenage girls remains twice that for white girls (Commonwealth Fund, 1999).

Pregnancy during adolescence can result in long-term health and social problems. Girls who are mothers before age 18 are less likely to continue in school, achieve a higher income level, or maintain marital relationships (Commonwealth Fund, 1999). But an even more worrisome problem of teenage pregnancy may be this: in only 8% of all teenage births and 1% of all births in the United States are both partners under age 18, that is legally "children." Consistent with the data for sexually transmitted diseases (including HIV/AIDS), too many adult men are having sex with teenage girls. In fact, on average, there is a 10-year age difference between the youngest teen mothers and their partners (Males, 1996).

Sexual and Physical Abuse

Adolescent girls are at greater risk of both physical and sexual abuse than boys; in the Commonwealth Survey of the Health of Adolescent Girls (Commonwealth Fund, 1999) more than one in five high-school girls said she had been physically or sexually abused (12% said they had been sexually abused, and 17% said they had been physically abused). Most abuse occurred at home (53%), took place more than once (65%), and the abuser was most often a family member (57%) or a family friend (13%). The rates of sexual abuse increase dramatically for girls between 10 and 14. Most studies concur that cases of adolescent abuse involve girls twice as often as boys, whereas there is a more equal balance between the sexes among cases involving victimization of preteens (Ackard & Neumark-Sztainer, 2003; Finkelhor & Dziuba-Leatherman, 1994). Recent media coverage on Internet predators may make it appear that girls are more endangered by strangers outside of their home. In reality, the vast majority of girls are victimized by someone they know quite well.

In the Commonwealth Survey, nearly 1 in 10 older girls reported abuse by dates or boyfriends. When date-forced sex is included in the count, 1 in 4 high-school girls reported some form of abuse. Additionally, 1 in 4 girls (presumably many of the same girls) wanted to leave home because of violence against them or someone else in the home. These data are consistent with other studies that conclude that about 20% to 30% of girls may be victims of sexual abuse (Finkelhor & Dziuba-Leatherman, 1994; Office of Justice Programs, 1998; Putnam, 2003). Fifty-eight percent of abused girls said they had wanted to leave home at some point because of violence, compared with just 18% of nonabused girls.

Because of different definitions and sampling methods, estimates of physical abuse of adolescent girls are harder to compare to the Commonwealth Survey. However, Gelles and Straus (1990) estimated that 6.9 million American children under age 18 were assaulted that year by parents (defined as kicking, biting, punching, choking, beating, and using weapons—these data do not include psychological maltreatment). It is widely believed that adolescent abuse is particularly underreported, and that authorities only learn about 1 in 7 cases.

It is important to note also that girls do not often experience only one form of violence; there is significant overlap, for example, between physical abuse and psychological maltreatment of children (Claussen & Crittenden, 1991; Vissing, Straus, Gelles, & Harrop, 1991), and woman abuse and child abuse (e.g., Straus, 1988). As a corollary, it needs to be reiterated that, while the victimization of girls is very serious indeed, the vast majority of girls remain unharmed. There is a notable overlap among girls experiencing poverty, despair, and injury.

Indeed, the Commonwealth Survey underscores these correlations, finding a strong relationship among impoverished homes, reports of abuse, fair or poor health status, and risky health behaviors. High-school girls who reported some form of abuse were approximately twice as likely to drink alcohol, to smoke cigarettes frequently, and to have used drugs in the past month. They were also far more likely to report eating disorders: 32% said they had binged or purged, more than double the rate (13%) of girls who did not report abuse, and were more than twice as likely to be depressed (46%) as girls who had not been abused (18%). Not surprisingly, abuse of adolescent girls poses significant medical, legal, and psychosocial problems for them, often with life-long consequences.

Depression and Suicide

The Commonwealth Fund Survey determined that 1 in 4 adolescent girls exhibit some depressive symptoms and 1 in 10 have severe depressive symptoms. These symptoms included: feeling like crying often, thinking about or planning suicide, feeling as though nothing will work out, feeling sad most of the time, hating oneself, feeling alone, not having any fun, not feeling loved, and not feeling as good as others. This study additionally revealed that black girls were least likely of all racial groups to exhibit depressive symptoms (17%) while Hispanic and Asian American girls had the highest rates (27% and 30% respectively), and white girls were in the middle range, at 22%. Most studies concur that, although the prevalence of depression is equal for boys and girls before puberty, adolescent girls have more than double the rates of depression found in boys (Waller et al., 2006).

It is quite clear, from numerous surveys, that many adolescents contemplate and attempt suicide. For example, The Centers for Disease Control estimate that, each year, about 3.5 million high school boys and girls have suicidal ideation; 2 million have made specific suicide plans; and over 1 million have made suicide attempts (Centers for Disease Control, 1991).

In the Commonwealth Fund Survey, overall 29% of girls agreed with the statement, "I think about killing myself but I would not do it." Among high-school girls, 1 in 3 had thought about suicide in the past two weeks and another 3% responded positively to the statement, "I want to kill myself." Gender differences are notable: among reported cases, adolescent girls attempt suicide four times as often as boys, but boys succeed four times more often than girls do (Lewisohn, Rohde, & Seeley, 1996). However, varying definitions of suicidality make it difficult to interpret these numbers.

Indeed, the data on female suicidal behavior are sobering but also somewhat confusing. As Males (1996) has pointed out, "While 10 percent of teen females are reported to have attempted suicide, only one in every 5,000 girls actually kills herself during her entire adolescence through age 19. That's 500 failed attempts for every suicide" (p. 240). It is quite likely that we don't know how to categorize and define the kind of hopelessness that girls describe. It sounds most like suicidality, and indeed to be conservative and safe, we must respond to that meaning. However, in fact, we may often really be hearing these girls communicating some message other than the wish to die; for example, rage at someone else, a cry for help, alienation, or despair (Straus, 1994).

Eating Disorders

Confronted with the weight gain associated with puberty and the intensification of gender role expectations, it is typical for girls to experience extreme body image dissatisfaction. By age 13, 53% of American girls are unhappy with their bodies; by age 17, 78% are dissatisfied (Brumberg, 1997). For too many, adolescent concerns about their physical appearance become all-consuming and eclipse concerns about other life goals.

Eating disorders pose a major health concern for adolescent girls. The Commonwealth Survey found that 1 in 6 girls in grades 5 through 12 said she had binged and purged; 7% said they had done so more than once a week. Eighteen percent of high-school girls reported that they had binged and purged, and 8% said they did so a few times a week or daily. Well over half (58%) of older girls said they had been on a diet, and 1 in 3 thought she was overweight. Other national studies similarly conclude that anorexia nervosa affects between 1 and 3% of all adolescent girls; bulimia affects 15% (Hoek, 1991; Lewinsohn, Hops, Roberts, Seeley, & Andrews, 1993). In addition, a large number of adolescent girls engage in eating patterns (such as extremely restrictive dieting, laxative abuse, vomiting, or binge eating) that although not severe enough to meet diagnostic criteria of anorexia or bulemia, represent clinically significant symptoms of eating disorders (Rogers, Resnick, Mitchell, & Blum, 1997).

Obesity among adolescent girls has, in fact, increased in recent years, though compared to the vast numbers who believe it, still only 21% of girls are actually statistically overweight (Centers for Disease Control, 1994). Not surprisingly, this increase in obesity accompanies a decrease in physical activity and an increase in caloric intake and television watching. One study of a nationally representative population of adolescents found that 10- to 15-year-olds who watch five or more hours of television per day are five times more likely to be overweight than adolescents who watch two or less hours per day (Gortmaker et al., 1996). Girls from lower socioeconomic households and girls who mature early are also at particular risk for being overweight (Litt, 1997). As girls enter high school, they are less likely to exercise and more likely to diet to control weight (Commonwealth Fund, 1999).

Drugs and Alcohol Use

In the dubious achievement category, more adolescent girls than boys started using marijuana, alcohol, and tobacco in 2004, and are now involved with these substances at rates comparable to those for adolescent boys (Substance Abuse and Mental Health Services Administration, 2006). Alcohol is the drug abused most by adolescents in the United States, more than cigarettes or other substances (Johnston, O'Malley, Bachman, & Schulenberg, 2005). In 2005, about 10.8 million adolescents aged 12 to 20 (28.2% of this age group) reported drinking alcohol in the past month. Nearly 7.2 million (18.8%) were binge drinkers, and 2.3 million (6%) were heavy drinkers. These figures have remained essentially the same since 2002 (Substance Abuse and Mental Health Services Administration, 2006). While more males than females overall under the age of 21 report using and abusing alcohol, among younger adolescents (ages 12 to 17) the percentage of females who are current drinkers (17.2%) is now higher than the percentage of males (15.9%) (Substance Abuse and Mental Health Services Administration, 2006). Similarly, according to a summary of three recent federal surveys, girls are also now binge drinking at rates greater than their male peers (Newes-Adeyi, Chen, Williams, & Faden, 2005). It is also noteworthy that the causes and consequences of alcohol consumption are different for girls and boys; girls are particularly vulnerable emotionally, mentally, and physically.

The rate of illegal drug use among adolescents overall has actually decreased dramatically since 1979, despite popular beliefs to the contrary (American Academy of Child and Adolescent Psychiatry, 1999; Johnston, O'Malley, & Bachman, 2003; Substance Abuse and Mental Health Services Administration, 2006; U.S. Department of Health and Human Services, 1999). Even in recent years, this downward trend has continued. Among adolescents ages 12 to 17, 11.6% were using illegal drugs in 2002; by 2005, use rates were around 10% for both boys and girls (Substance Abuse and Mental Health Services Administration, 2006). These data are generally encouraging.

Still, burgeoning numbers of intensive substance abuse treatment programs offer some support for the notion that our concern about adolescents is greater, adolescents who are using may be more intractably addicted than in the past, or that our outpatient strategies for managing adolescent substance use are too limited and inadequate for today's world. It is safe to say that drugs are more refined and varied than those available a generation ago, and still pose a significant concern for those working and living with teenagers. Interestingly, the best predictor to date of adolescent smoking, drinking, and substance abuse is still parental involvement with those substances (Males, 1996; U.S. Department of Health and Human Services, 1993).

Cigarette smoking is also a serious problem for teenagers; once hooked, more than 80% will smoke as adults. In 2005, 3.3 million (13.1%) of adolescents used a tobacco product in the last month, and 2.7 million (10.8%) used cigarettes (Substance Abuse and Mental Health Services Administration, 2006). Among these youths aged 12 to 17, current cigarette smoking in 2005 was equally prevalent among females (10.8%) and males (10.7%). The rate for both girls and boys has declined by several percentage points since 2002. As with other addictive substances, girls probably smoke for different reasons than boys, and appear to have a much quicker path to nicotine dependence. One recent study concluded that adolescent boys typically develop symptoms of nicotine dependence in 183 days, compared with just 21 days for adolescent girls (DiFranza, Savageau, Rigotti, Fletcher, Ockene, McNeill, et al., 2002).

There is some overlap in adolescent involvement with substances. In the Commonwealth Fund survey (1999), nearly one-third (30%) of older girls and one-third (33%) of older boys reported either smoking, drinking, or using drugs. Fifteen percent of older girls were engaged in at least two of these behaviors.

When asked why they smoked or drank, 66% of girls who reported smoking said they did so to relieve stress, as did 38% of those who reported drinking frequently. And 36% who reported drinking said they did so because it helped them to forget problems. Girls with depressive symptoms or who reported abuse were even more likely to turn to smoking or drinking for relief.

Anxiety and Panic

The anxiety disorders, in all their forms, describe by far the most common problems for adolescent girls. Researchers have put some effort into arguing about how much worry and fear is "normal" during adolescence. But given the world we live in, this seems like the wrong avenue for discourse. We could logically be concerned about girls who weren't anxious—maybe they're out of touch with reality. Nonclinical samples of adolescents today score as high on measures of anxiety as adolescents seen as inpatients in 1957 (Twenge, 2000). And severe anxiety still underlies many of the presenting problems we are asked to treat: It is in kids, in families, in communities, and in our social fabric. A lot of therapists are anxious, too. Thus it is a particularly difficult symptom to treat by counseling one girl at a time; she is usually anxious for a reason.

Millions of adolescents each year feel unsafe at home, in school, and in their communities. They are emotionally, physically, and sexually abused, neglected, homeless, hungry, unable to focus or learn, and witnesses to terrifying violence. If we take into account social phobias, school refusal, posttraumatic stress disorder, and obsessive–compulsive disorder, as well as the variety of generalized and specific anxiety disorders, we are likely to be describing a vast number of adolescent girls in a broad range of social contexts.

Self-Mutilation

Adolescent girls who self-harm are more numerous than most reports would suggest. Notably, many texts on adolescence for parents and for professionals barely mention this problem at all. Self-harm is not a diagnostic category in DSM–IV, nor is it routinely explored in research on other problems that are associated with it—trauma, suicidality, anger, anxiety, eating disorders, and depression, for example. Though reports of self-harm among adolescents in clinical samples are common (Linehan,

1993; Miller, 1994; Pike, 1995), one study places the incidence around 3% for adolescent girls (Garrison, Addy, McKeown, & Cuffe, 1993). Yet in a general high-school sample, 39% of students surveyed had engaged in self-mutilation (biting self, hitting self, cutting/carving skin) in the last year (Lloyd, 1998).

It is impossible to know the actual numbers of girls on a national scale because deliberate self-harm is often concealed by the self-harmers, and by their relatives and friends; it is seldom severe enough to require hospitalization by itself. We do know that the problem is significantly greater than published reports generally suggest (Smith, Cox, & Saradijian, 1999). We can also be confident that self-injurious behaviors are not just a symptom of "borderlines" as once believed, but a much more mainstream coping strategy. Many miserable girls appear to be "writing" messages to us on their bodies, even if there is only a very small chance we will notice and "read" them, and respond. In the absence of more adaptive self-soothing strategies, millions of girls have discovered that self harm provides a reliable short-term solution for them.

Delinquency

Girls are also involved with the juvenile justice system in significant numbers, although the meaning of this increase is a legitimate topic of debate. A decade ago, when police began engaging more aggressively in domestic violence cases, an increasing number of girls were arrested. The majority of girls in the juvenile justice system continue to be adjudicated for nonviolent status offenses like running away, truancy, and violating curfews. Indeed, FBI and Bureau of Justice Statistics reports show that girls' rates of violent felonies have been declining since 1995, as have their rates of murder and robbery since 1993, and school fights since 1992. Girl murder and robbery arrest rates stand at their lowest levels in 40 years (Males, 2006).

Despite a lot of hype about girl aggression and violence, even the 748,000 arrests of girls younger than 18 years old in 1997 represent just 26% of all juvenile arrests made that year (Acoca, 1999). While girls may be "gaining" on boys in their violent ways, the arrest rate for boys engaging in violent crimes is still five times that for girls (Acoca, 1999). Similarly, while girl gang involvement is also increasing, girls still make up only about 10% of the 846,000 estimated juveniles who are in gangs (Snyder &

Sickmund, 1999). Girls are acting out in significant numbers and more are getting caught doing it, but aggression and violence are still largely the province of boys.

Running Away

The National Incidence Study of Missing, Abducted, Runaway and Thrownaway Children (Hammer, Finkelhor, & Sedlak, 2002) reported that in 1999, an estimated 1,682,900 children (half females) had a runaway/thrownaway episode. Of these youth, 37% were missing from their caretakers, and only 21% were reported to authorities for purposes of locating them. Two-thirds of these youths were between ages of 15 and 17; 71% were endangered during their runaway episode. Most came from families of divorce or separation; only 28% lived with both (birth or adoptive) parents. Most runaways initially stayed with someone they knew (66%) or did so at some time during the episode (94%). Some had spent time in dangerous or unfamiliar situations: 29% spent at least part of the episode without a familiar and secure place to stay, and 11% spent at least one night without a place to sleep. Many runaways returned home within a day or two, but about half (52%) were gone for three days or more, and 25% were gone for a week or more. For about half of the runaways, the caretaker knew the child's whereabouts more than half the time the child was away from home. Most runaways had run before, with 34% having run away at least once before in the past 12 months. Some traveled a long distance; approximately 16% went more than 50 miles from home during the episode, and about 10% went more than 100 miles.

All reports conclude that many adolescents are at risk in their homes—even more than on the streets. Over 90% of adolescents who end up in shelters and on the streets are trying to escape physical, sexual, psychological, or emotional abuse (Acoca, 1999; Archer, 2005). However, the street is no sanctuary. For adolescents who do not return home in a few days or weeks, the statistics become increasingly grim. After one month, half of the runaways will resort to prostitution or other crime to support themselves; by the time they have spent six months on the street it will become much harder to rescue them and interest them in continuing their education, looking for employment, working on family problems, and giving up drugs. However, as with other acting out behaviors, it is possible to sense the hope inherent in running away; girls who are escaping even the most dangerous situations harbor the faith that they will be helped somewhere and somehow. Adolescents run expecting their lives to be better than they are at home.

Clearly, a significant minority (at least 20–30%) of adolescent girls are struggling mightily to get through the adolescent passage. They need our help, yet as the following chapter describes, the environments that are supposed to support and direct these girls are in disarray. Girls are paying a terrible price for systems in uproar and collapse, for communities that have no place for them, and for an exploitive culture that is poisoning them every day. There is so much to be done, and so much we can do.

Chapter 2: Thoughts for Intervention

- Ask about whether there was a time in her life before things got hard for her and what it was like. Ask whether the problems arrived suddenly or gradually. Put events in context for her and her family; find out how each views the "derailment," and listen to their different narratives.

- Think about opportunities that girls have to care for others. Ask them whether they see themselves as contributors; find ways they can give (as well as receive) help and make a difference in someone's life.

- Ask them what their parents do; have parents talk to adolescent girls about their work (and dreams); have girls see their parents at work.

- Talk with girls about how the media portray them. Get them talking about the value and cost of objectification.

- Discuss the ways that the consumer culture diminishes pleasure over the long run, how relationships are harder but matter more (while honoring the quick fix of "retail therapy.")

- Consider whether the expectations for this girl are fair or realistic. Ask her what she thinks. Educate concerned adults about her development (including the impact of her pruned prefrontal cortex on executive functioning and behavior). Help them understand and appreciate her unique developmental course. Lower the expectations bar so she can be more successful.

- Don't assume abstract reasoning abilities. Most girls are concrete problem-solvers.

- Ask more questions than you usually do about how she takes care of herself and her health: sleep habits, schedule, physical concerns. Help her learn about taking care of her body.
- Ask girls detailed questions about their friendships; find out what skills they need to make and sustain connections and provide opportunities for them to practice and develop social skills.
- Teach emotional literacy: Identifying, naming, understanding, and managing feelings.
- Reassure girls that they will get through the hard times and that their lives can get better.

CHAPTER THREE

SYSTEMS IN AN UPROAR

Carla is 14 and she's always been a complicated kid. She was adopted after spending her first two years in an eastern European orphanage and she had developmental difficulties from the start including learning, emotional, and behavioral problems. She acts out sexually and evinces no remorse when she gets in trouble with adults. She sneaks out of the house, hangs out with an older crowd, and behaves seductively with strangers. Her parents have sought help for her since she arrived in the United States but the onset of adolescence has presented innumerable new challenges for everyone. Her parents have tough decisions ahead about whether she'll be able to manage the large regional high school, and about how best to keep her safe—from her own poor impulses as much as from exploitation by others. Carla's therapy has to focus on improving her self-care to the extent this is possible, and also, perhaps more importantly, on developing the family, school, and community systems that might contain and support her.

An adolescent girl in crisis, like Carla, is part of a chaotic landslide, burying concerned adults and their good intentions on the way down. Add to the plunge inadequate resources and insufficient understanding of the unique needs of girls, and the crash at the bottom may seem inevitable.

Even under better social and political circumstances than we have today, the people and places surrounding teenagers tend to be overwhelmed. This is probably not a coincidence: the transition to adulthood is a tough job requiring a frequently exhausting team effort—with little immediate compensation for overtime. And delayed parenting heads hormonally surging girls into the fray with their hormonally depleting mothers, adding further dysregulation to the equation.

But the lack of resources available to reach girls is a serious problem. Now the team is under great strain: families, schools, and community agencies have too much to do and too little help to manage effectively. The supports designed to hold teenagers are fragile, at a time in history and development when girls most desperately need solid and safe connections.

Home

A primary developmental task of adolescence is to gain the skills and confidence necessary to leave home, or function as a reasonably responsible adult while remaining there. Both options are common today, and suggest a gradual step-up in planning and organization abilities over early adolescence. Ideally, the shift is almost imperceptible, with additional freedoms and responsibilities accruing as the years go on, resulting in a generally competent young woman. And most adolescent girls in the United States envision a time when they will be on their own; what seems remarkable at this point in history is the incoherence of the structures that are supposed to get them there.

While parents don't hold all the responsibility for launching adolescents, this transition is surely more complicated and difficult when the home base is fragmented, stressed, or has insufficient—or excessive—resources. It is hard to take off from a bumpy runway. Perhaps more than at any time in the past, many families with adolescents feel overloaded and underprepared. Even extremely well-intentioned and loving parents seem to be struggling more these days.

Single Parents, Divorce, and Remarriage

More than a quarter of the 38 million adolescents between the ages of 10 and 19 in the United States live in single-parent homes, more than half of which are poor (U.S. Bureau of the Census, 1997). One in five of these adolescents lives in a family with income at or below the poverty standard. Some researchers estimate that in the next decade, with the rise in single motherhood, and divorce trends leveling off around 50% for first marriages (and slightly higher for second marriages), a majority of children will live in a single-parent household at some point (Hernandez, 1993; Hetherington & Kelly, 2002).

Many of these children will also have to adjust to living with a stepparent and in a stepfamily. This may improve their economic situation while it also can create other problems. The domestic reality is this: most adolescents today will inevitably endure multiple transitions and adjustments around them, even as they are attempting to make sense of seismic internal changes. And the fact that divorce and remarriage are so prevalent does not necessarily make the adjustments any easier for the involved kids, or feel as "normal" as the demographics make it seem.

The literature on divorce in families with daughters suggests some additional data that is of concern. Among married couples with children, those with daughters are more likely to divorce than those with sons (Mott, 1994). And following divorce, fathers are more apt to stay involved with their sons (Mott, 1994; Seltzer & Brandreth, 1994; Simons, 1996). Taken together, these findings lead to a broad generalization about fathers having greater emotional investment in their boys.

Even without divorce, bonds between fathers and daughters may weaken during adolescence, particularly if the connection during preadolescence wasn't strong in the first place. Research into father–daughter relationships indicates that many girls do not feel close to their fathers and are unlikely to turn to them for help (Schonert-Reichl & Mullen, 1996). And when parents divorce, there is a common, if unfounded, belief that mothers can manage the complexity of adolescent daughters more empathetically. Fathers, feeling unneeded, may then retreat further from the melee.

In fact, though, the available, if limited, literature on positive father–daughter relationships points resoundingly toward the salutary effects of sustaining such contact through the teen years, including, and perhaps especially, postseparation (Apter, 1993; Hetherington, Bridges, & Insabella, 1998; Snarey, 1993). Close ties between fathers and daughters are positively associated with girls' school success, occupational competency, and sense of comfort in and mastery of the world around them.

Although half of all divorces occur early on in the first seven years of marriage, there has also been a significant increase in divorce among midlife couples—those most likely to be parenting teens. About 20% of all divorces involve women over 40, and this percentage is on the rise (Bogolub, 1995). Regardless of when parents divorce, most adolescents will need to live with often-dramatic changes in social, material, and emotional resources through their teen years.

The impact of divorce and remarriage on adolescents is well documented, but accounts are confusing and conflicting, with no simple way to summarize the findings. The easiest conclusion is: It depends. How much conflict has the adolescent endured up to that point? High conflict homes tend to result in worse outcomes for the children (Amato & Keith, 1991; Hetherington & Kelly, 2002) even without divorce. What are the supports and resources available before, during, and after the break-up? Adolescents who lose emotional and economic support as collateral damage of divorce will naturally have a harder time adjusting. What were the adolescent's relationships with her parents like anyway? Girls who felt love and support all along will be significantly less vulnerable. And how compromised and preoccupied are her parents in the weeks, months, and years after the separation? Parents who keep their children's interests in the fore help the adjustment go more smoothly. Does the fighting between parents subside? Adolescents with parents who get past the chronic conflict have better outcomes (Bogolub, 1995; Hetherington et al., 1998).

What internal resources does the adolescent have that will give her strength to cope with the transitions and losses? The research on resiliency indicates how individual characteristics like confidence, humor, an easy temperament, and intelligence can be important in overcoming the stress of parental divorce (Cohen-Sandler, 2005; Kalter, 1990). What other resources does she have that will offer her extra scaffolding and stability through the divorce transition? Siblings, extended families, friends, and neighbors can all ameliorate some of the stress created by divorce (Bogolub, 1995).

Our assumptions about the impact of separation and divorce shouldn't overwhelm our willingness to find out about the specifics. In turn, our capacity to support and intervene will be enhanced by an open mindedness to make inquiries without preconceived ideas or prejudice about how hard separation and divorce might be for a particular girl.

In fact, there are two contradictory beliefs about the impact of divorce on adolescents. On the one hand, many researchers have suggested that teens, with their greater comprehension of events surrounding marital break-up, feel the impact of these transitions more than younger children, particularly when the level of conflict is high (Forehand et al., 1991). The reasoning follows that older children become more enmeshed in parental disputes. And as they develop the ability to comprehend the opposing views of their parents, they may become more vulnerable to loyalty conflicts (Johnston, Kline, & Tschann, 1989). Internalization of responsibility as girls get older may increase the levels of anger, guilt, anxiety, helplessness, and low self-esteem they feel when their parents divorce (Wallerstein, Lewis, & Blakeslee, 2000).

Others surmise that because adolescents are better able to understand the reasons behind their parents' divorce, they may stay out of the middle and so it may be less painful for them (e.g., Hetherington, et al., 1998). Further, clinical observation and research data support the idea that many teen daughters may benefit from closer relationships with their divorced mothers (and sometimes fathers), enjoying greater intimacy and parental attention than before the separation (Apter, 1990). And although they run the risk of parentification when they have to step into adult roles, many daughters rise to the challenge and become more self-possessed and view themselves as more mature with the increase in responsibilities and expectations.

Of course, there may be other negative consequences that are not immediately apparent. Initial coping might, in some cases, be short-lived. At least one small longitudinal study suggests that after 25 years, outcomes for girls of divorced parents often look poorer, with newly emerging problems in sustaining relationships and direction (Wallerstein et al., 2000).

It is evident from the discourse on effects that divorce can be a major life transition for adolescents, and as such it will typically have an impact on normative developmental tasks, though for most these will be transitory. Some teens may initially exhibit many of the same behavior problems seen in younger children—sleep problems, increased anxiety, depression, irritability, or acting out. In addition, adolescents with divorcing parents are more likely than their peers with married parents to drop out of school, to be unemployed, to become sexually active at an earlier age, to have children out of wedlock, to be involved with delinquent activities and substance abuse, and to associate with antisocial peers (Conger & Chao, 1996; Demo & Acock, 1996; Elder & Russell, 1996; Hetherington et al., 1998; McLanahan & Sandefur, 1994; Simons, 1996). However, it is notable that these findings are correlational and do not describe the attendant social and economic forces at play.

Indeed, it must be underscored that not all adolescents have severe or enduring reactions to their parents' separation. With some support and resumption of the functioning of parents postdivorce, there may soon be no negative difference between them and their age mates from nondivorced families (Armistead et al., 1990; Barber & Eccles, 1992; Patten, 1999). In fact, divorce can actually benefit some adolescents, when it involves the departure of a particularly violent or dysfunctional parent (Barber

& Eccles, 1992). Further, meta-analysis of studies reveals that differences within groups of intact or divorced families are generally much larger than the differences between them (Barber & Eccles, 1992). And it is important to note that while divorce is associated with an adolescent's risk for a variety of problems, the vast majority of teens (75 to 80%) will not experience significant difficulties (Patten, 1999). In other words, while divorce can increase the likelihood of developmental difficulty, we can assume safely that most children of divorce will not have major problems.

It is perhaps more evident that parental separation and divorce can make adolescents particularly vulnerable by the collateral damage that they bring, for example through dislocation, decrease in family time, loss of resources, loss of contact with extended family, or even a fundamental change in identity. How do we disentangle the impact of divorce from all the other variables commonly experienced by these adolescents? For example, what are the secondary effects of prolonged exposure to family discord, father absence, economic distress, other life stresses like moves and changes in school, poor parent adjustment—or the impact of any short-term crisis for that matter? Circumstances less frequently make divorce the preferred alternative (with the exception of domestic violence or sexual abuse, for example), but it is quite evident that postdivorce adjustment depends on a variety of factors, both over the short- and long-term.

Parental Involvement

Most parents of adolescent girls are insufficiently involved with them. These parents are not confident in their strategies but simply keeping up with a cultural pace that holds little room for expectations for family time, especially in families with teenagers. It seems that contemporary parents have little idea about how much they are needed. Too many parents underestimate the importance of that old familiar hum of family life and routine that makes even older adolescents feel safe and held.

Notably though, the girls themselves in clinical interviews, in research studies, and in large-scale surveys claim they want more of their parents—though maybe they're not directly saying so (Rice, 1996; Taffel, 2005). Similarly, a national poll conducted for the White House Conference on Teenagers (2000) established that the top concern of adolescent respondents was, "not having enough time" with their parents. These data are compelling, and support a picture of girls struggling to get the attention and nurture of adults, though often in a very roundabout way.

And it seems that the problem of true parent involvement is complicated by two extremes of family life. At one end, overworked and exhausted parents have little time to spare anyway, and accept closed doors at the end of the day with both regret and relief. They take the "Keep Out" signs—and edgy interactions that ensue when they have to knock—as proof that they've made the right choice in not pushing for contact. In some homes with adolescents, family members spend their evenings staring at separate screens in different rooms, seldom interacting at all. This seems more like a landlord–tenant arrangement than family life.

These parents also may be struggling with a problem that psychologist William Doherty (2002) has called, "the consumer culture of childhood." Such parents do not really think they should make their children engage in family activities; for them even family meals, for example, may have become another "consumer option" that the adolescent seemingly has the right to opt in or out of. Doherty writes:

> If we see ourselves only as providers of services to our children (and indeed, this is one important part of parenting), we end up confused about our authority, anxious about displeasing our children, insecure about whether we are providing enough opportunities, and worried that we are not keeping up with the output of other parents. In a market economy, the service provider must offer what is newest and best, and at all costs must avoid disappointing the customer. When applied to the family, this is a recipe for insecure parents and entitled kids. (Doherty, 2000, p. 16)

Such parents disengage from the hard work of setting limits, negotiating, arguing, cajoling, and maintaining intimacy with their adolescents under the misguided, but persuasive, notion that this distance is what their daughters need (and have a right to demand). Parents may reason that the girls should have choices, or they'll be on their own in just a short while, or the specter of conflict threatens to weaken already tenuous bonds. Whatever the logic, some parents allow and actually facilitate the drift apart from their daughters even as they may feel sadness and disappointment about it.

At the other extreme, girls are overscheduled by anxious and competitive parents eager to provide their daughters with opportunity and added advantages (Doherty & Carlson, 2002; Elkind, 2001; Rosenfeld & Wise, 2000). These parents are involved with their adolescents, but the agenda is confused and stressed. Parents who are dissatisfied with their own lives may begin to live vicariously through the accomplishments of their children (Elkind, 2001). Or parents who have always micromanaged their kids, are unable to pull back or stop, even through high school, when the stakes are higher, not wanting to leave anything up to chance — or, maybe worse, to the poor organization of their teenagers.

For families determined to give their adolescents every conceivable extracurricular experience, the pressure on everyone is very intense. The deeper reflective dialogue about things that matter — thoughts, feelings, memories, beliefs, intentions — what might popularly be termed "quality teen time" — seems completely lost for them. The pace of life is hectic and requires planning, cell phones, and logistical prowess, with little time for connecting conversations. These girls are chronically exhausted — their fatigue seems akin to that of new mothers. They may have more parent attention than in more disengaged families, for example, spending some time riding in the car with their parents to sports or musical practice (at least until they get their own cars, or find rides with friends). Even so, they are not likely to be participating much in the deeper and more emotionally meaningful ways of belonging in a family.

We know from both research and common sense that kids need parent involvement. It remains a complicated and confusing formula to fill in the details of what the particulars of this might be for adolescent girls. It is clear, though, that the extremes are problematic and inadequate. Whether parents have opted for "lite" parenting by backing off too far, or "extreme" parenting by taking over too enthusiastically, their daughters may not be getting enough of the slower, richer mix of family life.

This is not such an easy mix to prescribe. Pediatrician Mel Levine (2005) has described a dozen ingredients of parenting that need to be balanced over the course of adolescence: praise/criticism, discipline/freedom, intervention/self-help, free play/programming, leisure/work, cultural assimilation/cultural insulation, individual pursuits/group activities, interaction with adults/interaction with peers, family life/life beyond the family, general abilities/specialized affinities and skills, body/mind, present/future. Levine believes there are optimal blends for each of these poles "to create just the right mixes" (p. 200) for particular adolescents. Concerned parents may feel like mad scientists in the laboratory coming up with the finest recipes for raising their daughters! And, alas, there is no final formula; as girls grow and change, the mixture required will need new ingredients in different proportions.

Many other researchers have similarly sought to determine the features of successful parental involvement. And although there is much variation among flourishing families, some general principles appear to cross class and culture. These fall loosely into the categories of monitoring, expectations, limits, routines and rituals, and warmth.

Monitoring

A sizable body of literature supports the logical notion that parental monitoring of adolescents has salutary developmental benefits. Monitoring generally includes: knowing about friends and peer activities (as reported by both parents and adolescents); spending time together, helping with schoolwork and being involved in school activities, and supervising more broadly (e.g., limiting television, checking homework, limiting going out with friends, knowing where the adolescent is when not at home).

In many studies, such parental monitoring is negatively correlated with adolescent drinking, marijuana use, sexual activity, delinquency, suicidality, and general risk-taking (Beck, Shattuck, Haynie, Crump, & Simons-Morton, 1999; Cottrell, et al., 2003; Falbo, Lein, & Amador, 2001; Flouri & Buchanan, 2002; McKnight & Loper, 2002). Parents who do not monitor their teenagers seem to be more likely to have kids who act out and feel unsafe. As a corollary, parental monitoring is positively associated with many successful outcomes: positive peer relationships, academic achievement and attendance, identity achievement, social–emotional adjustment, superior parent–adolescent communication, and capability beliefs (Aunola, Stattin, & Nurmi, 2000; Gustafson, 1997; Juang & Silbereisen, 2002; Sartor & Youniss, 2002; Shumow & Lomax, 2002; Updegraff, McHale, Crouter, & Kupanoff, 2001). Overall, these are robust data that support parents' comprehensive monitoring of adolescents: knowing where they are, whom they're with, and what they are doing. Such involvement appears to pay off in large dividends—although it can be arduous for parents to sustain this investment in the face of adolescent mobility, friction, and secrecy.

Expectations

How much it is reasonable to expect of adolescents is one of the great parenting mysteries that repeatedly plays out in therapy. Again, the extremes seem obviously problematic—expect too much and an adolescent girl disintegrates into a puddle of anxiety, frustration, and self-worthlessness.

Expect too little and she turns into a self-centered and ungrateful tyrant, miserable to herself and to others.

Such external concerns are further complicated by the fact that girls place different sorts of expectations on themselves. It is usual that they fall short of their aspirations for themselves—and are under considerable pressure to achieve according to some standards they imagine they should be able to attain. Less commonly, girls don't seem to expect much of themselves at all; they "just wanna have fun" as the old Cindy Lauper song goes. Clinically, girls often present as though they don't have real aspirations, but the inverse is more accurate—they live almost entirely in the land of self-disappointment. It is also particularly hard for adolescent girls to separate out their own voices—what they want for themselves—from the opinions and expectations of their parents. In an effort to make that distinction, they may act in entirely self-defeating ways, quitting teams or instruments, getting involved in tough relationships, or doing poorly in school, for example. Parents sometimes have to keep their enthusiasms in check so girls can stay connected to their own hearts' desires for achievement.

Therapists also inadequately advise parents about how much or what to expect from a particular girl. Developmental information needs to be integrated into the larger context of the adolescent's particulars: temperament, intelligence, resources, stressors, and culture. Comparisons—to siblings, neighbors, the ideal adolescent, the child she once was, the parent as an adolescent, or celebrities—are all equally odious. Expectations need to be reasonable for a particular girl in a specific time and place, and regularly fine tuned.

Reasonable expectations meet these four criteria: First, such expectations are clear and consistent. Both a girl and her parents should be able to articulate them, and reach at least a 90% level of agreement about how they are managed in the home. This agenda item can take up weeks of family therapy alone—it is sometimes astonishing how murky and fluid rules and roles can be. For example, expectations about grades, chores, involvement, manners, friends, and behavior can all be interpreted in myriad ways. Girls need to know what is expected of them.

Second, expectations have to be attainable as evidenced by the fact they have been met before in the not-too-distant-past. For example, parents can want their daughter to be a straight A student, but if she hasn't gotten an A since third grade, this expectation is not reasonable. However, if she can achieve Bs, albeit just in English, this might be more possible to expect. The bar has to be set so a girl can get over it.

Third, adults must be certain that the girl has all of the skills and resources necessary to meet the expectations. For example, she has to have both writing ability and stationary available so she can send a thank-you note for a birthday gift. However, if an adolescent also needs help organizing her time to fit in note writing, then, despite what anyone may say to the contrary, she still does not have what it takes to meet this expectation. It is also true that parents and teens usually spend more time fighting about these little tasks than it takes to actually accomplish them. Still, it is very likely that girls need more basic help than would seem necessary for completion of mundane chores like this. Parents can choose to argue or help, but they will be involved one way or the other. We make too many assumptions about what girls "should" be able to do on their own.

Thus, fourth, the support structure has to be sufficient to ensure that the expectation is met successfully. For example, parents need to both congratulate a girl who comes home on time and enforce relevant consequences if she comes home late. External expectations—those we place on adolescent girls—by definition require external monitoring and support. Simple behavioral principles that shape the habits of small children need to be asserted in adolescence as well. If parents want their daughter to act a certain way, they will need to follow up such expectations with investment of their own considerable energy, thought, and time. Therapists can and should help parents structure environments so girls may meet more expectations more consistently.

Limits

Even though research and commonsense concur that adolescents do better with clear and consistent limits, this may well be another area in which the current generation of parents seems to be dropping the ball. Typically the problem of limit setting begins before adolescence, but some parents who were courageous and sensible with their younger children seem to lose their bearings with the adolescent. This softer style is attributable, at least in part, to what William Doherty (2002) has called the "therapeutic culture of parenting" (p. 22). Doherty noted that, since the 1970s, parents have turned to experts who can advise them on how to speak with children to sound more like therapists than parents. Therapeutic parents do not speak judgmentally or angrily to their adolescents—and they do not set many limits either.

Doherty (2002) suggested that this trend toward therapeutic parenting has at its foundation three myths that currently dominate popular culture, and undermine parental willingness to exert authority over their adolescents. The first myth is that children and adolescents are too fragile, and will be somehow traumatized or become retaliatory if parents set limits with them. The second myth is that limits that force conformity will somehow stultify or damage adolescents' unique development and self-esteem. The third myth is that adolescents will have to learn to handle lots of freedom to make their own choices and mistakes; parents shouldn't try to have this influence anyway. Taken together, these myths explain a lot about how our current generation of parents tends to be so insecure about standing up to their adolescents.

And there are other reasons why it is difficult to set limits, too. These may include, for example: other parents aren't doing so; teen challenges wear parents down to a bare nub; it's almost impossible to come up with real consequences for adolescents who have everything they need; parents have trouble deciding what is really worth fighting for when every interaction can be an issue to debate; and, in busy times, enforcing consequences is a tribulation unto itself. Still, it is clear that good, involved parents set unmistakable limits, taking into consideration their own girl's health and safety, depending on her environment, level of skill, and maturity. And then they have to enforce the limits the next time, too.

Not infrequently, an acting-out girl is brought to therapy and this move in itself becomes the first real limit on her behavior. Family treatment works on many levels, including the most basic structural fact of it. Parents who get their daughters into therapy are, de facto setting a regular limit on her behavior every week or two. Of course, good therapy does much more, but limits that say something about safety and predictability are always a great place to start.

Routines and Rituals

One of the biggest casualties of the rush of contemporary life (through the days and out of childhood) is the loss of family routines and rituals. The surge ahead means that family dinners, celebrations, vacations, bedtimes, and special events get lost. Routines and rituals provide vital glue for development; without them adolescent girls are sent spinning into the ether. Such traditions offer the stability and connectedness girls crave. The rare family dinner is both real and emblematic of this loss.

Sit-down, leisurely dinners provide all the nourishment of good rituals—predictability, connection, identity, and enduring values. Girls who have regular family meals do better on an astonishing number of measures: nutritionally, emotionally, academically, and socially. Research shows that teens who eat dinner with their families several times a week are more likely to do well in school and less likely than other teens to have sex at young ages, get into fights, or be suspended from school. Frequent family dining is also correlated with developing healthy eating habits (Doherty & Carlson, 2002; Erlandson, 1997; Wylie, 1997). This pattern holds true regardless of a teen's sex, family structure, or family socioeconomic level.

Moreover, a survey conducted by the National Center on Addiction and Substance Abuse (2003) further determined that the more often children have dinner with their parents, the less likely they are to smoke, drink, or use illegal drugs. They are less stressed and are less frequently bored. These findings support family dinners, of course, but also suggest something larger: family routines and rituals are hugely important for the sense of security and well being that is fundamental to healthy development.

Steady Warmth

A quality shared by good parents of adolescents is their ability to wander around with their eyes open. They happen to be in the house during some of the four times their adolescents need them the most—when they get up in the morning, when they get home, at dinner, and when they go to bed (Doherty & Carlson, 2002). Adolescent girls talk to parents who are there when the girl is ready to talk.

But beyond that availability, it appears that successful families are able to maintain steady warmth into the more barometrically challenged time of adolescence. This translates into keeping up family traditions and identities—trips for ice cream, breakfast treats, car trips, those ways of being that offer comfort and reassurance to the adolescent. Steady warmth that doesn't change, even as adolescence takes over, lets girls know that even though they feel different, the floor underneath them can still support them. This is not as hard to carry out as it may seem; it can be as simple as tea occasionally made the way she likes it, a shared movie rental, or an admiring gaze across the room.

It is incumbent upon parents to set the emotional tone in their homes. Too often, the adolescent's anger or disengagement defines what it feels like for everyone who lives there. Emotional tone, for most adults, is a conscious decision about how we want to show up in the world as adults. We have formed prefrontal cortexes and years of practice; how we treat and react to teenagers can be a conscious decision much more of the time than most parents have considered. More often than many parents may realize, they can decide how to act to have the kind of home life they desire. They can set a warm emotional tone that feels safe, steady, and welcoming. This "hum" is as familiar and reassuring for girls as they venture forth and return again as it was when they were younger.

Normal Conflict

Parents frequently feel under sudden siege in their homes when adolescent girls begin trying out their newfound self-advocacy skills. Conscious of their girls' self-esteem, of their developing need to think for themselves, and of the generations of voiceless women who preceded them, parents can be at once proud and devastated that so much ire is coming their way. Still, they need to know how much of the anger in the home is "normal." Therapists have a very important role to play in helping parents sort out garden-variety limit testing, rebellion, and rudeness from real unhappiness, frustration, and anger.

For their part, girls frequently feel misunderstood—and in fact they are. While there usually are reasons for bad behavior, underlying motives are incomprehensible (or intolerable) for adults—and sometimes for the girls themselves. Empathic listening, tolerance, and selective arguing all go a long way to get through a tough few years. Therapy is effective when it teaches parents strategies for reading subtext and helps girls to recognize and manage their strong feelings. Until systems are in place, the conflict can seem untenable all around, and parents may react in a way that puts even greater distance between them and their girls. Such conflict may also not be normal at all and indicative of a deeper problem for the adolescent and the family.

For a sizable number of girls, home feels unsafe, unpredictable, and unwelcoming, exploitive or harsh, with too little supervision or too little intimacy, with too much anger or too high expectations. The balance is way off, and they are suffering as a result. These girls may feel better at school, with friends, and even on the streets. They stop growing and developing in the name of survival, and they escalate in their symptoms of distress until someone steps in to help. Therapeutic interventions for them can only focus on safety until this most basic human need is met. We rely upon their signs of rage and distress to signal to us that they need our concern and connection and that their parents need help, too.

School

The American junior high (or middle school) and high school were not designed to address even basic developmental needs of adolescent girls, much less to compensate for the deficits of home life for them. Yet, the burden on schools is enormous. While girls have made notable progress in schools over the past 20 years, many are still not getting the kind of support that they need to thrive there academically, physically, socially, or emotionally.

Equal Opportunity

A summary of a report released by the American Association of University Women (AAUW; 1998) indicates that, since Title IX, girls have made some important gains in schools. For example, girls are taking more math and science classes, enrolling in higher level honors and advanced placement classes, playing more sports, and participating in more extracurricular activities (though not as much as boys). Girls are also heading to college at higher rates; 57% of all bachelor's degrees are awarded to women (Conlin, 2003). Indeed, a kind of educational backlash has ensued, in which some researchers report that boys in school may be more at-risk than girls (Conlin, 2003; Sommers, 2000). This seems to be a silly debate; there should not be a faux competition here in which advances for girls mean peril for boys in a zero-sum game. Both genders appear to be suffering at the hands of an educational system that is falling short of meeting their needs, if for different reasons.

And despite the notable improvements, issues that interfere with students' ability to learn—sexual harassment, bullying, violence, crowding—continue to be quite significant for girls. These risk factors are particularly problematic for ethnic minority adolescents (Vasquez & de las Fuentes, 1999). The AAUW (1998) report also documents a drop in the self-esteem of high-school girls, which is of concern. This decline crosses racial and ethnic lines but is most dramatic for white girls, starting in 7th grade (55% of white elementary girls and just 22% of white high-school girls report being "happy as I am").

Moreover, gender bias in classroom and curriculum continues to be clearly evident (deZolt & Henning-Stout, 1999). The AAUW (1998) report concludes that boys still receive more attention in class and are allotted more time to talk. Teachers, regardless of their sex or race, interacted more with boys, gave them feedback that was more precise and useful, and provided them with more comments than girls received. Student–teacher interactions favored boys in accepting poor or even wrong answers, posing higher-level questions, providing positive attention, and responding to requests for help. This report concludes that, although teachers were not sensitive to the presence or impact of bias, they were amenable to training and could ameliorate their teaching style to become more equitable.

When the AAUW (1998) examined commonly used textbooks, materials, and activities, they found that girls continued to be stereotyped, invisible, misrepresented, or marginalized. Within patterns of course enrollment, tracking continues into the present time; boys are still in more higher level and advanced courses, especially in math and science, and boys and girls remain in gender-stereotypical vocational programs (Cain, 1999; deZolt & Henning-Stout, 1999). In one review of 20 years of research, the authors concluded that in the high-school years, many girls continue to avoid courses that will influence their future academic and career opportunities, including math, science, and technology (Sadker & Sadker, 1994). Taken together, these data provide convincing evidence for the differential treatment and experiences of girls and boys in school settings. And even with some improvements that are noteworthy, especially for more affluent girls, overall their participation in the classroom and in extracurricular activities is still not where it should be—nor are the girls as satisfied with themselves or their opportunities as they should be.

The AAUW (1995, 1998) has made some suggestions about how to improve the likelihood of success for girls in school based on a review of over 500 studies. The list of factors includes: nonsexist/nonracist materials and instructional techniques, lower levels of competition and higher levels of innovative learning in the classroom. Also, girls did better when they had good relationships in the school with caring adults whom they liked and were given attention and recognition for their efforts. Most of the studies reviewed mentioned the importance of relationships for those girls who did well.

These meta-analyses are supported by smaller, narrative studies that explore how girls view themselves in school. When adolescent girls talk about their experiences with teachers, they tell stories about their relationships, featuring a caring connection in the context of high expectations (deZolt & Henning-Stout, 1999). And all of the research points toward success for girls lying in a different and more personal direction than most schools have taken.

Crowding

At a point in development when girls need desperately to be known and seen, they head off for the regional middle or high school, where despite the efforts of some well-intentioned adults, they are largely anonymous and invisible. More than 70% of U.S. high-school students attend schools of more than 1,000 students according to the U.S. Department of Education (McNeill, 2000). Large middle schools are also on the increase. Between 1968 and 1996, middle schools of more than 800 students increased from 16 to 30% (McEwin, Dickinson, & Jenkins, 1996). Many schools in large urban areas like Miami and Los Angeles have enrollments of over 5,000 students.

Researchers say that large schools are a result of Americans' penchant for efficiency, economies of scale, and curricular choice, and their belief that it's cheaper to educate more students in one building (Allen, 2002). Large high schools also evolved to assimilate immigrants to become more efficient and productive citizen-workers in the U.S. economy (Lee & Smith, 1995). Whatever the historic reasons and benefits of large consolidated schools, they no longer work for anyone, least of all those students in impoverished communities (Allen, 2002). In fact, almost all of the relevant contemporary research suggests quite emphatically that girls do better in smaller, more personal schools where they can develop connections and be seen.

The impact of crowding is intensified by the general chaos of schedules and school life. Teachers do not have the luxury of relationship building in a multiperiod day. Rather, they are faced with responsibilities to deliver information, reward and punish, maintain competition, and often to follow preordained curricular requirements established by state and federal policies. Meanwhile, many girls are at sea, pushing through crowds to the locker, the next period, the cafeteria, and out of the building. An average girl can head through all of her middle- and high-school years and hardly be known by any adults at all. Such anonymity makes even the most marginal peer group more compelling for a lonely and isolated girl.

Social Supports

In the absence of much adult presence, girls naturally turn to their peers for even more support. This strategy can be wonderful; some girls have close and nurturing friendships that carry them through the adolescent passage in fine style. And as they progress through adolescence, girls are more likely to have exclusive friendships, and to rely heavily upon their best friends for help and guidance (Brown, Way, & Duff, 1999). Depending upon the school climate and social context—providing opportunities in and out of school for such connections—it is possible for adolescent girls to make and sustain the vital attachments they deeply desire.

More often, though, the peer culture produces significant stressors of its own. Without adult involvement—interpretation, mediation, attenuation—issues of popularity, conformity, and belonging can become overwhelming in themselves. There are at least three reasons why too much reliance on peers (instead of a balance between peers and adults) causes problems for girls. First, and as was discussed in Chapter 1, contemporary adolescent groups are highly fluid, changing from year-to-year during high school. Cliques and in-groups continue to be persistent in middle school (Evans & Eder, 1993; Merten, 1997) especially for white, middle-class girls. But by high school, group assignment diminishes and is replaced by significant fluidity.

Adolescent girls may change groups for a variety of reasons: to avoid activities (e.g., using drugs) they consider a problem; to explore new interests; to escape personal conflicts; or to create a new identity for themselves. The fluidity allows for more exploration and less of a strict adherence to old standards of popularity. But it also makes it harder to develop close, enduring intimate friendships with so many options available (Schneider & Stevenson, 1999). As a result, many girls report feeling somewhat aimless in high school; they lack a sense of connection and have few close friends with whom they feel comfortable discussing problems or sharing ideas.

A second concern, defined clearly by Taffel (2001, 2005) is the dysfunctional influence frequently provided by peers (and pop culture) in the absence of adults. Taffel describes this as the "second family" and argues persuasively that its effect on development is now much more powerful than the actual "first" family. As Taffel (2005) states:

. . . since the peer group is essentially rudderless, it exemplifies Murray Bowen's undifferentiated ego mass. Once in the group, some individuals have trouble developing their own independent interest and values; if the old family hierarchy kept adolescents from ever leaving home, the new second family discourages them from going home. This is especially so, not in high school as many think, but in the pressure-riddled middle school years. (p. 242)

Taffel notes further that the leader of the group is frequently one of the most disturbed, albeit charismatic members. Just as therapists may need to engage parents in treatment with adolescents from dysfunctional first families, now it may be difficult to help a member of a "second family" without gaining access to the leadership there.

This leads to a third and related concern about the limitations of peer social support for adolescent girls: bad advice. Girls who are marginalized or emotionally disturbed tend to gravitate toward peers who match them developmentally. Regardless of how long they adhere to a particular group ethos, girls who are struggling need to get above the lowest common denominator, and have in their lives someone a bit more stable and centered than they are. This is not to denigrate the importance of friends, but to emphasize some of the ways that a peer group is necessary but not sufficient for troubled adolescents.

Harassment

Girls continue to be harassed in very high numbers through middle and high schools across the country, despite statements of zero tolerance for such behavior and laws that prohibit it. Female high-school students report the highest degree of sexual harassment of all groups, and the most harassing and inappropriate scenarios (Loredo, Reid, & Deaux, 1995). In one large-scale study, 85% of girls in grades 8 to 11 reported some form of it (AAUW, 1993). Acts included, but were not limited to, such behaviors as sexual looks and comments; touching; grabbing and pinching; brushing up against a person in a sexual manner; mooning and flashing; being called gay, lesbian, or queer. Girls reported being sexually harassed by peers, teachers, administrators, and other school-related personnel.

With levels of harassment this high, it is a wonder that girls can focus on school at all. Indeed, according to the AAUW (1993) report, girls who had been harassed reported decreased desire to attend school, or to speak in class, poorer grades, and difficulty paying attention. In addition, they were self-conscious, embarrassed, frightened, less confident, and doubtful about whether they could have romantic relationships (deZolt & Henning-Stout, 1999). They also altered their way of functioning at school, avoiding certain locations, and places where they might see their harassers, and changing their friendships and activities if they felt it was necessary for their safety. Girls may not seek out support after being harassed if they are fearful or ashamed; schools may not necessarily respond satisfactorily when they do seek support (Lee, Croninger, Linn, & Chen, 1996). All in all, and even with legislation like the Safe Schools Act of 1994, schools are not necessarily safe places for many girls. The impact of harassment on their emotions and behavior is significant and of concern. Particularly for girls who are endangered at home, school can be a sanctuary—except when it isn't.

Community

Millions of adolescent girls are involved in activities and programs in their communities that may provide them with a chance for connection, skill building, physical challenge, healing, and fun. Good community-based programs are inherently therapeutic in that they promote positive adolescent development. Such programs provide: physical and psychological safety; appropriate structure; supportive relationships; opportunities to belong; positive social norms; support for efficacy and mentoring; opportunities for skill-building; and integration of family, school, and community efforts (Eccles & Appleton, 2002). Community supports are necessary to relieve some of the increasing burden on families and schools for rectifying problems of adolescents that are seemingly beyond family and school control. A push for community responsibility is predicated on the age-old assumption that to support adolescents effectively, the responsibility for raising them needs to be shared more broadly by the "village."

And despite well-documented benefits of participation, most of the community resources available to girls are understaffed, underfunded, unavailable in many communities, poorly linked by public access, or otherwise insufficient to the need (Carnegie Council on Adolescent Development, 1992; Newman, Fox, Flynn, & Christeson, 2000; Stanton-Salazar, 1997). Only a fraction of the adolescent girls who might benefit from some kind of therapeutic intervention will receive it, so the need for community resources looms even larger. Indeed, for many girls, community interventions may equal or exceed traditional treatment approaches in ameliorating their distress. Community-based interventions are relatively cost-efficient, can reach more girls, and have the additional assets of connecting girls to people and resources in their neighborhoods.

Possible community links (with researched advantages) for adolescent girls include:

Community Youth Organizations

There are over 17,000 different youth organizations in the United States (e.g., Girl Scouts, 4-H, Boys and Girls Clubs, Young Democrats). However, recent surveys of participation suggest that over 11 million adolescents are not engaged in any kind of after-school activities, despite the interest reported by a high percentage of these teens, and the well-documented benefits of involvement (Eccles & Appleton, 2002; Newman et al., 2000). Access to and the function of such programs varies dramatically across social class and racial and ethnic lines (Stanton-Salazar, 1997). Sadly, girls who might benefit most from after-school opportunities tend to have the least access to such programs.

Local youth organizations are hampered by the instability of program design and high staff turnover. Additional problems include frequent loss of funding, staff burnout (little salary and little career stake); a common occurrence of loss of an inspirational leader, causing the organization to essentially die out; and failure to create the conditions for youth commitment to the program (Davis & Tolan, 1993). Despite these problems, youth organizations may be a particularly effective method of primary prevention: they encourage social responsibility, can reach adolescents who may not have access or interest in other kinds of services, and provide the potential for development of connections and skills beyond home and school. A smaller number of these successful programs specifically address the needs of adolescent girls (DeZolt & Henning-Stout, 1999). An important component of competency and health-based therapies is helping girls feel more connected to their communities so it behooves us to know what the local resources are for the girls we are treating.

Organized Sports

Girls are involved in team competition in unprecedented numbers. In addition to the more obvious physical benefits, other advantages of such participation include a reduced involvement in sex, drugs, delinquency, cigarette smoking, and improved grades and time-management (Daley & Ryan, 2000; Pate, Trost, Lenn, & Dowda, 2000). Girls who participate in sports like gymnastics and ballet that emphasize staying at a certain weight are more vulnerable to eating disorders; other sports appear to promote more healthy eating habits (Pate et al., 2000; Sherwood, Neumark, Story, Bevhring, & Resnick, 2002). Girls in sports also articulate the importance of the adult role models and the social support of the team (Carnagie Council on Adolescent Development, 1992).

Disadvantages of sports include the unhealthy emphasis on winning; excessive levels of stress and overcompetitiveness; too much structure, undercutting creativity and spontaneity, and pressure from narcissistic parents (e.g., Pate et al., 2000). Clearly, differential effects are evident; there is a range of outcomes. Given the growing cohort of girls in sports, their potential for impact on a large number of adolescents, the social value given to participants, and their ready convenience as an intervention in so many communities, sports participation is particularly compelling as a potential mental health intervention.

Other Community Resources

Other formal community resources that may benefit girls, in communities where such resources may exist, include, for example, youth volunteer service opportunities; peer helping programs; mentor programs; work training programs; and religion-based programs (Davis & Tolan, 1993; Eccles & Appleton, 2002; deZolt & Hennings-Stout, 1999). These opportunities share the goal of connection by matching girls with interests and others who share them. Summarizing findings about community organizations that meet the needs of adolescent girls, deZolt and Hennings-Stout concluded that they're best when they:

> (a) provide positive, caring, and consistent role models of both sexes; (b) promote high yet realistic expectations in skill development; (c) promote the development of relation across class, gender, race, and ethnicity; (d) offer a range of experiences and topics that are of interest to girls, foster gender equity, or both; (e) encourage community involvement; and (f) involve the girls in settings in which they can be themselves, speak their truths, and find their own sources of power. (p. 264)

With so many communities without sufficient resources in a war-hampered economy, this summary may seem to read more like a holiday wish list. Yet it is clear that millions of girls do, and many more could, benefit from greater community involvement.

The real conclusion from this research is that we do know what girls need from their homes, schools, and communities. But, as the next chapter explores, we have social policies that deny access to the resources adolescents deserve and instead blame and marginalize them for getting into trouble. Until the profound cultural ambivalence toward teenage girls is acknowledged and addressed, and neighborhoods get the resources they need, homes, schools, and their communities will continue to be overwhelmed. Moreover, the mental health of girls will be severely and unnecessarily compromised.

Chapter 3: Thoughts for Intervention

- Draw a detailed family genogram and ask about relationships with extended and immediate family members. In cases of separation, divorce, dating, and remarriage of parents, ask about these relationships, too. For girls who are adopted or in foster care, make sure you find out about their birth families as well as any other psychological parents they may have.
- Find out from girls and their parents about the nature and extent of parent involvement. Is it parenting "lite" or parenting "extreme?"
- Ask girls what they would like from their parents in the way of time and interest.
- Find out about monitoring, expectations, limits, routines and rituals, and warmth. Does the family eat dinner together or do other things together that reinforce family connection or identity?
- Is the conflict extreme or developmentally normal? Do people feel safe?
- Is the girl taking classes that meet her educational needs and aspirations?
- Are there, or could there be, any adults in the school who know her and care about her?
- Draw a sociogram of her friendships in school. Review it periodically to help track changes and upheavals in her support system. Find out about the quality and complexity of relationships within the social group.

- Is the peer group helpful, neutral, or detrimental to her development?
- What extracurricular activities does she participate in (e.g., sports, music, work, volunteering, mentoring, etc.)? Therapy should not be the only after-school activity in her life. How invested is she in these activities? Is she doing not enough or too much? What are the benefits and problems with these activities for her?
- Is she involved in any other aspects of community life? (e.g., religious affiliation, Boys and Girls Club) Does she want to be?
- How are the systems—home, school, community—working to support her? Is there more that needs to be done to coordinate interventions?
- Who is on her "team?" Are there adults who know her and support her in each and all of her different realms?

CHAPTER FOUR

THE WAR ON GIRLS

Kiki is 12 and she's growing fast now, taller than almost everyone in her class. With her cropped black hair and blue eyes, she's becoming quite striking to look at, too. She's been a scrappy girl, with three older brothers and a working single mom, historically able to hold her own and then some. Suddenly though, she feels like a misfit, not belonging in her body, in her social group, on her streets, or in her home. People—that she knows and doesn't know—are reacting to her developing body, making comments about her appetite and her curves; Kiki's brothers now exclude her from their rough and tumble games. She has started to skip meals, to wear the extra-large baggy clothes the boys have discarded, and though she had begun to menstruate, her period has (happily for her) ceased. Kiki's mother noticed that her daughter seemed thinner, and chalked it up to the rapid growth. But at a visit to the pediatrician, Kiki confessed that her dieting had become obsessive. She was referred for therapy for anorexia, the disorder of female adolescence most emblematic also of the war on girls.

Kiki's diagnosis is best understood as a symptom of our times. Like many of the problems for which we treat adolescents, hers have been shaped and sustained by a cultural press that can diminish vulnerable girls literally to the vanishing point. It is incumbent upon therapists, educators, parents, and anyone who wants to make a difference in the lives of adolescent girls to understand the deleterious impact of both policy and advertising on their development.

Social policy for adolescent girls suffers from confusion, ambivalence, and neglect. While most citizens and policymakers know well that problems abound, the awareness has not gotten translated into sustained attention or policy-driven interventions. In fact, where adolescent girls are concerned, commerce trumps protection every time.

Such disregard is more striking in the context of a torrent of national studies that demonstrate significant needs. Numerous reports detail both the developmental threats and opportunities for contemporary adolescent girls. But despite well-documented public awareness, including quite specific accounts of serious hazards, the policy response has been limited. Perhaps not surprisingly, the greatest policy activity has centered on legislation designed to control their sexual behavior (Ehrhardt, 1996).

In a thorough analysis, Wilcox (1999) has detailed the histories of five areas of relevant legislation: (1) policies intended to prevent teen pregnancy through the provision of reproductive health services; (2) policies to provide children and youth with sexuality education; (3) policies to promote sexual abstinence among adolescents; (4) policies intended to limit adolescents' autonomy regarding reproductive health decisions; and (5) policies to create disincentives for teen pregnancy and childbearing.

Taken individually or in aggregate, these policies are not so much ambivalent as utterly hostile to girls. Each initiative has been turned on its head. For example, family planning policies were originally designed to assist teens in preventing unwanted births. Since the 1980s, they have been attacked and dismantled with the argument that the availability of confidential contraceptive services would make girls promiscuous and undermine parental authority. Sex education began with the intent of helping adolescents develop as healthy and informed sexual people. Now policymakers want to limit education to discussion of diseases and psychological damage from early sex. Taking concerns about too much education to the next level, these same policymakers have attempted to replace comprehensive sex education with abstinence only programs. Policies in recent years have similarly sought to place barriers in the way of girls' access to contraception and abortion. Most recently, the Bush administration has attempted to block over-the-counter access to emergency contraception for teenagers (the "morning after pill") that would prevent thousands of teen pregnancies a year.

Instead of sexual health, current policies for adolescent girls focus on restricting access to information and services (while scapegoating adolescents for high welfare costs). The failure of these policies is evident in the highest rates of teen pregnancy in the industrialized world and prevalence of sexually transmitted diseases among adolescents (Eng & Butler, 1996). The failure may also be reflected in a generation of voiceless girls who contend in despair with the most extreme mixed messages about their bodies and their sexuality.

Other areas of policy reform that affect girls have had a smaller impact but are also noteworthy. These include, for example, efforts in the juvenile justice system to address the unique needs of girls in gangs and female offenders; programs originating in the Centers for Disease Control that address violence and trauma; the U.S. Department of Health and Human Services' initiatives on runaway and homeless youth; and Title IX in schools that has opened up athletic opportunities for girls (Wilcox, 1999). Still, such initiatives seem fragmented and inadequate in scope given the complex underlying needs of girls within each of these areas.

The reasons for the lag in comprehensive policy are interesting and multifaceted, and have a direct bearing on the clinical presentation of girls. An exploration of policy pulls us away from the individual vision of psychopathology toward a broader cultural understanding of adolescent girls' symptoms. Arguably, many of the difficulties associated with adolescence are due more to social factors such as poverty, family stressors, and societal ambivalence toward youth than to some inevitable internal process, or particular characteristics of the girls themselves.

How then to explain the glaring policy gaps? Most adults are seemingly sympathetic to the difficulties inherent in being a teenage girl in our society. Both men and women remember their own uncertainty and confusion from that time, and concur that the world is a harder place now. It is widely accepted that adolescents today must deal with the wider availability of drugs and weapons, the power of the media and electronics, the uncertain economy for young people, and the fast pace of life in general. Adults probably understand that girls are under a lot of pressure to grow up fast, and that they have to contend with a lot of mixed messages about their roles in the world.

Perhaps such sympathetic adults are not blaming the girls, and are willing to place the brunt of responsibility for girls' problems on parents and schools. Even so, most will have only vague notions about how to intervene. We commonly take the forces of the marketplace as inevitable, and cannot see how to change them. It also appears that Americans do not put much stock in social policy interventions, which they regard as meddling. We may be unreceptive to public youth initiatives for a few reasons.

First, Americans are historically distrustful of large-scale public interventions to deal with problems of individual and family behavior or to develop individuals and families. In the United States, historically, it has been a last resort to use policy to improve social conditions, and it has only taken place when the problem could no longer be ignored (Walker, 1999).

Second, when public social policy is adopted as a strategy, we are not patient with it. If we suspect a policy is not solving problems or is perhaps creating other problems, we will abandon the initiative. Americans want to see their tax dollars going to immediate good use, and innovative programs lose traction and funding if they don't show rapid results.

Third, the social and political climate for reform needs to be "just so"—and different from what is out there now in the early 21st century. Conservative agendas prevail at this time—which is why there have been so many disempowering initiatives for girls. Beyond this, adolescent girls, a dubious, nonvoting constituency, simply do not seem to generate sufficient interest for a bigger place in the legislative agenda.

Policy momentum is generated when it taps into the immediate moral power of an issue or has a capacity to strike the "fairness" button for American leaders and the broader electorate. The sad truth is that people are not morally outraged on behalf of girls, and don't necessarily believe that public action is essential. Adults may see girls as hormonally driven and needing stricter parents, not as needing different environments to change their behavior. And, adults don't see this as a fairness issue, they may think that parents and neighborhoods need to change, not policies.

Key advocates also have to step up with significant resolve, resources, and political communication skills to get policies enacted. People need to be convinced that the problems of adolescent girls really are severe enough to garner a new level of resolve—teens and their problems really are different now from earlier generations. And these advocates will have a tough time: fostering positive development of girls is hard to translate into policy or operational terms, and probably sounds subversive to dominant cultural notions of femininity and girlhood.

Perhaps most of all, social policy is shaped by the availability of clear and compelling solutions. Adolescent girls' policy interventions have a ragged history. Policies driven by problems—teen pregnancy, drug abuse, and poor school performance—have a weak track record. This disappointing legacy has spurred a needed retreat from deficiency-oriented programming. More positive youth development approaches that focus on adolescents' assets and potentials appear to be significantly more successful (Benson, 2004).

Examples of youth development policies that help girls include mentoring and after-school programming. These interventions share many features that account for their public policy success and can serve as a template for the kind of legislation that seems more possible: they're basic, easy to visualize, doable, evocative of something beneficial adults may recall from the past, and they include "brand name" organizations (e.g., Big Brothers/Big Sisters, Boys and Girls Clubs).

Further, their power to shape policy is also tied to the potential to reduce negative behavior (for both boys and girls). These interventions attempt simultaneously to address a variety of priority youth issues—crime, drugs, pregnancy, school performance, and preparation for employment (Walker, 1999). These kinds of programs are appealing to policymakers because they address several areas of concern at once and have demonstrable benefits for large numbers of adolescents. They also represent a flicker of light in a fairly gloomy policy landscape.

There are more barriers to development and implementation of needed policies. Such obstacles tend to be more psychological and political in nature, having to do with the way girls are represented in the consciousness of adults, including: victim blame, ambivalence, scapegoating, and advertising.

Blaming the Victim

It is easy to believe that adolescent girls (and their parents) bring suffering on themselves. Girls are sexualized, for certain, but many (unlike Kiki) participate so eagerly in their objectification and look so grown up, it is likely that some adults (and peers) will hold them accountable for their effect on others. And if we extend sympathy to these girls, our next impulse is to hold parents entirely responsible for not nurturing and protecting them more effectively, for raising a girl "like that." The whole medical model of diagnosis is a monument to victim blaming—depression, eating problems, self-harm, anxiety—all of the "disorders" are supposed to reside in the psychology and biochemistry of the girl. We don't act on behalf of girls because we may fundamentally believe they have sufficient control over what happens to them; they're just making bad choices.

Ambivalence

Our cultural ambivalence toward girls has two parts. In general, we babyboomers despise our own inexorable aging, becoming the enemy of our youth. And we lean backwards toward adolescence, trying to navigate our lives as they do. We are just as self-involved, preoccupied with our needs and our happiness, our things. We are similarly fast-twitch, easily annoyed by the car in front of us, by the time the computer takes to boot up, by waiting for food in a restaurant. We are also naively smug because we have more stuff than people elsewhere in the world, and anxious because we don't have as much as we'd like. And perennial teenagers that we are, too, we'd like to think about other people, but often can't find the time.

It bothers us no end (if not always consciously) that teenagers get to look young and to have their whole lives ahead of them, to have summer vacations, shiny abundant hair, and tight skin. In other words, we are am- bivalent about them because we are not so sure we want the implications of their existence. If they are children, that makes us adults. If they are young, then we are old. We are jealous of their youth and beauty, even as we admire and attempt, fruitlessly, to emulate it.

But our cultural ambivalence toward girls in particular goes deeper than simple jealousy, into actual threat. How else to explain the tight bind the cul- ture has put girls in now? At the exact moment in time, developmentally and culturally, when girls could really show up, they are encouraged to disappear. They get the message clearly (from parents, teachers, peers, media, and pol- icymakers) to be quieter, smaller, thinner, and less competent even as they begin to feel big in every way. Girls know this is an impossible fine line to walk, making them incapable of pleasing everyone and themselves.

But how can they fully understand (and why should they have to) that they are a projective screen for the unfulfilled aspirations and desires of frus- trated adults? Social policies to control girl sexuality are real and also metaphorical. The metaphor is about keeping all their appetites in check, not just lust. By the time they are teenagers, girls learn to check their hunger, their power, and their true voices so no one feels threatened. It is not surpris- ing that they get frustrated and take it out on themselves (or other girls). Gendered problems like eating disorders, self-mutilation, and depression are understandable when seen through this lens. It is also, alas, clearer how the war on adolescent girls really does begin at the policy level, eliminating any chance girls will claim too much power over their own lives.

Scapegoating

The marginalization of girls serves a useful function for adults even as it renders girls invisible in terms of policy. Scapegoating accounts for the ris- ing alarms that girls are more menaced and menacing (while no large- scale interventions are proposed). Creating a pleasing image of the older generation by displacing blame onto the younger one may be one more disturbing motivation behind today's "mean girls" furor and attendant policies aimed at keeping them contained.

In fact, some researchers argue that it isn't young women but baby boomers who show the most frightening trends in problem behavior (Gluckman, 2002; Males, 2006). Claims about bad girls inevitably rely on adult commentators' selected anecdotes, generalizations from troubled girls in treatment, sanitized memories of a tranquil past, and omission of contradictory information (Males, 2006). These kinds of generalizations have, at root, a kind of discriminatory, misogynistic flavor. Indeed, we'd call it "prejudice" if it were used to describe any other group in society. And like all prejudice, such assertions enable us to look the other way rather than at our own contribution to the suffering.

Males (2006) noted that, for example, among adult women ages 30 to 59, felony arrest rates doubled and violence arrest rates soared by 220% since the mid-1970s. Today, a 40-year-old woman is much more likely to die from illegal drugs or be arrested for a serious crime than her high-school age daughter. But we do not hear anything about "mean middle-aged women" that resembles the outcry against adolescent girls. Indeed, the construction seems laughable, even though it is so.

This scapegoating of adolescent girls may allow us to wring our hands and do nothing about the problems that may, in fact, be just as much or more descriptive of adult dysfunction. In reality, adults benefit financially and psychologically from spreading misleading, negative stereotypes that demean politically powerless adolescents. In doing so, they also teach young people the value of bullying those who are weaker. Such cynical strategies allow us to abandon the pursuit of sensible social polices—for adults, too.

Public debate today that positions girls as either too young to know better or as primitive "mean" or "alpha" predators, denies them personhood, voice, or agency in the here and now. Scapegoating adolescent girls allows diversion of attention by a complacent, established America. Demographic myths about the behavior of girls and their culture-war trivialities helps U.S. policymakers avoid facing their own rage and violence.

Advertising and the Media

A point intimately connected to all of the preceding discussion of policy is the tenacious and insidious role of commerce in the lives of adolescent girls. Lest anyone forget, the point of advertising is to make people feel dissatisfied and hungry for things they don't have. Through whatever manipulative means necessary, they sell products, telling people in as many ways as imaginable that to be happy they need to consume material goods.

And adolescent girls are prime targets. Adolescents between 12 and 19 years of age spent $170 billion in 2002, or a weekly average of $101 per teenager (Schor, 2004). Teenage girls spend over $4 billion a year on cosmetics alone (Kilbourne, 1999). Girls can't escape: Advertising makes up about 70% of our newspapers and 40% of our mail. Advertising not only appears on radio and television, in our magazines and newspapers, but also surrounds us on billboards, on the sides of buildings, on public transportation, in the videos we rent, online, and when we're on hold on the telephone. Lecturer and author Jean Kilbourne noted that the average American will spend three years of her life watching television commercials. And even when girls think advertising is having no effect on their self-image and choices, they're wrong. As Crain (1997) ominously described:

> Only eight percent of an ad's message is received by the conscious mind: The rest is worked and reworked deep within the recesses of the brain, where a product's positioning and repositioning takes shape. (p. 25)

And the explicit message—to buy stuff—is couched in sexuality, exploitative racial imagery, and certain antisocial themes, appealing to the "cool" parts of girls. Marketers pit hip adolescents against boring adults, underscoring a trend toward antiadultism within the commercial world, and emphasizing that possessions are much more fun than adults could be. Media critic Mark Crispin Miller wrote about this strategy:

> It's part of the official advertising world view that your parents are creeps, teachers are nerds and idiots, authority figures are laughable, nobody can really understand kids except the corporate sponsor. That huge authority has, interestingly enough, emerged as the sort of tacit superhero of consumer culture. That's the coolest entity of all. (Schor, 2004, p. 54)

Marketers defend themselves against charges of antiadultism by arguing that they are promoting kid empowerment. The corporate message: kids and products are aligned together in a really great fun place, while parents, teachers, and other adults inhabit an oppressive, drab, and joyless world.

This kind of message is particularly compelling for adolescent girls who crave connections—with things as well as people. And they are especially likely to seek connection through alcohol, food, and cigarettes, partly as a response to disconnection, danger, and betrayal in human relationships. The problems of adolescent girls cannot be understood without recognizing that they are growing up in an unsupportive cultural environment, one clearly made more toxic by advertising.

As relatively new and inexperienced consumers, girls are prime targets for advertisers who do not hesitate to take advantage of their insecurities and anxieties, usually in the guise of offering solutions. Girls are told that what's most important about them is their perfume, their clothing, their bodies, their beauty. They get the message that they must be flawlessly beautiful and dangerously thin. Even more destructively, they get the message that this is possible, that with enough effort and sacrifice, they can achieve this ideal. Thus many girls spend enormous amounts of time and energy attempting to achieve something that is not only trivial but also completely unattainable. As Kilbourne (1999) has described:

> The glossy images of flawlessly beautiful and extremely thin women that surround us would not have the impact they do if we did not live in a culture that encourages us to believe we can and should remake our bodies into perfect commodities. These images play into the American belief of transformation and ever-new possibilities, no longer via hard work but via the purchase of the right products. (p. 132)

Kilbourne argued persuasively that young women are especially vulnerable to advertising because their bodies are already objectified and commodified—and this is especially true for traumatized girls who may gain some hope of control through pursuing the simple solutions suggested by ads.

Adolescent girls fantasize that objects will somehow transform their lives, giving them social standing and respect. The media images (so much more compelling than adults are) create this insatiable appetite for material goods. Girls are indoctrinated from before they can speak to believe that they will feel better if they have more stuff.

In reality, though, materialism actually saps a girl's sense of intrinsic self-worth. From the very beginning, advertising encourages kids to be on the lookout for more. Girls feel they're not good enough unless they have the "right stuff." No matter what economic story they have at home, they need more gear. The problem is that constantly needing more makes a girl feel empty inside: You are never enough unless you have enough. And there will always be a new style of Gap jeans, so it's an endless voyage. Girls begin to drown in a sea of objects; a mighty poor substitute for real connections.

Girls are also targeted by advertising to believe in an illusion of freedom and rebellion associated with products. Kilbourne (1999) wryly concluded:

> Desperate to be unique in a conformist culture, they follow the crowd right over the cliff—drinking, smoking, engaging in dangerous sex, compulsively shopping for recreation, stuffing and starving themselves. O brave new world where Addiction is Freedom and Conformity is Rebellion. (p. 310)

The genius of advertising is the position that those who resist this message can be labeled "antifreedom," lifestyle police, part of a Big Brother government, trying to tell everyone what to do. The alcohol, tobacco, and junk food lobbies have cleverly spent millions of dollars to keep the debate at the level of big government versus freedom lovers. And the girls, the "targets" of such insanity, are just faceless consumers who only matter for the money they will spend.

Girls in a Vise

The diametrically opposed stances of social policy and advertising hold girls in an intractable vise; depicting perfectly the impossible and suffocating contradictions girls live with. On one side we have policy and its institutions, upholding the status quo, viewing girls as nice, polite, patient, friendly, passive, childlike, virginal, quiet, girl-feminine. On the other, we have media and advertising, and their edgy, hypersexualized and violent girl images. In contrast, these girls are mean, rude, impatient, competitive, slutty, and daring—babe-feminine. Through the lens of the media (in advertising that they see 3,000 times a day), girls have an aura of sophistication and cool that makes them appear much older than they are.

And so in our culture, girls seemingly must pick a way of being, caricatures of real girls, and not possibly true to the multidimensional people they really are. The war on girls offers few strategies for them to defend themselves. Girls often valiantly struggle to resist stultifying norms and extreme expectations that do not feel accurate to their own experience, but such struggles have uneven results. The ideals of femininity prescribed in our split culture are patently crazy making. Pipher (1994) describes:

> Girls have long been trained to be feminine at considerable cost to their humanity. They have long been evaluated on the basis of appearance and caught in myriad double binds: achieve, but not too much; be polite, but be yourself; be feminine and adult; be aware of our cultural heritage but don't comment on the sexism. Another way to describe this femininity training is to call it false-self training. Girls are trained to be less than who they really are. They are trained to be what the culture wants of its young women, not what they themselves want to become. (p. 44)

As the values of white male greed continue to dominate discourse, the adolescent girl's agenda is suppressed and marginalized. Corporate wealth also monopolizes any attempts at debate; it corrupts politicians, and dictates policy. In such a culture, girls appear as fragments of their whole selves. The rage and despair of adolescent girls is perhaps the only sensible response to such insanity.

A Call to Action

Therapists cannot treat adolescent girls without maintaining a clear sense of the insidious role of policy and culture on functioning. Discussions of girls' identity development are based too often on narrowly defined notions of psychopathology and self-esteem, neglecting the social and political context of such suffering.

We also need to broaden our analysis beyond a simple emphasis on gender differences. There are vital interconnections among race, culture, social class, and sexuality. Thus, the structure of programs and policies devised to improve girls' lives needs to account for these complexities.

It is of particular concern that the voices of girls are rarely heard in research reports or in discussion of policies, or in advertising that affects their lives. These voices yearn for authentic connections, not just with things, but also with real and caring people. Too often our public policies reflect our cultural evasion of connection and of committed relationships—short-term solutions, abandonment of the poor, disabled, and mentally ill, refusal to provide health care to everyone—and silencing of girls. At a time when we desperately need to find a way to take care of one another and live together in one world, we tend to do exactly the opposite. In this, girls suffer, but they are not the only ones.

How can we relieve the cultural stranglehold on girls? Clearly, reforms in policy and media impact are necessary. Policy reforms will require intensive advocacy, lobbying, education, and applied research. The National Council for Research on Women (2002, p. 4) has offered five conclusions, summarized below, from their review of an extensive body of recent work on key issues in the lives of adolescent girls:

1. Policy needs to be sensitive to the ways gender interacts with other aspects of identity—race, ethnicity, social class (dis)ability, and the communities where they live—that influence girls' actions, attitudes and ultimately their futures.
2. Girls benefit from programs and strategies that build on their strengths and encourage them to explore meaningful possibilities for their futures.
3. We need a coherent research agenda that helps advocates and public officials understand and respond to girls' needs.
4. Girls need many concerned adults in their lives—parents, educators, professionals, and other community members should strengthen efforts to create a safe and nurturing climate that encourages girls to develop and pursue goals.
5. Adults should listen to what girls have to say about their own lives.

In many fields, including education, health care, athletics, and juvenile justice, adults have worked with some moderate success since the mid-1990s to create school and community based programs that provide support to many adolescent girls and that could be replicated. But we need to do much more, and to have longer-term funding commitments behind such efforts.

Resisting and fighting the marketing of adolescent girls requires a different, but equally comprehensive agenda. Global corporations may continue as the primary architects of girls' futures, but not necessarily so. Girls will need our help with this mighty defiance. As Schor (2004) noted, consumption of goods is arguably the activity our society deems most purely personal, outside the legitimate interest of government or society. Ironically, it is considered even more private than sex.

Governments do step in, from time to time, though not often. And since 1980, there has been a marked retreat from regulation. Thus, the control of consumption is back to parents, schools, and communities. They will have to help girls choose whether the consumer culture is for them or not. Some possible avenues of assistance include:

1. *Ad-free schools:* Congress should enact comprehensive legislation to restrict school commercialism. Advertising in schools violates a fundamental consumer right: to be able to escape marketing. Schor (2004) has suggested that such a federal act would prohibit sponsored educational materials, the use of brand names in text books, in-classroom ads, displays on school buses and other school property, and corporate-sponsored contests. It would also forbid giving market research firms access to adolescents during school hours.

2. *Parental cooperation:* Commerce and the second family insert themselves into the weak spots in family life. Individual parents can't help their girls as effectively alone and need to create more effective webs of communication among themselves. Around the country, for example, parents have formed Communities of Concern and signed the Safe Homes Pledge, promising that they will supervise gatherings at their home to prohibit minors from using alcohol, drugs, or firearms. Parent organizations in middle and high schools tend to be weak, but are also a potential rallying point for concerned adults. The main point is that there is strength in numbers; the more parents support one another to set limits on excess commerce and media, the easier it will be to help girls resist the peer pressure to engage in it. Advertising depends on the exclusion of adult reason and discourse for its profits; parents need to add themselves to the equation more forcefully.

3. *Find alternatives:* Girls who are not consumed by consuming are busy doing other things. Families, schools, and communities (and therapists) need to work harder to ensure that girls have

broader identities; that they do stuff, such as playing instruments, singing at church, babysitting, having part-time jobs, playing sports, volunteering, spending time with mentors, going to the "Y", reading books, acting in plays, joining clubs, and finding meaning and purpose outside of the mall and fashion magazines.

4. *Political activism:* Legislative, cultural, and social changes will only occur if enough people get involved. It makes sense that therapists join the growing and vocal opposition to the cynical forces of commerce. There are many types of organizations that promote anticommercialism (see Schor, 2004, Appendix B, for a contact list of a dozen). Perhaps it would also behoove us to examine the power of advertising in our own lives, too.

5. *Keep talking:* Maybe our best chance to take on these powerful second-family forces is through the things therapists do best— talking and listening. Talk to girls and parents about advertising, have girls bring in the images they find compelling and deconstruct them. Tell parents that even when girls roll their eyes in exasperation and fatigue, parents need to keep the dialogue going. Keep telling them that these ads make girls feel worse about themselves; that no one healthy really looks like that. The images lose some of their death grip when they are discussed and deconstructed. Watch the shows girls watch, listen to their music, and peruse their magazines. Talk about what is being sold, how it is being sold, and why.

H. L. Mencken once said, "For every complex problem there is an answer that is clear, simple, and wrong." The problems faced by adolescent girl do not have any quick fixes; the struggles are as multifaceted as the girls themselves. And at the policy level, we have intellectual and spiritual, as well as political, challenges ahead. Therapists have a vital role in helping to shape initiatives that meet girls' developmental needs. We must also keep in mind that girls are suffering because they are increasingly voiceless in a culture that is toxic to their growth. Whether their behavior is troubled or troubling, it is quite likely that oppressive cultural forces are also at work. Informed and effective therapy makes room for this broader ecological framework, including in the formulations and discussions the deleterious impact of policy and commerce on development.

Chapter 4: Thoughts for Intervention

- When a girl presents with a problem, can you (and she) see the cultural press on her contributing to it?

- Can you talk about the impact of culture on her with the girl and her parents? How can you bring the effects of social policy and commerce into the treatment? Are you willing to see her "problems" through this broader (nonmedical) lens?

- Are you aware of your own ambivalent or hostile feelings toward girls? Do they show up in treatment? How are you dealing with these feelings in your own life?

- Are you politically active on behalf of girls? What advocacy activities do you consider part of your job?

- How are you dealing with the social and commercial forces at work on your girl clients; how do you bring media and advertising into the treatment room?

- How much do you really know about adolescent culture? Do you read, listen to, and view any of the same media they are consuming?

- Are you helping girls develop alternative narratives to the antiadultism of advertising?

- What ideas about femininity do the girls you work with hold, and where do they come from? Is this part of your dialogue with them?

- Does the girl you are treating have connections to people and meaningful activities, or just to things? Can you help her develop more real connections?

- Help educate parents, get them in the same dialogues with girls; conversations that replace objects with deeper, multidimensional relationships.

II
Interventions:
Treating the Whole Girl

CHAPTER FIVE

TEN TIPS FROM THE TRENCHES: DOING GOOD WORK WITH GIRLS

Girls and their problems vary widely, and, as is evident from the myriad of strategies and interventions available to the practitioner, we can develop a vast spectrum of skills to treat them effectively. Still, there are some general principles of good practice with adolescent girls that underlie all the theories, techniques, research, and pizzazz. Once we're engaged with a real girl, our adherence to a particular school of thought often becomes impractical or useless as we strive to do what works best. It has been my experience that good therapy with adolescent girls is generally transtheoretical, no matter how precisely a case is conceptualized within a particular paradigm.

If pressed, I generally say my work draws mostly from developmental, relational, and systemic theories. But there are many times when I am also a narrative therapist, a dynamic therapist, a cognitive–behavioral therapist, and an existential–humanistic therapist, as the following chapters will describe. These categorizations, like the labels we apply to the girls we treat, frequently become moot when we find ourselves face to face with a girl who is sobbing, or stone-faced, or raging, or just yackity-yacking as girls sometimes do. Thus, when I talk about good practice with girls, I am not describing specific techniques but rather broad standards underpinning effective therapy. They are summarized here:

1. Make and Keep Promises

Adolescent girls often come to therapy without much experience with real adults. One bright 15-year-old contending with the relentless narcissism of her divorcing and dating parents observed to me recently that I was "the only grown up" she had ever met. It was an exaggeration, I think, but not much of one. Because therapy isn't usually a daily event, we have an opportunity to build trust more quickly when we find ways to make promises to girls, and then deliver the next week. I may ask them to bring in music, for example, so I'll promise to provide the boom box. Or when I have to go to a conference in DC, I'll promise to send a postcard of the Capitol. If we're doing a crafts or collage project, I'll promise to bring supplies we need and have them ready when a girl returns to my office. I promise to go to school meetings, to say certain things in family sessions, to remain hopeful, to keep confidentiality. And then on all these promises, I deliver.

Being consistent by doing what we say we will is important for adolescent girls because they experience so little internal or external predictability in their lives. Kept promises from the first moment give girls rapid messages that they are important to you even when they are not in front of you. This sort of object constancy sets a tone of trust and safety that can be hard to establish otherwise. And it sets you apart in a landscape otherwise marked by self-involved and forgetful adults who may not promise much nor keep the promises they do make.

For example, 13-year-old Hilary had grown up in the foster care system, so she knew precious little about adult follow-through. Developmentally, she was a young teen, still into horses and puzzles. Early on in our work I suggested that I might get a horse jigsaw puzzle for us to do together. She seemed mildly interested, so the following week, when she returned, I had it for her still in the cellophane, at the ready. She looked astonished, and said, "You got this for me?" We took it out and spread the pieces on a table in the corner of my office to work on from week to week. It was there so we could keep assembling it each time we met if she wanted to do it. When we completed the puzzle, we covered it in jigsaw glue and the next week, ecstatically, she took it home—a symbol of me and our time together that she could keep. This may sound like a fairly small example of promise keeping, but for Hilary it also provided some vital glued pieces for our relationship.

2. Admit Your Mistakes and Apologize

Most adolescents have precious little experience with adults apologizing to them. But like anyone else, girls appreciate it when we admit that we've made a mistake. It helps level the playing field and it affords them a respect that adults seldom feel like providing. It builds empathic attunement and gives them the chance to forgive us. I've found when I've apologized for messing up that adolescent girls can be surprisingly forgiving, even if often not of themselves. This fact can help therapy along, too. They'll forgive you readily for a mistake you made, and later, when they're being relentlessly hard on themselves, you can compare their sterner self-judgments with their kindness to you when you goofed up.

Some of my greatest therapy moments have come out of screw-ups. A couple of years ago, I gave appointments to two girls named Jessica at the same time. The moment I opened my office door, I realized my stupidity. Jessica One reached into her back pocket and flashed her appointment card, as though it were a front-row ticket to a concert. "It's my time, and I can prove it," she laughed. I asked her to hold on for a moment, and met sheepishly with Jessica Two, to touch base and reschedule. I apologized profusely, and when we met later that day, I apologized some more.

My work with Jessica One had a little spike of energy that day (she was the youngest of five sisters and enjoyed the sweet waiting-room victory for a few giddy minutes), but Jessica Two and I made a connection after I made a mistake, admitted it, and apologized to her. That subsequent hour of therapy with Jessica Two was the turning point for us, maybe because the playing field had suddenly leveled, and maybe because I was working hard to make repairs to this rupture. It's common wisdom that greater intimacy follows from mending a relationship. This isn't to suggest that I advocate wearing mismatched socks or showing up late on purpose. But these mistakes and missteps inevitably happen. And then we get to say we're sorry, and figure out what we'll do differently the next time.

3. Hold Hope

Somewhere between the Cinderella rescue fantasies, and the hard truth of girls' lives, many get lost in feelings of hopelessness and despair. They live too much in the present and in their emotional brains to feel confident about the future, about how to plan for it, and to envision the reality of it. This vision problem compounds their damaged sense of personal efficacy; without hope it is hard to feel confident. When I am with a girl who is floundering and seems desperately lost about how to take hold, I often intervene with a bold hopefulness. For these girls, I take my job seriously as a holder of hope for the future. I've come to understand that my confidence in my young clients and in their ability to heal is central to their developing an ability to believe in themselves.

Seventeen-year-old Marianne was in tremendous distress when we first met. She'd been at boarding school and had repeatedly gone to the infirmary to have her hearing checked and then her eyes, feeling she was hearing and seeing the wrong things. She felt tormented by horrible voices, and was afraid to go to sleep.

She called her parents one day in the middle of the fall term almost incoherent with fear, and they brought her home, not knowing what was wrong, but perceiving she was at the breaking point. I met with Marianne and her parents that day. I soon determined that she needed to be hospitalized for her safety and to get stabilized on medication. Before she left my office, I told her, "It won't always hurt like this. You'll feel better. I know you're not hopeful right now, so I'll hold the hope for you. Tell me when you can share in it with me. Until then, I'll be our holder of hope."

Marianne made rapid gains as an inpatient, and returned for several months of work with me afterward. When we were terminating and looking back on our work together, she recalled that she'd used my hope to get through the nightmare of being hospitalized and having to conquer the voices inside her head. She said, "I always remembered that you said you were hopeful that it would get better. That made a difference when I didn't know if I could keep going on."

4. Trust the Process

With adolescent girls, our impatience to *do* something to make a change in someone's life—to be transformative in a big way—can come across as criticism and disrespect. After all, if their problems were so easy to solve, they would have done it already. And sometimes girls interpret our agenda-setting ideas as power moves; we are then like other adults in their lives who think they know best and tell girls what to do. It is often a benign intention, wanting so much to be helpful, that can get both novice and more seasoned clinicians in trouble. Before we rush to intervene, we need to breathe deeply and attend closely to less conscious and intentional matters in the therapy room, what it feels like to be there (for both of us), what else is happening beneath the surface—into that limbic resonance that connects us, and deeper still. It's fundamentally important to trust the process, and to find a way to stay connected to girls over the path of the hours that we are with them. The course of therapy cannot be reduced to a series of plans and goals; it also takes place in tiny moments and in the crevices of a relationship. The "process" is happening even when (or maybe especially when) we are doing nothing at all.

Attending to the process is an idea that's become almost my mantra in my clinical supervision of graduate students. In this age of presto-chango technique and managed care, the process is too often a casualty of the pressure to make therapy as brief and problem-focused as possible. We forget that there's meaning everywhere, if we have the pluck and luck to discover it, and that it often flows out more freely when we're patient; honoring a girl's agenda over our own; sitting a while longer with our own uncertainty and discomfort. Regardless of whether adolescent girls are oppositional and challenging, or sweetly contented with us, we are too often tempted to take over and act rather than allowing the flow of the session to dictate what we'll do next.

One day just a few weeks into our meetings, 14-year-old Lucy and I were sitting together companionably. She was doodling on a big pad perched on her lap, not saying much to me, just occasional idle chatter accompanying her curlicues and the three-dimensional rendering of the word "Matt," a boy she was madly pursuing. I was beginning to squirm, and my personal demons were telling me that I ought to be "doing real therapy" with her now that we'd "established a relationship."

So I began to speak, quietly wondering about how I could be helpful to her, about whether we might now talk about some goals, about some problem-solving strategies she might like to learn. When I was done, Lucy looked up at me horrified, her lip quivering. For the first time since I'd known her, she silently began to cry. She regained her voice after a couple of interminable minutes and said, "This is the only place I have that I can just be me. Why do you have to fix that?"

I backpedaled fast, supporting her determination to be herself in other situations, too. I breathed deeply and leaned forward into the space between us. I reached for a colored pencil, and asked if I could color in a letter of Matt's name. As the sound of pencils scratching on paper filled the room, I realized anew that Lucy's healing depended in good part on my ability to trust our unique (if at times slow and seemingly dull) process in the therapy room. I don't always know what is, strictly speaking, "therapeutic"; sometimes all it takes is just being present. And sometimes just being present is harder than providing big-time interventions.

5. Identify Choices, Ask for Choices, Take Joy in Choices

Many teens feel that they have precious little say in their lives—it feels to them that someone is always telling them to go to school, do chores, eat dinner, do their homework, turn down the music, and get off the Internet. They're told to go to therapy, too—something else they didn't choose. Yet, self-control, which comes from the ability to make and follow through on our own choices, is the scaffolding that holds up so much of our lives.

With a sense of self-control, girls can develop self-esteem, have safe and intimate relationships, figure out how to succeed in school and work, and learn how to negotiate with their parents more effectively. Adolescent girls need to see themselves as capable of making choices, and caring adults need to help them choose, and notice when they do.

Donna was 18, drinking too much, and cutting herself. She was doing poorly in her first year of college and was feeling increasingly desperate about whether she'd ever be successful. She'd come into therapy and tell me about all the regrettable things she'd done the preceding week. It was quite evident in the narrative that she didn't see herself as proactive in any sphere in her life; the only control she believed she had involved choosing self-harm.

So I framed all the events she reported as choices. I asked, over and over again: Is this what you want? Is this how you want to show up in the world? What happens when you do? What happens when you don't? How true are you being to yourself in making this choice? How does it help you get the love and care you need and deserve? When she drank less, I congratulated her for making a good choice, and asked her how she was able to do it. These questions stemmed from my heartfelt belief that Donna had more control over her life than she believed. They steered Donna in the direction of finding the strong voice she might be able to identify and distinguish as the one she chose for her own.

6. When She's at a Loss for Words, Guess and Guess Again

Even though girls are supposed to be verbal and emotional, they're often surprisingly lost when describing their internal lives. Many girls, well into adolescence, remain concrete in their reasoning and have a limited vocabulary for describing their feelings. Cut off from anger, impelled by culture and family to present a smiling facade, they often really do not know how they feel. Therapists often are frustrated when they get the usual responses to the inevitable inquiry about how a teenage girl feels about something: "Fine," "I don't know," or strained silence.

At this juncture, I no longer think girls are being defensive or withholding when I receive one of these responses. Instead, I plunge ahead and guess. I frame my musings in general language: "Some girls I know might feel pretty angry about something like that." "I think I'd be pretty frustrated if I had to deal with this." "I know a girl who said she felt like crying an ocean when that happened to her." "I wonder if you might feel a little confused by this." I think such reflective dialogue about deeper feelings and what they might mean helps girls. They see me trying and when I guess right, they feel *felt*. They also begin to learn to draw meanings from feelings themselves. Guessing is really a brave foray into helping girls develop their own emotional intelligence and "mindsight," so they become increasingly able to know and articulate what they think and feel.

7. Base Expectations on Developmental Level, Not Chronological Age

If girls develop at different rates along so many concurrent lines in their physical, emotional, social, and cognitive paths, how do we know what are reasonable expectations and where to set the bar? One of the great challenges of work with adolescent girls is that they often enter treatment for adult-sized problems that they've attempted to solve with child-sized strategies. I believe that I'm treating an increasing number of anxiety disorders because our expectations for girls exceed what they're capable of delivering. This issue is particularly compelling when safety is concerned. We have hugely unrealistic cultural and societal aspirations for adolescent girls—wanting them to function independently and wisely long before they have the tools to do so. By the time a girl is 11 or 12, we may expect her to handle being alone for many hours a day, organize her school work, get dinner started, and manage herself in public with poise and maturity. Adults may become annoyed by a girl's "ditziness" or emotionality, express shock or dismay at her poor choices and judgment, or take her irritability as a personal affront. Because girls look like young adults, and can sound like them, too, we are too apt to forget that they are frequently overwhelmed by expectations that they can't consistently meet.

I remember meeting Margaret for the first time. She was an angry, unhappy, 13-year-old girl, who came to therapy with her father, her 9-year-old half-sister, Izzy, and her stepmother. Her family members had a long list of changes they wanted Margaret to make—to lie and argue less, be more respectful, do her chores, stop blaming Izzy for everything, and stop stealing from her stepmother. I asked Margaret the "miracle" question: Imagine that you're going to wake up tomorrow and a miracle had occurred overnight so all the problems that brought you here today were solved. What would you be seeing and doing differently so you would know that the miracle had happened? She thought briefly, and then her answer surprised me: "I wouldn't have to pick up Izzy at the bus stop after school and watch her every day until 6:00, so I could maybe do karate again. And I'd only have to get dinner ready a couple of nights a week." I realized then that the family expected Margaret to function as an adult and parent; they didn't see how these high expectations were causing this young, confused child to feel overwhelmed and frustrated. Her "miracle" was just to have a little free time of her own in the afternoon some of the time.

When I meet an adolescent girl for the first time, I assess her cognitive, social, emotional, and physical development, and consider what level of independence and responsibility—for herself and others—she can handle. I set the bar a little low at first, to be sure she's safe and competent to get over it. I educate the parents, who see an almost-grown woman before them, about the fact that this girl is still just a child.

Girls benefit from the temporary "loan" of an adult's executive functioning while their own brains are still undergoing major renovation—and so much of their behavior is controlled more by emotion than by reason. Even when girls say they are capable of behaving more independently, or deny wanting such support, adults should not take these statements at face value. The fact remains that evolution has given humans a very long period of dependence and childhood, and this simply can't be rushed, no matter how much adults need girls to grow up faster.

8. Build Teams

In today's America, the nuclear-family model is inadequate for raising adolescents. Parents are unable to function in all the roles needed by girls to develop safely into women or provide everything—supervision, nurturance, role-modeling, initiation into the adult world, education, and counsel—required to launch them into womanhood. With the powerful second family of pop and kid culture all around, girls need lots of adults to hold and support them — adults who can function as parents, friends, mentors, and elders. Clearly, a therapist who sees the girl for 50 minutes a week can't provide all the nonparental adult time she needs, either.

From the onset of treatment, I view myself as part of a team, adding adults as we go. One of my favorite team stories is about a very funny and maddening 14-year-old named Megan. She was diabetic, learning disabled, truant, and recently adopted by her long-term foster family. Megan had adults scrambling in all directions to support her and we added more when she was hospitalized for medical problems, and then still more when she attended a residential school.

One day a few months into treatment, Megan was bemoaning the fact that she had no one on her side, "Everyone is against me," she wailed. I glared at her, handed her my clipboard, and asked her to write down the names of people who'd tried to help her just in the past two weeks. We began with a truant officer, added the nurses on the inpatient unit, extended family, school personnel, her adoption worker, and a myriad of others. Megan counted happily to a team of 24 adults. She seemed quite pleased and laughed as I admonished her to carry this list with her *at all times,* so that she could never again say she was alone. Even in less complicated situations, girls need more adults in their lives, now that they so seldom have nearby extended families or a cohesive community to back them up.

9. Empathy, Empathy, Empathy

It isn't easy, when an adolescent girl aims a verbal bomb at us, to remain empathetic, but when we do, we run less of a risk of taking things too personally. Girls, even big, tough ones, have limited strategies for getting their needs met. They come to therapy following years of struggle and failure in relationships. We need to try not to be wounded or disappointed when they aren't good at being in therapy either.

Sally, a pistol of a girl, was 16. With hair she'd cut herself one afternoon, broad shoulders, and a fierce scowl, she was the terror of her suburban high school. People, literally, got out of her way when she walked down the hall. Teachers disliked her because she continually and relentlessly challenged their authority. She was sent to therapy after she swore at her English teacher one too many times and was suspended. The school hoped I could "help her be happier." I suspect they hoped I'd sedate her somehow, too.

Sally was a bright enough girl who had a couple of critical older brothers and parents who were overworked and exhausted. Her parents had trouble making it to therapy appointments together, but separately, both expressed bewilderment and frustration about their angry kid.

Because I prefer a girl who has some zip, I immediately liked Sally, and told her so the first chance I got. I admired her determination to be true to herself and to have a voice. So even after she used that voice to let me know I was wearing the "ugliest ass pair of shoes" she'd ever had to look at, I still liked her. And when she told me I was wasting her time and that her cat understood her better than I ever could, I still liked her. Ditto the comment about feeling that she was talking to drywall one day when I wasn't immediately responsive; I told her no one had ever compared me to drywall before. Even after she put her muddy boots on my couch and told me to "just shut up for a change," I was in there with her, liking her. I grimaced affectionately, and mutely waved her feet off the furniture. And then I asked another question about the "indie" rock she had on her iPod and listened hard to her answer.

Sally's actions were, I believe, creative attempts to share with me how rotten she felt, so I held (clung, really) onto my empathic connection and didn't let her push me away. Sally didn't know me well enough to despise me, and she needed an admiring adult who fit my description perfectly. I've finally learned, after years of being hurt and worried in such situations, that what was transpiring wasn't about me at all. My job with Sally, and other girls who use insults or verbal aggression as a way to get personal, was to reflect back a better way of staying connected.

Sally probably wanted a relationship with me more than most girls I've worked with. I had to keep remembering that her oppositional strategies were in the service of engagement. By doing that, I was able to tell her, "I love your spirit. When you talk like this, I know that there's someone in there worth fighting for. I admire that so much. The last thing I want to do is to send another shut-up woman out into the world. Promise me you'll fire me if I do that." Then, to try to engage her in the work of smoothing her rough edges so others would want to be there for her, I added, "But we need to do some work on your style and figure out together a way for you to develop a voice that people can hear. I can help you become a better Sally advocate."

Like many girls who are not used to people responding as I did, Sally redoubled her rejection of me, just to be sure I was sufficiently indefatigable. For a few weeks, she became even more adamant she didn't need some "nosy shrink" in her business, and challenged me still some more. But over time, her comments became part of our ritual way of being together: I'd go to the waiting room and hear about my shoes, I'd wait patiently while she read a magazine, she'd eventually wander in and sigh with ennui. Then she'd get down to work. Several months after I terminated with Sally, I got some high praise from her: she sent a friend to me for therapy (who told me she had instructions to check out my ugly ass shoes).

10. Don't Underestimate Your Role in an Adolescent Girl's Life

One of the biggest mistakes we can make is to devalue ourselves, or at least our importance to the girls we treat. Maybe adults come to therapy to fix particular problems. Adolescent girls don't; they want to be seen and heard. They want to feel felt. They usually want a relationship with you, even (or especially) if they say they don't.

Fifteen-year-old Marissa was a "multidiagnosed" girl I saw just three or four times, before losing her back into the system in which she'd spent her entire life. She came to me drug-addicted, with years in and out of foster care, a police record, and suicidal ideation. Her current placement was unstable because she wouldn't follow even the most reasonable rules in the home. Her foster parents had just about given up.

I hospitalized her to keep her safe when her despair grew so acute that she seemed a danger to herself. During her stay in the hospital, I sent her a silly greeting card, telling her I'd really enjoyed meeting her, and noting her strength to endure. Then I lost touch with her. I know now that Marissa wound up in juvenile detention until she turned 18.

Three years later, I was summoned out to my waiting area to greet a smiling young woman, who claimed to know me. She introduced herself as Marissa, the kid I'd hospitalized a few years back. She told me she'd always planned to see me when she got out of detention, because she'd kept the card I had sent her and wanted to let me know how important I had been to her. I was, and remain, flabbergasted.

These 10 lessons provide strong scaffolding for adolescent girl therapy. Regardless of presenting problems, theoretical frames, techniques, or diagnostic formulations, good treatment has some constant underpinnings. I have learned these many simple and vital lessons over many years, and I relearn a few of them every week. After many years of trying, I am still discovering who I am as a therapist for adolescent girls, honing that growing edge of attunement to myself as well as to the girls I treat. I now know that my job is to show up with my most patient, empathic, creative adult self. The best parts of me can help them sort through the confusion and find their authentic voices.

On my best days, I help adolescent girls to find their "selves" in the midst of the cacophony of other competing voices—parents, grandparents, teachers, friends, celebrities, and the loud insistence of popular culture. I know that clear speaking in therapy serves as a model for speaking truth elsewhere. Seeing, hearing, and feeling my best voice also strengthens me, and the connection between us.

CHAPTER SIX

GETTING CONNECTED

Sophie is 17 and her naïve parents have just caught her sleeping with her boyfriend. It turned out he had basically been living in the house with them; they'd go to bed early in the evening, and for months it seems he's been climbing in through the window when their light went out. He's involved with drugs, homeless, and a school dropout; they haven't liked him much from the beginning. Now they say he's banned entirely from the house. They'd like to say that Sophie can't see him but they think this is futile and would potentially sever their tenuous connection to her. Sophie's investment in high school is also fading; she's missed enough days already in the semester so it is likely she won't get credit for the term. They search her room and find drug paraphernalia; when questioned, she admits defiantly (or is it with relief that they have finally asked?) to regular marijuana use and some experimentation with other substances including cocaine and amphetamines. They have ascertained through the small-town grapevine that her boyfriend is probably a drug dealer; she doesn't deny it when they confront her about this.

The call to me is desperate. They don't know if they want her in the house if she won't follow rules, or if she'll even stay when they set stricter limits. They're uncertain they can even "make" her come to therapy, but they want to try, if it isn't already too late to save her. They're surprised when she comes without much of a struggle.

Sophie arrives for the first session flanked by her determined and terrified parents. She's filthy, frail, and blank-faced, looking more like a street-waif that a beloved youngest child. She observes me from under a shank of tangled hair that covers her eyes. In that first hour I cast my overtures to Sophie, trying to find the lure that will get her back. But it takes the next few months to hook her in. Sophie drops out of therapy and returns several times, she misses and comes late to appointments; she reaches out to me and then retreats. It takes about six months of this slipping and sliding before we begin to get some traction. I'm encouraged that she sees me a few times even after she leaves home and is living with her boyfriend in his car. But I lose her again for a couple of months, and I suspect she's just living on the street and too confused, drug-involved, and disorganized to attend regular appointments. Then, sadly, her mother gets diagnosed with cancer. This event galvanizes Sophie to step up in her life as nothing else has. She moves back home and calls me; it's her choice this time. She's absolutely devastated, and says in a tiny voice, "I'm ready now. Can I come back and try again?"

Most girls, like Sophie, end up benefiting from a therapeutic relationship. The healing connection evolves, sometimes surprisingly out of terrible beginnings—crisis, disengagement, reluctance, and rage. It can form instantly, or as happened with Sophie, in fits and starts, over time. Seeing a counselor is not usually the adolescent's idea in the first place (though they can be quite willing no matter whose solution it was). Whether or not a girl is "sent" for treatment, it is important to sort out the different agendas of involved people.

In the therapy of adults, it is transparently evident who the "identified patient" is. But in adolescent cases the referring person or institution also has a vested interest in your success. This makes agenda setting much murkier. For whom are you working? Parents, schools, courts, social service agencies, law enforcement, and communities all may need you to address their concerns. And the adolescent will likely have her own, very different story of what needs fixing. You'll need to keep a lot of customers satisfied. When I first met Sophie, for example, her stated agenda was getting her parents to back off; lucky for her though they were trying to head in the opposite direction.

Then there are additional thorny questions worth considering, which have no set answers. First there is the matter of theoretical framework. It is important to have a paradigm, a way of thinking about change, even if you don't follow it precisely or according to a manual every time. What is your comfort level with different approaches? For example, cognitive–behavioral therapy (CBT) is touted as widely effective for a variety of adolescent problems, but if you do not feel confident using it, or do not feel it is best for a particular situation, there's no need to restrict your intervention strategies to CBT. In fact, there are many methods that clearly work—and quite a few are even on the growing "list" of empirically supported therapies—for problems of adolescence (*all* in the context of a good, intentional relationship). Indeed, it matters more that you believe in the efficacy of your paradigm.

Solid interventions depend on the most salient specifics of the case, and how you apply your personality and your expertise to helping a particular girl. It is important to have some therapeutic skills, but we can get too bogged down in techniques and sacrifice healing connections in the process. The point here is that you should be conscious about how you proceed, knowing that there is no one-size-fits-all, and that there is important work to be done to set the tone for the treatment to come. Think about these issues and your rationale for your answers as they apply to an adolescent you plan to see:

- Will you try to include parents?
- Should you provide both family and individual treatment?
- Should you see parents and adolescents separately?
- What happens when the adolescent doesn't want her parents involved?
- What happens when the parent(s) don't want to be involved?
- How much confidentiality does she really want and need?
- Should peers be invited into sessions?
- Should you be functioning as part of a team?
- How much communication with the outside is beneficial; how much should a team even know about the therapy?

Answers to all of these questions can hinge on information about the referral, and the diagnostic and treatment decisions you will be making by the end of the first or second session. Even if there is no one right way to do business it helps to be conscious (as opposed to blindly diving in) from the very start.

The Referral

How girls get to your office is the first piece of information you will have to weave into the fabric of the treatment. The referral source can be the girl, if for example, you work in a school and she has literally knocked on the door. Usually though, it's an adult who makes the initial contact. This first information usually offers the most unfiltered, if not ultimately accurate, definition of the problem that you will hear, especially if there's a crisis. The person who calls or shows up in front of you will give you a straight-ahead definition: "I'm having panic attacks"; "She's cutting school"; "We're getting divorced"; "She's sneaking her boyfriend into the house and using drugs." That version of events can also end up having the most weight, even though it will ultimately be just one story out of many.

Luckily for us, we are not in a position to determine Truth (with a capital T) but only to find out as much as we can about how this is a problem, why it's a problem *now* (usually things have been bad for a while before someone asks for therapy so the timing of the referral can be informative), and how different parts of the system view the problem. Depending on how many definitions you can tolerate, you will benefit from hearing all the stories you can — from parents, teachers, friends, other adults, and, of course, from the girl herself. Ask yourself:

- Who gets to define the problem?
- Is the behavior more troubled (upsetting for the girl) or troubling (to others)?
- What will you do with competing agendas? (If you ask for different versions of Truth, you will find them).
- Will you treat the late adolescent, moving toward age 18 and legal adulthood, any differently? Consider, for example, confidentiality, agenda-setting, your role, the late adolescent's responsibility for scheduling, missing and paying for appointments, risky behavior, and family involvement.
- Will you treat an adolescent with a disengaged family? Under what circumstances will you tolerate the passivity or rejection of under-involved parents? When does parentless treatment become neglect or bad therapy?
- How will you set limits with an intrusive or controlling family? How will you respectfully stay in charge of the therapy?
- Who is the client in your cases (e.g., the girl, the family, the school, the courts, the social service agency, the residential treatment center)?
- Under what circumstances will you decide you cannot treat a girl? What are the limitations of your expertise and confidence?

- In cases of parental divorce or estrangement, foster care and later adoption, have you made psychological room for all the parents who are, by default, in the therapy, too?
- What other information will you need to make a treatment plan? How will you gain this information?

This is by no means an exhaustive list of concerns that you might have when an adolescent is about to walk in your door. But it should give you some sense that there are lots of worthy topics even before counseling begins.

Finding the Tipping Point: Is It a Problem?

Adolescent girls are often referred for treatment with a question that goes something like this: "Is this behavior we're seeing (pick one) Normal, Just a Phase, A Little Worrisome, or Serious?" There are obvious situations of course—acute trauma, suicide attempts, psychosis, self-mutilation, substance abuse, for example—where you'll say, "This sounds serious." And it's a myth that all girls must suffer in adolescence, so when someone expresses concern, there is likely to be a good reason for it, even in less dire circumstances. Many referrals, therefore, attain at least the "Worrisome" level just by the fact that someone close to a girl is indeed worried.

But assuming that most behaviors can be placed on a continuum, it can sometimes be a judgment call to decide where the tipping point lies. For example, a girl who is generally fairly anxious has a panic attack before a test. Should she be seen for therapy, assuming that you might be able to help her prevent another? Or a girl who is struggling a bit in her senior year also starts staying out an hour past curfew. Treat or wait to see if it's really an escalating problem?

And our cultural threshold for worry may be higher now. Consequently, many girls will be in deep distress by the time a referral gets made. In this period of history, it seems that a greater level of anxiety and disengagement may be the "new normal" (Taffel, 2005). We seem to expect kids to be different, tougher, today. They are disdainful and amused by those messages of love and peace we found so compelling when we were their age. Their cynical stance, combined with boomer parents' self-preoccupation, basically means that it can take a whole lot more alienation and distress for adults to register concern.

Further, how much anxiety a girl's behavior is going to generate among adults probably depends a lot on where she lives. There's much unevenness in referrals just based on race, class, cultural norms, access to resources, and availability of trained helpers. Our expectations for girls and our responses to their distress will vary tremendously depending on demographics and local options. Thus a middle-class girl who cuts classes may generate a therapy referral sooner than a poor girl who skips school altogether. The sad truth is that the tipping point for therapeutic concern is often based on external factors that have little to do with a girl's actual level of distress.

Still, in situations where we are uncertain, we sometimes help best by not rushing in and turning a girl into a "case." We can encourage the referring sources to stay vigilant and see whether the behavior is the beginning of a concerning trend, or just a developmental hiccup. Or we can make ourselves available to *them* to discuss their worries in the necessary perspectives of three general variables: taking a good developmental history, placing the problem in the larger picture of the girl's functioning, and getting a sense of the surrounding social context. We may also want to meet once or twice with the girl and her family just to become part of the baseline and establish a connection in case she struggles further down the road. Tipping point information includes:

Developmental History

Child and adolescent development isn't exactly linear. Despite some sequential developmental milestones, and some more enduring traits such as intelligence and temperament, there are many normal fluctuations in adolescent functioning. These progressions, plateaus, and regressions are what make a good history worth taking. When girls level off or go backward developmentally, it is usually for a known reason, and, most importantly, it is temporary.

Over time though, we can expect to see a forward progression of skills and functioning, broadly building sequentially along the way. Thus, when you are asking about developmental milestones and concerns, make sure also to note: duration of any past or recent developmental problems (in general, the longer and more intractable the symptoms/issues, the greater reason to intervene), and identifiable causes of problems such as conflict, divorce, death (in general, normal regression is expected in these kinds of circumstances). The main idea is that despite some ebbs, development is supposed to be mostly continuous and forward-progressing over time, even for adolescent girls.

Ask about physical, cognitive, social, and emotional development, collecting information from the girl, her parents, and any other collateral sources that you have available (e.g., school, social services, previous assessments). Use your own eyes and knowledge to begin to evaluate her developmental strengths and vulnerabilities, and how her developmental levels match up with general expectations for her chronological age.

Current Functioning

The distinction between normal and abnormal in adolescent behavior is complicated by the fact that there may be such variety in rates or patterns in the different areas of development. We are interested in how adolescents put all of these different pieces together, how they succeed in constructing and maintaining an increasingly consistent and coherent identity, made up of such parts as:

- Self-care (including attention to health, exercise, diet, sleep, and hygiene);
- Social skills (including developing ability to sustain connections with same- and opposite-sex peers, siblings, parents, and other adults);
- Psychological functioning (including affect, self-regulation, mood, attachment status, self-esteem, motivation, conscience, defense and coping behaviors, reality testing, problem-solving skills, and self awareness);
- Academic and vocational achievement (including ambition, motivation, future orientation, and consistency between ability and accomplishment);
- Passions and interests (including use of free time, relaxation, competence in self-defined areas, presence of activities that are or could help a girl feel engaged and successful somewhere in her life);
- Risky behaviors (including sexual activity, substance use, self-harm, suicidal gestures, thrill-seeking, fighting).

It is common for girls who are developing normally to have some variability across domains, of course. Nobody grows up all-of-a-piece. But as we decide on the urgency of intervention, we need to make note of how much spread there is among the different developmental trajectories. Additionally, if girls have more than a couple of areas of poor functioning, we should, correspondingly, have greater concern.

Social Context

Girls also may be functioning variably depending upon the demands of their different social settings. Schools, peers, family, part-time jobs, and after-school activities will all have different expectations and supports. Thus it is useful to inquire (of the girl, and others) about how she functions in these various environments. If a girl is only struggling in one place, you may still want to intervene, but with a sense that this may be more of a phase. The only way to gain a clear sense of a girl's strengths and vulnerabilities is to find out about how she is managing across the board in all of her places. When marked problems and compromised functioning emerge in multiple domains, it is more likely to be due to psychopathology than when problems are limited to a few areas or occur only in times of elevated stress.

Sick Girls and Bad Girls

The referral source, race, class, and community resources all have clout in defining the trajectory of the intervention. "Sick girls" are typically from at least the middle class, and white. If outpatient treatment doesn't ameliorate the problem, they are apt to be sent for a psychiatric hospitalization (paid for with private insurance). If their families have even greater resources, they may wind up in a therapeutic boarding school, or specialized residential treatment. We see even their acting-out behaviors (e.g., running away, substance abuse, sexual risk-taking) as evidence that they are in psychological distress; they are hurting themselves by their recklessness. Middle-class parents at the end of their tether still have other options, so they are still less apt to engage law enforcement or social services. The medical model prevails; these girls get treatment as the first line of intervention, and may also reap the benefit of other resources that only money can buy.

By contrast, poor and minority girls are much more apt to be referred through juvenile justice or some other disciplinary channel. These are the "bad girls" who are sent to counseling out of a primary concern for family or community safety. Adults are angry as well as worried. There are very compelling data indicating that increasing numbers of girls are being arrested, detained, and labeled as "violent" even as they seek to escape violent situations (Chessney-Lind & Belknap, 2004). So most of these bad girls getting into the system have traumatic histories of sexual and physical abuse and exposure to domestic violence. Thus, the "bad girls" are probably in as much, or more, psychological distress as the "sick girls," but will not get the same level of sympathy or support.

For these girls, therapy can be beneficial, but it is usually part of a list of restrictive expectations that may also include, for example, community service, adherence to a curfew, and checking in with someone associated with the court, such as a probation officer. Even more importantly, these girls are likely to be contending with many of the other obstacles attendant to poverty; their acting out is likely to be just one small brush fire in a forest of flames.

Treatment for both "sick girls" and "bad girls" then becomes a part of the web of services deemed necessary by adults to prevent out-of-home placement. Parents may want desperately to regain their authority, and some will work tenaciously to keep custody and connection to their daughters. Many times though, they are burdened by their own difficulties—poverty, substance use, violence, new relationships, narcissistic rage and disappointment, histories of abuse—and are well on their way to giving up. They just can't invest much of themselves in helping their girls. And no matter which referral avenue has been taken, girls without invested parents are most vulnerable and will need much more of a supportive team to even begin to compensate for all they have missed and lost.

The Team

Most girls, and especially those who are struggling, are suffering from a diagnosis that hasn't made its way into the DSM yet: Adult Deficit Disorder. They need more concerned and involved adults in their lives. Some girls have interdisciplinary treatment teams up and running. In these cases, it is our job to figure out how to be team players, staying in touch with the other members, and keeping it as organized and unified a team as we can muster.

But even for girls who are not part of a formal system of care, it helps from the very first session to imagine that we are still just one part of a de facto team. Often, too, it is useful to make sure you know (and they do, too) just who is on their virtual team—creating the feeling of a support system around a struggling girl. This can be conceptualized in a couple of useful ways; no matter how you think of it, just remember you can't help girls as effectively if you're impersonating the Lone Ranger.

Helping Hands

One useful exercise to do, early on, is to have a girl trace one of her hands on a piece of paper. Then enter a discussion with her about which adults are "there" for her. Come up with five people who hold and support her, writing the name and phone number on each finger. She can carry this list with her to remind her she isn't so alone.

If she cannot think of even a handful of caring names, this becomes a very salient piece of work for therapy. Note also, that names of other adolescents don't count here—they can go on another hand if she wishes to include them. Girls need nurturing *adults* in their lives and naming just five is a minimal expectation. Of course, girls who flourish and are resilient have many supportive relationships in their lives; how could it be any other way? Thus you may want to begin by ensuring that you quickly become a finger on their "helping hand," and that there's even some overflow of possible names. Some other adults you might consider include:

- Parents/Foster Parents
- Extended family: grandparents, aunts and uncles, older cousins, relatives
- Adult siblings
- Teachers
- Other school personnel: counselors, nurses, coaches, staff
- Other systems personnel: social workers, physicians, nurses, juvenile service officers, youth workers, counselors
- Community supports: coaches, music teachers, "Y" workers, Big Sisters, mentors
- Religious leaders
- Neighbors and family friends

TEAM Up

Another way to configure adults around a girl is through the different roles that they might play in her life. Beyond the jobs of parents, or therapists, some girls benefit from having a more formalized and supportive team to hold and guide them. And parents are often relieved to learn this: it is unreasonable to expect that (often single) parents can provide all adult roles and functions for contemporary adolescent girls. The team doesn't have to be just a random group of adults the adolescent describes as supportive, but an actual set of identified adults who work together for her. A useful acronym is TEAM; as you pull together the component parts, you will be forming a very solid circle of adults around a girl. Some of the roles you may want to recruit adults to fulfill include treatment, education, advocacy, and mentoring:

Treatment

What are the available interventions that have a therapeutic intent? Some possibilities include: individual, group, and family treatment, social-skills training, self-help groups, relaxation training, or therapeutic programs such as specialized improvisational theater, ropes courses, or wilderness experiences. Of course, this might just be you fulfilling a few of these functions. But if a girl needs other kinds of treatment, those providers can also be teammates for her.

Education

Is the school program optimal for the needs of the adolescent or is there more we can do? Does she have an Individualized Education Plan (IEP), or does she need one? What other educational supports might be helpful? Consider tutoring, extracurricular activities, in school counseling, or volunteer opportunities that give her more contact with supportive adults in the school. Who is her "person" in the school setting who can help her manage there?

Advocacy

Who speaks for the adolescent best, or helps her speak most eloquently on her own behalf? Are any of the people she has identified on her Helping Hand good advocates for her? It may help for girls to have a *lead* advocate. Optimally, a parent can serve this role, supported by the other members of the team. But if a parent is not interested or capable, such a designation fits well within our job description. Moreover, one of our biggest goals for adolescent girls is teaching them how to advocate well for themselves.

Mentoring

There are several compelling studies supporting the idea that girls benefit from having mentors (Denmark, 1999; Philip & Hendry, 1996). A mentor can be a Big Sister, a coach, a youth worker, a tutor, an older peer, or someone who is good at what they like to do. Girls also find mentors in former baby sitters, aunts, family friends, and teachers. Mentors function as special friends, encouraging positive risk-taking, appropriate choices, and self-development. They may also serve as a mediator between the girl and her family when necessary.

Parents and the Team

The TEAM is a 21st-century response to the problem of the weak nuclear family and the emergence of the vigorous and insidious "second family." Parents, all by themselves, can no longer be expected to provide everything a girl needs to grow strong and healthy. And as a rule, adolescent girls thrive when they have more adults in their supportive circle, whether these comprise an informal "helping hand" of adults, or a more formal group organized by role functions. Optimally, the TEAM supports the parent(s) in doing their jobs, too. Only in Western culture do we expect the impossible from a nuclear family to go it alone raising their adolescent girls. The TEAM assists parents with essential functions—monitoring, communication, guidance, stimulation, love—so that adolescent girls can have enough caring adults in their lives to begin to heal.

How Much Confidentiality Do Girls Need?

From the outset, and even if we believe in teamwork, we usually promise girls a tremendous amount of privacy from their parents and others. We establish rules of confidentiality that are derived from adult treatment, reassuring girls that unless they are harming themselves or others, they have a sacred space with us. The problem here is that most adolescents have too much privacy. They are yearning for more contact with their parents and with more people, but we unwittingly undermine this desire by reinforcing the distance between them and adults. In a brilliant reversal of strategy, Taffel (2005) described a much better approach:

> Because the second family is such a powerful force, I now view confidentiality from a different perspective. The statement I casually make at the beginning of the interview (which often goes unheard), and then again toward the end of our time (when it has more meaning), reflects this perspective: *"If there's anything you don't want me to tell your parents, let me know."* The foreground and background are switched from the message "Except for immediate danger, this space is 100% private," to "This relationship is going to help you get more of what you want *and* help your parents become more effective with you." I continue: *"Anything you want kept just with me we'll talk about. I'll never say anything to your parents unless we've gone over it first."* (p. 44)

Taffel (2005) notes that adolescents are generally accepting of this arrangement. He suggests that contemporary teens believe that they are sufficiently in charge of the flow of information not to be too concerned, that they may forget it, or that they're skeptical but willing to give it a try. In any event, very few reject the plan.

I have employed similar strategies over the years, with even less finesse, and don't believe I've lost a single adolescent client due to this change in emphasis. I also believe it helps me form a necessary alliance with parents who perceive that I am there to help them know their daughter better and am not just trying to have a closer relationship with her than they do.

It turns out that mothers (and sometimes fathers) who worry about their girls are (frequently embarrassed) snoops. They sense something is amiss and feel compelled to rummage in backpacks, pocketbooks, journals, and notebooks for signs and information. They read postcards, look in the history record on the computer to see where their girls have been surfing. They penetrate the fortress of a girl's room for clues about who she is. Many parents are desperate to know their daughters more, to feel closer and more trusting. We need to find out a way to honor this impulse from within the therapeutic relationship; it can be mirrored in the reverse energy of a girl's secrecy. It is often the case that very private girls also want to be known better by their parents, though they may not know that this is even possible. They've fallen prey to that mythical cultural imperative that they shouldn't let their parents see them too closely. It's a piece of some kind of phony generational warfare that does no one (except maybe commerce) any good.

When a girl gives you information you want and need her to share with her parents—maybe about drugs, health issues, significant peer conflict, sexual activity, victimization—you have several immediate choices, including keeping it in the therapy room. The beauty of not rushing into a blanket promise of confidentiality from the outset is that you'll be in a fine position to consider these issues with the adolescent girl, and together decide on a course of action toward disclosure if that is in her best interest:

- Ask her to tell them, discussing and role-playing how she'll proceed. Make sure you have agreed upon a time-frame for the disclosure so it doesn't drag out indefinitely.
- Offer to be with her when she tells them, supporting her and buffering the experience for everyone.
- Offer to be the spokesperson, while she is in the room.
- Offer to tell them when she is not present, to help them plan for how to best proceed on her behalf.
- Give her the menu of possibilities and help her weigh her options.

The point of the early days of therapy is to set the stage for success. If it is possible in the circumstances, helping girls communicate safely with their parents is an essential component to build in from the outset.

The Late Adolescent

Of course, the rules don't stay the same all the way through therapy—we usually feel a lot more comfortable talking candidly to parents when a girl is 12 years old than when she's 17. Overall, a more permissive confidentiality policy makes a lot of sense though, even through later adolescence. Teenagers need their parents all the way into emerging adulthood, and beyond. The increase in vulnerability to psychopathology, risky behavior, and acute distress for late adolescents (in that 16–20 age range) should be sufficient evidence that they need more parental presence, not less. Parents may misinterpret the acting out and regressive behavior of their older girls as proof that it is time to leave home, that they are ready to disengage. But as Terri Apter (2001) clearly notes about such regression, "Usually, however, it is a sign of *anxiety* about leaving home, of leaving behind childhood status" (p. 40). We do best when we put expectations for maturity aside and try to understand what a girl needs in the way of enduring connection and support, even as she gets older.

Still, we must continue to balance the developing need for autonomy and voice with our more paternalistic (and maternalistic) concerns about a girl as she approaches those cultural-legal landmarks of 18 or 21. We engage with older girls with a different kind of authenticity, perhaps letting them hear the competing voices in our heads about wanting to tell them what to do, to help them problem-solve, and to support them in their choices, conceding readily that it's up to them. Still, it needs to be underscored that many struggling older adolescents also need greater adult presence in their lives, and this means adults who are ready to both listen to and advise them.

Sadly, too, there are many families that run out of steam with older adolescents; parents who intentionally disengage as their daughter grows up, and simply want to be done with the job by the time she's 18 years old. There are also families that have been, for a myriad of reasons, unable or unwilling to give girls enough of what they need for a long time. These are the *up-and-out"* cases. We tell such girls, though maybe not in so many words,

> Your parents are doing the best they can, even though it may well feel to you like you could have used more support. Sometimes the match between what girls need and parents offer isn't a perfect one. And you still have to get on with your own life. Given the likelihood that we won't be getting your parents to make any dramatic changes, let's figure out what you'll need at this point from them, the rest of the team, and me to help you get up and out.

Therapy with older adolescents is more complicated—for them and for us. The stakes are higher, the other side of the threshold is closer, the rules are shakier, and the need for autonomy greater. And still, although it may seem paradoxical, girls cannot separate or individuate without sustained connection and support from caring adults.

Lead with Competence

From the point of the referral onward, you'll need to be hunting down, learning all about, and helping to develop sources of competence and pleasure in girls' lives. A growing literature on "positive youth development" supports the notion that we should not just focus on deficits and pathology when we work with adolescents, but also their strengths and resources; building mental health is not just getting rid of mental illness but fostering assets, too (Commission on Positive Youth Development, 2005). It is therefore important to consider how we build strength and optimism into the treatment we render. Taffel (2005) recommends getting adolescents to talk about their interests as the second question asked. He suggests that the first question, about reason for attendance, is usually a dead-ender anyway. Similarly, psychologist Robert Brooks (1994) talks about interventions that foster "islands of competence"—areas of interest that are (or could be) sources of strength or accomplishment. He notes that troubled kids are frequently "drowning in an ocean of inadequacy" (p. 549). It makes sense to find out about a girl's sources of strength and pride, if she has them, and to figure out how to develop them if she doesn't.

Most therapists know that the content of early sessions shouldn't be entirely negative. Still a switch in emphasis at the very outset can help girls become less defensive and more engaged. Some approaches might include:

Finding Interests and Talents

Your first mission in therapy is getting to know what girls like to do. So you can understand what they tell you, and keep a discussion going, you may have to do a little homework: listening to popular music, watching television, going to the movies, surfing the web, visiting the mall, reading magazines, and asking a lot of dumb questions in and out of sessions. Pursue details with gusto, even if it means finding out more about Johnny Depp, "emo" rock, or Wicca than you knew was possible. This doesn't mean you're supposed to become cooler than you already are, or turn into some kind of a chum, but that, as an interested and compassionate adult, you're willing to learn about her; you're curious and want to know more about what's important in her world. Girls may also have some special abilities that they may not share immediately. Is there an area of their life in which they have some extra skill (whether or not they still use it)? For example, have they been involved with sports, music, art, the outdoors, dance, theater, babysitting, or writing? Sometimes girls have given up old passions and interests that with time, they may be able to return to or build upon.

Focusing on Friendships

Girls at all points along the popularity spectrum place a high value on their friendships. It is very useful to get girls to complete a "friend web" which is a kind of sociogram that illustrates the complexity of their relationships; it is likely, especially with younger adolescents, these will evolve rapidly over time, and depict considerable emotional investment. Take out a large piece of paper. Write her name in a circle in the center. Agree that different lengths of lines will describe how close she feels to different friends, and that single straight lines between others indicates they are also friendly with each other. Have double lines for closer alliances and jagged lines for acrimonious relations, or use colored markers to key different levels of closeness in the group. Track over time how the friend web evolves, her reactions to it, and how she understands what is happening with both social alliances and social aggression in her peer group. Girls are generally very interested in these webs and you will get a lot of information about how they see themselves, their social problem-solving skills, and their support system, all at once.

Hearing about School

Of course, it's okay to ask about school, too, especially if you know it's a source of relative pride, but if you're uncertain, keep the questions fairly general so the conversation doesn't devolve into rapid-fire questions generating only terse yes or no answers, or worse the disclosure of mounting shameful failures. Find out what she likes and does well and what she loathes and struggles with. Ask how her interest in school has changed over the years and what she misses about elementary school. Girls usually find the transition to the impersonal atmosphere of junior high and high school quite jarring if they've been in a cozier local elementary school. Find out if she has any adults in school who really know her, or

whom she likes, and why. If she has a known learning or attention problem, keep the focus on whether the interventions are helping adequately
with it. If you suspect that she might have greater school difficulties, file
your worries away for a later date, or consider getting her evaluated sometime. In this first meeting, she needs mostly to hear she's going to be okay.
It won't necessarily help just yet to test out your hypothesis that she may
have a math disability. But keep in mind that school problems can really
compound issues for a struggling girl.

Family Matters

With just a little prompting, girls may be very interested in talking about
their parents and siblings. Feel free to ask them direct questions about
what people are like, what they do, and what they find most appealing
and annoying about them. Since most girls do not live in conventional
two-parent families, be sure to make room in your questioning for the family members not in the home, and other kinds of relationships with extended family and stepfamily members, too. If you're comfortable using
a genogram, it can be a great visual aid to learning about the girl's understanding of her family setup and relations among members. It also gives
you a distraction from the rapid fire interrogations that some girls find
uncomfortable — instead, together you're doing a joint project of filling
in a genogram.

You might gain some additional information through asking circular
questions that get girls to describe the interactions of family members
around a particular problem (Tomm, 1988). Sometimes the indirection of
circularity can also be more comfortable for an adolescent who feels put
on the spot. For example, if a girl has been depressed, some circular questions about her family might include:

- When you get depressed, whom do you show it to?
- When your mother notices you are depressed, how do you know?
- What do you do when your mother shows you she knows you are
  depressed?
- Who is more worried about your depression, mom or dad?
- When your mother is hovering over you, what does your father do?
- Who do you imagine would be most upset if you were so sad you
  didn't go to school?

Finding Meaning

Girls are starved for meaning, for something real to sink their teeth into, for authentic connection. We waste both of our times by asking frustrating, and to them, idiotic, questions like, "How did that make you feel?" or, "Why did you behave that way?" or "What does your mother think about your grades?" or any of our other therapeutic inquisitions. If you can find just one real thing that might matter to a girl in the first session, you're on the road. If she can say, "I just want my parents to hear me when I talk to them," or describe how it feels to be with her friends, or detail for you how she trained her puppy, and she sees you understand, you are taking the therapy to that deeper place. You are sharing with her what has value and purpose in her life. You might ask, for example:

- Who is the most important person in your life? Tell me about her or him.
- If you had a day or a week to do exactly as you liked, and money wasn't a problem, tell me about how you'd pass the time.
- If you had a special power and could cure a problem with the world, what would you fix? What are some of the other ideas that come to mind?
- What is something special that has happened to you in the last couple of years you'll never forget?
- Let's imagine that this therapy is a total success and we've done the work we needed to do together. Tell me about what's different in your life, and what you're doing differently.
- Where would you rather be right now, and what would you be doing there?
- Tell me about what you like in this world: music, art, fashion, magazines, books, friends, TV shows, stores, foods, animals, games, and why you like it.

Rising to the Challenge

The problems that girls bring to therapy must be tough or they would have solved them already. We need to take seriously a girl's struggle and be careful to avoid oversimplifying a treatment course. Our own humility goes a long way in helping girls see us as three-dimensional and authentic. But even as we can express our own doubt, confusion, or uncertainty, we will also want to convey a willingness and determination to persevere. Resilient people see obstacles as inevitable parts of life, not as sources of irrevocable defeat. We model this style of being in the world from the first contact. We give them the reassurance that, yes, this is hard, and we'll get through it *together*.

Controlling Ourselves

Girls often feel so out of control in their own lives that they latch onto troubled and harmful venues for exerting whatever power they can. They may also hold back from engaging in treatment as a way of preserving the little self-esteem and dignity they feel they have left, or attempt to control us instead. We can offer them rare validation by respecting their struggle to take hold of their own lives. We need to notice and admire what they *are* doing to manage their lives. And we have an important job to do in controlling ourselves in the first (and subsequent) sessions. We need to keep open, curious, and interested in them, attending to our countertransference, and letting them lead as they can. We set the emotional tone in the room. Our dignity and full engagement enables treatment to proceed from a higher path, and also, not incidentally, offers them the safety of a controlled (but not controlling) relationship.

Staying Cautiously Optimistic

Sometimes when girls feel overwhelmed, they are unable to garner much hope that things will ever get better. Yet it helps them become more resilient having even a small glimmer of faith in the future. One of the wonders of good therapy is the way that the relationship can hold so much potential for girls. You might offer them a bit of your own optimism to tide them over, saying something like,

> I know you are feeling pretty overwhelmed right now, and maybe thinking things aren't going to get better, even with therapy. But I'm more optimistic than that, and I intend to hold the hope in here for both of us. It has been my experience that as long as *somebody* in the room holds hope, things can get better. I'll do this a while and then I'm confident that you'll be able to become cautiously optimistic yourself.

Talking about Problems

At some point, so that everyone in the room has the same information about the concerns that brought a girl to treatment, you will probably have to talk about the problems, too. One wonderful strategy for engaging girls in problem discussions comes from the narrative therapy approach (White & Epston, 1990). Narrative therapists "externalize" problems—they make the problem a separate entity that a person is working to resist and overcome. By objectifying (and sometimes even giving a special name to) the problem, a girl and her family can then talk about how the problem has an impact on their lives (what these theorists call "problem-saturated stories," or "dominant stories"). The girl stops *being* the problem—she is not depressed, for example, but she struggles with depression.

More importantly, this strategy enables us to ask about times when the problem isn't dominating. We then have the opportunity to talk about "unique outcomes," asking, for example, about times when a girl was able to resist depression. These "alternative stories" provide rich material for subsequent sessions, strengthening a girl's strategies for managing her life better.

The advantages of talking about the referral problem in this way are many: By describing the problem as a destructive intruder on a girl's life, the girl and her family may be better able to work together against the problem instead of against the girl. Narrative questioning also uses the language of rebellion and resistance, which are inherently appealing to many girls. We inquire, for example, how she stood up for herself when depression tried to stop her from getting up in the morning; how she used her power and courage to fight it. The technique doesn't dwell on where the problem came from, but rather on the current negative consequences: the way the problem is making life miserable for the girl and disrupting her relationships with her family and friends.

Within this framework, you find out about the problem in two ways. White and Epston (1990) called these "relative influence questions." The first set of questions explores the influence of the problem on a girl's life and relationships; for example, by asking how depression has interfered with her schoolwork and friendships. The second set encourages girls to "map their own influence in the life of the problem" (White & Epston, p. 42). For example, you could ask about how a girl mobilized to go to a party even though depression made her want her to stay home.

These questions help get girls unstuck because they establish a relationship with the problem that is fluid and bidirectional. Relative influence questions enable girls to reflect on what the problem does to them, and their own effect on it. Such questions are especially helpful in the initial sessions because they pull for alternative, more rewarding stories of selves and relationships. They delve into the problems, not to get mired in them, but to challenge them, and to get therapy headed where we want it to go: helping girls take hold of their own lives.

Other Problem Questions

If narrative approaches are not comfortable for you, there are perfectly nice, straightforward ways to ask about problems:

- Tell me about the problem that brings you here today?
- Who sees this as a problem? Is it a problem for you?
- How long has it been a problem for them? For you?
- How did it begin?
- Tell me about how you've managed it since then. What are some of the times it has been easier and harder to handle?
- What do you see as some of the reasons this is a problem?
- What else is happening in your life that is stressful that may be contributing here? What changes have taken place in your life recently that I should know about?
- Are there other concerns your parents and friends have?
- What's going well in your life? What do you like to do? Is the problem interfering with your pleasure in life?
- Tell me about school, your friends, your family, your hobbies and interests? How are the problems showing up in these areas?

The main point about problem talking is that it shouldn't be all you do in the first sessions, nor does it have to be a deeply probing discussion. Get the information that you may need so you can proceed with building a supportive relationship. Maintain a curious stance, trying not to be so intrusive that a girl will feel shamed, embarrassed, or violated by your questions.

Getting Adolescent Girls to Come Back Next Time

Girls often appear more reluctant than they really are. They may appear resistant when they are actually feeling anxious and defended; after all you are a stranger, asking a lot of questions that they may not know the answers to, may not be able to put words to, may be really upset about, or may even feel retraumatized by. Still, it is important to make it worth their while to see you again, or at least to give them enough reason to be at least a little curious about returning.

Some girls do not have a choice about being in treatment in the first place—they are mandated through an IEP or a court order, for example. Or perhaps they have engaged in such risky or antisocial behavior that therapy is the last gasp before out-of-home placement. Still other girls are made to see a therapist because perhaps they've been suicidal, self-harming, or substance abusing, and it is psychologically imperative they do so. Many more girls feel they have no choice because their parents, schools, probation officers, or social workers are "making them go."

In all of these cases, you still want to encourage them to make choices that they do have. Even girls who have been coerced or mandated into treatment probably have some idea about what they need to make their lives better. Even if it isn't their idea to come, they can still give you advice about how to be helpful to them. Adolescents are looking for someone who can meet their needs, and they will not stick around otherwise. Taffel (2005) further suggested that adolescents today are more apt to view therapy as another "product" they are purchasing. He notes:

> Treating kids as sophisticated consumers, and defining your relationship as a service is necessary to move matters forward. Since millennium adolescents are adept at identifying needs yet often inept at meeting them, it makes sense to end a first interview with the question, "How can I help you?" (p. 41)

You might say something like, "I know it isn't up to you to be here, but given that, let's figure out how to make the time useful to you." You can ask questions that suggest a girl does know what she needs:

- How can we make this worth your while?
- What do you need to happen to make your life better?

- If you woke up tomorrow and the problems of your life were gone, what would be different? What would you be doing differently? Who would be the first to notice the changes?
- How would you like your social life to be different? What do you want to change with your friends?
- If you could do a makeover, not just of your body, but of the way you handle things, what would you change about yourself?
- How could your home life be better for you? What do people there need to do differently to support you?
- If you had a magic wand and could wave it over your life and change one thing about it, what would that be?
- If I turn out to be a great addition to your life, and you really end up liking therapy, what do you suppose I might have done to earn such acclaim from you?

When you feel family therapy is indicated, and the adolescent is reluctant about participating in it, you do not want to get into a tussle over this. Fishel (1999) proposed this lovely monologue to circumvent a potential power struggle:

> I would be really worried if you had been eager to come here today. I would know that there was something seriously wrong with you if you thought this was a great place to be. I mean, no self-respecting teenager should want to be here. So I will be really perplexed if you *want* to come back. However, I don't think your parents should be meeting without you and possibly making decisions that will affect your life, without you being here to offer your version. I think you are too old to let changes in your life happen behind your back. So if you decide to return, I will never mistake that as a sign that you like being here, or want to be here but only as a sign that you don't want your parents to go too far off the track in making changes that will affect you. (p. 77)

This sort of statement honors an adolescent's desire for respect and control while setting the stage for a face-saving return to therapy.

Another approach to getting an adolescent to return is to make a verbal contract for a few visits at a time, thus reassuring her that seeing you will not be a life sentence. It also helps to suggest some topics for the "next time." Have her bring in pictures, favorite CDs, her poetry or art, her brother, her friends, or even her dog—anything to make the next appointment an event to anticipate more and dread less. Offer to supply something she might enjoy—cards, a snack, materials for collage—let her know you really do want to see her again and that it could even be a little fun to meet.

Crisis Interviewing

If a girl and her family are in an immediate and acute crisis—following a suicide attempt or a run-away episode, for example—much of the above content is irrelevant until you have ascertained her safety and made a plan with the family for how to proceed. The basic crisis interview has three components:

- *Stay entirely in the "here and now."* Focus on the precipitating factors that led to the crisis—who, what, where, when, why, and how. Find out about the severity of the effect, the timeline, and the events leading up to coming to see you. Ask about subjective reactions to the event, to find out how she felt about what happened at the time, and how she feels about it now. If parents are involved, also find out about their subjective emotional states.

As the story comes out, and the emotional pitch is lowered, you can move onto the larger context of the crisis—when things began to go wrong, how events led up to it. You want to know how long she has felt vulnerable, even before this particular event. Try to maintain some kind of coherent, chronological narrative. If she has begun to stabilize at all, she will be able to tell a story about her life that makes sense. If she is still in active crisis, you will see this in both her affect and her cognitive disorganization.

- *Evaluate the current predicament:* Make a "decision statement" about what you think is currently going on and the areas of greatest ongoing concern. In this statement, you will attempt to synthesize the most important information you have heard, and give the girl and her family a sense of how you plan to proceed. You may want to describe the way you see the problem in terms of the "core dilemma" or quandary she's struggling with. Ask the girl if you're on the right track, and settle on a single problem that needs addressing first. For example, "It sounds like you were just at the end of your rope and couldn't think of anything else to do to feel better and get your mother to see how miserable you felt. Do we agree that the first thing we need to do is to be sure she can hear you, and that you both feel safe at home together?"

- *Develop a contract for working together:* Set up a working plan that specifies the following: what you will do, what the girl and her parents are going to do, and what others might be expected to accomplish as well. Be as specific and concrete as possible. The contract need only extend a week or two into the future; girls in crisis need immediate, short-term plans to help them feel better: "You are going to talk with your mom every night for a half hour. I am going to meet with you on Tuesday and both you and your mom on Thursday, and I am going to teach you strategies for self-soothing and problem solving, and give you and your mom better communication techniques. We are going to get your dad and big brother involved next week so they can become good supports for you, too."

In this general approach, you can get a crisis situation evaluated relatively quickly, negotiating and implementing a short-term plan in conjunction with the adolescent girl and her family. If you cannot get a coherent story or a safe agreement for how to proceed, you'll have to consider hospitalization to help stabilize her. Even if this is the case, you will still be ahead of the curve when you begin therapy later. You'll have seen the girl at her most distressed and vulnerable and taken action to help her and she'll know that.

Whether or not a girl is in acute crisis, throughout the referral and first session or two you will be making decisions about diagnosis and treatment. To do this best, you will need to be confident both in the assessment you have done (or have available) and in the multiple sources of data you are collecting from the "team." The first couple of sessions, along with some collateral information, provide the foundation for all that follows.

Note that diagnosis of adolescent girls is helpful to you only as it guides and informs your subsequent intervention, so you don't have to be so preoccupied with that at first. To get started, your mission is simply to get to know a girl, and begin to form a connection with her. Most girls do not fit neatly into one diagnostic box anyway. But keep your evaluative eyes and ears open. Through your developing relationship, you will be making more accurate and increasingly informed judgments about a girl, what she needs from you, and from all the people and domains of her life. Your interventions will have to be tailored to her individual concerns, strengths, and vulnerabilities, so you need to know all about them. And a solid relationship is not just the starting point but the main point.

The following chapters describe diagnostic considerations and interventions for some of the most vexing problems we see in therapy, beginning with some of the internalizing disorders.

CHAPTER SEVEN

TROUBLED BEHAVIORS I:
AFFECTIVE DISORDERS
AND ANXIETY DISORDERS

The old adage that girls act "in" and boys act "out" has some truth to it. Indeed, many of the "internalizing" or troubled behavior problems disproportionately affect girls. And the interventions with them have to be tailored to their ways of being in the world: their need for relationship, their struggle with authenticity in the face of expectations, and their often-limited strategies for problem solving. In the next three chapters there will be descriptions of some of the most common troubled presentations of adolescent girls, and suggestions for how to intervene, both on the spot and over a longer period of time.

Affective Disorders

Girls who have affective disorders most often suffer from Dysthymia, Major Depression, Bipolar Disorder, and/or Cyclothymia. Although suicidal girls tend to be included in this category, they are not necessarily, strictly speaking, depressed; girl suicidality can have variable motivations.

Dysthymia

Nicole was always a serious, thoughtful girl. Her parents have photos of her staring pensively at the camera; they remember working hard to get her to laugh, even as a baby. By the time she was in elementary school, her older sister had nicknamed her "Neyeore", which she derived from the despondent donkey Eyeore of Winnie the Pooh. Nicole would worry about disasters happening to family members. She'd go to birthday parties only to return home and report all the disappointments that she'd faced: the cake wasn't chocolate, the present she brought wasn't nice enough, the games they'd played were dull. Her family grew accustomed to Nicole's style of living in the world, and when she complained about school or friends, they listened patiently, with a distant ear. Part way through high school, though, Nicole started feeling shortchanged by her moodiness. She requested therapy to deal with her chronic sadness and irritability saying thoughtfully, "When I'm happy, I want to feel happier."

Nicole is a dysthymic adolescent. Dysthymia is a mild form of depression that has a more chronic course. Some girls have been sad for so long that they seem to have dysthymic personalities; it is like living with Eyeore for their families. Dysthymia is a low mood that is felt for most of the time on most days, and can continue for years. In fact, for a diagnosis of dysthymia, the unhappiness needs to have endured for over a year pretty much unabated. In adolescence, the average duration is four years (Koplewicz, 2002)—this suggests that such adolescents spend a significant chunk of their teen years depressed.

This prolonged sadness has implications for girls' social, emotional, and academic functioning in the present and so into the future. And since girls can be moody and lethargic anyway, dysthymia can be hard to diagnose. It complicates the picture further that girls may also be anxious, substance abusing, or eating disordered—these problems can both be the cause and consequence of depression, and invariably make it worse. Usually dysthymic girls will retreat rather than talk about how they feel— maybe they don't have the language or the audience. Or maybe it seems almost normal to them to feel crummy since it has gone on for so long. In any event, it is also tougher for adults to intervene if girls aren't complaining specifically about feeling miserable.

Depression in adults and adolescents can look quite similar. For example, both may be fatigued, reclusive, indecisive, hopeless, lose interest in activities they formerly enjoyed, act self-critically, have difficulty concentrating, have a worsening of mood as the day progresses, feel unloved and unlovable, have sleep and eating disturbances, an increase in physical complaints, a decrease in attention to hygiene, a sense of a foreshortened future, and feelings of agitation. This long list is a fairly standard outline of how depression shows up.

But the symptoms of depression in adolescents can also be different from adult presentations. They may include irritability, anger, and aggression, too. The quality of dysthymia in an adolescent girl is more one of being out of sorts, seemingly inconsolable; she's quickly triggered and painfully slow to settle back down. She is even more sensitive than usual to slights by friends and lovers. While adults may experience either a loss or an increase in appetite and sleep, most dysthymic and depressed girls eat and sleep more than before. They almost always seem anxious, too — about social matters, and about leaving the house or their parents for example. They may have been cautious, anxious younger girls who did not step up developmentally to new challenges and become increasingly despondent. Or they may have been managing well before adolescence, but seem to cave under the weight of all the new expectations.

Dysthymic and depressed girls are also more prone to somatic complaints — lots of aches and pains, headaches, stomachaches, more acute PMS symptoms. Unlike adults, they may keep their libidos, or even increase in their sexual interest and activity. In fact, one of the most important differences between depression in adolescents and adults is that in adolescents it isn't such a monolithic, intractable presence (Commission on Adolescent Depression and Bipolar Disorder, 2005; Koplewicz, 2002). Depressed girls seem to rally now and then. They'll be moping for hours, then seem jolly talking on the phone with a friend, or cheerful going out for a few hours. But if it's dysthymia or major depression, the dark pall will return. And unlike dysthymic or depressed adults, girls are particularly reactive to their social environments; their depressive symptoms may come and go a bit depending on what is happening in the rest of their lives.

Major Depression

Antoinette is a girl who expects a lot of herself. She studies more than she probably has to, and is a loyal friend to her 10th grade peers. Her mother is a single parent, and she relies a lot on Antoinette to help with younger siblings, walking the two family dogs, and getting dinner on the table. Antoinette also plays the flute and takes karate lessons after school. It seems like a lot of responsibility, but she doesn't feel it is too much for her.

To her way of thinking, the problem is Henry, her first true love who dumped her seemingly for no reason and her best friend, Ruby, who started going out with Henry the next day. Bereft of both significant relationships, Antoinette began to plummet. She had crying jags that lasted for hours, and barely studied at all. She told herself and others that maybe she deserved to be treated like this. She didn't take the dogs for after school walks, and became increasingly irritable with her mother and little brothers. She slept in the afternoon and right after dinner where she just picked at her food. One of her teachers noticed the downward change in Antionette, and sent her to the guidance counselor, who then referred her to me for therapy.

Although it can be difficult to distinguish dysthymia from major depression (and these problems from normal variability in mood in adolescents), most experts agree that the differences are important to highlight. The major distinctions are: (1) *Severity:* if symptoms are notable but still relatively mild, and not dramatically different than they've been over a long while, it is more likely to be dysthymia. (2) *Impaired functioning:* dysthymic girls may continue to function at a minimally expected level and won't have bizarre or incoherent thoughts; impaired functioning and thinking problems are found more commonly with major depression. (3) *Intensity:* if symptoms fluctuate over a long period, it is more likely to be dysthymia. In major depression, the symptoms will be unremitting for a couple of weeks with less variability overall. (4) *Duration:* adolescent major depressive episodes typically last on average between 7 and 9 months; dysthymia can stick around for years (Commission on Adolescent Depression and Bipolar Disorder, 2005; Koplewicz, 2002).

Even with these guidelines in mind, it can still be hard to know whether the worry, and intervention, is warranted. The real issues here are how bad a girl is feeling and how hard it has become for her to bounce back from the inevitable disappointments and stresses of life. None of the symptoms in and of themselves are significant—most teenagers will have most of them at some point in time; the duration and number of these symptoms together tells us if a girl has crossed the line into major depression. In the case of Antoinette, the onset and intractability of the symptoms suggested a depressive episode; indeed she evinced most of the more serious symptoms.

Early detection is vital to help with speedy recovery, so it is useful to have a checklist handy, and to go through it with multiple sources, not just the adolescent herself. In a period of over two weeks consider how many of these problems have surfaced (the more problems and the longer they have lingered means cause for greater concern):

- Did she lose interest in things she used to enjoy?
- Did she withdraw, isolating herself from friends and family? Did she feel lonely?

- Is she complaining about boredom more than usual?
- Has there been a significant drop in performance in school; is she apathetic about it? (In school this apathy can seem like laziness, gloominess, negativity—or it can be mistaken as a phase or as a part of her dour temperament.)
- For more than two weeks, has she seemed "down in the dumps?" Has she been crying a lot? Saying she's miserable or unhappy?
- Has she started to act out, be reckless, and take more risks than usual? Is she abusing drugs or alcohol?
- Does she have more than the usual number of headaches, stomachaches, colds, and physical ailments?
- Does she seem especially fatigued for no good reason? Is she just sitting around doing nothing because she's so tired?
- Is she more irritable, agitated—does she seem more impulsive and volatile than usual?
- Is she having more difficulty concentrating? Is she more restless?
- Is she expressing feelings of worthlessness, hopelessness, sharing thoughts of death, suicide plans? Is she relentlessly self-critical and self-effacing? Does she say she hates herself? That she can never be as good as other kids? That she does everything wrong?
- Are there significant change in sleeping or eating patterns (usually more of both)?
- Is she extremely sensitive to rejection or failure?
- Does she believe that she is unworthy of love?

The differential diagnosis between dysthymia and major depression is ultimately less important than the fact that a depression is noticed and we intervene to interrupt its insidious course.

Bipolar Disorder

Victoria's got genetic loading on both sides of her family for affective disorders. Her mother had postpartum depression and also suffers from major depression, and Victoria has two paternal uncles and a grandfather who have been diagnosed with bipolar disorder. Her father committed suicide when she was just a baby; her mother is convinced he was manic when he died, although he had never been diagnosed as such. When

Vicky was younger, she was treated for both depression and ADHD. No-tably, she's gone through extended periods of sleeplessness, averaging, at times, just a couple of hours a night throughout her 18 years. This fall, away at college, she stopped sleeping almost entirely as she grew increas-ingly expansive and manic. Her thinking became significantly disorgan-ized. Vicky's behavior escalated until she was arrested for assaulting a policeman when he tried to stop her from singing loudly outside her dor-mitory at two in the morning. Following this incident, Vicky was hospi-talized briefly, and discharged to home, psychopharmalogical consulta-tion, and outpatient treatment.

Bipolar disorder has become increasingly common as a diagnosis in adolescence in recent years. Even though, as seemed likely for Victoria, it is thought to have a strong genetic component, bipolar disorder affects around just 1% of the population. Still, it is more widely diagnosed than these strictures might suggest. Many clinicians now believe that in the past it was incorrectly identified because professionals and parents can be con-fused at its inception. After all, most girls have pretty dramatic mood swings. Bipolar disorder can also present as a sudden onset of bizarre symptoms, including psychotic thinking (e.g., disordered and incoherent expression of thoughts, strange beliefs that no one else shares, and hallu-cinations); excessive substance abuse, and sleep disorders also can both trigger and be symptomatic of mania. When adolescents are treated for these kinds of symptoms, clinicians may instead think of schizophrenia, intoxication and withdrawal, or a severe stress reaction to other emotional problems. Further, between 70 and 90% of adolescents diagnosed with bipolar disorder also have other diagnoses (Koplewicz, 2002). Some there-fore believe that adolescent bipolar disorder has previously been signifi-cantly underdiagnosed and overlooked.

Recently, however, researchers have recognized several clinical fea-tures likely to be associated with adolescent bipolar disorder which may help in its diagnosis. These include: the *sudden* onset of symptoms, a much earlier diagnosis of depression in a girl's history, and psychotic thinking; in addition, pharmacologically induced hypomania and a three-generation family history of bipolar disorder are also strong indicators (Commission on Adolescent Depression and Bipolar Disorder, 2005).

Researchers note that *childhood* bipolar disorder is distinguished by more rapid cycling of moods, with a more chronic and mixed manic pre-sentation (Geller & Luby, 1997; Wozniak et al., 1995). By contrast, the diagnostic criteria for adolescents are the same as for adults. Bipolar Disorder has two major types. In *Bipolar I*, there is an identified manic episode, or a mixed manic and depressive episode, usually with a period of depression, too. In *Bipolar II*, there is not a full-fledged manic episode, but rather a briefer, less disruptive hypomanic phase intermixed with periods of depression. Adolescents with Bipolar I are more likely to be hospitalized and treated with mood stabilizing drugs. Though bipolar disorder usually begins with an episode of depression, manic symptoms can also be the first sign of it. These include:

- Abrupt or gradual changes in mood including "delusions of grandeur" (she may speak of super powers); great increase in energy with significant decrease in need for sleep; rapid, pressured speech—she'll be talking too much and too fast, zooming from topic-to-topic, and hard to interrupt; and extreme investment in new projects to the exclusion of usual activities and relationships.
- Increased libido with a tendency toward uncharacteristic promiscuity and sexual acting out.
- A new recklessness and disregard for safety. She may be experimenting with drugs, having unprotected sex, abusing drugs and alcohol, driving carelessly, or otherwise behaving in an unsafe fashion.

Although adolescents with bipolar disorder do cycle more rapidly than adults, they still may have swings of significant—at least a week—duration. And the range is greater than the "normal" moodiness of adolescent girls—the highs and lows are more extreme and potentially self-destructive.

Cyclothymia

Alyssa, now just 15, has become exhausting to live with. Her moodiness is so unpredictable that her whole family says they're "walking on eggshells" just to get through a weekend with her. At dinner, for example, she laughs hysterically at something no one else finds funny until milk comes out of her nose and then she gets banished from the table. She also sometimes rages until her younger sister is in tears, cowering in her room. Alyssa realizes that people are upset with her after she's gone way too far. She then falls into a deep despair from which she'll take a few days to recover. Alyssa is a sensitive girl, so she'll apologize repeatedly after she upsets people; even this act of contrition is tiring for her family. She just doesn't seem to learn from these episodes, or to be able to control them. The whole cycle from extreme to extreme begins again too soon.

Cyclothymia is a milder (and more common) form of bipolar disorder—the way that dysthymia is a milder and more prevalent form of major depression. For this diagnosis, adolescents need to have had hypomania numerous times over the past year, and similarly, periods with some depressive symptoms. In cyclothymic adolescents, there can be no more than a two-month period without mood problems during a two-year period. Although these mood cycles are more rapid and less severe than in bipolar disorder, they still need to exceed the usual adolescent swings and cause some kind of disturbance in social, academic or family functioning.

Intervention

For girls like Nicole, Antoinette, Victoria, and Alyssa, who appear to have affective disorders, you will want to ask very clear and direct questions about specific behaviors that will suggest to you what kind of problem you'll be treating. If you are too general in your inquiry, you may not get at the core symptoms that will help you decide if a girl is going through a phase or has a significant problem, or what, exactly the problem is. Ask, for example:

- How many hours did you sleep last night?
- How about the night before?
- Is this different from a few weeks ago?
- How long does it take you to fall asleep?
- Do you wake during the night?
- How long does it take to fall back to sleep?
- How do you feel when you wake up in the morning?
- When are you most tired during the day?
- How's your appetite? What have you eaten today?
- Is your appetite any different now from a few weeks ago?
- Have you noticed any difference in your ability to concentrate?

- How's your schoolwork? Is this different from a few weeks ago?
- Do you have friends? How often are you seeing them? Do you call them? How often? Do they call you? What do you do for fun on the weekends? Is this the same as before?
- What are your interests/hobbies/extracurricular activities? Are you doing these? How much time are you spending on them? Is this a change for you?
- How much time do you spend crying or feeling like crying?
- What is making you sad? Are you sadder than you've been?
- Are you more upset, irritated, annoyed, or grumpy than you have been? For how long have you noticed this change?
- Do you wonder if you'll feel better, or do you know you'll get through this hard time?
- Are there things you're looking forward to? Tell me about them.
- Are you getting high more now? Do you think you're self-medicating for depression?
- Are you sexually active? Have you noticed any change in your sexual interest?

The more pointed and precise questions you ask, the more valuable information you will get. It may not be a surprise to the girl that she's depressed. More often, it is the advent of a manic episode that is harder for her to fathom. Manic girls may have trouble slowing down enough to even hear your concern. If they are unsafe, you may need to consider hospitalization and medication to help them use what therapy has to offer.

The best treatment for all of the different affective disorders is basically the same; typically a focused kind of psychotherapy with adjunctive antidepressants and mood stabilizing medication as needed (see Chapter 12 for a detailed discussion of the role of medication).

Psychotherapy for affective disorders typically has a combination of three components to it: education, cognitive–behavioral strategies for coping, and interpersonal therapy.

Education

Education is vital so that girls understand the variety of factors that may have led to, or increased their vulnerability to depression. It is helpful to frame the discussion using a biopsychosocial approach so girls and their families can understand the connection among the forces at work.

At the biological level, girls need to know about the role of genetics (a family history of depression/bipolar disorder increases the likelihood of its occurrence) of temperament (quieter, more fearful children may be at greater risk than more cheerful, extroverted ones, for example), and of brain structure and functioning (depressed brains appear to be chemically different in the amount of available serotonin, for example). While biology is not destiny, it is an important factor in understanding why one girl may be more vulnerable than another to depression.

At the psychological level, girls are struggling to cope with and manage both a stressful physiology and a stressful environment. They have to handle their thoughts and feelings about their changing bodies, their evolving relationships with parents and friends, their sexual orientation, and their future. And if their internal reactivity isn't enough to precipitate a depressive episode, social stressors abound that can also trip them up.

Indeed, stress plays a prominent role in most theories of depression; a powerful, empirical link exists between stressful life events and depression in adolescents (Compas, Grant, & Ey, 1994). These findings appear to be particularly strong for girls (Commission on Adolescent Depression and Bipolar Disorder, 2005). Some stressors that have been found repeatedly to be associated with increased rates of depression for girls include: child abuse, sexual abuse, poverty, disappointments, losses, separations, interpersonal conflicts, and rejection (Commission on Adolescent Depression and Bipolar Disorder, 2005). Given the frequency of studies citing gender as a variable, it is also evident that being a girl is in itself a precipitant. And these factors are cumulative; the more stressors, the greater the risk. Girls are reassured to know that they have reasons for feeling as lousy as they do; in some ways it is perfectly understandable that they are suffering.

A broad range of family communication, structure, and functioning problems has also been implicated. Notably the family link between interpersonal vulnerability and depression is bidirectional (Gotlib & Hammen, 1992). Families with a depressed member provide less support, and sustain more conflict; such dysfunction increases an adolescent's risk of developing depression. But depressed girls are themselves more difficult to live with and befriend, which also results in greater problems in their social network. And every one of these biopsychosocial factors all interact with one another. Education about all the parts of depression helps girls and their parents understand the connections among brain, behavior, and the environment.

Cognitive–Behavioral Therapy

Cognitive–behavioral therapy (CBT) is most researched and touted as the preferred approach for treating adolescent affective disorders, despite a lack of evidence that it is uniquely beneficial for them (Commission on Adolescent Depression and Bipolar Disorder, 2005). CBT is based on the idea that depression comes from having negative and unrealistic perceptions about self, the world, and the future. The therapy focuses on correcting these mistaken thought patterns, and helping girls engage in more pleasurable activities.

While many depressed girls are unwilling or unable to participate fully in all of the homework assignments and self-monitoring of thoughts and activities required by CBT, it is still very useful for therapists to understand the principles of it, and to attempt, in the context of the relationship, to help girls look at their strategies for coping that maintain or alleviate the depression. For example, girls who are depressed have numerous "Automatic Thoughts" in the course of a day that they utterly believe are factual. These "ATs" are highly negative and self-fulfilling and include most commonly, for example, *all-or none thinking* (believing that things will either be perfect or disasterous); *mind reading* (believing she knows how someone else thinks or feels without any supporting evidence); *catastrophizing* (believing that the worst has, or is about to, happen); *would/should/could* (believing that whatever has happened or will happen is inadequate, or not worth trying); *disqualifying the positive* (minimizing accomplishments, negating compliments); and, *probability overestimation* (believing a low-probability event is really a sure thing).

Within the context of the therapeutic relationship, therapists can gently describe and question these ATs, asking for the evidence that supports or refutes them. Depressed girls need help in problem solving, challenging their ATs, and coming up with a concrete plan for turning the ATs into hypotheses that can be tested. In the process of this, therapists give girls new tools for thinking and responding in the present moment, while giving the message that they believe the depressed interpretation of events is not the only one available.

Interpersonal Therapy for Adolescents

Interpersonal therapy for adolescents (IPT-A) is another intervention strategy with solid empirical support and excellent clinical sense for treatment of affective disorders (Mufson, Weissman, Moreau, & Garfinkel, 1999). Any therapy that focuses on relationship has an immediate advantage for adolescent girls, no matter what the presenting problem or stated theoretical framework might be. Although CBT has the most research supporting it, there is ample and growing evidence that IPT-A may be even more effective for them than CBT (Rossello & Bernal, 1999).

IPT-A is a time-limited, focused psychotherapy that addresses common adolescent developmental issues that are closely related to depression: separation from parents, authority and autonomy issues in the parent–teen relationship, development of dyadic interpersonal relationships, peer pressure, loss, and issues related to single-parent families.

The therapist in IPT is quite active, exploring these issues with the adolescent very much in the context of the therapeutic relationship. IPT therapists work from the assumption that the impact of depression is greatest in how it plays out in social relationships; the depressed adolescent becomes more disappointed and frustrated with life in general when her connections to friends and family diminish. By exploring the effects of a girl's behavior within the therapy itself, she can learn more about the ways that she acts in relationships that make them hard for her. If her relationships improve, her depression will then abate.

This strategy is inherently intelligent for girls who generally want connections with others above all else. It links the depressed mood to problems in identified areas and ties an improvement in mood to constructive changes in communication and social problem solving. It also gives girls a chance to practice in vivo in the context of a safe and supportive relationship (Mufson et al., 1999). Therapists also get to be more three-dimensional and less of a technician than with CBT; they'll go to schools, talk with girls between sessions, do whatever it takes to break old patterns of negative interactions in the world outside of the office. Depressed girls need to become more internally regulated. This happens best when they learn problem solving and self-soothing strategies in the context of a supportive and authentic relationship.

Suicide Attempts

Abigail is 13 and she's grounded again. This time she got poor grades and then lied about her plans, saying she stayed for "homework club" after school to meet with teachers so she could catch up. Instead she made another bad choice and went to a high-school boy's house when no adults were home. She was deceitful about that too, even after his mother called to report it to her father and Abigail was completely busted. Her father was furious about all the lying and frightened about what she was doing unsupervised with this older boy. He saw her "going down the tubes." Abigail's father responded in the way he thought made the most sense given the severity of the infractions: he grounded her for a month.

To Abigail's impulsive way of looking at her life, a month was akin to a death sentence, so she might as well just die. She was also bitter about her father's involvement in her life "only when I'm in trouble." She went into the bathroom and ingested the contents of a bottle of Tylenol, which luckily was not full. She began throwing up, and experienced severe abdominal pain. Terrified, Abigail told her father what she had done. She was rushed to the hospital and doctors pumped her stomach. She did not suffer from liver damage although if she had waited longer to get help she might have died.

Most girl suicide attempters do not resort to the most violent and lethal means to kill themselves. They're unlikely, for example, to use firearms or other weapons, or intentionally to drive their cars off of the road, or jump from a high place. As such, most of their attempts have been more aptly termed *parasuicidal*. While all attempts must be taken seriously, the depressed wish to die is only one of a long list of reasons for the gesture. There are at least 10 other dynamics underlying girl suicide attempts—none of which is mutually exclusive from the others.

1. *Anger turned inward.* These adolescents are actually enraged with someone or something else but are unable to express it outwardly. They may fear rejection or retaliation or they may have developed a corresponding sense of self-worthlessness that precludes entitlement to strong feelings. In some families, girls are given little permission for such powerful expressions, and feelings thus build up with no place to go. For these adolescents, the suicide attempt is really the enactment of hostility aimed elsewhere.

2. *Manipulation.* Girls who cannot get their needs met through direct and nonviolent means may resort to a suicide attempt without necessarily thinking about killing themselves at all. Manipulative suicidal girls seek to gain attention, to influence the behavior of others, to send a mes-

sage, or to punish others—ultimately to gain power in a situation in which they feel powerless. The suicidal act is a dramatic, controlling one that ensures them center stage for a time.

3. *A cry for help.* The suicide attempt that serves as a cry for help is usually not lethal. Girls who attempt suicide for this purpose typically feel much better after therapy begins because they are then finally getting the support they desired all along (but couldn't ask for in a way they could be heard). A suicidal cry for help is often a last-ditch effort when other methods of finding ways to make changes have failed. Of course, because adolescents who engage in more parasuicidal acts are not pharmacologists (or otherwise capable of determining the tipping point of lethality in these gestures) they cannot gauge accurately the level of intensity that they need to cry for help, but not die. Still, the fortunate ones, like Abigail, let someone know, before too long, that they have harmed themselves and need help.

4. *Psychosis.* For between 10 and 15% of suicidal adolescents, the attempt is apparently more of a desperate means to relieve increasing internal tension and confusion than a reaction to external stress. Diminished contact with reality can be particularly terrifying when accompanied by persecutory voices telling adolescents to kill themselves. Abuse of hallucinogens can also cause an adolescent to become suicidal, making "bad trips" particularly dangerous. When girls are suicidal, it is important to find out if a thought disorder or recreational drugs have anything to do with it.

5. *The suicidal game.* For some girls, toying with death is a game reinforced by the glamour and attention it attracts from peers and adults. These adolescents are not motivated in therapy and tend to minimize the "big deal" that others make of their attempts. Some girls are particularly flamboyant in their risky behavior—driving recklessly, cutting themselves in exposed places like their necks and arms, walking on train tracks with friends when a train is coming—and they deny they are afraid of death in any way, even when confronted with the possible consequences of their behavior. Their lives may be sufficiently empty that the thrill of walking on the edge seems worth the extreme risk.

6. *A reaction to loss.* Some depressed girls have experienced the death of a beloved relative, friend, or pet, and feel that life is not worth living without them. They may harbor fantasies, either consciously or unconsciously, that after they die they will join their loved ones again. Girls

with religious beliefs that describe an afterlife where people are reunited, may be particularly relieved by such fantasies when their lives feel sad and lonely.

7. *Life is too hard.* For some girls, the motivation for suicide is to stop unendurable pain and conflict. Death may be seen as the only option left, but it is really the end of problems—not the end of life—that these adolescents seek. They lack the skills necessary to address their anguish in a more functional manner. Seen in this light, suicide is really just a coping strategy, albeit a potentially fatal one.

8. *Rage and revenge.* Some girls are consciously punitive in their suicidal behavior. More than just wanting to manipulate or get attention from someone, they seek to teach a lesson, or somehow to get even, using their potential death as a club with which to bludgeon others. Since retaliation is the primary motive, these adolescents don't actually want to die but rather to terrify someone. In these cases, the anger is expressed on both sides of the conflict, and the suicide attempt is an escalation of words and actions that are increasingly violent. Homicidal thoughts may also be present—expressed by both the suicidal adolescent and others in the family. Girls who are rageful use the suicide attempt to convey the sentiment, "You'll be sorry when I'm gone; you'll see how badly you treated me."

9. *Imitation and suggestibility.* If adolescents are already at some risk for suicide, they may be more vulnerable to the news that others—celebrities, peers, or relatives—have attempted or committed suicide. Ample research supports contagion effects for both attempted and completed suicides (Commission on Adolescent Suicide Prevention, 2005). Some girls get caught up in the dangerous whirl, whether through media coverage or direct knowledge of a suicide.

10. *Alienation.* Some girls do not necessarily perform a single suicidal act, but rather behave in a chronically disengaged and self-destructive pattern that could at any time result in death. Social factors like poverty, parental and family conflict, problems with peers, and school difficulties may interact reciprocally with some adolescents' feelings of powerlessness, loss of hope, and isolation. As they become increasingly disenfranchised and disconnected from the mainstream, their interest in and ability to self protect diminishes. They may then place themselves at greater risk by, for example, abusing drugs (including alcohol and cigarettes), running away, having indiscriminate or unprotected sex, or engaging in thrill-seek-

ing suicidal games. They may also give up and do something overtly suicidal. Hopelessness and disengagement underlie these types of parasuicidal behavior.

Suicidal girls share some general developmental characteristics. This is not to say, of course, that all girls who have these qualities will be suicidal. But there are adolescents who are more vulnerable to this (potentially) permanent solution to a temporary problem. Prevention and intervention efforts might focus on some of these particular problems:

Suicide attempters are less able to *tolerate frustration*. This may be due to temperament, or a result of adult indulgence, or just developmental immaturity. But such girls, like Abigail, are liable to resort to quick action to attempt to manage discomfort or pain.

Perhaps this goes without saying, but girls who attempt suicide also tend to be unable to *plan future actions*. They're concrete reasoners, who live too much in the present. It is hard for them to visualize events even a few weeks ahead, much less to take orderly steps to get there. They rely heavily on external structure and support to help contain an impulsive mindset.

Prior to a suicide attempt, these girls may also have been *prone to aggressive or violent outbursts*. The impulsivity can cause some very poor choices along the way. In their reactivity, these girls often have a particularly extreme and passionate way of coping. Some girls hold themselves in such low esteem that the notion of self-care or self-protection seems very alien. In these cases, it isn't surprising that they may be willing to hurt others, too.

Given how impulsive suicide-attempters seem to be, it is noteworthy that they frequently have considerable *difficulty making decisions*. Perhaps an impulsive style is a way of warding off the uncertainty and frustration necessary for a considered decision. Whatever the reason, these girls often seem overwhelmed by choices, and struggle to take hold in a more thoughtful manner. Therapy can help such girls articulate what they want and need; something they may not even know.

Suicidal girls are also less able to *assess situations realistically*. Cognitive distortions, low self-esteem, negative automatic thoughts, and dysfunctional attitudes are all more common in suicidal adolescents leading them to jump to faulty conclusions about events and consequences. Such girls have unrealistic expectations, leading to repeated disappointments and pessimistic thinking. They may take a bad exchange with a chum as irrefutable evidence that they will never have any friends, or a break-up as proof they are forever unlovable. In Abigail's situation, she was not able to see either that her irresponsible behavior called for a consequence or that the consequence was not, in fact, akin to a death sentence. Some girls' ability to define and explain events is compromised by negative thoughts about themselves and the world they inhabit, and weak logical analysis.

Girls who resort to suicide may also share other experiences that render them more vulnerable. Girls who suffer the loss of parent before age 12 may maintain a perception that death is compelling. Parent–child conflict, and a perceived lack of family support are also common in suicidal girls (Wagner, Silverman, & Martin, 2003). Physical abuse and sexual abuse both contribute significantly to suicidal thoughts and behaviors (Johnson et al., 2002). Other stressors including peer and romantic relationship problems, bullying, legal problems, and academic failure are also all associated with increased suicidality (Commission on Adolescent Suicide Prevention, 2005).

Girls who are in the process of questioning their sexual orientation, coming out as lesbians, or identifying as lesbian or bisexual, are similarly more vulnerable; stigmatization, victimization, isolation, and parental rejection have all been identified as contributing factors (McDaniel, Purcell, & D'Augelli, 2001). A growing but mixed body of research suggests that vulnerable girls may also be adversely influenced by the media—both in the way suicides are reported and in media influence via confusing and depressing images of girls (Commission on Adolescent Suicide Prevention, 2005).

Individual factors that have also been implicated in girl suicide attempts include: psychopathology, especially depression and panic disorder; biological and genetic variables including parental psychopathology and higher levels of serotonin receptor expression; and the extreme hormonal shifts of adolescence (Commission on Adolescent Suicide Prevention, 2005). These variables seem less significant than others in explaining the vulnerability of some girls to suicide, but remain on many lists for their interest to the medical establishment.

Intervention

In cases like Abigail's, the suicide attempt is in the past, but suicidal intent still needs to be assessed in an ongoing manner. At the same time, the focus can also turn to improving self-soothing and problem solving strategies, and family communication. In other situations where you may suspect suicidal ideation or intent, you must first conduct an evaluation. The purpose of a good screening is both to determine whether an emergency response is indicated and to make a coherent treatment plan with the adolescent. Some general ideas for such a screening might include:

- A thorough mental status examination that explores the girl's current mood, behavior, and cognitive state.
- Current assessment of suicidal intent (before an act):
  — Is there any thought of suicide?
  — What would be the purpose of the attempt (as stated and understood clinically)?
  — Is there a specific plan to commit suicide?
  — Is the plan clear and specific, or vague and bizarre?
  — Does she have access to the means to implement the plan?
  — Has there ever been an active attempt to carry out the plan?
  — What are her expectations regarding the fatality of the act? How reversible would it be—friends nearby, medical attention might save her?
  — How forthcoming and comfortable does she seem to be in sharing this information? How confident are you that she's reporting honestly?
  — Is she willing to make a safety contract with you?
- Current assessment of suicidal intent (after an act):
  — Did she do as much as she thought would be lethal?
  — How serious is this as a suicide attempt?
  — Is she ambivalent about living?
  — How does she visualize death?
  — How premeditated was the attempt?
  — How many previous attempts have there been?
  — Were drugs and alcohol involved?
  — What was the communicative intent of the act?
  — How effective was it in communicating what was intended?
  — What are the reactions of significant others?
  — Is she willing to make a safety contract with you?

The Safety Contract

Also known as a "no-suicide contract," the safety contract is a valuable supplement to ongoing treatment with adolescent girls. It is controversial only insofar as therapists may be lulled into believing that a signed contract eliminates suicide risk, or it somehow becomes more important as a risk-management tool than an actual relationship (Range et al., 2002). The contract works best as just one part of a comprehensive evaluation and treatment plan; a good contract provides specific behavioral alternatives to suicide and underscores what the therapist will be doing to support the adolescent. A safety contract commonly includes the following negotiated components (Buelow & Range, 2001; Drew, 2001):

- A specific statement not to harm or kill oneself.
- A specific duration of time.
- Contingency plans if contract conditions cannot be kept (e.g., talking with the therapist or parents if thoughts of suicide should occur during the time of the contract).
- Formal statements of treatment goals.
- The responsibilities of each signatory.

In the first couple of sessions, the therapist needs to become a calm ally to the adolescent and her family, seeking to understand the motivations and the stressors as well as what resources there are.

The therapy that follows employs the same triad of emphases described for treatment of affective disorders—education, cognitive restructuring (improving problem-solving skills), and relationship building (improving communication and interactions with significant friends and family members). Therapists of suicidal girls must reassure them (and their families) that talking about suicidal feelings is okay, that depressed—or anxious, confused, enraged—people do get better with treatment, and that you will help them stay safe. Families need to be involved to whatever extent is possible, with a focus on improving communication, involvement, and age-appropriate expectations. And as with mania or any other problem in which safety may be compromised, good therapy also ensures that the environment is providing significant structure and support to hold and contain the fragile girl. If not, she will need to be hospitalized until her safety can be better assured.

Anxiety Disorders

Most people (especially adolescents) are anxious these days—it is so prevalent that this period in the early 21st century may even prove to be the "age of anxiety." Curiously, it's probably more worrisome to find a girl with no anxiety at all! Indeed, mild anxiety has played an important evolutionary role for humans, signaling that some kind of self-protective action is required to ensure safety. And because anxiety exists on a continuum, it is hard to know where the tipping point is, or whether severe anxiety is really pathology at all. Perhaps it is just the extreme expression of a common trait.

But anxiety clearly becomes symptomatic when it prevents or limits developmentally appropriate adaptive behavior (Klein & Pine, 2001). And the diagnostic threshold is also crossed when an adolescent can't recover from anxiety in a reasonable amount of time, even when the provoking situation is absent. Girls can be a little anxious, but they should be flexible, too. Thus, a girl who is fearful in a new social situation is behaving as might be expected. However, if she becomes ruminative about the experience for days afterwards, or avoids such social opportunities in the future, this is cause for concern.

Difficulties in separating "normal" from "pathological" anxiety are perhaps more problematic for epidemiological studies than in specific instances. Adolescent girls with anxiety disorders who end up in treatment typically suffer from markedly impairing anxiety, and there is little ambiguity about determining if their level of anxiety is normal or not. This section describes four of the most common kinds of anxiety disorders: Panic Disorder, Phobias, Obsessive–Compulsive Disorder, and Generalized Anxiety Disorder. Posttraumatic stress disorder is also considered an anxiety disorder in the DSM–IV. But it is such a significant concern for adolescent girls (and it is also, arguably, a dissociative disorder) that it is discussed separately, in Chapter 9.

Panic Disorder

Georgia has always been shy in social situations. She doesn't like speaking in front of groups, and sticks to her home base and a couple of friends she's had since elementary school so she doesn't get that panicky feeling. She's been able to avoid class presentations for the most part until this year. Now her final marks in U.S. History for her 11th grade year are dependent upon a 10-minute oral report, so she has to speak in front of the class. As the date approaches, she feels impending dread and fear. Objectively speaking, she's reasonably prepared, but is sure she'll fail. The day of the presentation, she hyperventilates so severely and becomes so agitated that, just as she had feared, she actually passes out. She is rushed to the hospital (and successfully escapes the dreaded presentation). Once all the other medical possibilities are eliminated, her doctor determines that she's had a major panic attack. She concedes that since she was in middle school, she's had many similar experiences though none this dramatic.

The cardinal feature of a panic attack is the sudden onset of intense fear associated with a multitude of bodily symptoms that have no apparent explanation (Hayward & Collier, 1996). These symptoms typically include rapid heart rate, shortness of breath, choking sensations, and sweating, or a feeling of depersonalization. Panic disorder usually begins in adolescence. It is usually preceded by sporadic, isolated episodes of anxiety, increasing in intensity. Panic reactions in children and younger adolescents are different because they usually have a known trigger; the essential element of this diagnosis is the spontaneous and unprovoked nature of the attack.

When girls have a panic disorder, they have recurring panic attacks. Their fear of another attack becomes a defining way of being in the world for them. They may reorganize their lives so they can avoid situations where they would feel panicky, and feel compelled to pile on worry about the embarrassing and frightening implications after such an attack. Untreated, it is common for girls to become agoraphobic by the time they are young adults; their world gets smaller and smaller as they attempt to control their terror.

Phobias

Amy's parents divorced when she was 11. Now she's 16 and her father has recently moved across the country. There is no way to see him unless she gets on an airplane. But she just can't make herself do it. She really wants to see his new life, but she's just terrified. The last time she flew, she was so physically ill and shaken afterwards that she took a bus back home again. She has come to therapy on her own with one goal: to overcome her phobia about flying so she can visit her father.

Phobias are marked and excessive fears of certain animals, objects, activities, or situations (e.g., dogs, spiders, dark, school, heights, crowds, other people, flying), to the point that any exposure to them—even just in thoughts—precipitates extreme anxiety and panic. This fear is so intense that it interferes with functioning, or becomes acutely distressing for the adolescent. Girls may have irrational fears; these only become phobias when the girl does all she can to avoid the source of it. For example, a nonphobic girl can be afraid of the dark but still be willing to go upstairs at night alone and turn on the lights herself. Other girls may not enjoy flying, but they still make themselves get on the plane.

Obsessive–Compulsive Disorder

Thirteen-year-old Kayla is taking longer to get ready for school every day. She is spending hours in the shower, and uses several towels to get dry. The whole laundry and soap situation at home is out of control. She has also developed elaborate rituals for getting into and out of the car because she can't touch the doors, and she is late to classes because she needs to walk in a particular pattern that is not necessarily the direct route from room to room. She's always been an anxious child, but in recent months her symptoms have escalated, and by the time she comes to therapy, she's functioning quite poorly everywhere.

The diagnosis of OCD is made when an adolescent has intrusive thoughts, urges, and images (obsessions) that cause her significant distress or anxiety. To relieve the internal pressure that builds up, adolescents with OCD perform rituals (compulsions) that can be either behavioral or mental. Younger adolescents seem to be primarily compulsive; for example, spending considerable time involved in elaborate cleaning, checking, ordering, or counting rituals. They may not be able to articulate what, if any, obsessions are driving the behavior.

As they get older, adolescents are increasingly willing and able to describe the obsessive thoughts that accompany their compulsions (Commission on Adolescent Anxiety Disorders, 2005). They also know that the intrusive thoughts are irrational and consume an unreasonable amount of time. Most obsessive thoughts center on issues of contamination (Kayla's preoccupation) sexual or aggressive imagery, repeated doubts, or a need for order. Even though there is a strong neurological basis for OCD (and it is frequently accompanied by other neurological problems like tics and ADHD), it can be as responsive to intervention as other anxiety disorders.

Additionally, as with other anxiety disorders, there are known medications that work best in concert with psychotherapy.

Generalized Anxiety Disorder

Crystal comes from a long line of worriers on both sides of her family, and she's really thorough about it. She worries all day long, sometimes without respite. She worries about herself, her friends, her parents, her sisters, her pets, her house, and the world. In our first session, I had a little head cold, and she worried about me, too. Crystal is only 14, but she sounds like an old lady in the way she frets. She has chewed her cuticles until they bleed, and before she goes to bed, she needs to know about everything that might happen the next day. Her mother called my voice-mail late one night to schedule an appointment. It had taken two full hours to get Crystal to calm down from hearing that she had a routine physical scheduled for the next day. She "flipped out" because she hadn't known it was on the calendar.

A diagnosis of generalized anxiety disorder (GAD) is given to adolescents who worry about the big and little parts of their lives, somewhat unremittingly. As with depression, more girls than boys have GAD (Commission on Adolescent Anxiety Disorders, 2005). They fret about schoolwork, money, their appearance, the future, relationships, injury, and disaster. Girls with GAD are even more self-conscious than their age peers, with worries far out of proportion to what a situation seems to warrant. These girls are often perfectionists; even if they are quite competent, they remain very shaky about how they appear and how they perform. They may be particularly apprehensive about upcoming events that hold uncertainty or novelty for them, seeking out repeated reassurances. Girls with GAD also frequently describe restlessness, difficulty concentrating, fatigue, irritability, insomnia, and preoccupation with immediate and past events (Hayward & Collier, 1996). A sense of apprehension follows them on most days, and they cannot control it.

Although most anxious adolescents do not meet the full diagnostic criteria for GAD, they do have some (or many) of the features of it. GAD shares a lot of characteristics with both other anxiety disorders and with depression. In adolescent girls, it is extremely common for both anxiety and depression to be present together (Commission on Adolescent Anxiety Disorders, 2005). Thus it is probably not surprising that when we treat depressed girls, they become less anxious and vice versa.

Intervention

Treatment of adolescent anxiety disorders often requires both individual and family therapy; adjunctive group treatment and psychopharmacology are also frequently beneficial.

As with treatment of depression, a combined psychoeducational, cognitive–behavioral, and more relational therapy works very well. From the onset, girls need to develop a safe, trusting relationship in which to explore and better understand their fears. Psychoeducation about the nature of anxiety in adolescence in general (and the specific manifestation of it for the particular adolescent) helps to provide a context for the work. This is followed by some specific strategies for relieving the most acute symptoms. Adolescent anxiety is invariably embedded in developmental concerns—relationship confusion, family conflict, school issues, identity problems—and these deeper issues also need to be discussed as they arise.

One of the hazards of more doctrinaire CBT interventions for anxiety is their almost-exclusive focus on evident symptoms. Although these strategies can help a girl like Georgia to keep panic somewhat at bay, or Amy to get onto a plane, anxious girls need more than symptom relief (although this is sometimes a great place to start). We must also attend to their health, the parts of their lives that go well, the skills they have or might develop. We attack anxiety from all directions—mind, body, family, skills, and connections. Good anxiety therapy does it all—CBT, insight, competencies, and relationships.

CBT for anxiety generally follows several broad principles:

Training, Education, and Skill-Building

During initial sessions, the anxious adolescent learns to distinguish among various bodily reactions that are specific to her anxiety (e.g., rapid heart rate, difficulty breathing, light-headedness). Coupled with this awareness, she is taught relaxation exercises designed to help her gain control over these physiological and muscular responses to anxiety (Bourne, 2005; King, Hamilton, & Ollendick, 1994).

Next, adolescents are taught how to identify and modify their anxious thoughts (e.g., "It has to be perfect," "I am going to die," "I have to count to 100 now"). The idea is not to give a pep rally, or argue about the negative self-talk, but gently to challenge the distorted thinking so that girls become able to examine, test out, and reduce these thoughts. Consequently, they may be able to generate more realistic and less negative self-statements, and create a plan to cope with their concerns (Commission on Adolescent Anxiety Disorders, 2005). It can also be helpful to teach girls to rate their thoughts and fears along a continuum of severity or reality. For example, they can describe their anxiety on a 1 to 10 scale, where 1 is perfectly calm and 10 is a full-blown panic attack. They can then practice taking it down a notch using relaxation and cognitive restructuring exercises.

Anxious girls need better problem-solving skills, no matter what type of anxiety disorder they may have. They need to recognize problems, brainstorm, and generate alternatives so that they can manage their anxiety, weigh the consequences of each possible alternative, and then choose and follow through with a plan. These are complicated and challenging steps to learn, and girls need close support to accomplish them.

The therapist is a mentor and guide during all of the phases of learning to problem solve. Since some anxiety in life can be expected, the therapist must concede that a little worry about problems and challenges is okay. Anxious girls may have absurdly high standards for themselves and be unforgiving and critical if they don't match up. Thus, it is particularly important for the therapist to help girls judge more accurately the effectiveness of their efforts, and learn to reward themselves for handling anxiety in new ways — even if not entirely successful every time. The support is both for the new cognitions and for the developing adolescent.

Exposure Exercises

In the next phase of anxiety treatment, most therapists focus on a variety of exposure exercises in which adolescents begin to practice their new self-soothing and problem-solving skills. Exposure is very gradual, beginning with imaginary scenarios (think about touching a car door, visualize an airplane, imagine yourself in front of the class), to lower-anxiety situations (touch a car door and wash a short while afterwards, look at pictures of airplanes, give the talk in the empty classroom), to increasingly stressful anxiety exposure. The therapist assists every step of the way in preparing for actual exposure to the feared object or situation by discussing troubling aspects of it, working through steps of the plan, backing up, reaffirming relaxation and cognitive strategies, and role-playing and rehearsing how the next step will go.

In vivo exposures are extremely important (touching car doors without washing immediately, walking onto parked airplanes without intending to travel by air, standing in front of a few friends in the classroom) because they provide the adolescent with safe but real opportunities to practice. And, after an in vivo practice session, the therapist can help girls evaluate what went well, what didn't, and encourage them to feel good about the effort. The steps toward the actual experience need to be collaborative, so that the experiences are personally meaningful for the adolescent.

We also need to remain confident that these strategies are going to be helpful; there's a lot of good evidence that the only way to conquer anxiety is to face it head on, have the unwanted feelings, and learn to cope with them. Like all imaginary monsters, anxieties get smaller when they are faced and known better. As psychologist Reid Wilson (2006) astutely observes, "The problems we suffer with anxiety often continue not because we have symptoms, but because we resist the fact that we're experiencing symptoms—doing our utmost to block out the symptoms rather than getting to know them a little bit" (p. 68).

Homework

Traditional CBT employs homework to support the work in therapy. Some girls are motivated to cooperate with homework, but *many* are not. If speed of recovery is the only goal, their reticence to practice on their own is a disappointment. But if a therapeutic relationship can be the context for richer development and growth, the lack of homework compliance is of little consequence, and should be dropped from the expectations.

If it works for the adolescent and the therapy, homework can include, for example, maintaining daily records of ongoing activities, making time for pleasant events and mastery experiences, keeping track of automatic thoughts, practicing new self-statements, and making time for progressive muscle relaxation. Girls who learn to use scaling techniques in therapy (rate your level of anxiety on a 1 to 10 scale, and see if you can bring it down one point) can also practice using rating scales in between sessions. Sometimes, when a therapy is going well, and even without assignments, girls take home strategies that are practiced in the office.

Treating the Whole Girl

Alongside of the hard work of CBT—facing fears and practicing new skills—we need to keep attending to the therapeutic relationship, and to the larger questions of life as an adolescent girl. We should cede our agenda regularly to what is on their minds: to the developing identity con-

cerns, to family issues (especially since anxiety tends to run in families—
a girl with a lot of anxiety is probably not the only one in the home who
feels that way), and to the defensive structure that a girl has developed to
try to stay safe. We make ourselves available to talk about the latest social
struggles and about her weekend plans. We also make sure she is finding
sources of pleasure, passion, and success in other places in her life.

Thus, interwoven into the phases of CBT, therapy follows a more relational and dynamic course, giving girls ample time to lead as well as to
follow in setting agendas for the time together. We must not only attend to
their fears but also to their hopes and desires, and to building our relationship with them in the therapy room.

Beyond individual work, effective treatment for anxiety also addresses
family and school expectations and supports. Teach parents the same self-
soothing and problem-solving strategies you're imparting to their daughters (no one has too many ways to feel better, and they may even thank you
for the tools). And make sure you're communicating with the team; this
next level of coordinated adult support can, by itself, help an anxious girl
feel safer and calmer.

As with depression, anxiety disorders feed on isolation and self-
condemnation. Anxious girls are usually upset about feeling that way,
compounding their misery. Thus the therapeutic and team relationships
can go a long way in reconnecting girls both to the stronger parts of themselves and to others who care about them. And no therapy is complete
without building on strengths and competencies. Girls who are more confident in one sphere of their lives have better foundations for facing their
fear. They may also come to see themselves as more competent as they become better problem solvers and self-soothers, and worthy of the love and
admiration of nurturing adults like you.

CHAPTER EIGHT

TROUBLED BEHAVIORS II: EATING DISORDERS AND SELF-MUTILATION

Eating disorders and self-mutilation are now common and mainstream symptoms, likely to be encountered by everyone treating adolescent girls. These self-harming behaviors are both real and emblematic of the particularly complicated relationships that girls today have with their bodies, with their social supports, and with our compelling but toxic culture. Effective therapy offfers a safe and healing connection, helps them find the vocabulary and a voice to describe powerful and unspoken feelings, and provides more adaptive, self-soothing, and problem-solving strategies.

Eating Disorders

Most girls in the United States struggle with body dissatisfaction. By age 13, 53% of American girls are unhappy with their bodies; by age 17, 78% are dissatisfied (Brumberg, 1997). There is some notable variation across race and class—the obsession with weight appears to be trickling down from girls who live closest to power and authority. Overall, though, it is safe to say that most girls are preoccupied with their bodies. And while only a smaller percentage of all girls will develop a diagnosable eating disorder, many seen in treatment for other issues will still be on the continuum, dabbling in potentially hazardous excesses of dieting, overeating, bingeing, starving, and throwing up.

The pervasive problem of negative body images among adolescent girls may be understood in part as their attempt to live within the perceived safety of an ideal image that looms large in the culture, rather than in the vulnerability, vitality (and confusion) of their female bodies. This ideal is, of course, unattainable. It's about 5'9" and weighs less than the lowest weight considered healthy for that height. It has ample breasts (even though this is so unlikely in the absence of other body fat). Whatever its racial or ethnic origin, it also has patrician Anglo features (Rodin, 1992; Tolman & Debold, 1994). When girls focus on such an impossible and dangerous vision for themselves, they not only end up with negative self- and body images, but with abundances of wasted mental and psychological time. And as Naomi Wolf (1994) notes, "hunger checkmates power" every time (p. 101). Girls who are hyperfocusing on food, weight, and body dissatisfaction are not taking hold of their own lives, much less changing the world.

Girls succumb to this culture of thinness partly due to its omnipresence in our society (Heinberg, 1996). It is hard to see any compelling alternatives out there without looking hard. The obsession with food, weight, and appearance does not just serve to drive multibillion-dollar industries or to make women insecure (though these are clearly significant motivators). Additionally, as feminist theory suggests, the glorification of waiflike, emaciated girls as the ideal woman is a further example of a patriarchal society's rewarding and idealizing the weak and incapable woman over the strong and independent one (Gilbert & Thompson, 1996; N. Wolf, 1991). The cultural fixation on female thinness is not about health or beauty but an obsession about female obedience. The bottom line they need to know about is this: powerless women are regarded the soul of perfection.

With such a dominant—and dominating—cultural message, our understanding of eating disorders must therefore extend well beyond the individual girl, and her family. As Naomi Wolf (1994) points out:

> Economic and political retaliation against female appetite is far stronger at this point than family dynamics. This can no longer be explained as a private issue. If suddenly 60–80% of college women can't eat, it's hard to believe that suddenly 60–80% of their families are dysfunctional in this particular way. (p. 100)

Still, even though we must have a sociocultural analysis of eating disorders, we continue to have to treat girls and their families, too. In fact, short of dramatic changes in social policy and media influence that drive the marketplace, preventing eating disordered behavior in girls is going to be nearly impossible. Since most girls diet at some time, are preoccupied with their weight, binge, and starve some, too, we also have to be prepared to intervene. And even secondary prevention—keeping eating problems from getting worse—can be difficult; an eating disorder can snowball out of control right under your eyes. Appetite starts as something the girl can control in her life, but there's a turning point, and with the vengeance of an addiction, an eating disorder starts running her life instead.

Researchers have observed a consistently strong relationship between girls' negative body images—worry and displeasure about how they look—and other signs of psychological distress (Allgood-Merton, Lewinsohn, & Hops, 1990; Tolman & Debold, 1994). Girls who have negative body images suffer from all manner of eating disorders and are more likely to be depressed and to be suicidal. These associations seem to go both ways—unhappy girls feel worse about their bodies; girls with poor body images feel lousy, too. Adults have reason for concern about the body preoccupations of unhappy girls, even if they are not manifesting a full-blown eating disorder.

And it is important to note, even if obvious, the problem of food never goes away because eating is essential for survival. Unlike the recovery from most other disorders, girls must face the pleasures and perils of food and all it represents, every day as long as they live.

Anorexia Nervosa

Savannah's on the fast track to the Ivy League. She's in all advanced placement (AP) classes and it's just her junior year. She's also hugely disciplined, taking dance classes five days a week after school, as she has been for many years; and she holds down a part-time job on the weekends working as a hostess at a local restaurant. Savannah is tenacious and she likes to "run things." She is coeditor of her high-school yearbook and writes for the school newspaper. Last summer she had a job helping build houses for homeless people. She's a small girl, but she can swing a hammer, too. Her parents are rightfully proud of her accomplishments. Because she's always danced, Savannah has been strong and slender her whole life. She also wears her clothes in layers, so it wasn't until the summer on a vacation by the lake when Savannah was in a swimsuit that her mother noticed that her daughter was rail thin. And because of the family's busy schedule with erratic mealtimes, Savannah's self-starvation had gone unobserved for many months. By the time the family came to my office, Savannah weighed well under 100 pounds, and was facing a struggle with anorexia that lasted through her freshman year in college.

Anorexia causes a severely distorted body image that has girls seeing themselves as overweight even when they're dangerously thin. Some warning signs include food refusal, compulsive exercise, and unusual habits (e.g., cooking lavish meals they don't eat, refusing to eat in front of others, talking about food excessively). Girls struggling with anorexia lose large amounts of weight (for the DSM diagnosis, they should be 15 to 25% below normal weight); they appear to be willing to starve to death. Like Savannah, girls with anorexia also tend to be controlling and perfectionistic, although not necessarily so. For example, some girls turn to these food-limiting strategies because they have so little control elsewhere in their lives.

Bulimia Nervosa

In contrast to Savannah, Mariah has endured a lifelong fight against feeling fat and ugly. She's now in middle school, and at age 12 her shape is changing, much to her continual dismay. In another era, people would have said she was voluptuous, but for 2007, she just feels obese and disfigured. Mariah has a learning disability, and she struggles in school academically. Indeed, there are few places and activities where she finds satisfaction in her life. She says she thinks about her weight "Ninety-eight percent of the time she is awake." She has never been with the "popular crowd," but yearns for this distinction. In reality, she has a couple of friends in school, but doesn't feel particularly close to them. Mariah doesn't enjoy sports or other exercise; she spends most of her free time hanging out at home, lonely and aimless. By the time Mariah confessed to her guidance counselor that she had been bingeing and purging after school, she had lost and gained the same 10 pounds many times over. Mariah's mother was horrified to learn this; indeed, like many parents, she hadn't a clue.

Bulimics eat excessively, then purge (what some girls colloquially refer to as "scarf and barf"). Their strategies for purging can include vomiting, laxatives, enemas, and exercise. Bulimics tend to be secretive, and ashamed, disgusted, and relieved once their stomachs are empty. In general, bulimics are impulsive but also guilt-ridden, caught up in a terrible cycle without end.

Compulsive Overeating

Sandy is struggling this year more than she ever has in her life. She's in her local community college and living at home. She had gotten into schools at a distance from home, but changed plans at the end of the summer when her beloved grandmother became very sick, and Sandy didn't want to leave her. Most of Sandy's friends have moved away, and the classes she's taking aren't that great. She finds herself with lots of time to worry and feel dissatisfied with her life. Sandy has always enjoyed cooking; she's taken this over for her mother. As the year has progressed, Sandy has increasingly turned to food for comfort. At first she would just make a little too much, and eat the leftovers in the kitchen. But after her grandmother died, she has just been eating "everything that isn't nailed down." She tells me she can eat a whole large pizza by herself without even noticing that she has done so. Sandy self-referred to me to talk about grieving for her grandmother; the compulsive overeating came up rather unexpectedly as we sorted out her limited self care and self soothing strategies.

Compulsive overeaters binge and feel ashamed, but don't purge. They tend to have poor coping strategies and low self-esteem. In recent years Binge Eating Disorder (BED) has gained some clinical attention; BED may make its way into the next edition of the DSM. Binge eaters do not seem primarily motivated by anxiety about being overweight, though they do have body image disturbances similar to those who suffer from the other eating disorders (Thompson, Heinberg, Altabe, & Tantleff-Dunn, 1999). And like Sandy, they don't have many internal resources in times of stress. In the absence of other solutions, food provides immediate comfort.

Intervention

An evaluation of girls' attitudes and behaviors toward food, eating, and body image needs to be a part of all early sessions with them, no matter what the presenting problem. Often the girl in your office doesn't think she has an eating disorder. Or even if she realizes she has an eating problem, she may not be that interested in, or be ashamed about, addressing it. Like Sandy, some girls are dealing with other problems that are upsetting; they believe the eating issues will disappear once more pressing matters are addressed. Indeed, the eating disorder is often a solution to these other issues. So frequently, an eating disorder lurks behind other presenting issues—school stress, peer problems, low self-esteem, family conflict, and increased anxiety, can all be a screen covering disordered eating.

Ask general questions that help to lift this screen. Don't be satisfied just discussing the "presenting problem." After you get some information about that, perhaps in the next few weeks, especially if you sense that weight and body issues are more salient to her struggles, ask more questions. The point of the assessment is to get a handle on the big picture: what the problems are, how they show up in her life, and how big they are—to the girl, to her family, and in your own estimation. Sometimes girls are tentative or ashamed about these discussions, but more often they are quite comfortable talking about dieting and body issues. And if you're willing to understand that eating disorders can be both problems in themselves and strategies for managing problems, you will have richer conversations about them.

Numerous research studies confirm what most of us suspect: for adolescent girls, feelings about their appearance are the greatest predictor of self-esteem and general self-worth (Eccles, Barber, Jozefowicz, Malenchuk, & Vida, 1999; Harter, 1990; O'Dea, 2006). If a girl begins to describe eating and body concerns, or if you suspect that she may be struggling with weight and body issues, do not be shy, as time goes on, about asking more pointed questions about the times she has decided to lose weight and what prompted these decisions.

At this session or the next, you might also inquire about the initial motivations for weight loss, and whether they changed or evolved over time. It is important to know what a girl hopes to gain from losing weight (no pun intended). Ask about goals—specific weights or sizes, and how she'll react if she's told it's too little. Girls get attached to particular numbers— 110 pounds, size 6 pants, for example—and these numbers become very powerful in fueling their resistance to gaining weight.

Find out also whether she has turned to the web for help losing weight. While numerous sites seriously consider health and recovery, there are many more "pro-anorexia" sites that actually *support* eating-disordered behavior. Recent research suggests that many girls use the web to learn new weight loss and purging techniques (Wilson, Peebles, Hardy, & Litt, 2006). Results indicate that girls with eating disorders who used the web faced longer illnesses and more frequent hospitalizations than their non-web browsing peers. You will need to know if a girl you are treating is hearing a lot of information that directly contradicts what you have to offer.

The reactions of others are also important to assess. It is quite common that girls feel rewarded, at first, by both family and friends. Significant others praise them for eating more healthy foods and appearing to be fitter, and it's all good news to hear. It is abundantly evident that we live in a culture that rewards girls for thinness and the self-discipline that goes along with maintaining it. However, parents and even peers may make a quick shift toward fear and anger if weight loss goes too far.

And the power struggles in families with eating-disordered girls can reach epic proportions. You'll also want to know about the impact of weight loss on home-life health, self-esteem, school, relationships, and outside interests. Remember that when girls are feeling out of control in areas that have nothing to do with their size at all, they'll turn to eating/not eating as a solution. The line of inquiry you might pursue could include:

- Are you worrying about your body weight or body image? Can you tell me about it?

- Tell me about your decision to lose weight? What was happening at that time that led you to this choice?

- How did you go about losing weight? Describe what you've tried so far to lose weight: restrict calories, count calories, carbohydrates, grams of fat laxatives, drugs, exercise. What is your goal weight? How did you decide on this number? How did you stick to it? When you went over it, what happened?

- Are you exercising regularly? How much? What happens when you can't or don't exercise?

- Have you binged, just eaten so much you felt you were out of control? What did you do after this? How often has this happened? What do you consider a binge, in quantity and calorie amounts?

- Have you thrown up your food intentionally? Tell me about the strategies you've used to throw up. How often do you purge? Tell me about the triggers for this. Have you ever noticed blood in your vomit?

- Have you used laxatives, diet pills, appetite suppressants, or speed to help with weight loss? Which methods? How much? How effective do you think they were? What were the triggers for using these drugs? How did you learn about these strategies?

- What have been your highest and lowest weights? How did you feel when you weighed the most and the least?

- What is your favorite weight? Why is this the best weight for you?

- Who has noticed your weight loss? How have they reacted? How does that make you feel?

- Have you been trying to hide your weight loss? Why? How did you do that?

- Have you noticed any connections between your dieting strategies and other stress in your life?
- What else do you do to help you feel in control, and to take care of yourself?

Prevailing research and clinical wisdom argue in favor of two general approaches, together or in some kind of integration for treatment of eating disorders. Either method follows well from a general assessment as described above. And all interventions for eating disorders also benefit from teamwork. The specific team members may include, for example, school guidance counselors, pediatricians, nutritionists, child psychiatrists, friends, and of course, parents. A collaborative treatment approach works the best, one that connects with the whole girl: mind, body, relationships, and culture.

The first set of strategies combines different possible elements of cognitive–behavioral therapy (CBT), interpersonal therapy (IPT), family therapy, and group work. The underlying premise of these approaches is that eating-disordered girls must deal with personal problems regarding feelings, thoughts, and interpersonal relationships. Techniques can include systematic desensitization, social skills training, relationship building, assertiveness training, relaxation, and education. The second approach is narrative therapy.

CBT Strategies

CBT strategies are employed to combat a distorted body image, erroneous beliefs and assumptions, and misinterpretation of environmental messages. Girls are helped to replace cognitive distortions and overgeneralizations by considering alternatives. Therapist questions attempt to challenge the old cognitions (e.g., Do you really think one piece of candy will immediately convert into stomach fat? How can you have control over your life and also eat? What do these magazines tell you about your self-worth?)

As with most CBT, techniques can include homework, practicing, journaling, learning about self-talk, and identifying triggers. These interventions can help girls develop needed problem-solving and self-soothing skills. Therapists also may use some aspects of systematic desensitization. Exposure, relaxation exercises, and 1 to 10 scaling techniques can help decrease a girl's worries about gaining weight, having to buy larger clothes, and being criticized. The goal is to begin to gently challenge her all-or-none thinking by promoting shades of gray, and to reduce the attendant anxiety by giving her new coping strategies.

Social Skills

Social skills training may also be beneficial in the treatment of eating disorders, helping with deficits in social skills, assertiveness, interpersonal communication, and basic problem solving. The goal of social skills training is to give girls a better sense of self-control, develop meaningful connections, and help them become more effective in living outside of their eating disorder. Groups for girls with eating disorders can be quite helpful in developing more authentic and aware social coping strategies. Groups can also help diminish the shame and loneliness often prevalent with some eating disorders.

Interpersonal Therapy

Along these lines, interpersonal therapy (IPT) has an interesting application to eating problems (Fairburn, 1997). The focus of this application of IPT is exclusively on identifying and modifying current interpersonal problems, with little or no attention directed to the preoccupation with shape and weight. Specific eating problems are viewed as a means of understanding the interpersonal context that is assumed to be maintaining them. Girls' sense of personal identity is interpersonally constructed, with self-esteem strongly influenced by positive relationships. Thus, the focus on developing greater social competence and awareness through relationship (in both CBT and IPT) is likely to be a key ingredient in healing.

Family Therapy

Family therapy for eating disorders has four general goals, no matter which systemic framework is followed: To help a girl find a way to achieve greater developmental separation from the family without the feared loss of all connection to them; to help her state personal needs and feelings clearly; to help her get permission from her mother to be separate or different from her; and to facilitate direct communication between the parents so the daughter is not needed as a facilitator, or a distracter from other problems they may have.

Typically, family therapy needs to be an integral part of treatment with eating disordered girls. Both parents and siblings will be deeply affected by anorexia and bulimia. A power struggle between parents wanting their daughters to eat and the anorexic agenda not to eat is almost inevitable at some point. For some girls, the onset of eating disorders, coinciding with puberty as it frequently does, can function as an avoidance of maturation, and all that it entails. Thus the struggle is not just around whether to eat, but whether to grow up and to individuate from parents. The girl and her parents are then in a shared bind of not knowing how much independence she really wants or can handle given her endangered health.

Narrative Therapy

Narrative therapy is a very useful approach because it takes into consideration the larger sociopolitical perspective on eating disorders, thus providing a critical avenue for effective treatment. As discussed briefly in Chapter 6, the narrative strategy describes eating disorders by externalizing the symptoms, separating them from the girl (White & Epston, 1990). Externalization helps a girl acknowledge her problem, develop insight about it, and explore the negative effects of the problem on her life. The girl is helped to fight the problem instead of her parents, friends, and therapists. This strategy also eliminates blame: instead of holding the girl and her parents culpable, the problem itself gets blamed for the suffering.

The narrative approach is also inherently respectful, indicating from the outset that the girl and her family are the experts. This strategy strengthens girls' voices in a culture that seeks to silence them. In the view of narrative therapy, the voices of anorexia and bulimia repeat those of the larger society, similarly asking that the adolescent silently defer to their demands and expecting unchallenged loyalty. Through therapy, girls are encouraged, by contrast, to take a stand on their own behalf (White, 1986).

Some examples of narrative questions include:

- Suzie, how do you know when anorexia or bulimia is around?
- How does it make itself known to you? What does it say to you? How does it make you feel?
- When you are talking to me, are you talking for yourself, or is anorexia talking for you?
- If anorexia starts talking for you or stops you from speaking for yourself, would you consider that you were being gagged?
- Is anorexia, in a manner of speaking, talking you into punishing and torturing yourself? Would you agree that it is putting you in a concentration camp?
- Why do you think this anorexia has forbidden you to have life, liberty, freedom, and happiness?
- On what grounds is anorexia denying you your freedom?
- What are its charges against you?

- Were you given an opportunity to defend yourself?
- Do you consider that justice is being done in your case?
- How much of your life does anorexia now own? You say it is taking up 80% of your time. Would you like it to take up less of your life?
- If you were to have more time, what would you like to put back in your life?

The narrative strategies allow girls to disentangle themselves from the disorders they are fighting, to see themselves as capable of such a struggle. The questions asked in narrative work are open, collaborative, and curious. They indicate that the girl is the expert on her eating disorder. Narrative therapists believe that girls get stuck because they lack the emotional vocabulary or narrative skills to make a story that is not constraining; the intervention develops these.

Although most of the questions above suggest negative effects, you should not be surprised to hear that girls have many positive associations to their eating disorders, and deny the negatives quite contentiously. For example, they may experience a degree of control over weight gain and this makes them feel better, at least temporarily. In fact they may report that anorexia and bulimia assure them that they are superior to their overweight peers because they are stronger in their ability to keep weight down. Of course, this sense of power is false because eating disorders take over their lives, diminishing their worlds literally to the vanishing point.

In any event, the therapist has to be open to all the stories; we want to help them tell new ones, not control or blame them for how they see things. As they develop a trusting relationship with you, they may be able to describe more of the negative effects. These generally include: the amount of time the eating disorder takes up, isolation from peers, poor self-esteem, family conflict, hunger, and other physical problems.

The first questions, then, attempt to identify the dominant stories that limit an adolescent's repertoire, how she sees herself and her world, how the issues with eating attempt to solve a perceived problem. In the responses, the therapist listens for any marginalized narratives that contain in them more possibility, and works to amplify these. These alternative stories are less problem-saturated and describe the times when girls were able to resist and outsmart the tyranny of the eating disorder. The focus of the work shifts rapidly to expanding and amplifying those instances of rebellion.

Dominant stories include beliefs that the girls (and their families) have about themselves as well as any cultural stories that may be influencing a family. For example, girls and families are influenced by what they believe about the period of adolescence for girls, and whether they expect that unhappiness, turbulence, crisis—and dieting—are inevitable. Many dominant narratives about adolescent girls contain a strong element of confusion and despair, especially about how they feel toward their bodies. Thus, even when a girl has an eating disorder, it may have to become extremely disabling before she can make room for other stories.

Good narrative questions are designed to amplify the extent of damage and havoc the problems have wreaked on girls' lives, and any unique outcomes—times when she resisted the problem's pull, when the problem did not dominate her life. Through close attention to these unique outcomes, therapists engage in *reconstruction*, thereby helping girls and families to reauthor the stories they tell about their lives.

The narrative therapist asks girls to speculate about what made it possible at those times to resist the dictates of the dominant story—when she ate, or handed in a paper that wasn't perfect, for example. Subsequently those unusual moments of resistance are enlarged and added to by more of the stories that feature the client as competent and free of the stranglehold of the eating disorder.

One of the aspects of narrative therapy that makes it uniquely wonderful for girls with eating disorders is the way that it is both personal and political. The therapist and client may create or find an audience for these new stories—for example, they may make a tape, give a talk, develop a newsletter, or consult to other girls about their strategies for winning the eating-disorder struggle. Girls become advocates of change for others. Indeed, the "Anti-Anorexia/Anti-Bulimia League has a worldwide presence on the web and can be a valuable resource for both therapists and girls with eating disorders, replacing the allure of the "pro-anorexia" sites with comparable social support. Regardless of whether therapists choose to use CBT, IPT, narrative, or some other integrative approach, it is clear that when it comes to eating disorders, we should not pathologize the girl. Our interventions should also explore with girls aspects of the toxic culture that may be fostering and perpetuating their suffering.

Self-Mutilation

Nadine is 17 and she's got a trauma history that includes molestation by a babysitter when she was 7 years old, and, more recently, a rape by a schoolmate that began with consensual kissing at a drunken party a year ago. Her parents live in the same house, but they're estranged; she and her mother seem to be one "team," and her father and younger brother band together on another. Her father knows about the rape but he's busy coaching her brother's year-round basketball teams and has never mentioned it to her. A few days before I met Nadine, she had a screaming fight with her mother, who then retreated from her, which Nadine termed, "the old silent treatment." Beyond distraught, Nadine went into her room with a paring knife, and sliced her forearm dozens of times. Her mother found her bleeding and sobbing in the bathroom two hours later. A couple of the wounds were severe enough to require stitches; her entire arm was bandaged by a physician in the emergency room. Nadine admits to cutting herself on and off over the past five years, often in response to family conflict, or peer problems. Since the rape, she has self-harmed many times. Her mother has known about three of these, spread out sufficiently for her to be able to hope, each time, that Nadine wouldn't do that again.

Self-injurious behavior among adolescent girls is likely much more prevalent than any estimates may suggest (Egan, 1997; Favazza, 1998; Smith, Cox, & Saradjian, 1999). In the general population, estimates of self-injury hover around 4%; in some high school studies, it's more like 14%. Among psychotherapy patients (of all ages) the percentage rises to about 20%; among adolescent and emerging adult young females, this percentage is likely to be much higher still. Those of us who see large numbers of adolescent girls in psychotherapy know that self-mutilation (SM) is a major, if often hidden, problem for a huge range of adolescent girls (and not only a reaction to trauma or major dysfunction as it was for Nadine).

Self-mutilation has not attained its own diagnostic status yet. In fact, it mostly shows up in the DSM as just one symptom of borderline personality disorder; a label not even possible to apply to the evolving character development of young adolescents. Too many clinicians still trivialize it as mere scratching, or attention-seeking behavior. For a long time, too, self-mutilation has also been misidentified as a suicidal gesture, which it is not. Indeed, when girls deny suicidal intent, the implication of this seems to be that they are instead just being manipulative, and should not be "rewarded" (Solomon & Farrand, 1996). In these mistaken analyses, if it is not accidental or suicidal behavior, girls should just get motivated and knock it off. But as many therapists working with adolescent girls know, self-injury is, in fact, a very real and serious problem unto itself, possible to address, but not simple at all.

SM refers to the deliberate, direct destruction or alteration of body tissue without conscious suicidal intent (Favazza, 1998). The intentionality of the act distinguishes it from accidents; interestingly, self-mutilators who accidentally cut or burn themselves feel as much pain and discomfort as anyone else (Favazza, 1998). SM is also a direct act as opposed to indirect injury caused by, for example, smoking, drinking, or self-starvation.

Making a distinction between acceptable and unacceptable self-mutilation is complicated. There are numerous socially encouraged practices of self-harm—for example, hair plucking, cosmetic surgery, body piercing, skin bronzing, smoking, alcohol consumption, and participation in dangerous sports. In general it might be argued that there is broad cultural support for some kinds of self-harm.

And throughout the world, there are religiously and culturally sanctioned rituals and practices that cause significant injury (Favazza, 1998); these are not considered pathological, though they are clearly harmful. In recent years, adolescent girls in the United States have gotten tattooed, branded, and pierced all over—eyebrows, nipples, tongues, chins, cheeks, every inch of the ears, navels, genitalia, and nose. The overwhelming majority of these girls believe that this variety of SM is attractive, gains them attention and group status, and provokes adults—all perfectly adaptive reasons to self-harm.

Thus, defining SM as a problem for girls means finding the place where it crosses from acceptable to problematic behavior. Concerning acts can include: cutting, stabbing, scratching, scraping the skin, gnawing, biting the inside of the mouth, picking at wounds, burning by heat or chemicals, pulling hair out, hitting self, head banging, cutting of circulation, and ingesting toxins to cause pain but not death.

But although they are worrisome and dangerous, these behaviors may not be entirely as maladaptive or disordered as they may seem. Indeed, a compelling perspective on motivation suggests that *girls self-harm to make it possible to live* (Smith, Cox, & Saradjian, 1999; Solomon & Farrand, 1996). Solomon and Farrand note that ". . . it can more usefully be understood as an adaptive act and as a means of survival borne of the will to carry on, despite overwhelming feelings of helplessness, despair and self-hatred" (p. 111).

We now know that girls self-harm to find relief for painful states of consciousness so they can cope with other aspects of living. Rather than attention seeking, most try to hide wounds or describe them as accidental. In one survey of 240 self-injurers, body harm was spread out: 74% to arms,

44% to legs, 25% to abdomens, 23% to heads, 18% to chest, and 8% to genitals (Favazza, 1998).

Many therapists (and self-injuring girls) concur that girls resort to cutting to cope with emotional tension, enabling them to control and regulate overwhelming affect (Machoian, 2001; Suyemoto, & Kountz, 2000). By transforming emotional pain into physical pain, and releasing it that way, girls get momentary relief from the internal pressure. Feelings of self-loathing and low self-esteem can fuel justification that self-harm is the only way to relieve the tension. Biological theory holds that SM then becomes something of an addictive drug. SM increases levels of endogenous opiates in the body, which results in feeling high for a brief time. Girls, who are not learning other strategies for coping, then return to SM to get those endorphins back again (Simeon et al., 1992). After SM, girls frequently report a feeling of release, calm, and pleasure.

And girls describe feeling little if any pain when they are harming themselves, even when they are inflicting severe injury. The biological theory may also help explain how this can be so—endogenous opiates are also natural painkillers. It is also very likely that girls who self-harm are capable of extreme dissociative states. They report being completely cut off at the time of self-injury, noting something like, "It isn't me doing it, I'm watching it being done." Judith Herman (1992) theorizes that, in fact, the act of self-harm is a way to break a dissociative trance, by giving this major jolt to the body. For example, the color shock of seeing blood may contribute to the end of dissociation.

Other theories abound about motivation to self-mutilate, mostly taken from research on adults who self-injure. These include:

Anger Turned Inward

Girls and women who are socialized to contain angry feelings may harm themselves instead. The poet Adrienne Rich writes, "Most women have not even begun to touch this anger except to drive it inward like a rusty nail." Many girls who self-harm are quite cut off from the rage they're feeling toward parents or peers.

Self-Punishment

Another common explanation for SM is self-punishment. Girls feel guilty about their strong feelings, and then may use self-harm as a punishment for having them. This payback seems to relieve their guilt in a strange way. Indeed, SM can be the way girls justify anger at themselves for failing in relationships. Some describe lives in which, even as young children, they have been made to feel responsible for everything, including their relationship with their parents. Further, it is also common for survivors of abuse to take on the beliefs of the perpetrators—that they are bad or evil and thus deserving of harm.

Survivor Guilt

Another precipitant of SM may be a kind of survivor guilt. For example, girls who witness domestic violence against their mothers may feel helpless and guilty that they were not the ones who were hurt.

Punishing Someone Else

As with suicide attempts, some self-harm can be a communication to show family members that they have hurt a girl; that she is hurting, that damage has been done to her. In this way, SM is both an effort to harm the self and others all at once.

Traumatic Reenactment

Virtually all self-injury involves breaking the skin. In cases of trauma, girls may both do to themselves what was done to them, and then care for and soothe the skin—thus they additionally take on the role of comforter.

Other Explanations

There are numerous other models of self-destructive behaviors in girls and women, which examine character structures and personality disorders, psychosis, acute trauma, and attachment histories. Recent efforts have emphasized the multidimensionality of SM for adolescent girls (Suymeoto & Kountz, 2000; Yip, 2005). For example, Yip explores the various pathways to SM. She notes that the process of self-cutting can follow a predictable pattern: First, external adversities pile up. These include, for example, interpersonal conflict, traumatic events, or feeling rejected or misunderstood. The internal stress attendant on these factors mounts accordingly and becomes intolerable. Girls resort to cutting to release pent-up emotions, thus gaining a sense of release and control. A multidimensional model also considers the influences of parents, peers, and the sociocultural context in supporting and thwarting the need to self-harm.

It must be underscored that the function and meaning of SM for girls is not the same as in adults, who tend to have more traumatic histories (van der Kolk, Perry, & Herman, 1991). Indeed, in one of the rare studies that addresses diagnoses of adolescents who self-injure, researchers found that adjustment disorder was very common suggesting that, for adolescent girls, SM is frequently related to temporary, and current stressors, and not necessarily deep underlying psychopathology (Suymeoto & MacDonald, 1995). The point here is that all kinds of adolescent girls self-injure—those with histories of trauma and disrupted parental care, as well as those with more transient relationship problems and developmental difficulties.

Indeed, a significant factor for girls appears to be the subjective experience of not feeling heard through more conventional means. In one narrative study of girls who cut, a dominant theme that emerged was the way that cutting gained an audience and a response when their speaking voices failed. They felt better not just because they had immediate relief from psychic pain, but when the self-injurious behavior actually communicated to someone how badly they were suffering (Machoian, 2001). Thus, SM is complex in the way that it is both so often secretive and shameful as well as being a form of desperate communication. Machoian writes, "The girls' self-injury becomes a relational strategy in service of self-preservation, wherein, paradoxically, they hurt themselves in an effort to help themselves" (p. 27). For self-harmers to heal, supportive and caring connections have to interrupt the ultimately destructive cycle of self-harm.

Intervention

In the initial session, or when you discover the SM behaviors you need to begin by making sense of the personal significance of them for the girl. Even with all the ideas and theories out there, it is the girl's ideas and theories that are the most important: what problems is she attempting to solve through self-harm? Make sure you validate her beliefs and emotions—make connections between the external events and the internal pressure so she doesn't feel crazy, alienated, invalidated, or retraumatized. Make sure you find out:

- How long has she been hurting herself?
- What does she do to hurt herself?
- Why does she do it?
- When and where does she usually injure herself?
- How often?
- How did she learn to hurt herself?
- What is it like to talk about it with someone?
- Does it hurt when she injures herself? Afterwards?
- How does she take care of her wounds?
- How open is she about her self-injurious behavior?
- Does she want to stop self-harming?
- What does she think would be helpful?

Once self-injury is disclosed or identified, the therapist must seek to assess its severity and to understand the girl's perspective about it. The therapist must not be afraid to ask for as many details as possible—though don't rush it. You do not want girls to disclose so much that they feel even more out of control.

SM is often highly ritualized and it is helpful to know about the ritual—what leads up to it, what happens during it, and afterwards. Assessment should also include how much control she has over the self-harm, its degree of objective severity and danger, and whether the girl (or anyone in her family) acknowledges it as a problem. Of particular importance is whether the self-harm has been escalating, whether she is compulsively drawn to it, and whether she is able to stop (Courtois, 1999). Even though it seems paradoxical, the therapeutic stance must convey that the behavior is both self-injurious *and* self-protective. Be careful about how you ask these questions so that you convey concern and a genuine desire to understand the role and function of the behavior.

Although not all girls who self-harm have a trauma history, it is common enough so that the assessment phase should also include some questions about historical events that might have been traumatic or at least extremely upsetting for them. Girls who are dissociative or alexithymic (unable to recognize, differentiate, identify, or name internal affective states) may only have self-harm as an available strategy for handling internal pressure.

Therapy for self-harm integrates the best that CBT, narrative, and interpersonal therapies have to offer. Begin to understand the self-harm cycle of negative thoughts, feelings, and behaviors—the most vulnerable times when self-harm becomes tempting (these are akin to CBT strategies for getting to know a girl's faulty schemas). Also, probe the exceptions: what she does differently when she doesn't self-harm under stress. In this early phase of work, treatment participation can include a no-harm (or, if this is not possible, a harm-reduction) contract, a list of alternatives, writing assignments, and an impulse-control log.

Note though, that with self-harm, we do usually need to begin with a harm reduction contract, rather than expecting that a girl will give up her primary and most-effective self-soothing strategy. For example, find out if she'll self harm a little less frequently, and try other strategies some of the time. Or if she'll be willing to use cleaner methods, and take better care of wounds she has inflicted. Or ask if she'll try squeezing ice or consider some other less invasive and yet physically painful alternative first. Sometimes, a gradual but steady increase in contract expectations can be both more realistic and more respectful. She'll feel the behavior is more under her control this way—you are helping her identify it as a choice she is making, implying that there are other choices for her, too.

If girls are willing, keeping records can be very useful; if you remain open and curious, rather than being a "school teacher" about setting the tasks, she may be more willing to both write down information and share it with you. She needs to learn what her patterns of self-harm are. Some questions she might answer include:

- What was happening before she began to feel so bad?
- How long was the build-up to the episode?
- What is the role of anger (was she angry with someone else? Who and why?)
- What is happening when the build-up *doesn't* lead to self-harm?

Journaling helps both as a self-soothing strategy and a way to document pressures, feelings, and triggers. Some girls who have the urge to cut learn to write about the feelings instead of acting on them. And then perhaps, the urge will have passed. Girls are more likely to keep journals when they have confidence that parents will not "snoop" and confront them about the entries. Of course, parents will often legitimately be very worried about their self-harming daughters. To the extent it is possible (and safe), parents need to be kept sufficiently informed about therapeutic strategies so they can trust the progress. Family sessions may also help diminish understandable parental anxiety.

Once the self-injurious behavior has become more infrequent, you will be able to get into the deeper underlying problems: trauma, school problems, family problems, inadequate problem solving, and self-soothing strategies. But the first goal is at least to reduce, if not entirely stop the self-harm. And while adult treatment for SM can take years, many girls who can learn a few better strategies for coping and communicating heal much more quickly than that.

It is vital to emphasize that this must be a therapy for feelings as well as thoughts: it is feelings that lead to self-harm. Girls need to know what they are feeling. Even though they may live this way, they are not emotionally numb, cut-off, or dead, but they have trouble finding the language for putting internal experience into words. Girls need to learn how to differentiate between thoughts and feelings, and between feelings and actions. Through discussion, questions, relaxation, scaling, practice, and writing, you can teach girls to tolerate feelings of different intensities. Get into lots of details about feelings with them, all the textures, locations, and nuances you can inquire about:

- Where in your body do you feel the tension?
- What are the physical sensations you experience?
- What is your image of the emotion (e.g., is it a huge rock, a sharp object, a tear, an ache, a blanket, a vise, etc.).
- When have you felt this way before?

Because expressing feelings is so difficult for these girls, consider more expressive and symbolic forms of therapy—painting, movement, music, sculpture, sand-tray therapies—any way to get the feelings out from inside.

Researchers and therapists agree that one of the most therapeutically relevant dynamics of the self-harming adolescent is her difficulty verbalizing (and feeling in control of) emotions and needs. Therapy therefore is really also about helping girls *communicate* effectively. In the context of the therapeutic relationship, girls can develop the ability to articulate emotions and needs, and learn to use alternative behaviors to cope with and communicate about them. Further, we can help girls get others to meet their needs, too.

Girls must learn that they do have feelings, know what they are, put them into words, *and* get others to help. New skills needed to interrupt patterns of self-harm include:

- *Safety.* Girls need to have a safe relationship. Optimally, they should have more safe connections than just the one in therapy, but it's a fine place to start. They will benefit from the experience of empathy and from developing a trusting connection to someone who can listen hard, has reasonable boundaries, and sets fair expectations.

- *Distraction.* Some girls find they can distract themselves enough to get through a crisis without self-harming. You may be able to help a girl come up with rituals that she is willing to follow before she "allows" herself to self-harm. Sometimes these interventions are sufficient to avert the self-harm. It is perhaps paradoxical that by giving themselves permission to self-harm, but following rituals before they do so, they get the sense of control they need to overcome the urge to self-harm. Other distractions might include, for example, finding activities that are incompatible with self-harm — contacting someone, going out, taking a bubble bath, making dinner for the family. Similarly, teaching girls relaxation exercises — tapes, meditation, yoga, or tai chi, for example, may over the long run become a distracter technique. The point is to be doing an activity that cannot at the same time be self-injuring.

- *Positive substitution.* When girls feel upset, they are unable to recall positive emotions. You can help them make a "Rainy Day Box" in which they put ticket stubs, written accounts of good times, happy photos, letters, and any other affirmative documentation. Then when they feel the internal pressure building, they can go through these memories, substituting the pleasant associations to those experiences for the overwhelming negative feelings. Another very helpful strategy of positive substitution involves taking a soft sponge, and dripping warm water over the part of the body where harm had been intended. For example, if a girl cuts her forearm, have her squeeze warm water over it, staying fully conscious and noting all her feelings, including those of self-love and care instead of dissociated self-harm.

- *Grounding.* Girls can learn how to stay present and become less cut off from their feelings. In stressful situations, they need to practice staying oriented in the moment, remaining in their bodies, and knowing, naming, and regulating unbearable affective states. The more you can help a girl handle rather than dissociate from stress, the less likely she will be too resort to SM.

- *Recognizing and avoiding triggers.* By recording all the situations, thoughts, and feelings that lead up to an episode of self-harm, girls can figure out what their self-harm triggers are. Then they have a better shot at avoiding or minimizing the situations that increase their vulnerability. They also have something very useful to talk about in therapy; these triggers tend to be connected to most of the major developmental issues faced by adolescents—identity, loneliness, hurt, peers, family, and worries about the future.

- *Improving self-care skills.* Girls who self-harm tend to be disconnected not only from their feelings of pain and distress, but also from normal bodily cues that indicate hunger, thirst, fatigue, cold, illness, or even odor. Therapists and families have to work together to support girls in taking more general care of themselves—eating well, getting enough rest, staying in bed when unwell, dressing for the weather, and attending to personal hygiene.

- *Language skills.* Most of all, girls must learn to talk about themselves. Girls have to learn to modulate and integrate feelings into everyday life. Instead of ridding themselves of affect through physical pain, or disconnecting from it through dissociation, self-harmers have to learn the fine skills of containment and of verbal expression.

- *Relationship.* Girls do get better when they have a therapist to talk to. As van der Kolk (1989) concluded in his study of self-harming adults, "All subjects attributed their improvement to having found a safe therapeutic relationship" (p. 404). We need to help girls develop better communication and coping skills so they can also have other productive and nurturing relationships with family, friends, and others in their lives.

Ultimately, through relationship we give girls the support and strength to find the words to describe their internal pain, and our best selves to help them learn to contain and express overwhelming feelings. It is our job to help girls translate the language of self-harm into words and to hear them tenderly.

CHAPTER NINE

TROUBLED BEHAVIORS III:
ATTACHMENT AND
TRAUMA PROBLEMS

Attachment and trauma problems constitute a serious and often-hidden cause of emotional and behavioral difficulties for adolescents. Girls with histories of trauma and attachment disruption show up in every conceivable diagnostic category, invariably presenting with a veritable witches' brew of issues and concerns. We need to do a better job recognizing the root cause of this vast distress so we can be most helpful.

Attachment Problems

Lydia has been seeing therapists on and off since she was 3 years old after she attacked her day-care provider. She is now 16, and in long-term foster care with wonderful, committed foster parents who first began providing respite care for her when she was 11, and then made a full-time commitment to her when she was 12. Lydia has gone to 10 schools, lived in seven homes, been hospitalized and spent time in a group home, too. Lydia's mother had a drinking problem, and chose abusive boyfriends over her six children; the oldest four are either in foster care or have been adopted, the two babies are just beginning their inevitable journey into the foster care system. Lydia is glad she knows where her mother is, and worries about her little brothers, but doesn't want to return to her mother's care. Indeed, from the beginning, Lydia was the child with the strength to tell people when her mother was drunk, or someone was being hurt in the home, including herself. This remarkable ability to speak up has been a double-edged sword because over the years it has both kept Lydia safe and repelled people with her seeming lack of sensitivity to others' feelings. Although she used to run away, Lydia has stayed put for the past year and she seems to be stabilizing with her foster parents. She also now willingly comes to see me. Happily, after four years together, I am getting signals that our connections are deepening. I was encouraged, after we had missed a couple of weeks, that when she began the session she said, "Wow, two weeks is a long time. I have so much to tell you."

Attachment difficulties can be caused by many different kinds of disruptions in care. The most obvious reasons are early abuse and neglect, entry into foster care, and movement around the foster care system, where, as for Lydia, the problems with the child–parent relationship have been obvious. Similarly, loss of parental functioning due to incapacitating physical or mental illness (including, for example, postpartum and other major depression, acute anxiety disorders, or psychosis) substance abuse, acrimonious divorce, or death are also frequently associated with attachment problems. But girls also may experience attachment disruption when, for example, they have medical conditions requiring invasive procedures or extended hospitalizations; a caregiver is gone for extended periods of time for any reason; parents have their own troubled attachment histories and have difficulty comprehending the unique developmental needs of their child; or there is a particularly bad fit between a child's temperament and the parenting style.

Indeed, it is also arguable that this postmodern era, with the loss of family time, replacement of relationships with commerce and electronics, and ramped up expectations, is a virtual petri dish for growing attachment difficulties in children and adolescents. It is likely that most therapists treating adolescent girls are seeing many more attachment disturbances than they realize, crossing boundaries of race, class and family structure.

While there is a diagnostic category for Reactive Attachment Disorder, it is extremely limited in its scope and utility for adolescents. Attachment (and attachment difficulty) really describes what is happening in a relationship, and is not, strictly speaking just about an individual. Further, attachment trauma problems are better understood as early pathways to other vulnerabilities and diagnoses, with a powerful developmental impact. They can show up in adolescence as anxiety and other internalizing disorders, as well as oppositional defiant disorder and other externalizing problems. Later in life, they may appear to be personality disorders. The role of attachment in subsequent healthy and pathological development is much broader than the kind of restrictive categorization provided by the DSM (Carlson, Sampson, & Sroufe, 2003).

Recent research suggests that a future DSM diagnostic category, "Developmental Trauma Disorder" (van der Kolk, 2005), may more accurately capture the complex attachment-trauma problems endured by many adolescents. This proposed diagnostic system aims to address the cumulative developmental impact of multiple exposures to interpersonal trauma, thereby making it a more accurate category than either reactive attachment disorder or posttraumatic stress disorder (PTSD) for these teens. As van der Kolk (2005) has described

> The PTSD diagnosis does not capture the developmental impact of childhood trauma: the complex disruptions of affect regulation; the disturbed attachment patterns; the rapid behavioral regressions and shifts in emotional states; the loss of autonomous strivings; the aggressive behavior against self and others; the failure to achieve developmental competencies; the loss of bodily regulation in the areas of sleep, food, and self-care; the altered schemas of the world; the anticipatory behavior and traumatic expectations; the multiple somatic problems, from gastrointestinal distress to headaches; the apparent lack of awareness of danger and resulting self-endangering behaviors; the self-hatred and self-blame, and the chronic feelings of ineffectiveness. (p. 406)

It is also likely that there are many kinds of attachment disturbances. In the current diagnostic system, to have an attachment problem a child must be either (1) excessively inhibited, hypervigilant, or ambivalent toward caregivers, or (2) totally indiscriminate, or totally unable to form a relationship. However, large-scale studies of attachment disordered children demonstrate that such rigid categories are not sufficient to capture the complexity of child behavior (Sroufe, Egland, Carlson, & Collins, 2005). The causes and consequences of disturbed adolescent attachments are even less amenable to these narrow descriptions.

Consider a girl's attachment style as you take a history and attempt to form a trusting relationship with her, but do not require that she demonstrate a pure form of *avoidant* or *indiscriminate* attachment for you to be concerned about it. For example, some girls with avoidant histories can seem quite enthusiastic about the social scene at middle school. Or a girl who appears to have no preferences for one adult over another, may, in fact have some developing selectivity, however slight it may be. These adolescents wouldn't meet diagnostic criteria, but they'd still evince plenty of signs of disturbed attachment.

And also note that there are some other kinds of troubled attachments that mean a girl is in distress. These include: exaggerated attachment, inhibited attachment, aggressive attachment, attachment with role-reversal, and attachment with psychosomatic symptoms (Brisch, 2004). When girls present with these problems, it can be very helpful to think in terms of their troubled attachment histories even without a full blown attachment disorder diagnosis.

Exaggerated Attachment

These girls are not separating and individuating at all, or so it seems. They tend to be excessively clingy, and are demonstrably uninterested in trying new age-expected activities. They don't go to dances, or get their driver's permits, or go out on the weekends. It isn't simply that they're homebodies; they get markedly upset when pushed to leave their attachment figure (usually a mother, though not necessarily). When they are around her, they seem visibly relieved; they're easily calmed and steadied in her presence. These girls don't enjoy individual therapy, at least initially; they're guarded, tense, and suspicious of attempts to pull them away from home. Parents report that historically, they may have reacted to separations with excessive emotional distress. They'd cry, rage, and panic, and become inconsolable. Attempting to keep a lid on this level of separation anxiety, parents may have rearranged their schedules and lives, including home schooling if necessary. These girls tend to have fewer separations because their reaction to them is so violent. In cases of exaggerated attachment, girls have difficulty leaving their primary caretaker all the way through their adolescence and beyond. Their development is seriously impeded.

Inhibited Attachment

These are the girls that are "too good to be true." They're compulsively compliant and so they react to separation with no resistance at all if this is what is expected of them. There is very likely some physical violence in their past: they express desire for attachment cautiously and with reticence. In their experience, they have come to expect protection accompanied by threats of violence. These girls may not challenge limits as might be expected for their age, and they'll stay close by if they feel they must. However, in therapy, away from these turbulent attachment figures, such girls do open up. They are seemingly eager to express their feelings and do so much more freely and openly than might be expected if you see them first with their parents.

Aggressive Attachment

Girls with aggressive attachments frequently come into treatment with the diagnosis of Oppositional Defiant Disorder (ODD). They appear to organize their attachment relationships around excessive verbal and even physical assault. It is as if they save the worst of themselves for the adult they love the most. Notably, they are not oppositional and defiant in other ways or with other people, so that label is inaccurate. They don't have the other features of antisocial girls, just this interpersonal aggression with one or two people. With help and support, they may calm down quickly, and then the attachment can develop in a healthier way. But these are hard situations to treat because it is a lot to ask of adults to remain empathic and available when they are emotionally or even physically hurt. It is more likely that the wounded adult will become rejecting—the very thing the girl fears the most. Then, commonly, such girls will turn the aggression onto themselves, through dangerous and self-destructive behaviors.

Attachment with Role Reversal

The parentified teenage girl has an attachment disturbance as well. Such girls take on the roles and responsibilities ordinarily assumed by a parent, including everything from major purchase decisions, to housework, to discipline. In these instances, it is common that parents are having significant mental or physical difficulties and are quite dependent on the daughter to take care of them in any way she can. For her part, the girl can be caring, but she can also behave in significantly punitive and controlling ways.

Importantly, her own development is shelved as she devotes substantial time and energy to caretaking. These girls will change their plans at a moment's notice if they think they are expected at home. But their needs for nurture and help are not reciprocated. In therapy, we must remain respectful of the astonishing maturity exhibited by parentified girls while carving out a place where they can have a relationship in which they learn how to receive care.

Attachment Disorder in Psychosomatic Symptoms

Adolescent girl attachment disturbances also can show up in a range of vague physical problems that are of concern. They may attempt to get attachment needs met through frequent visits to the school nurse or family physician. Some girls just don't feel well much of the time, even though there may be little medical evidence for their suffering. They get stomachaches and headaches, and may feel nauseated or dizzy. Interestingly, such girls seem to overreact to small amounts of pain, crying when they get a splinter, for example. But they will then be incredibly stoical (perhaps dissociated) when faced with real pain, like stepping on a hornet's nest. Girls who have somatic attachment problems also can have extreme physical reactions; some stop growing altogether (Stanhope, Wilks, & Hamill, 1994). Much like the Failure to Thrive (FTT) infant, a girl with "psychosocial dwarfism" stops growing while she lives within the troubled attachment relationship. And also like babies with FTT, girls with psychosocial dwarfism are able to resume development when moved from a home that is toxic for them and given healthier and safer adults with whom to connect.

Essential Ingredients of Attachment Relationships

Daniel Siegel (1999) has described the neurodevelopment of attachment in an infant. He talked about the qualities in those early relationships that foster attachment: contingent communication, reflective dialogue, repair, emotional communication, and coherent narratives. These five "ingredients" can readily be applied to our work in treating adolescent girls with attachment disturbances.

Contingent Communication

Good parents are able to react to their child's signals in a reasonably accurate way. In infancy, this is what Stern (1985) has called "the dance of attunement," the collaborative interaction that shapes a baby's sense of self and security. In successful contingent communication, a child vocalizes, cries, or acts in particular ways that an attuned caregiver readily notices. The caregiver tries to understand what these signals mean to the child, and then uses this information to respond quickly and effectively. And this is a dance that continues throughout life; people need to have their thoughts and feelings validated even after they have words to describe them.

Adolescent girls with troubled attachment histories likely won't have had much experience with effective contingent communication, and may no longer expect that they can get their needs met directly. In the past, caregivers may have responded to them too much from their adult points of view, denying the different reality held by the girl. Or they may have emphasized noncontingent communication in the home, seemingly caring little about what the girl needs. These parents may spend more time interrogating and judging, for example. Some adults, trying hard, focus on the content of what is being communicated, without digging deeper to understand what it means to the girl, and this, too, can make communication feel disconnected for her.

But therapy is a great place to begin to help girls with contingent communication. That early and essential feedback loop can be shaped and amplified in therapy every time you try to explore, join, and understand what is happening for her and respond accordingly:

- Observe her behavior: "You just sighed, sounding so weary. Can you tell me about that sigh?" "You seem full of energy today." "It seems like you just want to sit quietly today and not answer a lot of questions."
- Reflect on her impact on you: "You're so angry, I can hardly keep up with what you're saying. I really want to understand about everything that happened, so I need you to take a couple breaths and slow down."
- Ask questions to understand better what she is feeling and thinking: "How come that happened?" "Tell me more about that." "That sounds terrible. What did you do next?" "On a scale of 1 to 10, how frightened were you?"
- Use your body language to demonstrate attunement: Mirror her position and affect, or lean forward, nod, stay empathically engaged, respond with encouragement in your voice, show her you are following in the dance.

Reflective Dialogue

Reflective dialogue is that deeper kind of conversation between children and caregivers that leads to what Siegel (1999) called "mindsight." These are conversations between children and parents that go beyond objects and the logistics of daily living, past calling kids to dinner or finding the remote, getting their shoes on, and getting their homework done. Reflective dialogue includes the deeper layer of communication, exchanging with children thoughts, feelings, perceptions, sensations, memories, attitudes, beliefs, and intentions—actually getting to know the internal process of their minds (Siegel & Hartzall, 2003). This process creates a kind of image of the child's mind within the caring adult's mind. Over time, it also enables children to predict and explain how others might be thinking and feeling behind their actions.

The mindsight that evolves from reflective dialogue is arguably the cornerstone of compassion and empathy, qualities inherent to good therapy with adolescents. Mindsight requires an ability to perceive the internal experience of another person and make sense of that imagined experience. With mindsight, we offer compassionate responses that reflect our understanding and concern. As importantly, this process may also help girls develop greater compassion for themselves, and become more empathically attuned to others. Reflective dialogue questions might include:

- *Thoughts:* "Tell me how you think about that one." "What image comes to mind when you think about that."
- *Feelings:* "What did you like most about that?" "What is the most memorable aspect of that trip?" "What does that song mean to you?" "At the risk of sounding like a shrink, how do you feel about it?" "Was that a good time for you?"
- *Sensations:* "How does your stomach feel right now?" "Where in your body are you carrying that feeling?" "What did your body register when that happened?" "What do you think your body is trying to tell you?"
- *Perceptions:* "What's the difference between how this seems and what really happened?" "Can you think of some reasons why he might have said that to you?" "Do you think you'll stay this mad?" "How do you think I'm thinking about this?" "When she calmed down, was she any easier to talk to?"
- *Memories:* "What do you remember about that?" "I remember last week you talked about Diane, what's happening with her?" "Your mom said that this happened; can you tell me how you remember it?"

- *Beliefs:* "What do you think about why that happened?" "How do you think that works?" "How are you thinking differently about that now?" "Why do you think your mother was so upset?" "What do you think people were saying at the party?"
- *Attitudes:* "What were you thinking and feeling when you had that meltdown?" "What do you like so much about coming home to an empty house?" "What's your attitude toward the math teacher now that you did so well last term?"
- *Intentions:* "What were you planning to accomplish when you asked that question?" "Did the girls react well when you sat down at the table with the cookies?" "Did you want your mom to know that you were scared?

Repair

Throughout life, beginning at the very start, even great parents mess up. And because parents aren't perfectly attuned, rupture is inevitable. Rupture happens when parents are preoccupied, set limits that thwart a child's desire, become angry or frightening, or just miss on a communication and the child feels unheard. When the disconnection is extreme, for example, when parents become emotionally or physically abusive, the distress and shame for the child can become overwhelming and intense. Siegel and Hartzall (2003) call these "toxic ruptures." It is harder to reconnect after these frightening experiences; the more often they occur, the less likely that a parent will be able to repair fully next time. In the end, though, no matter what kind of rupture it is, the goal is to achieve a new level of alignment where both parent and child feel understood, and parents acknowledge fully their role in it. In the repair process, a child learns that, although interactions can be stressful, they can also lead to greater intimacy.

Adolescent girls, who are familiar with toxic ruptures through difficult and traumatic experiences with adults, may be anticipating them to the point of self-fulfilling prophecy. The closer these girls feel to an adult, the more certain they may become that the adult will frighten, shame, and disappoint them as others always have. They then may act in ways that ensure there will be a rupture of some kind—behaving defiantly, missing appointments, breaking rules; generally setting up a situation where there will be conflict or confrontation.

And even if they don't act upon these sad expectations, it is likely that, mere mortals that we are, we'll let them down, anyway, and they'll experience rupture with us through our own exquisite imperfection. We'll be late for an appointment, forget something they told us, ask a dumb question, slip up, fall down, or be distracted. Ultimately, the fact of the ruptures in therapy with these girls are less important than the act of repair, which serves as a new template for how people apologize, grow, and move on. Indeed, if no mistakes are made, and no chances for repair are found, it will be a long slow therapy going nowhere. We get closer to girls when we have the opportunity to repair ruptures in connection with them. We say, for example:

- "I'm sorry I was late today. I know that you worked hard to get here on time. I see that you were angry that I wasn't ready when you were. I can't promise it will never happen again, but I'll try, and I know you feel better when we meet on time."
- "I'm really not getting it today, am I? I just know that if you give it another try, and I listen harder, your message will get through. I really want to understand what you're saying and I know it is very frustrating to talk to someone who doesn't get it."
- "I can see you're still upset with me for speaking with your teacher when she called. I know you really want to keep things private. I just need to reassure you that I didn't tell her anything else than what we discussed last week. I see you're not ready yet to let this go, but I hope you can find a way to forgive me because I really care about you, and I did what I had to as a responsible team member."
- "I don't want to fight with you about these rules. I'm sorry we're struggling like this. I really want us to feel good about each other again. Let's talk about it some more."
- "This is a really tough time for you, and even though you're not so sure, I am on your side. Tell me more about what I can do to prove to you I do care."

Emotional Attunement

Daniel Siegel (1999) had a great expression to describe emotional communication; he said that people want to "feel felt." By this he meant that people need to have someone attuned to their emotional states. When the primary emotions of two minds are empathically connected, they experience a kind of alignment that helps them feel joined at a deeper level. He wrote, "So much of what happens in relationships is about a process of resonance in which the emotional state of one person reverberates in that of the other" (Siegel & Hartzell, 2003, p. 65).

Parents who create securely attached children have the capacity to communicate emotionally with them, reflecting accurately how their children feel. Parents share in pleasure by mirroring and amplifying joy and excitement. They also share in pain by soothing fear, sadness, and anger. This sharing is helpful and it teaches the child that emotions are tolerable internally. A child who "feels felt" also learns to self-soothe.

By contrast, many of the girls we treat who have suffered from attachment-trauma problems, have not had relationships where they were taught anything about emotional communication. They have had their feelings invalidated, ignored, manipulated, and denied. They may be so disengaged from what they are experiencing internally, that they may no longer even know how they feel, much less put it into words or explain why. This, too, is a large component of good attachment therapy. Emotional relating makes possible all the other kinds of dialogue you will have, enabling a level of collaborative, integrative communication that is not possible otherwise. Siegel and Hartzell (2003) described seven qualities that enhance this kind of connection, all with notable applications to treatment, which I outline below. Consider how you incorporate these qualities into your empathic understanding of the girls you're treating:

- *Awareness:* In therapy we are aware both of our own feelings and bodily responses, and the verbal and nonverbal messages that girls send us. We use this awareness to stay present and authentic with them, to stay in control of ourselves, and to be as empathically available as we can.

- *Attunement:* Awareness enables us to allow our states of mind to align with theirs, so we can do more than just listen to them; we can experience a direct connection with them. This attunement is filled with sharing of nonverbal signals, including tone of voice, eye contact, facial expressions, gestures, and the timing and intensity of our responses.

- *Empathy:* With these adolescents, it can be very trying to remain empathic as they put our tenacity to the test. But when we open our mind and heart, to sense and feel the world from their point of view and empathize with their experiences, we do much better work with them. When we align ourselves with them, we begin to build the foundation for a deeper empathic connection.

- *Expression:* We need to be very conscious of our expressions with these wary adolescents, communicating our internal responses with care and respect. We offer them continuous feedback both on how we are feeling, and how we understand what they are doing and saying.

- *Joining:* Good therapy attains a level of comfort and connectedness with a girl, includes sharing openly in the give-and-take of communication, and both verbal and nonverbal connections. We need to be particularly mindful about joining with girls with attachment trauma, as this will be a novel and difficult—if essential—task to accomplish. Often the work of joining is accomplished not through interrogation but mutual activity—a puzzle, a game, or an art project, for example.

- *Clarification:* Guess, and guess again. The objective is to "get it" about how the girl is thinking and feeling; to help make sense of her experience. Really work to be clear about how she sees it. She may not even know herself, but keep trying anyway.

- *Sovereignty:* With these adolescent girls, we are aiming toward a realistic empowerment. We indicate, through word and action, that we respect the dignity and separateness of a girl's mind. She will expect you try to control her, and she'll seek to control you, too if that's her model for how the world works. Thus it will be useful for us to help girls foster their independent thinking, helping them learn about things over which we do acknowledge their sovereignty.

Coherent Narratives

From about the age of 2, personal stories become a vital part of self-development. These stories, that help us make sense of our lives, require the integrated work of both hemispheres of the brain; coherent narrative depends on the blending of the left-side drive to explain and the right side storage of autobiographical, social, and emotional information (Siegel, 1999). Indeed, parents who can tell a logical and meaningful story that makes sense of life experiences are much more likely to have securely attached children, and to be securely attached themselves. Conversely, insecurely attached parents produce disorganized and dysregulated narratives and, typically, insecurely attached children.

However, it is very important to note that there is more variability in attachment patterns over the years than this simple equation might imply. It is true that, if nothing adverse happens—no losses, abuse, change in sensitivity of caregiving—a securely attached infant will become a securely attached adolescent and adult. Similarly, if nothing new and good happens, an insecure infant is quite likely to grow up and become the avoidant, ambivalent, or disorganized adolescent you may be treating.

But here's the good news: fascinating recent research on adults (with important implications for our work with adolescents) suggests that attachment styles are actually more flexible than previously believed. Under proper circumstances, someone who had attachment trauma as a child can attain "earned secure" status (Phelps, Belsky, & Crnic, 1998; Roisman, Padron, Sroufe, & Egeland, 2002). These "earned secure" adults have come to make sense of their lives, in the context of a sensitive, responsive, and caring relationship with another adult. They have someone who can help them construct meaning by developing that coherent narrative.

In other words, infants and children with attachment trauma problems can subsequently become more securely connected. They'll need a very special relationship with someone who can help them understand what has happened to them in their lives, how it made them feel, what they did to survive, and who they want to be. This narrative has to be informed by clear thinking and the equally important emotional and autobiographical aspects of experience. This makes it a tougher task for a younger child, but more plausible for an adolescent to accomplish.

Such a narrative, explored with a safe adult, such as a therapist, begins to integrate the functions of the brain and connects these processes over time, making meaning in the past, present, and future. Siegel (1999) and others suggest that this personal story telling in the context of a safe relationship heals not just the girl but may actually mend her brain, enabling it to grow new synapses and better integrate information across the hemispheres. These ideas challenge us to make therapy with these adolescents the kind of safe and productive environment that turns around a terrible trajectory.

Coherent Narrative Therapy

Using a mesh of attachment therapy and narrative approaches, we can become coauthors for the complicated and confusing stories adolescents tell. We help girls turn the fragments of memories, incomprehensible pain, experiences that registered in their bodies before they had recall, and magical early thinking into tales of triumph, and purpose (Kagan, 2004). The new narratives help them move from helpless victim to determined survivor, from weakling to hero. We help girls remember and hold history, manage the present *and* imagine and plan for the future.

This is slow therapy, founded in the hard work of contingent communication, reflective dialogue, repair, and emotional attunement as a girl struggles to develop sufficient trust in you, and faith in herself to persevere. The suggested questions that follow are adapted from Siegel and Hartzell's (2003) list of self-help questions for parents looking back on their attachment histories. These are the kinds of considerations that begin to shape a story, and not necessarily questions you should ask verbatim. They'll give you an idea of some of the details that can contribute to a coherent narrative:

- What was it like when you were little? Who was in your family? Who took care of you?
- Tell me about the relationship with your parents over the years. How did it change as you went from being a baby to a toddler to a little kid to a big kid? What's it like now?
- How do your relationships with each of your parents differ? How are they the same? Are there ways you try to be like your mom? Like your dad? Are there ways you try to be different?
- Did you ever feel rejected, threatened, or hurt by either of your parents? Were there other really bad times in your life, times that felt overwhelming? Really sad? Really scary? Traumatic?
- Do any of those experiences feel really alive for you, like it was just yesterday they happened? Do they continue to influence your life? Your relationships?
- How did your parents discipline you when you were little? How do they do it now? How did it work? What (if any) is the impact of that on how you are feeling and managing your life now?
- Do you recall your earliest separations from your parents? What happened and what was it like for you? How long did they last? Did that feel very long to you?
- Did anyone really important to you die when you were younger? What was that like for you? How does that loss affect you now?

- How did your parents communicate with you when you were happy and excited as a little kid? Did they join with you in your enthusiasm? How do they respond now? How about when you were distressed or unhappy? What would happen? What happens now? Did each of your parents handle your emotions differently? How?
- Tell me about other people who took care of you and were important to you when you were growing up. Tell me about what those relationships were like, and what they are like now. Are there important people you no longer see? What happened to them?
- Who besides your parents is special in your life now? What is it about them that you value? How can they help you now?
- How do you think your experiences as a baby and little kid are affecting your relationships now? Do you find yourself doing things, like not trusting people, because of what happened to you?
- Do you want to change some of the ways you handle stress and people even though it's hard because of old patterns?
- Tell me about the future. What do you want to do? What kinds of relationships do you want to have? What will you need in the way of skills and support to get there?

The Anxiety/Executive Functioning/Attachment Trauma Triad

Adolescents with attachment trauma problems tend to have a constellation of related problems that are hard to separate. Indeed, because the difficulties are so interwoven, it is possible that a specific intervention will improve overall functioning. If the development of coherent narrative seems beyond the realm of possibility, you might first want to work on other compromised areas. These should include both reducing anxiety and improving executive functioning. All the while, you'll be building the essential therapeutic connection. Down the road, coherent narrative work may then be more useful and productive.

Anxiety

Clinical reports and research indicate strongly that no matter how else they present, these girls are hugely anxious (Hughes, 1998; Maerlander,

Isquitt, Racusin, Sengupta, & Straus, 2004). They may be so overwhelmed internally that they cannot begin to develop external relationships. Thus it can be helpful to treat them first with both therapy and medication, specifically focusing on their high levels of anxiety.

Executive Functioning

Another near universal characteristic of these girls is their significant deficit in self-regulation and problem solving (Maerlander et al., 2004). It is likely that their lack of self-control, cognitive inflexibility, and difficulty in planning ahead impede their ability to form and sustain relationships. Similarly, these executive functioning deficits are also associated with anxiety. It is probable, though, that if they could become better problem solvers, they would be less anxious. These improvements, in turn, would make it more possible for them to make and sustain trusting relationships. And it certainly won't hurt them to have a more rounded executive, and less anxiety, even if development of coherent narratives remains a more distant goal.

Attachment Trauma

Kelsey was sexually abused by three different men over the years, and she's now 18 and in a relationship with yet another man who is violent and sexually abusive. She sees how this is harming her, but she feels incapable of breaking free. He doesn't know she's in therapy and wouldn't like it; when she misses appointments I can't even call her to find out if she's okay. Kelsey's got some grit though; she invariably calls me to reschedule.

Kelsey escaped from her mother's home almost a year ago, and moved in with him; a classic case of going from the frying pan into the fire. Now she's pregnant; her doctor referred her to me for therapy since she's obviously young and emotionally unstable. Parenting will be especially challenging for her. With a baby to think about though, Kelsey *is* more available to exploring her "story," she wants to be a better mother than the one she had. She has little traction though, because the most fundamental prerequisite for trauma therapy, safety, can't be met. Still, I continue to be hopeful. She's gotten a high school diploma, and she is saving a little tip money that her boyfriend doesn't know about. Kelsey is contemplating a better path for herself, and with my help, she's dissociating less. We don't have a lot of months left, but it's slow and steady work. Along with a maternal aunt, a couple of girl friends, her doctor, and the outreach nurse assigned to her case, we've got a viable team, helping Kelsey take hold of her own life.

While attachment disturbance and trauma do not invariably go together, there is considerable overlap. Girls with attachment problems are frequently traumatized; girls with traumatic experiences often develop attachment difficulties. However, even without attachment complications, girls who endure trauma often suffer profoundly and for a long time.

Trauma generally refers to an experience of overwhelming horror, fear, or pain, along with helplessness. Typical examples include car accidents, rape, psychological, physical, and sexual abuse and neglect, exposure to disaster such as a house fire or tornado, and witnessing violence.

For a full posttraumatic stress disorder (PTSD) diagnosis, four separate criteria have to be met: (1) experience of an event outside the range of usual human experiences that would be markedly distressing to anyone; (2) re-experiencing of the event (e.g., traumatic dreams, recollections, sudden reexperiencing of events, acute distress at reminders); (3) numbing/avoidance of reminders (e.g., efforts to avoid feelings, detachment from others and activities, diminished affect; (4) persistent arousal (e.g., difficulty falling or staying asleep, difficulty concentrating, hypervigilance, exaggerated startle response, physiological reactivity to cues). Further, these symptoms have to last over a month; under a month is considered a normal crisis reaction.

For reasons of development and individual experience, adolescent trauma does not always meet the complete measure of adult PTSD. More commonly, teens tend to have just some of these symptoms, and some others not specified here. Notably, recent research concludes that posttraumatic symptoms in adolescence are manifested primarily through maladaptive behaviors, such as substance abuse, running away from home, serious school attendance problems, and peer difficulties (Johnson, 1998).

Adolescents also take more risks than other age groups and find themselves more often in potentially traumatic situations. Because their mental structures are changing so rapidly, it is also likely that their responses to stress are more diverse. And since they may keep traumatic events private, their distress often transmutes into other behaviors before we notice it. As a consequence, adolescent girls can be traumatized and present with a full complement of internalizing and externalizing problems; the traumatic origins of their behavior problems may be overlooked entirely.

Further, Terr (1991) suggested that trauma really takes on two distinct forms for children and adolescents. Type I disorders, which follow from unanticipated single events, are characterized by full, detailed memories of the event; "omens" or attempts to develop a reason for the trauma or how it could have been averted; and misperceptions. Adolescents misperceive traumatic events because they may suffer from peculiar time distortions, visual hallucinations, and misidentifications after a single, intense, unexpected shock.

Type II disorders—also described more recently as complex trauma—follow from long-standing or repeated exposure to extreme external events. One primary characteristic of type II disorders is the child or adolescent's attempts to preserve and protect the self from painful feelings, memories, and experiences engendered by the trauma. Many experts (Briere, 1992; Pearce & Pezzot-Pearce, 1997; Terr, 1991) describe the functionality of such dissociative coping; they note that it serves as the child's adaptive accommodation to early victimization that enables her to survive.

Terr (1991) identified three major characteristics of type II disorders: rage, psychic numbing (leading to extreme memory lapses), and dissociation. Recently, research on complex trauma indicates more far-reaching sequelae spanning multiple domains of impairment, including attachment, biology, affect regulation, dissociation, behavioral control, cognition, and self-concept (Cook, Blaustein, Spinazolla, & van der Kolk, 2003). Thus, particularly extreme events in childhood and adolescence may often lead to different types of traumatic impact, and many kinds of outcomes are possible (Cook et al., 2003; Greenwald, 2000; Pearce & Pezzot-Pearce, 1997).

There is ample evidence that traumatic events have the potential for more or less severe effects on all aspects of adolescent functioning—including cognitive, behavioral, physical, emotional, neurological, moral, and spiritual development (Gil, 1996). Regardless of diagnostic specificity, trauma takes a toll on development. Notice how it reverberates in three different ways in girls' lives; when we intervene, we consider all of these:

Experience
What is their experience of the problems they have? How do they describe the trauma and their strategies for coping? Depending on such variables as temperament, supports, previous functioning, kind of trauma, and overall functioning, girls will have widely disparate experiences of similar events. It is important not to jump to conclusions based on how you might

expect someone to experience a comparable trauma; try to discover her unique perceptions about it.

Ongoing Expression

How does she show she is suffering? Depending on the age when the trauma began, and their coping strategies, girls express their ongoing misery in various ways. For example, a girl with early sexual abuse may still wet the bed or be sexually preoccupied, while a girl who was in a car accident may want to tell her "story" over and over again, and have sleep problems. Such behaviors give us important information about the nature, duration, and age of the trauma, and an adolescent's stress and resilience.

Enduring Effects

How did her environment change as a result of the trauma? Was anyone injured, incarcerated, killed? Did she enter the foster care system? Do family problems escalate? Does her emotional and behavioral difficulty lead to social and school changes? What other interventions does she need to participate in besides attending therapy? It is very important to realize that trauma doesn't get "resolved" in some tidy way; a girl's life is changed as a result of it. But she can learn to make meaning of it, compartmentalize it, and continue to grow and develop.

There are also some important principles of trauma work with adolescent girls that require special attention. These include:

- *Safety.* One of the very true adages about this therapy is the expression that, "all trauma is recent." Traumatized girls have a damaged sense of time. Their bodies are tightly wired into fight-or-flight mode, and they tend to be hypervigilant, and more easily triggered into acute fear because they are constantly prepared for it. In these circumstances, it isn't possible to make a therapeutic connection; girls are safe only if they feel it. Talk about safety with them, what they need, what it feels like, how they know if they are safe or not. They need to be safe in their homes, in their classrooms, in their communities and in your office to begin to heal from the impact of trauma. If you cannot guarantee this most basic need, then the intervention you are providing is restricted to helping a girl live less dangerously. This sort of risk management approach to treatment can be beneficial, but it is not, strictly speaking, therapy.

- *Security*. Within the therapy and girl's lives, we also need to increase the level of daily predictability, limiting surprises as much as possible. Traumatized girls benefit tremendously from structure and routine; they need lots of consistency. Benevolent adults should take charge of the big decisions, perhaps at a preadolescent level of direction for a time. If you do weekly therapy, try to give them a set day and time. Within sessions, establish a rhythm, with predictable rituals that define the beginning, middle, and end of the hour. Begin with a check-in, end with a favorite cut from a CD—decide together what routines should develop. Taffel (2005) talks about the value of developing ritual in therapy with adolescents: "It expresses the uniqueness of the relationship, the comfort and predictability of your space together" (p. 60). And remember: a setting the adolescent can count on lowers her stress and makes connection possible.

- *Acceptance*. Traumatized adolescent girls may act in ways that ensure they will be rejected. Although this behavior is counterintuitive, trauma robs girls of a sense of self-efficacy and self-control. In response, they sometimes take charge in the only way they can, by pushing away supports. The task for therapy is to figure out how to accept the adolescent and reject her behavior. Remember, if a girl doesn't feel loved (or worthy of love) she will act unlovable.

  And acceptance is tougher because these girls are prone to extreme thinking; they don't modulate their reactions well due to their state of physiological arousal. Consequently, they experience even small rejections as total rejections. The safe holding environment of your office and your relationship can begin to provide a traumatized girl with a feeling of acceptance that may help her accept herself again.

- *Belonging*. For a traumatized girl to stick to therapy, she has to believe she belongs there. This doesn't mean she's unwell, but rather the space you cocreate is one that feels good to her. The sense of welcoming includes surface factors like comfortable furniture, warm colors, good snacks, interesting (to her) activities. Belonging is also about feeling welcomed by you, how well you do finding the girl temporarily buried under all the past problems. Express pleasure in being with her, in seeing her again, in her special characteristics that you value the most. Tell her, "I love your spirit."

"You made me such a special CD; I'm listening to it all the time." "I'm so glad you're here." "Wow do you have a lot of courage." "I'm looking forward to seeing you next week." "I'm going to miss you." In so many words, tell her often that she belongs.

- *Trust.* Perhaps the greatest interpersonal toll of trauma is the loss of trust—in herself, in adults, and even in the world. It is hard not to overgeneralize when your body is in a state of preparedness for danger. So girls need lots of encouragement and nudging to rely on others. They have to give people a chance not to let them down.

  With girls who have lost trust through earlier attachment trauma, consider teaching them the Trust Cycle. Draw a circle on a piece of paper. At the top (the 12:00 position if it were a clock), write "*Need.*" Explain that when they were younger, and they had a need—they were hungry or lonely, for example—they became very uncomfortable (or even if they were older, they may have had a need to be protected and cared for). Draw an arrow to the "3:00" spot. Write "*Emotional Response.*" Describe how babies cry and scream to communicate that they have a need (or whatever you know they may have done to signal their need for care and protection). Draw another arrow heading to the bottom of the circle, the "6:00" place. Write "*Gratification.*" Tell them that in the best of circumstances someone responds to the baby the right way and takes care of the need—feeds and holds the baby, for example (or cuddles and protects the older child from harm). Move the arrow up to the "9:00" area and write "*Trust.*" Say that every time a baby (or anyone) has a need, communicates it, and gets it gratified, she builds a little more trust.

  In no way should this exercise be used for parent bashing. Make sure you remain respectful: "Because your mom was only 16, and a kid herself, she couldn't always meet your needs. So even before you could talk, you started to think that the world wasn't a very trustworthy place. And now, when you need to have people in your life who are trustworthy, your mind and body tell you, Don't Do It. But you're safe now, and people are working to be sure you get your needs met. We have to help you relearn this Trust Cycle." In this way, we can provide traumatized girls with a visual image of what happens to them as they struggle to get close to people.

Therapy is a great place to relearn trust. If you make a promise, keep it. Trust also contains elements of respect. Make sure you expect that she'll treat you respectfully and that you'll do the same for her. And as with all work with girls, be authentic. One of the side effects of all that anxiety is a more finely tuned "phony-detector." If you are not genuine, she'll know it even before you do, and you'll instantly be less trustworthy as a result. Finally, persevere. Trust is a long hard road that will need to be traversed and tested many times before it gets smoother.

- *Relationships.* Of course traumatized girls need safe, stable, predictable relationships where no one is used or abused. In therapy, this relationship is a mutual connection that maintains high expectations and high tolerance. You will need to keep inviting a girl back to try again, and maintaining an adult tone of warmth and forgiveness. If parents or foster parents are available and invested, they should naturally be included some of the time. Traumatized girls need a solid home base most of all.

  But if parents are only marginally interested (and this is sadly sometimes the case), you become even more important as a role model and attachment figure. One of the most robust findings in the trauma and resiliency research is the overwhelming conclusion that resilient adolescents have had at least one person in their lives "who accepted them unconditionally regardless of their temperamental idiosyncrasies, personal attractiveness, or intelligence" (Werner, 1988, p. 5). If there is no one else, that person can be you. And even if there are other trustworthy adults, these girls need more.

  As for all girls, peer relationships are also very important, but trauma has a deleterious effect on this area of development, too. Thus, another principle of trauma work is particularly ensuring that they have the social skills and social opportunities to make and keep friends. This is not a side objective; indeed for many traumatized girls, getting better is highly dependent on diminishing their feelings of isolation and difference. Find them social opportunities that elevate their "game" a little, pulling them in from the edges. Look in their schools, religious institutions, and communities for ideas — youth groups, social skills groups, ropes courses, theater groups, choirs, and teams all can have value for a marginalized girl needing peers.

- *Self-Awareness.* We learn about ourselves mostly in the mirror of others; girls come to see who they are through our eyes. And they typically enter therapy struggling with a negative reflection; trauma can wreak havoc on a self. We use words and gestures to externalize what we see. These new descriptions broaden a girl's sense of her efficacy and her hope. Some ways we help expand a girl's positive self-awareness:

  — Use games, activities, and interactions to challenge concretely a girl's negative self-estimation. Offer behavioral evidence of her strengths: "You learned how to play that card game very quickly." "You're a good sport when you win (or don't)." "You hung in really well with that tough family session today. I was impressed." "You are really getting good at telling and showing me how you're feeling." "You have such a great sense of humor, that really cracks me up" (or laugh appreciatively).

  — Encourage a girl to try new activities. Both within therapy and outside, help girls to broaden their definitions of who they are—what they do, and know how to do. Trauma tends to make girls feel tentative and powerless. Combined with the general uncertainty of adolescence, the impact of trauma can diminish a girl's world practically to the vanishing point. Mastery of new skills can help girls see themselves in a new and better light.

  — See the world through her eyes. Share a journal back and forth—have her write about experiences that you respond to in writing; have her take pictures of things and people that matter, and help her make a scrapbook; have her draw pictures; make her own board games—anything that gives you greater knowledge of how she sees herself in her places.

Trauma Work Is Also Grief Work

Traumatized adolescents are grieving adolescents. These girls have sustained unfathomable losses—through deaths, moves, injury, incarceration of family members, foster care, and part of childhood itself through premature awareness of adult weakness and cruelty. Just remember, they will have profound sadness in them no matter how they present, no matter how many behavior problems they have, no matter how infuriating they may be.

No Lone Rangers

The circle of adults is important for all adolescent girls, but for girls with attachment trauma problems, establishing a strong support system can make all of the difference in outcome. Never be the only extracurricular activity in a traumatized girl's life. Make sure they are doing more: tutoring, social-skills groups, jobs, trumpet lessons, volunteering at a nursing home, assisting a veterinarian, whatever you and she can think of that breaks isolation and gives her more caring adults. Making these links work is sometimes the most valuable aspect of the therapy. These connections to competence and community can make all the difference in healing. Because traumatized kids are complex, they need to experience success in a range of systems and places.

The Essential Link Between Disrupted and Normal Development

Although we tend to make statements about the overall impact of trauma, it is usually more helpful to look at strengths and delays in different domains; making an assessment of emotional, cognitive, social, and physiological functioning. It is entirely common for traumatized girls to be struggling in several areas at once, if not all across the board. As we learn about how they problem solve, self-soothe, and get along with peers and adults, we get a sense of "how old" they are. Because we want to set up expectations that are helpful and realistic, we must meet traumatized girls at their *developmental level and attend less to chronological age*. In this way, we address delays through building attainable competencies and skills.

It is important to note, also, that trauma can lead to both delays *and* distortions in development. Thus, a girl who has the social skills of a 10-year-old, may not next act like she's 11. It is more likely that, as she builds a trusting relationship and develops some strategies for managing her anxiety, and learns a bit about social problem solving, that she'll seem more her own age, but with some idiosyncrasies. She may, for example, have a better time with peers, but be uninterested in dating. Or she'll depend on a couple of close chums but be unusually reticent about going out with a larger group. Her empathy for others may demonstrate maturity beyond her years, while her insight into her own motivations may be very undeveloped. The main point is that as she becomes more competent in each of these domains, she will feel better, and the trauma will then be less central in her life. She will come to see that it doesn't have to define who she is, but rather is just one kind of experience in a lifetime of challenges and opportunities.

Trauma Therapy

Attachment problems and trauma also have many commonalities for intervention. Traumatized girls need to develop safe, trusting relationships in order to heal, too. There is some controversy among clinicians about whether a girl has to be able to "tell her trauma story" in order to heal. It is entirely possible, particularly with Type II traumas, that she may not remember many specifics about what happened. A detailed reconstruction of events, feelings, sensations, and chronologies and release of pent-up emotion is virtually impossible in these cases.

Still, much work can be done without Colombo-like pursuit of "the trauma story" in favor of a more general narrative approach exploring the broader self-story that may have some trauma elements in it. In any event, good trauma therapy begins with a secure and predictable relationship, and a girl with a strong set of problem-solving and self-soothing strategies. So the first part of the work is dedicated to making both the story and a happy life possible.

It is indeed likely that down the road, at some point, a girl will need to talk more about what happened to her, and perhaps recall as many specifics as she can, adding meaning to her life now as she reconstructs the trauma. You should certainly be available to hearing whatever elements she chooses to share, but not push for it too hard. As Beverly James (1989) noted, "The goal is to have traumatized children reach the point where they can say something like, 'Yes, that happened to me. That's how I felt and how I behaved when it happened. This is how I understand it all now. I won't really forget it happened, but I don't always have to think about it either'" (p. 49).

The general point is to be available to recalled events as they arise, but first and foremost to build a therapeutic relationship and competencies. So when a girl is ready to talk about what happened to her, and what it may mean for her self-concept, relationships, and worldviews, she is strong enough to manage the horror and despair of it. You have to create a safe holding environment before you should hear a trauma story, so when it arrives a girl doesn't fall to pieces, become dissociated or panic in the telling. It is also essential that when she does speak about trauma, she is telling her story to *you*; healing depends upon the specificity of this attachment relationship.

There are numerous more specialized techniques that aid this basic framework for treatment. You may want to consider getting some specialized training in, for example, eye movement desensitization and reprocessing (EMDR), Sand Tray Therapy, or hypnosis. But even without a lot of extra training, a solid and compassionate adolescent therapist can learn to do good trauma work. Trauma can't be forgotten. It can only be contained so that life can go on. Both our empathic presence and specific skills help traumatized girls to persevere. And nothing works better to heal the wounds of attachment trauma than the salve of a safe, predictable, and nurturing relationship.

Chapter Ten

Troubled Behaviors IV:
Social Aggression, ADHD,
and Oppositional-Defiant Disorder

The popular press has covered the rise in girl aggression and acting-out in recent years because it is interesting news. Since the mid-1980s, there has reportedly been an increase in girls engaging in externalizing "boy-type" behaviors, thus bringing them ever more into the public eye. And ample longitudinal data gathered in this interval support the fear that for girls early acting out leads to a myriad of negative outcomes as they head into adolescence and young adulthood. The more common form of girl anger—relational aggression—is also associated with physical aggression; a growing number of girls engage in both kinds. Girls who act out get in trouble with peers, teachers, parents, and the law.

Girls engaging in disruptive behavior and fights are at risk for being rejected by peers; they feel alienated and unsupported in their relationships; they struggle academically, affiliating with other more marginal peers; they become involved in more antisocial behaviors; they choose antisocial romantic partners, initiating and receiving partner violence; they become teen mothers, have children with a greater than usual number of health problems, and they are less sensitive and responsive as parents (see Putallaz & Bierman, 2004 for a fuller account of all of these problems). Thus as girls act out more, they get onto a path that makes them particularly vulnerable to a vast range of emotional and social difficulties.

Most studies demonstrate that boys are more aggressive than girls, and are more likely to be given externalizing diagnoses including ADHD, Oppositional Defiant Disorder, and Conduct Disorder (Hinshaw & Anderson, 1996). Further, boys' early aggressive behavior predicts subsequent antisocial outcomes, such as fighting and stealing, whereas girls' early aggressive behavior predicts subsequent internalizing problems, such as depression and anxiety (Conway, 2005). Girls with disruptive behavior disorders are more likely to have one or more comorbid disorders as well, including ADHD, anxiety and depression, somatization disorder, substance use disorders, antisocial personality disorder and learning disabilities (McMahon & Wells, 1998). These differences underscore the need for increased attention to early detection of behavior disorders in girls.

Feminist research has attempted to shed some light on the differences in the ways that boys and girls act out. One approach has been to include a more gender-sensitive conceptualization of aggression (Crick, 1995). According to this model, children use aggressive behaviors that most effectively harm the social goals of their peers. Boys use physical aggression to harm the instrumental goals of other boys, whereas girls often use covert, relational forms of aggression to obstruct or frustrate the relational goals of other girls. Girls withhold friendship, ignore others, spread rumors, gossip, and elicit peer rejection of another child (Conway, 2005).

Findings using this model indicate that when relationally aggressive behaviors are included in assessments of aggression, gender differences disappear (Crick & Rose, 2000). Boys and girls demonstrate nearly equivalent rates of aggression; boys have high rates of physically aggressive behavior and girls evince high rates of relationally aggressive behavior. However, that said, it seems absurd to argue that boys and girls are equally aggressive, given that these behaviors are so different in form. As Underwood (2003) has argued, "it seems much more interesting to focus on other questions, such as the meaning of these behaviors for girls and for boys, how they might relate differently to girls' and boys' social functioning, and their developmental origins and outcomes" (p. 234). Further, once we understand what social aggression is, and how it operates, we need to devise interventions that are gender sensitive. Treatment for victims and perpetrators of relational aggression is not necessarily the same as strategies for reducing more overt aggression.

Social Aggression

Maureen is not yet 12 but her name comes up repeatedly in meetings about problem students. She's got a few friends who follow her loyally, and a path of destruction behind her; mothers of other girls call the school and each other to commiserate. Maureen isn't exactly a traditional bully; in fact, she's a beautiful, soft-spoken girl with careful manners. But she excludes one girl whenever she's in a threesome, and her loyalties are fickle. So a girl who is Maureen's best friend one day can easily fall from grace and be dropped in a subtle but unmistakable way the next. The expected seat won't be available in the lunchroom, or the promised call that evening doesn't come. Maureen's mother hears about these affronts from other parents and the school, but she supports her daughter down the line, and thinks that the kids should "just work it out themselves." Thus, it's up to school counselors to mediate and patch up the next "victim" who knocks, in tears, on their doors.

After almost a whole year of this social aggression, the tables turned, and the little group of victimized girls organized against Maureen. She was, of course, devastated. Their vindication was more precontemplated than the invasion of Iraq. The girls got online for a group chat, and Maureen was "inadvertently" copied in on the vicious exchange. Eventually, unable to repair the damage on her own, and ill with indignation, Maureen went to guidance herself and asked if she could talk to a therapist. Her mother reluctantly agreed because Maureen appeared to be so unhinged by this total rejection from her peers. Maureen (and, interestingly, also her mother) struggled to see the connection between her practice of social aggression and her own victimization. They felt the retribution was much meaner than anything she had ever done. Maureen's homeroom teacher told me that none of the girls, "did a stitch of work for a solid month when all this was going on."

The findings that victims and perpetrators of social aggression are at higher risk for emotional and behavioral problems are very robust. These data are consistent in longitudinal studies, prospective and retrospective studies, and clinical samples, looking at aggressive girls and their victims within gender and across gender (Underwood, 2003). Perpetrating social aggression is related to peer rejection, loneliness, depression, and social isolation; victims of social aggression are also more depressed, isolated, and have lower self-esteem (Paquette & Underwood, 1999). Most adult women have their own stories of social aggression from middle and high school, noting that adults either did not know about their struggles, or did not intervene. They describe their victimization (and offending) with a vividness and immediacy that shows the wounds haven't entirely healed, many, many years later. Social aggression can be insidious.

Girls need to learn how to become more assertive and straightforward in resolving their interpersonal difficulties. In adolescence, they face increased pressure to mask straightforward expressions of anger. It is likely that they then engage in social aggression because they have so few options of acting on these strong feelings—anger, contempt, or desire for dominance. So we best help girls by giving them more skills and strategies for coping, and by structuring environments that lower opportunities and tolerance for relational aggression.

Intervention

Research in social aggression is recent. Thus we know relatively little about the best methods of intervention. Several interesting directions we might take include:

- *Parent Training.* Sensitize parents to how children may learn social aggression by observing marital difficulties. While the research data on this is slim, it seems reasonable to speculate that if adolescents observe parents (or other family members) attempting to hurt each other by triangulating others in conflicts, or by threatening to withdraw from the relationship, this might increase the likelihood of girls engaging similarly with peers (Underwood, 2003). We do know, quite clearly, in any event, that exposure to marital conflict is associated more generally with psychological problems. Treatment of parents can also provide them with information and modeling for more direct communication strategies. Parents are often cited as the first line of defense against social aggression; active listening and proactive parenting can be very helpful in teaching girls the benefits of direct communication (Simmons, 2002). Like Maureen's mother, many parents take a noninterventionist stance when it might help for them to get more engaged in helping their daughters with social problem solving.

- *Social Competence.* Socially competent girls are less likely to be aggressive. Social competence includes, for example, encoding relevant social cues, accurately interpreting those social cues, generating effective solutions to interpersonal problems, realistically anticipating consequences and potential obstacles to one's actions, and translating social decisions into effective behavior. These behaviors can all be shaped and learned through modeling, teaching, practice, and reinforcement.

Social–cognitive interventions can help teach girls more benign interpretations in ambiguous social situations: For example, research shows that girls high on relational aggression tend to overattribute hostility when they can't read what someone's intentions are. We can help girls learn to interpret social cues, clarify social goals, and expectations for relationships (Underwood, 2003). Some other modifiable social cognitions might include: preoccupation with others' perceptions—in line with David Elkind's "imaginary audience" (Elkind, 1967); rumination—girls tend to think obsessively about relationships and relational aggression (Owens, Slee, & Shute, 2001); and rejection-sensitivity—rejection-sensitive girls may be more likely to perceive social slights and more likely to respond by harming others by social exclusion, relationship manipulation, and spreading rumors (Underwood, 2003).

- *Assertiveness Training.* Theorists believe that social aggression is associated with the tension that girls carry between experiences of rage and the desire to dissemble negative emotions. Thus, assertiveness training can teach girls to express their needs and desires more directly, and to accept that conflict is a natural part of relationships. Therapy can help girls role play how to confront rumor spreading, or social exclusion, for example. Girls don't need to learn to fight physically, but to become more comfortable directly voicing their concerns and asserting their social goals.

- *Encourage Kindness.* Research also shows that we can do a better job harnessing girls' distaste for social aggression. Girls dislike girls who engage in it (French, Jansen, & Pidada, 2002). They can, in fact, be taught to stop excluding and manipulating peers—parents, teachers, and counselors all have a role. We can teach girls to interrupt malicious gossip. Peers do have the power to resist negative evaluations of others. Girls can be educated to take on this role, with role-playing and help in finding specific strategies for intervening in a negative spiral of discourse. In *Odd Girl Out*, Simmons (2002) concluded:

> Girls have a critical role to play in changing the culture of their cliques and friendships. After all, most of us hate this way of life. I can't count the number of girls who told me they'd rather be beaten up than ignored or cut down spiritually by their peers. We need to abandon the belief that doing this is natural or unavoidable. It isn't. We can change. (p. 252)

- *Combat Isolation.* Loneliness can be a marker or a cause of girls' vulnerability, but either way we need to be even more concerned about girls who are isolated and spend too much time alone. Girls need to develop and maintain social skills.
  - *Increase Belonging.* Provide multiple opportunities for girls to feel connected (Underwood, 2003). If girls in middle childhood and early adolescence affirm their own sense of belonging by social aggression, then one way to reduce it might be to offer multiple frameworks within which girls can be accepted. Girls who engage in a broader array of activities may have more venues for social acceptance. Too often, by middle school, girls feel as if there is only one possible group for them to belong to, and if they are not in it, they are doomed.
  - *Reduce Boredom.* Engage girls in more structured activities. Social aggression is also a consequence of boredom, and too much unsupervised time. Sports, drama, music, service organizations, and clubs may foster competence and growth and decrease social aggression.
  - *Depersonalize Competition.* Compared to boys, girls tend to be less experienced with competition and are less comfortable with negotiating rules and roles in organized activities (Underwood, 2003). They tend to take competitive behavior personally when playing games and sports. They are relatively unfamiliar with coping with winning and losing, so have more negative feelings in competitive situations. It follows that if girls had more experience in competitive organized activities, they might become more comfortable handling both these organized contexts and their friendship conflicts.
  - *Develop Defenders.* We can teach specific peers to actively defend victims. Research shows that there are many roles girls play in these interactions: assistant, reinforcer, defender, outsider, in addition to bully and victim (Underwood, 2003). Some adolescents naturally take on the defender role and, interestingly, they tend to be popular girls. We could foster their instincts to interrupt social aggression.
  - *Face It.* Address social aggression when you see it, even as part of therapy. Help girls understand and name it. Don't ignore it just because no one has a broken bone. This means calling attention to social aggression in casual conversations with girls,

helping schools develop more detailed antibullying policies, guiding parents, and providing girls with skills and resources to find another path. Our individual and cultural tolerance for indirect aggression fosters its expression.

— *Support Mean Girls.* As we go deeper in understanding the significance of social aggression, we learn that it may not always be maladaptive. Is a girl tough in order to survive a hostile environment, or is it the only way she has available to be visible and accounted for? Was she a victim before she became a bully? Relational aggression can serve a girls' important needs. Be sure that you have thoughts about how she can meet these needs in other ways.

— *Question Categories.* Explore these false dichotomies of good and nice girls versus bad and mean girls. Make room for all of the other ways of being in the world. Help the girls you treat become more three-dimensional in their own minds—not just victims and bullies, real and fake, sweet and spicy. When they speak with confident voices, they are much less likely to fall back on exclusionary categories that artificially inflate their sense of belonging. Have conversations with them about how limiting this discourse can be for all of us.

In reality, relational aggression is a social and cultural issue that is associated with many, if not all, other disorders with which adolescent girls struggle. As such, it can be viewed as an underlying current running beneath the range of both internalizing and externalizing behavior problems. Therefore therapists need to keep intervention for relational aggression in mind even as they treat other disorders.

Attention Deficit Hyperactivity Disorder

Kim has a wonderful imagination. As a little girl, her room was a virtual horse world, filled with little plastic stables, jumps, and other horse paraphernalia. She lives in a rural area and she's been riding and working in the barn practically since she could walk. She's a great stable worker, strong and energetic. In the early grades in school, Kim's report cards would mention that she sometimes seemed a little "dreamy," "absent-minded," "forgetful," and "spacey." She'd do all right on assignments, and she's always been very likeable, never a behavior problem at all. The general consensus has been that she just didn't try hard enough. By high school, Kim's grades began to sink, even though she continued to be an able horsewoman, and a fun and creative friend. Teachers began to treat her like a slacker, and lowered expectations and levels of classes. Though she seldom read, she enjoyed writing stories, and made plans for going to college, in spite of her dislike for school. At home, though, she mostly just watched television. Her parents decided to get Kim evaluated for a learning disability. They couldn't understand why such an obviously bright and inventive girl was doing so poorly. The test results came back unequivocally: Kim had ADHD-Inattentive Type. She was referred for medication and therapy. It seemed like a miracle: the next semester, her lowest grade was a B, and she was becoming more cheerful and confident by the day.

ADHD is the diagnostic label used to describe children who exhibit developmentally extreme levels of inattention, or hyperactivity, or both. As with disruptive behavior disorders, most of the research (and concern) about ADHD focuses on boys and includes very few girls in the discussion. As a result, much of what we know about ADHD is based on how it shows up in boys' troubled behavior patterns. There are only a few exceptions to this limited perspective (Biederman, Kwon, Aleardi, & Chouinard, 2005; Nadeau, Littman, & Quinn, 1999); efforts to understand girls are increasing but only in recent years. Importantly, current research on girls demonstrates that they may be significantly underdiagnosed for ADHD.

The prevalence of ADHD in the general population has been estimated at about 3 to 7%. But male to female ratios vary widely, ranging from 9:1 to 2:1 (American Psychiatric Association, 2002; Biederman et al., 2005). Prevalence estimates are inconsistent for many reasons, including the use of different criteria, methods of data collection, source of information, symptom threshold parameters, and sample characteristics. Studies have variously used parents, teachers, doctors, and children, both alone and in combination, as primary informants to make the diagnosis (Jackson & King, 2004). But girls with ADHD have gotten precious little of this scholarly focus. Related to this lack of research interest, girls with ADHD have also received much less clinical attention than they deserve.

Reasons for Underdiagnosis

- Girls are more likely to be inattentive than hyperactive (Biederman, Mick, Faraone, & Braaten 2002); they may just seem "spacey."

- ADHD in girls is less likely to be associated with problems in school, or a learning disability in reading or mathematics (Biederman et al., 2002). Therefore, school-testing referrals may not include questions about attention.
- Girls may have fewer attendant behavior problems, working hard to hide their problems in school and to conform to adult expectations.
- Girls are often diagnosed as anxious or depressed; they may also have ADHD.
- Bright girls compensate longer, thus managing until the expectations bar gets raised much later in high school. Highly intelligent girls with ADHD can be the most difficult to notice until they can no longer manage the level of organization and planning required by the upper grades.
- Questionnaires used to screen ADHD emphasize "boy" symptoms of hyperactivity, impulsivity, and defiance.
- People tend to think of ADHD as a boy problem; four to five boys continue to be referred for evaluation for every girl. Recent research confirms the idea that disruptive behavior disorders drive referrals in pediatric ADHD, leading to a disproportionate number of evaluated and diagnosed boys (Biederman et al., 2005).

Nadeau (2005) describes the three types of ADHD as they appear in girls who may have ADHD: "Tomboys," "Daydreamers," and "Chatty Kathys." She notes that hyperactive girls are often called "tomboys" (although certainly not all rough and tumble girls are hyperactive). These ADHD "tomboys" like to be on the go, take more risks, and enjoy competitive sports. Although they may not have major behavior problems, they may be very disorganized, rush around, and keep their rooms and possessions in a mess. Parents and teachers may not suspect ADHD, seeing them as immature, undisciplined, and just not academically inclined.

"Daydreamers" with ADHD are inattentive, shy, and quiet (Nadeau, 2005). Teachers may not notice their inattention in class because these girls do not make a scene. They may even seem to be listening while their minds wander away. But they can be very anxious about school because they don't focus and miss so much. They are forgetful and disorganized in completing their work, and fret as deadlines approach. Daydreamers with ADHD have trouble completing assignments; they may stare into space when they sit at their desks unless a parent or teacher keeps them on task. Nadeau notes that these girls often also have symptoms of depression and anxiety, and, because they seem spaced out, may appear less intelligent than they really are. Kim was a daydreaming girl.

The "Chatty Kathy's" with ADHD are both inattentive and hyperactive. They have more energy than the daydreamers but do not necessarily take the risks that "tomboys" do (Nadeau, 2005). Nadeau noted,

> Often these girls are hyper-talkative, rather than hyperactive. They are "silly, " excitable and overemotional. They chatter constantly in class and have trouble staying quiet even when they are disciplined for talking. They interrupt others frequently and jump from topic to topic in conversation. (p. 3)

Yet it should also be noted that these same girls are often social leaders. They can be lots of fun to be around. They're exciting, energetic, have lots to say, and may use humor to mask their problems.

Help Making the Diagnosis

The best way to diagnose ADHD is to gather data from many different sources, using both interviews and questionnaires. Take a detailed developmental history, and talk to parents, teachers, friends, and girls themselves. If you are not in a situation where you can make this diagnosis, you can still gather some information and share it as part of your referral. Make sure you look more closely at inattention as opposed to pure hyperactivity. To help you decide if a more thorough evaluation is warranted, you might consider asking some ADHD-type questions, noting that the more affirmative responses you get, the greater the likelihood of a problem. These responses alone are insufficient for a full diagnosis. You can ask:

- Does she fail to give close attention to details?
- Does she make lots of careless errors in her schoolwork?
- Does she seem to be daydreaming when spoken to?
- Does she have trouble following through on instructions?
- Does she have inordinate difficulty organizing tasks and activities?
- Does she talk excessively? Does she interrupt, blurt, or intrude on others?
- Does she lose things necessary for completion of tasks or activities?
- Is she easily distracted? Do people say she's "spacey?"

- Is she usually late?
- Does she wait until the last minute to begin tasks and assignments?
- Does she have rapid and drastic mood changes? Does she overreact?
- Does she struggle to remember what she read?
- Does she have trouble falling asleep and waking up?
- Is she impatient, easily frustrated, and repeatedly surprised that she's "messed up again?"
- Does she fidget, doodle, and seem restless? Do people say she's "hyper?"

Reasons for Concern

Girls with undiagnosed ADHD have additional, compounding problems as well. You may be inferring a possible ADHD diagnosis from these other concerning behaviors, Remember that it is common for these girls to be viewed as space cadets, airheads, and mediocre, unmotivated students. The long and intensive academic day is a tremendous challenge for them just to survive, much less be able to excel at academic work. They may also have trouble sticking with extracurricular activities. Consequently, their self-esteem takes a hit all around; they don't have the extra support to study subjects that hold little intrinsic interest, or to develop special talents and passions. They then may feel like quitters and doubt whether they have the ability to succeed at much at all.

The social impact of ADHD can be significant all the way through childhood, but it tends to be greatest in high school as girls attempt to function more autonomously. The ways in which they feel and behave "differently" may show up more at a time in life when fitting in can be paramount. Girls with ADHD are susceptible to dangerous or self-destructive behavior because they may be impulsive, and the desire to fit in can be very compelling.

Girls with ADHD may be at particular risk for sexual acting out and substance abuse (Nadeau, 2005; Wilens et al., 2002). They may be more likely to become pregnant (Arnold, 1996), and to seek sexual attention to compensate for feelings of inadequacy elsewhere in their lives. Since they tend to behave impulsively and may have added trouble planning, they're also vulnerable to making poor choices about partners and maintaining adequate protection from pregnancy and STDs. For similar reasons of impulsivity, risk-taking, and social anxiety, these girls also have a higher risk for substance abuse and other addictive behaviors (Biederman, Faraone, Mick, & Williamson, 1999).

Further, girls with ADHD have an increased difficulty meeting social expectations. Consider the constraints on ways that girls are expected to be tidy, controlled, passive (feminine), sensitive and compliant, and then imagine how ADHD might interfere with each and every one of these ideals. Most girls with ADHD are aware of how popular girls behave, but they just can't deliver that level of self-control. This knowledge contributes geometrically to their anxiety and despair. Similarly, they may seem relatively immature in their social and emotional skills; pressure to behave in a mature, responsible fashion can feel hopelessly overwhelming. They just may not have the executive functioning to maintain the level of self-control of their age peers.

Girls with ADHD tend to be highly reactive. They feel things intensely and instantly. With hormonal fluctuations in the mix in adolescence, the tendency toward emotional dysregulation is even greater for these girls. They may strike out impulsively when their feelings are hurt, perhaps overreacting and making thoughtless observations. These girls also may get over it faster, and are ready to forgive and forget soon after the dramatic episode is concluded. The emotional roller coaster they are on can be very hard to live with.

Intervention

- *Educate.* Explain to parents, teachers, and girls about ADHD and how it shows up differently for girls. Teach them about how it affects their lives, and reassure them that there are many strategies and supports available. The diagnosis of ADHD can itself be therapeutic because it provides an alternate explanation for problem behavior. Make sure parents and adolescent girls avail themselves of a growing body of information, in books and on the web, about girls with ADHD.

- *Discuss risky behaviors.* Make sure parents are on board with open discussions about safe sex, the risks of pregnancy, expectations about smoking, drugs, and drinking. Support them all in keeping her safe.

- *Build significant structure into a girl's day.* Such structure can include, for example, lists, reminders, schedules, calendars, assignment books, palm pilots, study spaces, and increased adult presence. Basic behavioral techniques help to reduce tension and conflict and clarify expectations and consequences but they need to be realistic for parents to enforce, too. Family therapy can help parents:

— Make sure rules are clear.

— Make sure rewards and penalties are clear.

— Provide a consistent schedule at home for meals, study time, television, and other activities.

— Provide warnings before transitions (do so in therapy as well).

— Encourage the use of self-time out, provide girls with a way to retreat if they feel that they are going to have a meltdown.

— Find alternatives to arguing.

— Explain goals and ideals to keep the "big picture" in mind.

— Break large tasks down into smaller, very concrete tasks.

— Give frequent praise and feedback for attempts to get it right.

• *Teach self-soothing strategies.* ADHD feels emotionally overwhelming, no matter what subtype a girl may have. Girls need to learn stress management techniques. They should be encouraged to give themselves down time to regroup after they have pushed themselves. Remember that the reactions of a girl with ADHD can be even more extreme during times of stress, fatigue, hunger, or PMS. They have an added vulnerability that makes the emotional roller coaster seem like a particularly wild ride.

• *Develop executive functions.* ADHD is associated with significant deficits in executive functioning, including for example: shifting from one mindset to another; organization and planning; working memory; and separating emotions from thoughts (Reid & Krasnegor, 1996). If girls are amenable, CBT techniques can help modify and provide insight into these problems with EF. Notably, it can also provide these girls with improved cognitive coping strategies. They can benefit from modifying and altering their self-defeating and inaccurate attributions about why they struggle to function, and coming up with more productive and affirming alternatives.

• *Make sure girls have islands of competence*—sources of pleasure and pride in their lives.

• *Provide coaching* (or help the family find a coach). Hallowell (1996) talks about "HOPE" coaching as another important treatment strategy. The acronym helps describe the steps that a coach/therapist might follow:

H stands for *Hello*: get her attention. The girl needs to focus at the start.

O means *Objectives*: ask for three main objectives for the day (or week). This question helps girls set priorities, making goals more attainable.

P looks for *Plans*: find out what her plans are for achieving these objectives. Stating what the plans are also increases the likelihood they will be accomplished.

E is for *Encouragement*: end the coaching session by providing extra support to counter all of the negativity a girl with ADHD receives from the environment and also herself. Hallowell calls this encouragement "An injection of positivity." (p. 111)

- *Refer for a medication consult.* While not all girls with ADHD require medication, many benefit from having it as an adjunct to therapy and increased external structure of their lives. But note that medication without modifications in the environment and better coping strategies is much less effective and not recommended. Girls with (and without!) ADHD need to learn how to have better problem solving and self-soothing abilities; medication can help but can't give girls skills and structure in their lives.

- *Add supports for more stressful days of the month.* Recent research suggests that girls with ADHD have a tougher time managing the hormonal shifts associated with their menstrual cycles (Nadeau, 2005). In such girls, PMS increases the intensity of emotional reactions, irritability, and frustration. Medical and psychosocial interventions to help with the hormonal swings can also be helpful.

Oppositional Defiant Disorder

Monica is 16 and she's in nearly constant trouble at home and at school. Her parents have raised four other children, and they seem to have run out of steam with Monica. They say they've "tried everything" and "nothing works" to keep her in line. If they ask her to do anything, the discussion usually devolves rapidly into a shouting and swearing match—on both sides. Monica stays out as late as she likes, even though the family's apartment is in an impoverished and dangerous area, and sometimes gets high before getting on the bus in the morning. Her friends are older; many are dropouts. When she gets to school, she doesn't do much work, and talks back to the teachers. She's now in a special school for adolescents with behavior problems because her public school felt she was too disruptive. She's disrespectful, but to her way of thinking, she hasn't had many adults in her life who have acted in ways that merit her respect, nor has she gotten much herself.

Monica also has a learning disability that makes school tough for her. She fantasizes about the day she can be on her own if her parents would just sign her out of school. She's angry and irritable about all the impingements on her freedom, but she has little in the way of plans or expectations for herself and how she might survive without her parents and school to help her. Surprisingly, she really seems to like therapy (though it is true also that she gets out of school to see me); she uses our time together to describe the dangers and injustices of the week. She problem solves like a much younger child, and much of her mouthiness seems like bravado covering anxious and confused thinking.

Oppositional Defiant Disorder (ODD) describes a series of behaviors that characterize many adolescent girls—arguing with adults, losing their temper, deliberately irritating others, being spiteful and vindictive, being actively defiant and noncompliant with rules, being easily annoyed, being angry or resentful, and blaming others. To earn the diagnosis, girls must show this recurrent pattern of negativistic, defiant, disobedient, and hostile behavior toward authority figures for at least six months—though they need just four problems from the list to fit the diagnosis.

ODD is one of the more controversial diagnoses. The debate about ODD is clouded further by the fact that relatively little is known about girls with ODD (and disruptive behavior disorders in general). A large body of research exists, but almost all of the literature describes male, or mostly male, samples (Kann & Hanna, 2000). In contrast to rates of relational and overt aggression, which show robust gender differences across childhood and adolescence, rates of oppositional behavior show only limited (in favor of girls) or non-significant gender differences in most studies (Bierman et al., 2004; Zahn-Waxler, 1993). Both adolescent boys and girls can be oppositional and defiant to adults.

There seem to be three perspectives on ODD. The first view is that it is a serious disruptive disorder, not as severe as conduct disorder (CD) but on the continuum and worthy of its own behavior category, Untreated, it too is associated with numerous risky outcomes, leading to a lifetime of social dysfunction, antisocial behavior, and poor adjustment (Kazdin, 1995).

The second perspective is that ODD is frequently a misdiagnosis of another problem. For example, physically and sexually abused girls often act out in a variety of ways and so are diagnosed as oppositional-defiant instead of traumatized (Chessney-Lind & Belknap, 2004). Similarly, adolescents with attachment difficulties stemming from loss and dislocation are also apt to behave poorly with adults, and are frequently labeled with ODD. In such cases, interventions are potentially motivated less out of concern and empathy than from a need to get behavior under better adult control. There is also a strong correlation between ODD and other internalizing disorders in girls, suggesting that symptoms of anxiety, depression, and bipolar disorder can also show up as adolescent girl defiance (Costello, Mustillo, Erkanli, Keeler, & Angold, 2003). For example, Stark, Dempsey, and Christopher (1993) found that depressed adolescents were not often just angry and irritable, but also demonstrated, "negativism, uncooperativeness, sulking, a belligerent attitude . . . [and] . . . decreased academic performance, social withdrawal, antisocial behavior, and increased drug and alcohol use" (p. 116). These teens could readily have an ODD diagnosis, too.

The high degree of overlap between ADHD and ODD further suggests that many girls with oppositional behaviors may have, at their root, untreated attention difficulties (Kruesi et al., 1992; McMahon & Wells, 1998). Indeed, it is often only when a girl with ADHD acts out that her attention deficits are detected. Thus, some clinicians note that when adolescent girls become disruptive, they may really be expressing some other underlying problems through these more observable symptoms.

The third viewpoint goes a step further and holds that there is really no such thing as ODD; it is the invention of drug and insurance companies, treatment facilities, and disengaged adults. Mike Males (1999), one of the severest critics of ODD, says it should be called "Kids with Insurance Disorder," or "Not Getting Along with Affluent Parents Disorder." Breggin and Breggin (1995) further noted that ODD is also suspect in that it is characterized by symptoms that are more upsetting to others than to the adolescent with the diagnosis. They state: "The 'illness' consists of being disruptive to the lives of adults—a definition that seems tailored for social control" (p. 56). From this perspective, adolescents are referred for treatment when they are annoying or disruptive to caretakers who aren't doing their jobs well.

Such critics suggest that such diagnosis and "naming" of problems is significant not only because it leads to potentially life-transforming interventions like placement and medication, but because it creates a stigmatizing label that diverts our focus and blame onto the adolescents where it may not belong. As Ballou (1995) has pointed out: "Naming is a powerful act. Naming clinically defines and directs attention to certain things and away from other things" (p. 42). Those who argue that there is no such thing as ODD maintain that poor parenting and lousy environments are often the unnamed source of distress. And for girls who have a cultural mandate to behave in a "ladylike fashion," ODD labels may be rendered as another method of silencing them.

But the more fundamental problem underlying the debate about ODD is the failure to evolve a diagnostic system that accounts for either gender expectations or child development. Nowhere in the diagnostic nomenclature is an adequate explanation of the difference between "misbehavior" that is the result of intentional, planned acting out, and an adolescent's lack of particular developmental skills. The abilities to self-regulate, self-soothe, and control impulses require both biological maturation and social conditions that help a girl learn and practice such abilities. As in Monica's case, unreasonable expectations, insufficient resources, inflexible and coercive adults, stress, and anxiety can all lead to problem behaviors and insufficient opportunity to learn about other ways of being in the world. Girls who end up oppositional and defiant may have good reason for it. And if the interventions that follow from the diagnosis are punitive or sedating, they miss the developmental mark entirely.

And it is hugely evident that sexism, ageism, and racism all contribute to disruptive behaviors in adolescent girls, but these "isms" have no place in our labeling system. Thus the ODD diagnosis is particularly onerous because it may individualize a problem whose origin is so clearly socially constructed. The implications of this for adolescents of color are of particular concern, black girls (and boys) with a diagnosis of ODD are more frequently punished in the legal system for their misbehavior without regard for its cause (Porter, 2005). Diagnostic schemas that insure positive interventions rather than punishment and incarceration for poor and minority girls have yet to be developed.

Whether or not we agree on the specific diagnosis for a girl who acts out, we still need to help her (and her family) handle the conflict in a more constructive manner. And such interventions need to follow from general practice and good sense because there are no published interventions to date that are designed specifically for girls with ODD, although boy programs abound (Kann & Hanna, 2000). It appears that some combination of individual, group, and family therapy along with connections to school and community are most beneficial for ODD adolescents as a whole (Hanna, Hanna, & Keys, 1999). Before you do anything, think about *why* a girl is behaving so badly. Consider:

- *Development:* Are expectations for behavior commensurate with what she has the skill and maturity to deliver?
- *Parenting:* Is she going toe-to-toe with an equally inflexible or immature adult? Is there any adult presence in her life that can help turn it around for her?
- *Environment:* Is she doing what she can to survive intolerable discrimination and adversity? Are there resources to support better behavior?
- *History:* Is there a history of traumatic events that would cause her to defend herself from intimacy?
- *Other diagnoses:* Is the oppositional behavior a symptom of depression, anxiety, ADHD, or some other emotional, learning, or social problem?
- *Family problems:* Is she acting out distress, like marital discord, that needs attention?

Remember that your intervention will follow from your understanding of the problem; do not assume a girl chooses to misbehave. While that level of premeditation is possible, it is much less likely than an ODD diagnosis would suggest. Further, any positive, or at least neutral, reframe of motivation can help families respond differently to the behavior. As ODD expert Ross Greene (1998) observed: "If you interpret a child's behavior as planned, intentional, and purposeful, then labels such as 'stubborn,' 'manipulative,' 'coercive,' 'bratty,' 'attention seeking,' 'controlling,' 'resistant,' and 'defiant' will sound perfectly reasonable to you, and popular strategies aimed at motivating compliant behavior and 'teaching the child who's boss' will make perfect sense" (p. 14). Adolescent girls act out for a myriad of reasons; it is our job to help them (and their parents) understand what these reasons may be.

Intervention

Individual Connection

As with all adolescent girl treatment, a compassionate style is essential for work with ODD girls. They will seek to control you, and the relationship, expecting and setting up familiar negative patterns of interaction. Your ability to manage angry, frustrated, and defensive countertransference to foster a safe and supportive connection is more than the prerequisite for treatment—it may very well be the ingredient missing in her life. The temptation with these girls (and the implicit or explicit request from parents and others) is to help police them by setting up tighter behavioral consequences, and "working on" their failures from the week. Girls with ODD features can be empathic challenges for us. A successful therapy begins with our ability to see the world through their angry, frustrated, and disappointed eyes.

Cognitive Problem Solving

Within the context of a safe and supportive relationship, most girls with ODD benefit from the process of developing better social problem solving skills. Their provocative strategies often stem from developmental skill deficits—they don't know how to behave otherwise, even if they would want to. Thus, therapeutic techniques, including modeling, practicing, rehearsing, and role-playing, help girls learn new strategies for managing social situations. Girls can learn how to behave better through understanding and developing the skills involved in positive interactions.

Social Skills Training

Some girls also may benefit from structured group therapy as an adjunct to individual work, where they learn and practice clear and assertive methods for interacting with others in the context of peer engagement and reinforcement. Whether the cause of their social deficit is trauma, inexperience, or some other problem, it is generally the case that girls with ODD have immature and ineffective strategies for making and sustaining friendships. Girls who are socially successful feel more competent and act out less.

Parent Training.

Many researchers maintain that disruptive behaviors in the home are maintained by maladaptive interactions between parents and children (Kazdin, 1995). Parent training has a vast literature supporting its use;

however, it tends to be more effective in changing management styles with younger children. Parents of ODD adolescents tend to be less motivated and more hopeless about being effective. One technique, "The Three Baskets" has proven useful; it is taken from Ross Greene's (1998) work with ODD children.

- *The Three Baskets.* Arguably, families with oppositional adolescents do better with everyone in the room learning how to change how they handle interactions at home. Still, many parents benefit from support in changing patterns of responding to their daughters. Most fundamentally, they need to learn how to pick their battles. Greene (1998) described several strategies for parents of younger defiant children that translate up in age reasonably well. One of the most effective is teaching parents how to pick battles in a more systematic manner. Parents learn to decide in which of three "baskets" to place problematic adolescent behavior. "Basket A" has the fewest concerns, and is nonnegotiable. Here, parents are encouraged to select matters of health and safety, for example; the very few issues that are worth the most ugly fights. However, parents should only use Basket A if they have a good ability to enforce the limits they set. For example, parents may want to establish rules about smoking or drug use, but can only maintain these in the home. In such cases, they need to be encouraged to use Basket B for these issues.

  Basket B is particularly important for adolescent girls; it includes issues that are very high priorities but are best resolved by communication, negotiation, and compromise instead of parental edict. For some families, Basket B issues might include, for example, curfews, chores, family activities, mealtimes, room cleaning, and religious activities. These are items that matter, but aren't life-or-death concerns.

  The truth is that both parents and their ODD girls usually have terrible negotiating skills. You can help improve their communication strategies as part of your individual and family work with them. Be aware though that such parents often have trouble with the idea of reaching solutions this way. They'll need support and education in letting go of struggles and the need to exert parental authority as a matter of course. It is hard for some to concede the principle that children "should" just obey their parents. Once they decide that an issue is not Basket A material, though, they need to make a conscious decision if they want to either negotiate Basket B) or give it up (Basket C); the overarching idea is *not* to precipitate a huge conflagration (what Greene calls a "meltdown" in younger kids — this can be descriptive for some adolescent girls as well).

Basket C is for any issue that can be taken off the agenda for a while, matters that ultimately aren't worth fighting about, or even struggling and negotiating over for a time. Poor eating habits, messy rooms, even homework can go into Basket C; parents might be encouraged to ignore swearing and bedtimes, too. The point of loading baskets B and especially C is to reduce frustration on both sides, and to develop better communication in the home. With less conflict, and improved negotiation skills, families have the chance to develop more adaptive and enjoyable ways of being together. Reinforce the idea with parents that they are not "giving in" but just exerting parental authority in a more judicious and effective manner.

You can also help them find and notice times when the conflict in the home is reduced; suggest to them opportunities for more positive interactions in the course of the week. For example, Monica and her father started going to the dump together on Saturdays as they had when she was little. Monica and her mother had an occasional movie night where they watched scary films and sat close together on the couch. These were small changes but they helped to turn around the momentum somewhat in the home.

Family Therapy

It is often useful to weave family therapy with individual work as adolescent girls will tolerate. You will have to be fairly heavy-handed in early family sessions, managing the flow of information like an air-traffic controller. You may want to set ground rules that include a "speaking stick" — only the person holding it can talk—and direct people to deliver negative messages to you, and positive information to each other. You can also end sessions, or ask some people to leave if you feel the struggle is escalating too rapidly. Make sure you have a very small and rehearsed agenda for the session, so that people can accomplish something in it.

For example, you may want to have separate meetings with the adolescent and the parents to decide what topic needs family time. Discuss what their positions will be, and get a sense of the direction of the session. For example, if the topic is curfew, find out what the parents' bottom line is going to be, and where there might be some negotiating room (e.g., weeknights versus weekends, or going out with a specific plan versus hanging out). Tell the family at the outset of the meeting that you will be keeping the discussion to the specific agenda, and then make sure you hold them to it. Encourage patience if possible, and notice any positive steps. Parents of ODD adolescents tend to be at the end of their ropes by the time they seek therapy; they may not be very invested in it. But they need to engage to the extent they are capable, and everyone benefits from a little encouragement. This means dads, too. Benevolent father involvement (if it is possible to cultivate) can make all the difference in a successful course of treatment with these girls.

Coaching/Mentoring

Girls with ODD often respond most defiantly with their parents and may be able to develop less adversarial relationships with other adults. In keeping with the spirit of the TEAM approach outlined previously, girls with ODD sometimes thrive with a coach or mentor who can help them with some of the policing of homework and expectations while parents are learning better strategies. Girls with ODD need more adults in their lives, and their parents need more support from the community to keep them safe. As described earlier, a mentor can be a Big Sister, a coach, a youth worker, a tutor, an older peer, or someone who is good at what a girl likes to do. Girls also find coaches or mentors in former babysitters, aunts, family friends, and teachers. Coaches and mentors for girls with ODD function as special friends, encouraging positive risk-taking, appropriate choices, and self-development. They may also serve from time to time as a mediator between the girl and her family. Whether or not these mentors serve in some formal way on a treatment team, their established presence in girls' lives can make a big difference in supporting the goals of the treatment—helping girls feel better and behave more competently.

Changes in School

While some oppositional girls do well in school and then melt down when they get home, more commonly, they are relatively unsuccessful in that environment, too. If you are treating a girl for ODD who is doing poorly or failing in school it is quite possible that she is struggling with undetected attention and learning problems. Are there parts of her education a girl enjoys and can do well in? Should she be in harder or easier classes? A different type of school? Vocational instead of college courses? Does she need more individual time in the day with a safe school person? Sometimes girls come home from school so miserable and frustrated, they blow up when they walk in the door; we need to help ameliorate such situations.

Medication

While there is no medication for a problem that causes other people, more distress than the patient, it is, as has been discussed, quite common for girls with a diagnosis of ODD to have other problems, too. For example, a depressed girl who is sleeping poorly is likely to be quite irritable. Medication that helps her depressed mood, may also make her easier to live with. Similarly, girls with untreated ADHD can seem disrespectful and agitated. Make sure you look beneath the ODD to determine if there are some underlying issues that might be addressed by medication.

I Love Your Spirit, Let's Work on Your Style

Ultimately the fact that girls are fighting can be a fabulous sign; it means they believe they are worth fighting for. Even though parents might be skeptical while in the fray, it is always better for girls to be defiant than hopeless. Emphasize to girls that their feisty spirit is admirable. You do not want to send one more silenced woman out into the world. But tell them that your job together is to work on their style. They need to develop a way to get their message across more clearly and with less strife. This is where a good supportive and problem-solving therapy can make all the difference.

CHAPTER ELEVEN

TROUBLED BEHAVIORS V: SEX, CONDUCT DISORDERS, AND SUBSTANCE ABUSE

Girls seem to be acting out more and getting into more trouble than in previous generations—even as they face many of the same pressures to conform and behave as we did in our youth. But there has been so much media hype about the more severe forms of girl misbehavior that it is now hard to sort through the hyperbole about what is really going on. Is girl violence really catching up to boys' violence? Is promiscuity happening earlier and in epidemic proportions? Are girls abusing more drugs at younger ages, too? The spate of "bad girls" books that have recently been published, along with numerous newspaper and magazine articles suggest that we have a rampant societal disaster on our hands—which we appear to be mostly wringing and waving about in an almost titillated response.

Yet, at the same time as the popular press is busy tarring an entire generation of girls for their sex, violence, and drug use, the U.S. Centers for Disease Control and Prevention (CDC) issued its 2005 national report on youth risk behavior, and arrived at a very different conclusion about the very *same* concerns (National Youth Risk Behavior Survey; YRBS). This study examined the risk behaviors of 14,000 high school students and compared the data to students in the early 1990s, noting significant *improvement*. The lead researcher concludes: "We're very encouraged about the progress we've made during the past 15 years in decreasing the prevalence of health-risk behaviors. . . . The most encouraging news from the 2005 YRBS has been the overall improvements over time in risk behaviors related to *sexual activity, injuries and violence, and tobacco and alcohol use*" (italics mine; U.S. Centers for Disease Control and Prevention, 2006).

Yet these actual findings have not done much to quell the popularly held images of adolescent girls being increasingly wild and out of control.

Thus while this chapter will address treatment for the troubling problems of sex, conduct disorder, and substance abuse, it will also necessarily explore how and why these issues appear to be so vexing for adults in our current social climate. And even though it is arguable that treating severe acting out is still high-stakes work, we need to be able to tailor our interventions to reflect the experiences of the girls themselves, considering also their developmental levels, family expectations, and community resources.

Sex

Charlotte is 16 and she's in her first real romantic relationship. She loves Jeremy, who's basically a good kid if not at her level academically. They've been spending practically all their free time together, and her grades are slipping in the critical junior year of high school. Charlotte's mother calls me worried that Charlotte is obsessed with Jeremy, and that she'll become sexually active before she's ready. The three of us meet to discuss what it means to "be ready" and whether Charlotte's mom gets to decide this for her daughter. They have an unusually open relationship, and Charlotte listens in a kindly fashion to her mother's concerns. Even so, it is clear that Charlotte will decide for herself when and if she wants to have intercourse with Jeremy. Charlotte comes to see me a few months later, and she's devastated. They did, as seemed likely, become more sexual. But then, Jeremy "got all weird," and broke up with her. She says she didn't enjoy the sex with him anyway, but she missed their other kinds of intimacy. She expresses disappointment that there was so much hype about sex that didn't come near her expectations for it.

There is virtually nothing written about therapy with adolescent girls for sexual problems. Indeed as Deborah Tolman (2001) has wryly noted, "female adolescent sexual dysfunction is an oxymoron" (p. 197). Most of the time that adults consider sexual acting out to be an issue, we are talking about the social and physical consequences of girls' bad choices and not the complexity of these decisions for the girls. We are not, by and large, thinking much about girls' sexual feelings or about the ways they are learning about their bodies and their sense of sexual agency, which severely limits our conversations with them. Good treatment needs to make room for both the complexity of the choices girls are making, and the consequences of these choices.

Sexual Activity of Adolescent Girls

Most of the survey data collected describes the activity of adolescent girls over the age of 14; there is relatively sparse statistical information available about the sexual experiences of middle school-aged girls. Still the most recent survey from the National Center for Health Statistics provides some interesting and even surprising information about adolescent sexual behavior in the 15- to 19-year group (Mosher, Chandra, & Jones, 2005). These data suggest that girls are actually engaging in later and better protected sexual activity than 10 years ago. Many of our fears and wild anecdotes about girl sexuality are unsupported by actual data.

Even now, in the 21st century, we continue as a society to struggle with extreme binary boxes into which we must fit complex biopsychosocial phenomena such as adolescent female sexuality. At the most basic of these forced-choice scenarios, we depict, for example, boys who are out-of-control predators and girls who must defend their bodies, without acknowledgment of their own sexual interest. In this construction, girls have a lousy choice — they must either disregard their own desire or risk too much. Dangers that sexually active girls face include, for example, violence, pregnancy, disease, ridicule, and ostracism. By contrast, there is relatively little corresponding downside for boys becoming sexually active.

The different trajectories for sexual development between boys and girls have led to the "two cultures of childhood" (Maccoby, 1998), one where boys are groomed for sexual entitlement, and girls are acculturated into a strange dance that seemingly includes both sexual accommodation and "sexual gatekeeping;" they're also responsible for controlling their own and their male partners' sexual behaviors. The old double standard seems to have diminished precious little. And it requires that girls explore their sexuality from within an impossible bind: they need to be simultaneously passive and actively resistant. No wonder so many girls we treat express confusion and guilt about how to handle their sexual feelings.

An interesting and growing body of literature discusses and deconstructs this stultifying heterosexual paradigm (Brown & Gilligan, 1992; Fine, 1988; K. Martin, 1994; Muehlenhard & Peterson, 2005; Tolman,

1994). These writers persuasively argue that, in adolescence, girls learn to look at, rather than experience, themselves. They know themselves from the perspective of men (or the dominant culture, or patriarchy) and lose touch with their own bodily feelings and desires. The cultural strictures are echoed by parents and peers, in schools, and in the sex ed curriculum where girls are taught more about male libido than about their own sexuality. These researchers further suggest importantly, that if an adolescent girl can be fully present in her sexual experiences and choices then she has a higher level of agency in her whole life. The ability to make responsible and self-affirming sexual decisions is, in fact, a central factor in competent and integrated adolescent identity.

But as Michelle Fine (1988) argued almost two decades ago, there has been little space in the discourse for girls' pleasure. This striking omission seems readily associated with the abject failure of abstinence programs. Interventions that strive solely to delay or prevent sexual intercourse are likely hindered by the fact that girls also perceive correctly that there are also overwhelmingly positive aspects of sexual experience.

Desire

Anyone who spends a few minutes with adolescent girls knows that their hormones are in operation, that they are feeling new and compelling needs in their bodies that are sources of great interest and excitement. This new awareness and identity of sexual being is not a big part of sex education in school, though among peers it may be discussed in great detail. This emerging aspect of identity is complicated by the dual experience that girls have of being both the object of, and the subject of sexual desire. Fine (1988) wrote:

> The adolescent female rarely reflects simply on sexuality. Her sense of sexuality is informed by peers, culture, religion, violence, history, passion, authority, rebellion, body, past and future, and gender and racial relations of power. The adolescent woman herself assumes a dual consciousness—at once taken with the excitement of actual/anticipated sexuality and consumed with anxiety and worry. While too few safe spaces exist for adolescent women's exploration of sexual subjectivities, there are all too many dangerous spots for their exploitation. (p. 35)

As Fine clearly describes, girls have few places in which they can begin to unpack and make meanings of all of the complicated and conflicting sexual feelings that they have. Therapy can be a unique experience for them if it provides the space and opportunity for them to develop their own stories about how they feel.

Ambivalence

However, these narratives will invariably hold multiple forms of ambivalence; there is no way, culturally speaking, that they can fail to do so. Imagine trying to sort through sexual arousal and attraction, but also feelings of guilt, and fear of harm to one's public image. Or maybe sexual activity will enhance this image, but the risk of pregnancy and STDs is great. Maybe sexual intimacy will bring a relationship closer, but there is always the possibility, as for Charlotte, that it won't.

There are many forms that ambivalence can take. Thus when we begin to enter the subjective world of adolescent girls, desire is only one experience they may have, and it will likely be hemmed in by numerous other conflicting feelings. Girls can both want and not want to engage sexually, or want the sex but not the consequences (pregnancy, disease, a bad reputation), or want the consequences (a relationship, satisfying the desire of a boy, avoiding conflict) but not the sex, or even want the sex but not consent to it (Muehlenhard & Peterson, 2005). When we ask girls (as many researchers and clinicians do) if they wanted to be sexual, we may be missing the opportunity for a much deeper and more nuanced dialogue about what we mean by "wanting."

Even more confusing for girls, and related to the whole disturbing topic of date rape, girls frequently engage in consensual unwanted sex, and in nonconsensual wanted sex, too. Impett and Peplau (2003) confirm that women too frequently have consensual unwanted sex, perhaps to avoid relationship tension, or to promote intimacy. However, it seems likely that there is not much room along the continuum between unwanted consensual sex and unwanted coercive sex for many girls. Thus it can be troubling for girls to stand up for what they do or don't want when there are so many impingements on simple desire.

One of the defenses in date rape cases is frequently that the victim "wanted" to have sex. However, this doesn't mean that girls are ambivalent, and here the line *is* clear: It doesn't matter if she *wanted* sex; if she did not *consent*, then it was rape. We need to help girls distinguish for themselves the difference between wanting and consenting (Muehlenhard & Peterson, 2005). This distinction also helps to clarify the confusion and self-blame felt by too many rape victims.

Girls and Oral Sex

Parents and educators frequently express concern about the reported rise in oral sex among schoolgirls. In the late 1990s, as if we didn't have enough to worry about already, the media began to stir up a huge hype about young teenagers and their seemingly rampant interest in fellatio. This fascination (perhaps via some prurient interest in our former president) seems to be traceable to a 1999 cover story in *The Washington Post* that ran under the headline, "Parents Are Alarmed by an Unsettling New Fad in Middle Schools: Oral Sex" (Stepp, 1999). The article featured alleged parties in a suburban school where boys and girls engaged in heavy petting and oral sex. This same piece discussed reports received "through the student grapevine" of fellatio in a hall at school and even on a school bus. National survey data indicate that, in fact, only 4% of adolescents 13 to 14 years of age report engaging in oral sex, and only 25% of 15-year-old girls report engaging in oral sex. The overall percentage increases dramatically, as expected, with age (Mosher, Chandra, & Jones, 2005). Among adolescents also, there is a greater gender balance for both giving and receiving oral sex than commonly believed. There is also room in these data to wonder about the reporting veracity of younger teens; boys report overall more oral sex experience than girls do, but *both* boys and girls were more likely to report receiving oral sex than giving it.

These data, along with plain common sense, indicate that the exciting story is based almost entirely in unfounded hysteria. Alas it has since been reified on Oprah, with discussions of "rainbow parties" where 8th grade girls wearing different colors of lipstick supposedly took turns servicing the same boy, and then this titillating little "news" item was rehashed repeatedly in other print and electronic media, too. There has been precious little documentation ever presented to support any aspect of this so-called news, which on the face of it appear ludicrous, with all due respect to studly 13-year-old boys and the nonsmudge lipstick industry. And what are we to make of the percolating adult anxiety suggested by it all?

Parents naturally want to protect their daughters from exploitation, but overworry about oral sex itself may not be the best place to start. This is not to trivialize the sexual victimization and exploitation of girls (at the root of too much early sexual behavior for girls), nor to minimize the fact that early sexual activity will likely not help their self-esteem or development. Still, it is hard to see how adolescent girls will ever benefit from a portrayal as either wild sex vixens, or helpless victims of boy desire as the current popular objectified discourse would have it. And as the data suggest, it is very unlikely that the "problem" of teenage oral sex is increasing anyway. Thus, good parenting, like good therapy, focuses on safety, choices, and the real, whole girl in conversation.

Sexual Orientation

Awareness of sexual orientation frequently emerges in adolescence. In one large-scale study, 88.2% of 7th to 12th grade students described themselves as "mostly or totally heterosexual, 10.7% as being "unsure" or "questioning of their sexual orientation, 0.7% as bisexual, and 0.4% as mostly or totally homosexual. The percentage of students who were "unsure" declined steadily with age, from 26% of 12-year-olds to 5% of 18-year-olds (Remafedi, Resnick, Blum, & Harris, 1992). In a related exploration of adolescents and young adults ages 14 to 21, Rosario et al. (1996) concluded that the average age girls are certain they are lesbian is 15.9 years (the average age boys know they are gay is a bit younger: 14.6 years). These data are complemented by the survey results of the National Center for Health Statistics; 11% of girls in the 15 to 19 age group claimed to have had same-sex encounters (Mosher, Chandra, & Jones, 2005).

Despite the possibility for exploration and some fluidity in sexual identity, the transition to adolescence for most girls (and boys) is typically the time of entry into the institution of compulsory heterosexuality (Thorne, 1993). Therapist assumptions of heterosexuality make it harder for girls who are thinking and feeling otherwise. The problem of not expecting deviation from gender norms is compounded by the fact that when girls are not perfectly straight, too many of us have a limited understanding of either the process of self-discovery or the possible outcomes and variations in experience.

We typically begin treatment expecting a girl to be interested in boys, to want to look and act feminine, and that she will have a female gender identity. We may share a cultural misunderstanding of these three different aspects of gender: gender identity (female, male, transgendered), sex typing (feminine, masculine, androgenyous, undifferentiated), and sexual orientation (same sex, other sex, both sexes). These three aspects are independent of each other (Basow & Rubin, 1999; Bem, 1993; Brown, 1995). Masculine females can be heterosexual and lesbians can have a female gender identity and feminine personality traits. Of course, most girls don't have all of these distinctions sorted out before therapy begins. But if they're questioning, or bisexual, or lesbian, or feel transgendered, or masculine, or androgenyous, our heterocentric line of inquiry will be frustrating at best—and probably disrespectful and alienating.

The emergence of a lesbian or bisexual identity is an ongoing process, rather than a single event, and discussions with girls need to be open to this exploration. Assumptions that girls will want to be sexually attractive to gain boys' attention may be implicit in our thinking and inquiry. Such bias will short-circuit open dialogue with girls who are learning that they do not necessarily follow the dominant culture's sexual scripts.

And notably, retrospective accounts from lesbians often indicate that they felt "different" even before adolescence, though these feelings increased over their teen years (Savin-Williams, 1995). While verbal, physical, and sexual harassment of lesbian students is widespread in U.S. high schools, "coming out" can also be associated with feelings of positive self-worth for girls. In fact, girls who know they are gay at an early age may have particularly high self-esteem (Savin-Williams, 1995). The important bottom line here is not to imagine that the old hetero stories apply, and to enter into the conversation with a girl in such a way that all of her possibilities can be explored should she want or need to talk about them. For example, if you're talking about sexuality, you can ask, for example:

- Are there any boys—or girls—that you've been interested in?
- Have you given thought to your sexual orientation?
- Do you think of yourself as all female, or do you have some more boyish traits, too?
- How comfortable are you with being a girl?
- What is the attitude in your group about lesbians and gays? Do you feel safe exploring these aspects of your identity?
- How would your parents react if they knew we were talking about gender identity and sexual orientation?

Sexual Violence

Good decision making is supported in part when we help girls develop the radar and strategies for coping with unwanted sexual activity, so that, to the extent it is possible, they can realize and refuse it. Particularly for younger adolescents, there is ample evidence to suggest that the line between sexual activity and sexual assault is not as clear as we might think. For example, the Alan Guttmacher Institute (1994) reports that "some 74% of women who had intercourse before age 14 and 60% of those who had sex before age 15 reported having sex involuntarily" (p. 22). Another related factor here is coercion by an older male. The power differentials in these relationships with adult men are inherently abusive even when girls do not perceive them as such. With girls, our assessment of safety in sexual situations is paramount. Our work strives to empower girls to make good decisions. But we must also move in as best we can to protect them when they are unable to make their own safe choices.

Of course, such shielding is not always possible. Some girls have no one looking out for them—parents, child protection, school, and community have all let them down. And despite our best efforts, they remain vulnerable to exploitation until they, too, come to believe they deserve to be safe, or act out in ways that require adults to respond and contain them.

Pregnancy

Teen pregnancy is another hot-button topic for adults, and therapists who treat adolescent girls with any regularity are sure to encounter it, or at least a share of anxiety about it. It is notable that in this area, too, that there has been such a marked decrease in the face of popular belief to the contrary. Between 1988 and 2000, the rate dropped by 22%, and, more importantly, fell by 28% since peaking in 1990 (Alan Guttmacher Institute, 2004). Similarly, the abortion rate has declined dramatically in this same period of time, falling from 46 to 33%—a decline of more than one quarter (Alan Guttmacher Institute, 2004). Though even with the lower incidence, the United States still holds the dubious honor of having the highest teen pregnancy rate of all developed countries.

Therapists need to know the facts about pregnancy, contraception, abortion and STDs. We're not expected to be expert in sex education, or to lecture girls, but such knowledge can be useful in guiding thoughtful discussions with them. Despite getting most of their information from peers, and being a little vague on key details, they frequently think they're better informed than we are. Sometimes they are, which can be awkward at best.

Unprotected teen sexual activity that leads to pregnancy (and STDs) is a major concern because it creates so many tough choices at best, and potentially so many increased developmental and health risks for both the girls and their babies. But the problem of pregnancy that has changed is not, as is commonly believed, the increase in adolescent parenthood but the rate of *single parenting*—at all ages. And here the problem becomes more one of poverty itself than pregnancy and early childbearing.

Currently, unintended pregnancy and teen parenting are mostly issues for poor urban adolescent girls who may lack a sense of social or sexual entitlement, are less apt to use birth control, and who hold traditional notions of what it means to be female (Basow & Rubin, 1999; Fine, 1988). Adolescent girls who devalue their abilities, or whose perception of their economic and social situations becomes the basis for hopelessness, may be more likely to yearn for or accept pregnancy as a means toward satisfaction and achievement than do other girls (Basow & Rubin, 1999).

The real incentives for girls to delay pregnancy and childbirth—having a realistic chance of going to college or otherwise sharing in the national wealth—do work. As Marion Wright Edelman, former president of the Children's Defense Fund is often quoted as saying, "The best contraception is a real future." The lowest fertility rates occur among black and white adolescents who have the best alternatives to motherhood, including education, employment, and economic independence (McBride-Murray, 1996).

But the sad fact is that it is a lie to tell a poor young woman (white or black; two thirds of teen mothers are white) that she should wait to have children, work hard now, and then she'll be better off in a couple years. A teenager who has a baby is usually hugely disadvantaged already. Early childbearing may make a bad situation worse, but it doesn't cause the despair and poverty in these girls' lives. Socioeconomic status is particularly relevant in any discussion about early childbearing because low-income mothers may see few options for identity development beyond motherhood.

Therapy for adolescent girls should venture further into discussions about pregnancy risk and outcome than it typically does. These conversations will have many component parts. Indeed they tap into the deepest realm of a girl's identity, capacity for being planful, and sense of personal agency.

At the most fundamental level, a girl has to face the fact that she will be sexually active. This foresight may be difficult for her due to ambivalence, limited ability to imagine the future, and outright denial. Along with this, girls have to understand how to prevent pregnancy (and STDs) and have access to adequate contraception. Further, the possibility of pregnancy needs to be personalized so that she can see clearly the ways it would be a negative event for her (especially for girls who say they *want* to get pregnant). The perceived costs—emotional, familial, relationship, economic, health, educational, developmental, social—need to be discussed in detail, so the girl can fully weigh these (each time she considers being sexually active) against the annoyances and costs of using birth control. And, for those girls who believe that a baby will love them and solve other problems in their lives, these discussions need to be affirming and persuasive in even larger ways.

It is helpful, of course, to get parents on board, at least generally, before we have these discussions with their daughters. The point here is not to undermine parental authority, or to keep parents out of the discussion as an operating principle. But we'll sometimes risk the ire of parents, who for religious, moral, or personal reasons do not want their children discussing sex in therapy. On these life-transforming (or imperiling) topics, we still need to weigh carefully our own responsibilities to our adolescent clients. As in so many areas, the lack of knowledge about pregnancy prevention is lack of agency, too.

So despite discomfort (parents', girls', and our own), forge ahead on the topic of girls' sexuality. In therapy we need to convey several messages: that girls have the right to be healthy, sexual beings, to set sexual limits for themselves that are respected by their partners, and to make informed decisions. In order for this to happen, we must begin to equip girls with knowledge about sex, help them explore their own attitudes and values, and teach them the behavioral skills they'll need to protect themselves.

Intervention

- Talk with girls about the range of reasons to have sex, to not have sex, to be ambivalent.
- Ask for very concrete details—who, what, where, when, what happened next, how was she feeling? Don't assume you know anything.
- Do not frame the discussion in terms of sexual intercourse, because sexuality is not an event but a fluid and multidimensional part of a girl's identity.
- Help her sort through her underlying needs—including desire—but also how sexual intimacy may be used to increase self-esteem, combat loneliness, fulfill her sense of what it means to be a woman,

express anger, alleviate boredom, become dissociated, keep a boyfriend, or just to be held.

- Even apart from their own desire, girls may be in a double bind—to be simultaneously passive and actively resistant—make sure your discussion has room for confusion and guilt too.

- Explore her meanings—how she explains and thinks about sexual acts and sexuality, and help her make sense of her decision-making process before she chooses to be sexual.

- Explore your own values about this, your squeamishness—girls are frequently more matter-of-fact about all of this than we are.

- Don't be afraid to give advice, based on what you hear from the girl's ambivalence, "Well it could be fun, but afterwards you might not feel so great about hooking up." "The way you're talking about this, you sound so much less important than he does." "It sounds like part of you isn't so sure about this. I'm very curious about how that part views your plans." "Remember last time how you were really sad when we talked about this?" "Tell me the arguments pro and con: what would make it a great choice or a disaster?"

- Don't be judgmental. Frame your reactions: "Here's what I think . . ." "It's your choice, of course, but . . ." This is what I imagine will happen if . . ." "This makes me wonder . . ." "How about this idea . . .?"

- Make sure you know some basic facts about sex, reproduction, and STDs, birth control, and local culture—especially what her parents value and peers expect.

- These conversations are essential even if they can be hard to have for good reasons. Girls need a place to explore their attitudes and beliefs about sexuality. They need to be taught specific methods to resist unwanted sexual advances and they need an opportunity to practice these skills in an unthreatening situation.

- Talk about agency and choices with girls. Find out how they think they hold power in their sexual decisions, even if it seems to you they seem to be taking risks and ceding control.

- Don't assume heterosexuality.

- Make sure the girls you treat also know about pregnancy prevention and STDs.

- Encourage parents to learn about and understand adolescent girl sexuality to the extent they are willing and able.

Conduct Disorder

Allie tells me that her first memory is from age 3, eating pudding from a spoon that was burnt on the bottom from cooking crack cocaine. Her mother still drinks and uses drugs and doesn't care what Allie does with her time. Allie's father is very strict and physically punishing when he's around. But he has outside girlfriends, and he comes and goes. He expects her to take care of her little brother if he's not there. Lately she's refused; it's not her job. Allie is on probation for assaulting two girls, landing one of them in the hospital. She also went after the arresting officer who could have pressed additional charges. She was high when she was fighting, but claims she would do it again if she felt she had to.

Allie's been expelled from her regular public school for truancy, hitting a teacher, and getting into fights with peers on school property. She attends a collaborative school a couple of times a week, when she's not too tired from staying out. Allie shares her mother's drugs and alcohol, and skips the mandatory urine tests with no seeming consequences. Her probation officer has a hundred other cases, many more severe than Allie's; she appears to be invisible to the system. No amount of acting out or probation violations seem to have any effect on adults who might remove her to a more restrictive setting. Allie comes to speak with me one Friday when a dangerous young man in her neighborhood has threatened her life. She is scared to go home and uncertain about how to proceed. She is, characteristically, unwilling to consider any of the safety plans that I come up with. Her vulnerability makes her even more defiant, even as she asks for help. Her mother comes to get her so she doesn't have to walk home alone. It won't keep her safe all weekend, but it's the best we come up with for the time being.

Conduct Disorder (CD) is now the second most common of psychiatric diagnoses for adolescent girls (Loeber, Burke, Lahey, Winters, & Zera, 2000) with prevalence rates varying from 0.8% to 16% depending on the study and sample (Zoccolillo, 1993). Adolescents with Conduct Disorder display a persistent pattern of violating the rights of others and accepted social norms and rules. There are two types, distinguished by the developmental period when behaviors appear. The childhood-onset type (before 10 years) is much more common in boys, and typically features much more overt and confrontational antisocial behavior along with early diagnoses of ADHD and ODD. The adolescent-onset type (after 10 years) is more common in girls, and is associated with fewer aggressive and confrontational behaviors.

These gender differences have led some researchers to suggest that girls who develop antisocial behavior may follow a "delayed-onset pathway" (Silverthorn & Frick, 1999). In this schema, CD girls have many of the same developmental vulnerabilities and environmental stressors as boys, but don't evince antisocial behavior until later. It is also worth noting that children with adolescent-onset CD usually have a better prognosis than children with childhood-onset CD (Bloomquist, 1996).

It is widely agreed that boys are more heavily involved in serious antisocial behavior than girls, regardless of time of onset of CD. Epidemiological studies fairly consistently conclude that conduct disorder is evident in boys four times as often as it is in girls (Cohen et al., 1993). Even so, recent research and policy is increasingly focused on girl aggression and violence (Artz, 1998; Garbarino, 2006; Odgers & Moretti, 2002; Silverthorn & Frick, 1999) and the different developmental problems for CD boys and girls (Moffitt, Caspi, Rutter, & Silva, 2001; Putallaz & Bierman, 2004). Interestingly, one review of the literature concludes that girls who commit offenses similar to those of boys are much more likely to be referred for psychiatric treatment (as opposed to being routed through the criminal justice system) and are then disproportionately diagnosed with CD (Hartwig & Myers, 2003).

It is difficult to make sense of all the conflicting reports of increasing antisocial behavior in girls, with researchers contending that it is both overreported (Males, 2006) and underreported (Delligatti, Akin-Little, & Little, 2003). Researchers speculate about how similar behaviors in boys and girls (e.g., displays of anger, nonempathic responses, fighting) may get noticed and reported differently in the community. Gender differences in socialization and aggression that lead to a male bias in the actual diagnostic criteria for CD (with more items tapping direct aggression) also contribute to the confusion.

There are notable differences in the trajectories toward CD for boys and girls. For example, some of the life events that lead to antisocial acting out appear to be different for girls (e.g., severe physical and sexual abuse), and the kinds of behaviors they evince that are of concern also tend to vary from the more violent presentations of boys. Indeed, it is important to keep in mind, even with the evident prevalence of girl CD, that girls continue to be way more likely to be victims than offenders and are quite underrepresented as perpetrators of serious forms of overt aggression. They are also much more likely to have other mental health disorders. For example, in one study comparing male and female juvenile offenders, the prevalence was 84% of girls with other diagnosed disorders versus just 27% for boys (Timmons-Mitchell et al., 1997).

Still, so many popular books are now published about the rise in girl aggression; the idea of female brutality seems to have gained the momentum of a true urban legend. And while troubled girls may be exhibiting distress in significant ways, their violence is *not*, as we commonly believe, dramatically increasing. In fact, as Males (2006) has argued vehemently to the contrary:

> FBI and BJS reports show that girls' rates of violent felonies have been declining since 1995, as have their rates of murder and robbery since 1993 and school fights since 1992. Girl murder and robbery arrest rates stand at their lowest levels in 40 years. . . . The argument that girls are more violent rests on the decade-old increase in girls' assault arrests. . . . If more arrests for assault prove that violence is rising, then mothers are becoming violent twice as fast as their daughters. . . . The past assault arrest increase among girls that [recent authors of books on girl aggression] trumpet actually occurred among both sexes and all ages and tracked stronger policing of domestic abuse. (p. 34)

Thus most girls who meet criteria for a diagnosis of Conduct Disorder (CD) do so without exhibiting violent behavior. To be CD diagnosed, a girl must demonstrate the presence and persistence of at least three of these 15 behaviors: physical fighting, destruction of property, telling lies, running away from home, truancy, stealing (with or without confrontation with a victim), bullying, carrying or using a weapon, setting fires, breaking and entering, cruelty to people or animals, violating parental curfews, and forcing sex on someone.

Studies show that, from this list girls with CD most commonly exhibit the following behaviors: lying, truancy, running away, and stealing without confrontation (Loeber et al., 2000; Zoccolillo & Rogers, 1991). Compared to other girls, girls with CD also report more violent behaviors, but they are still less violent than CD boys. In most samples, even when these girls have delinquency charges and arrests against them, only a very few will have been convicted of serious offenses (Loeber et al., 2000; Moffitt, Caspi, Rutter, & Silva, 2001; Zoccolillo & Rogers, 1991). It is much more common that girls with conduct problems will enter the legal system as "status offenders;" that is they will have gotten in trouble for behaviors that would be permissible if they were over 18 years of age. For example, "running away," a very common indicator of female CD, is called "traveling" when an adult does it.

And girls with CD may or may not be adjudicated as delinquent; girls get this diagnosis when they have engaged in antisocial acts for six months whether or not they have been arrested. Conversely, a girl who commits a delinquent act may or may not meet the full criteria for CD.

Although the research on boys with CD is vaster, we now know a fair amount about the causes, effects, and treatments for girls with this disorder. And we also know that the diagnosis is associated with serious problems over a longer haul; untreated, these girls are likely to struggle even more as adults. Compared to girls without CD, girls with CD are more likely to be suicidal (Chesney-Lind & Shelden, 1998), and to engage in early sexual experimentation (Acoca, 1999). They will also have higher school dropout rates, criminality, greater difficulty in obtaining and keeping jobs, more relationship and marital problems, and a higher incidence of substance dependence, depression, and antisocial personality disorder (Bardone, Moffitt, Caspi, & Dickson, 1996; Moffitt et al., 2001; Zoccolillo & Rogers, 1991).

They are also more likely to become poor parents: to choose an antisocial mate; smoke and use substances during pregnancy; be less sensitive to their infants; more irritated by normal infant behavior (e.g., crying); to continue to smoke and use substances; to provide less stimulation to their young children; to remain poor; to have multiple partners in the home; and to be harsh and inconsistent with discipline. Zoccolillo, Paquette, Azar, Côté, and Tremblay (2004) provide a more thorough description of parenting liabilities in women who had a CD diagnosis as adolescents. The disorder itself seems to create the very conditions necessary for the disorder to rise again in the next generation. Thus effective therapy must take into consideration the entire biopsychosocialcultural spectrum of factors that may contribute to it.

Biological/Familial Influence

CD has been described as a familial disorder, probably with both genetic and shared environmental effects (Rhee & Waldman, 2002). Genetically informative studies (of twins and adopted children) have consistently demonstrated a heritable component to CD (Rutter, 2001). But these data are confusing: how do we interpret an adolescent's "risk" for CD, if one or both of her parents also carry this diagnosis? Some researchers suggest that even one symptom of parental CD may increase the probability of poor child outcomes (Loeber et al., 2000; Robins & Regier, 1991). For now, this question of nature versus nurture cannot be answered. Though as with much in psychology, the conclusion is likely to include an ongoing interaction between biology and environment.

It does seem likely that some children are more vulnerable to poor parenting than others. For example, CD is more common in children with learning and attention problems, limited cognitive abilities, and other "internalizing" problems like anxiety and depression (Bloomquist, 1996). But for girls, the problems of vulnerability are frequently compounded by high rates of physical, sexual, and emotional abuse (Acoca & Dedel, 1998). Thus they may be particularly at-risk if they have individual and familial risk factors exacerbated by traumatic exposure.

Parental psychopathology also clearly contributes to the development of CD; these girls overwhelmingly tend to have parents with emotional and behavioral problems of their own. Other common family and environmental characteristics include: fathers with antisocial characteristics, mothers who are depressed, and one or both parents with substance abuse issues. The range of predictable other stresses are altogether common for many childhood problems: financial difficulties, marital and relationship problems and poor parenting practices (i.e., ineffective, coercive, harsh, and unsupportive) (Bloomquist, 1996; Zoccolillo et al., 2004). In numerous studies, girls with CD are found to come from significantly more chaotic families than similarly diagnosed boys (Chamberlain & Reid, 1998; Henry et al., 1993).

Other Factors

Girls who are vulnerable to CD also have increased risk due to problems with peers, schools, and communities. It is widely noted that adolescent girls who show antisocial behavior tend to associate with deviant peers (Dishion, 2000) and have adopted a set of values that define antisocial activities as appropriate. Their friendship styles encourage or mutually reinforce delinquent behavior, and the quality of these friendships is marked by higher levels of conflict, jealousy, impulsivity, anger, and competition (Chesney-Lind, 1998; Colder & Stice, 1998). Girls with CD may also have endured significant peer rejection; if they are socially isolated, they may seek out other marginalized adolescents for company (Katz,

2000). Perhaps not surprisingly then, effective interventions for CD girls need to help them develop and maintain peer relations with nonmarginalized or delinquent age mates, and create environments for them that promote social competence.

Schools also pose risks for girls vulnerable for CD. School-related risk factors include attending school where little emphasis is placed on academic work, poor physical condition of the school building, and infrequent use of teacher praise, low teacher expectancy, and teacher unavailability to deal with students' problems. Teachers may also overlook some of the early problematic behavior in girls, including escalating relational aggression, before it develops into CD (Delligatti, Akin-Little, & Little, 2003). Apart from the seemingly intractable correlations between these factors and poverty schools in general, there are still points for intervention.

For example, vulnerable girls benefit from opportunities for greater attachment and connection within the school. These alienated girls need more adult involvement, and more positive interaction within the school day. A school psychologist, a special teacher, a nurse, or a social worker might provide such contact and guidance, offering a little encouragement and support.

The communities of girls with CD tend to be less amenable to intervention, offering still more of the deleterious and grinding effects of poverty on development and opportunity. In this vein, CD girls tend to come from more urban settings, where neighborhoods are distressed and disorganized (Katz, 2000). There are typically insufficient social supports and available activities for youth are sorely lacking. Stressed communities don't create CD in girls, but they may well compound feelings of anger and disconnection in girls already vulnerable to it.

Intervention

Many interventions for CD adolescents target cognitive and social risk factors (Dodge, 1993), and parenting practices—helping parents manage adolescent behavior and helping adolescents and parents communicate more clearly (Patterson, Reid, & Dishion, 1992). These strategies likely have limited long-term efficacy for a variety of reasons, including the fact that the etiology and maintenance of CD is multidimensional, linked to characteristics of adolescents, family, peers, schools, and neighborhoods (Conger, Reuter, & Conger, 2000; Keiley, 2002). For this reason, treatments that target the entire family, and the larger systems around the family, often yield more encouraging results.

And as discussed, CD in adolescent girls is further complicated by other problems, particularly trauma, and frequently includes other internalizing disorders such as depression and anxiety. Thus, treatment of girl CD requires thorough diagnosis and a broader ecological and systemic framework for interventions.

Four levels of outpatient intervention in some combination are efficacious for treating children with CD: Individual therapy, parent training, family therapy, and home-based interventions (Kazdin, 1998). None of these has been designed specifically for adolescent CD girls. However, taken together, these strategies have substantial track records for efficacy with CD adolescents in general (Kann & Hanna, 2000; Kazdin, 1998; Kernberg & Chazan, 1991).

Additionally, social and problem-solving skills groups also have significant theoretical support. Girls who are socially competent have opportunities to develop and expand their social skills with nondelinquent peers. Further, girls who have access to environments that promote prosocial behavior are much less likely to exhibit CD behaviors in the present and after they become adults (Weissberg, Caplan, & Harwood, 1991). Thus group interventions for adolescent girls that improve their ability to make and sustain friendships, and include more socially adept peer models, hold some promise as part of a menu of multisystemic interventions.

Out of home alternatives should also be considered when outpatient care does not change the symptomatic adolescent and her family. We have a vast array of out-of-home alternatives to consider that may be more effective, at least over the short run (e.g., therapeutic foster care, residential treatment, hospitalization). These alternatives are discussed in detail in Chapter 13.

Within the individual and family therapy you may be providing, consider these more specific strategies:

- Explore themes in individual treatment with CD girls including: the meaning of intimacy; conflict and its resolution; experiences of self; anger; fear and intimidation; self-worth; goals and aspirations; growing up female; role models; and friendships (Artz, 1998). Make sure when you talk about a girl's anger you are also empathically connecting with the underlying hurt she may feel for the suffering she has endured.

- Increase resilience and competence. The vulnerability of girls with CD is often overlooked. Interventions should strive to increase resilience to counterbalance so many risk factors in these girls' lives: positive attention, improved relationships with at least one caregiver, other caring adults outside of the home, confidence and optimism, improved self esteem through competence in an identified area, social cognitive abilities and improved executive functioning, external stimulation, structure, support and monitoring, and community activities (Rutter, 2001).

An interesting new holistic model of treatment of CD girls that focuses more on developing such protective factors is called The Wheel of Wellness (Hartwig & Myers, 2003). This model is based in Adlerian theory and draws from multiple disciplines. The Wheel of Wellness describes five life tasks that are fundamental for a healthy life: spirituality, self-direction, work and leisure, friendship, and love. Myers, Sweeney, and Witmer (2000) describe four phases of intervention using this treatment approach: introducing the model and defining wellness for the particular girl; assessing her wellness in the five areas; implementing a treatment plan by identifying the areas to work on; and evaluating short- and long-term progress.

The Wheel of Wellness allows for a girl's own sense of meaning to emerge, incorporating both her values and her cognitive style (Hartwig & Myers, 2003). It also permits individual tailoring of intervention to the specific environment and therapeutic paradigm. For example, it is possible to maintain a wellness perspective while integrating CBT and interpersonal strategies. It has advantages over models that focus exclusively on pathology and weakness, and offers instead a proactive, rather than a reactive, approach to CD behavior:

- *Keep a sense of humor.* Girls with CD tend to have tough lives, without much levity or fun in them. Humor is a way into greater intimacy that therapists might consider under the circumstances. Find opportunities to laugh at yourself, and at the craziness of life—not, of course, at the girl or at others.
- *Keep it simple.* Don't ask or explain anything that takes more than a sentence or two if you want to stay connected. Girls with CD will not stay tuned to complicated questions or, god forbid, long lectures.

- *Avoid power struggles at all costs.* Research shows that defiant adolescents arouse in adults frustration, resentment, callousness, disgust, apathy, and abhorrence about the adolescent's activities and beliefs (Hanna & Hunt, 1999). Your countertransference needs close monitoring with girls with CD who may perceive that pushing you away serves them best. Some strategies for avoiding power struggles include:
  — Prevent a struggle by predicting one.
  — Tell the girl how you're feeling, praising her for getting you so frustrated.
  — Ask her for advice on how she manages herself so carefully. You can say, "You're great at reading me. Are you as good with other people? How do you do it?"
  — Apologize for pushing too hard, and tell her you're going to try harder to help her.
  — Use your sense of humor to laugh at the absurdity of the situation.
- *Don't believe the apathy and disengagement are real,* but honor their presence in the room. Acknowledge that she isn't entirely invested in therapy, and that at least a part of her doesn't want to spend seemingly useless time going over a painful and upsetting history.
  — *Do persona work.* When you make room for the part that doesn't care, also open the discussion so you can get to know other "parts" of a girl. Tell her, "We all have different parts that feel differently and behave differently depending on where we are. I'd love to get to know the other parts of you." For example, you can ask, "I wonder if there's a part of you that's really mad about having all these appointments? Is there a part that feels sad that you're in so much trouble? Tell me about the part of you that protects your friends." Most girls are able to identify a few "personas." You can draw a diagram, with the girl's name in the middle, and the personas surrounding her core self. Then you can ask to speak to different parts and ask for their opinions.
  — *Externalize the "bully."* As with the externalizing exercises used by narrative therapists, you can also "name" the part of a girl that gets into trouble and thus diminish its' relative control over her life. Allie calls that troublesome persona of hers, "The

Hornet," and sometimes I check in to see how Hornet is feeling about her coming to me with worries she has. I also let her know when I think Hornet is setting up to sting me, and ask if I might speak to her "friend" part for a brief consultation on how to proceed.

— *Compare real self/fake self.* Another way into helping girls see that they are more complex and caring than they may first reveal is described by Hanna and Hunt (1999). This technique helps adolescents become more authentic and honest with themselves and in therapy. Draw two columns on a sheet of paper, labeling them "Fake Self" and "Real Self." Fill in the fake self column first, asking, "What do you want other people to believe about you?" Then after the girl generates a few responses (e.g., I can kick anybody's ass; Nothing hurts me: I can get any guy I want; I don't care what happens; I can handle the drugs I do), ask her, "What is really true about yourself that you do not tell anyone else?" She may then reveal the underlying doubts (e.g., Sometimes I get my ass kicked; I get really hurt when people let me down; there are guys who don't want me; I am unhappy a lot of the time; I'm scared by the times I can't remember what happened when I was high). Showing a girl that she is engaged in self-deception can be motivating. It can also allow you to help her see she has lots of ways of being in the world, and not just a single, exterior one.

— *Follow the story down the road.* Sometimes girls with CD spin stories that appear to be distorted or dramatized—if not outright fabricated. I used to challenge them with facts and logic of my own, but this method got them deeper into their defiant stance, and left me holding the doubt and pain for them. Now I don't worry about the truth of it as much; I want her to discover and hold her own ambivalence.

When you're following the story, you'll maintain a stance of admiration and curiosity. You can say, for example, "And then what happened next?" "Were people really scared?" "Wow, you really know how to handle yourself in tough situations." "Were your friends impressed with your reaction?" "You sound like you don't take 'no' from anyone!" "You *broke* a computer!?"

At some point, your questions can open the way for her ambivalence. Ask more detailed questions that get a bit underneath the text of the story. "So after you stayed out all night partying, how did you feel in the morning?" "What happened when you went to school?" "Could you understand what teachers were saying?" "Can you remember what you were feeling when you hit the policeman? Was part of you a little scared about what he might do?" "I thought you liked using that computer?" The point here is to use her own inflated narrative, shaping your questions to find the more genuine marginalized stories that are lurking below the surface. The goal is for her to own the whole story, including the parts of it that render her more vulnerable and doubtful about how she's proceeding with her life.

- *Talk about choices.* Girls with CD are often masters of externalization of blame and responsibility. Even when they are caught breaking rules, they can be quite emphatic about being framed, or victimized by someone else. When we tell girls they are making choices with their lives, we place the responsibility for self-control squarely back on their shoulders. We can say, for example, "Tell me about how that choice to skip school worked for you? Is there anything about it that worked? That didn't work?" "I'm glad you made the choice to stay in therapy today." "How did you make the choice to go out past your curfew knowing that probation might be checking up?" "When you go to the party tonight, will you choose to use drugs?"

- *Talk about freedom.* Challenge girls' willingness to cede their freedom to other people whom they allow to upset them (Hanna & Hunt, 1999). When a girl is becoming reactive to some perceived slight or injustice, say to her, calmly, "It's too bad that you don't have any freedom." If she argues or asks what you mean, reply, "I think that the other person/the situation is in control of your life right now, not you. If you react like this, it means they have control, not you." "If they can 'make you' this upset, then they have the control." You can practice and model self-control with her as she learns better strategies for managing her anxiety when she's feeling threatened.

It should be underscored that individual work with adolescent girls is just one part of a complete intervention that works for girls with CD. Keep in mind that changes in her environment—family, friends, medication, school modifications, community resources—will also be important to any extent they can be mobilized to support her. Girls with CD are *extremely* difficult to treat in the absence of these concurrent systemic interventions.

Substance Abuse

Stacey is a senior in high school and she's getting high on marijuana every day. She experiments with other drugs—prescription drugs like Klonopin and Ritalin, and street drugs like speed, cocaine, and LSD. She tells me she really likes cocaine and wishes it wasn't so expensive. She thinks it's an improvement over all the speed she was doing. It's more affordable, but it makes her sick. Stacey maintains the illusion that she's got lots of choices; what she uses, how much, and when, but I'm not so sure at all. Her parents know she's involved with drugs and they're worried, though they don't really know the extent of her substance abuse.

Stacey has a big group of friends who hang out in the park in the center of the small town where she lives, and drop in at the apartments of the few kids who are on their own now. They are all similarly disengaged adolescents, with lots of free time and seemingly little direction. But they support one another, and when she is having a bad day, or a drug-related problem, she feels like they "have her back" more than any adults would. The police know who Stacey is, as they do the other regulars in the park, but she has been able to stay mostly below their radar up until last month. At that time, she was at a friend's apartment with a large group of kids; neighbors smelled marijuana and called the police. Along with the other stoned adolescents, Stacey was arrested. Her parents then picked her up at the police station. They called me the next day. They're seriously contemplating mortgaging the house and "sending her to boot camp" depending on what happens with the litigation. Stacey hasn't yet had her day in court; it is likely that she will be put on probation but there is no certainty about the outcome. Even with the specter of possibly going to jail, or to boot camp, she is still unwilling to stop using.

Stacey's school attendance is also becoming a problem and she can't miss many more days without forfeiting the year. She says she would like to graduate, and seems dimly aware that a high school diploma might be useful down the line. Apart from her friends and her drugs, Stacey has few other interests or sources of pleasure in her life. She wanders vaguely into therapy sessions, and seems more like a lost 9-year-old in her concrete reasoning and bland, disorganized presentation. Stacey is a little frightened by the police involvement, and by failing in school. That's the total leverage I have at the outset. I'm absolutely thrilled when she agrees to "use a little less" as part of an experiment we'll do together. She says she's self-medicating for a "boring life," but doesn't argue when I tell her I'm betting she's an anxious and confused kid, too. She's considering going to a Narcotics Anonymous meeting also for our "research;" she'll go and tell me how she thinks she's different from the other adolescents who attend.

Adolescents have always taken risks, and so it seems safe to suggest that they always will. Neuroscience has even given us solid structural and biochemical explanations for the seductiveness of risks in general (and substance use in particular) for the adolescent brain (Spear, 2000; Strauch, 2003; Yurgelun-Todd, 1998).

In some ways, adolescent substance use also makes a great deal of sense in the absence of other rituals or markers that help children become adults. In the course of adolescence, a child's simple awareness of the present needs to metamorphose somehow into the more complex, multifaceted consciousness of the adult. In this light, the altered states of mind brought about by using substances (although perhaps not the only or preferred pathway) may even facilitate this transition.

Additionally, many forms of recreational drug use (for example, alcohol and cigarettes) are defined as legal for adults but illegal for adolescents, and adolescents who use such drugs may well perceive that they are progressing toward more sophisticated and adult social roles. Indeed it is plausible to consider that the combination of neurological vulnerability, developmental trajectory, and social press makes some experimentation with substances practically inevitable.

Moreover, throughout the world and history, humans have used drugs, with a vast range of intentions and benefits. True, drugs can be abused and this is cause for concern, but they can also be used without abuse. In fact, tobacco is the only drug for which abusers clearly outnumber users (Duncan, Nicholson, Clifford, Hawkins, & Petosa, 1994).

There are numerous studies concluding that some kinds of drug use are not inherently detrimental to adolescents and may, in fact, have some benefit. For example, Sheldler and Block (1990) compared the psychological health of adolescents who were abstainers, experimenters, or frequent users of illicit drugs. They found that experimenters were the psychologically healthiest of the three groups. Similarly, Clifford and colleagues (1991) described a curvilinear relationship between illicit drug use and a broad measure of life satisfaction, with the highest levels of life satisfaction among moderate drug users and lower levels of life satisfaction among both nonusers and heavy users. In still another much older, but interesting study, this one using college student subjects, marijuana users had better social skills, a broader range of interests, and more concern for the feelings of others than did nonusers (Hogan, Mankin, Conway, & Fox, 1970).

These reports underscore problems with traditional definitions of adolescent substance abuse that do not differentiate accurately between use and abuse. This failure to distinguish benign — or even beneficial — casual and experimental use from more serious abuse and addiction make it difficult to interpret accurately the data on the adolescent drug abuse problem. Further, as some policy experts have argued:

> . . . because most prevalence surveys do not measure harm but use, evaluating prevention programs as failures or successes using the criterion of an increase or decrease in the overall number of people using a particular drug may be fallacious. Logically, it is possible for user rates to increase while, via appropriate interventions, harm rates fall. (Moore & Saunders, 1991, p. 33)

Considerations about treatment and prevention need to accommodate a broader and more balanced understanding of the "problems" of adolescent substance use.

Definitions

Drug abuse can be defined as the use of a drug that causes adverse physical, psychological, economic, legal, or social consequences to the user or to others affected by the user's behavior (Rinaldi, Steindler, Wilford, & Goodwin 1988). However, the interaction between a drug and the circumstances around its use makes it difficult to identify the line between abusive and nonabusive use for all users. Numerous factors mediate an adolescent's response to drugs including age, sex, socioeconomic status, family support and distress, trauma, ethnic and cultural group, religious observation, types and combinations of use, levels of exposure, individual health status, and related risk behaviors, among others (Cheung, 2000; Poole & Dell, 2005). Most adolescents reduce their substance use when they learn their limits, get older, and begin to assume other responsibilities like work and parenting (Laursen & Brasler, 2002).

It is likely that, in fact, an adolescent's ability to use a drug in a con-trolled, nonabusive manner lies on a continuum. At one end, people are nearly helpless victims of the pharmacological properties of the drug, and for them use has become compulsive, uncontrollable, and problematic; users at the other end of the continuum are able to make informed choices, experiment judiciously, and weigh the benefits of the drug against its harmful consequences. Those who argue for this less dichotomized approach (Erickson, Riley, Cheung, & Ohare, 1997) look beyond the con-fines of the medical model to understand the range of ways that adoles-cents engage with substances.

Further, although the current clinical diagnostic system for substance abuse and substance dependence may assist clinicians in identifying ado-lescents with pathological patterns of substance use, the DSM-IV-TR cri-teria were developed for adults and have not even been established as ap-plicable to adolescents (Martin & Winters, 1998; American Psychiatric Association, 2002). Generally speaking, however, the clinical diagnosis of *substance abuse* requires evidence of a maladaptive pattern of substance use with clinically significant levels of impairment or distress. Impairment means an inability to meet major role obligations, leading to reduced functioning in one or more significant areas of life, risk-taking behavior, an increase in the likelihood of legal problems due to possession, and ex-posure to hazardous situations. *Substance dependence* requires a substan-tial degree of involvement with a substance as evidenced by the adoles-cent's meeting at least three criteria from a group of seven, such as withdrawal, tolerance, and loss of control over use (American Academy of Child and Adolescent Psychiatry, 2004).

Very few adolescents actually meet the DSM criteria for substance de-pendence. When asked about their reasons for use, adolescents talk about "numbing the pain of abuse and neglect," "being accepted," "peer pres-sure," "taking control of my own life," "for relaxation and pleasure," "chill-ing," "improving my self-image," "being curious, stressed or bored," and "asserting myself." (Laursen & Brasler, 2002). Girls tend to self-medicate with tobacco, alcohol, and drugs to improve mood, increase confidence, reduce tension, cope with problems, lose inhibitions, enhance sex, or lose weight (Poole & Dell, 2005). It seem clear that we need a better system for describing adolescent substance use and abuse, one that doesn't just downsize definitions of adult patterns.

Indeed, when it comes to helping adolescents, the current disease model that informs our definitions seems sadly limited in other ways, too.

It dichotomizes drugs into licit and illicit, or hard drugs (with abuse potential) and soft drugs (without abuse potential), or addictive and nonaddictive, or simply good versus bad. It creates absurd must-pick-one arguments also about whether adolescent drug use is just morally and legally objectionable, or a serious biologically based medical illness. Under this binary set of definitions, there is a unitary solution—abstinence.

This limiting and limited approach, which has featured dismal policy failures like the War on Drugs, Just Say "No," and highly punitive responses to drug users, has done little to stem adolescent substance use despite huge investments of federal funds. Many researchers have argued, on the contrary, that the traditional prohibitionist model is doomed by the arbitrary way drugs are divided into licit and illicit ones, the marginalization of drug users, straining of the criminal justice system, infringements on the rights of citizens, indirect sustenance of a black market, and ultimately the inability to curb the availability and consumption of illegal drugs (Erickson et al., 1997). Whether or not we fear there is also a biological basis to addiction, we need to employ definitions that are more inclusive of a broader understanding of adolescent substance use and abuse.

Indeed, other parts of the world have taken a more critical look at their drug policies and are working to establish criteria that the United States would also do well to consider. For example, in Great Britain, current debate centers on replacing the existing drug classification system with an "index of harms" that would include alcohol and tobacco, which cause significantly more risk and fatality than other drugs (Topping, 2007). The progressive policies of the Netherlands are also well known. The number of addicts in the Netherlands is low compared to the rest of Europe, and considerably lower than in France, the United Kingdom, Italy, Spain, and Switzerland. Further, Dutch rates of drug use are lower than United States rates in every category (Drug Policy Alliance, 2007). As the United States' war on drugs continues to yield less impressive results, we would benefit greatly from a comparable shift toward more promising harm reduction strategies.

Incidence and Prevalence

Ascertaining actual incidence and prevalence for different substances is complex, as is interpreting what the data mean at any point in time.

But the statistics provided by the Substance Abuse and Mental Health Services Administration (2006) provide one convincing thumbnail sketch. These data taken together suggest some very encouraging trends overall among adolescent substance use. They should also caution us against speaking too easily about an "epidemic" of adolescent substance abuse in this country; indeed rates have dropped significantly since their peak in the late 1970s (Johnston, O'Malley, & Bachman, 2003), and are now at the lowest point since then. Under 10% of all adolescents between ages 12 and 17 are now abusing drugs (Substance Abuse and Mental Health Services Administration, 2006).

This is not to trivialize the very serious problems that girls may have when their use does get out of hand, or in any way to endorse such use. But thoughtful intervention requires balanced comprehension of the problem within the culture. This means also that it should be noteworthy that for every measure of adolescent substance use, the incidence and prevalence patterns for adults are of significantly more concern. Indeed, if there is a drug abuse crisis today, adults are causing it, not adolescents.

Special Problems for Girls and Women

Women are particularly vulnerable to the physical effects of alcohol, tobacco, and other drugs. Although women in general have lower levels of use and problematic use compared with men for the majority of substances, it is well documented that they are at greater risk of developing health-related problems. Given the rates of use among youth for some substances and that adolescence is a time of brain and hormonal maturation, it is important to note that the consequences of substance use can have both short- and long-term effects for girls in particular.

Alcohol
Women develop alcohol-related liver disease earlier, and after a shorter history of use than men. Women who drink heavily are also at higher risk for hypertension, brain shrinkage and impairment, breast cancer, gastric ulcers, and osteoporosis (bone health in adolescent girls who drink is dramatically compromised). Even low-level alcohol use can disrupt normal menstrual cycles. Women risk having a child affected by Fetal Alcohol Spectrum Disorder due to heavy drinking in pregnancy. Notably, girls and women also have a higher chance than boys and men of being harmed by

others who are drinking (Emanuele, Wezeman, & Emanuele, 2003; Poole & Dell, 2005).

Tobacco

The numerous health risks of smoking—heart disease, respiratory diseases, cancer—are shared by men and women. Women get a different type of lung cancer than men, one that progresses more quickly. Women smokers are also more vulnerable to breast and cervical cancer. There is also extensive information available about the serious reproductive health consequences of smoking for women (British Medical Association, 2004). These include, for example, decreased fertility, early menopause, more symptomatic menstruation, and hormonal problems; women who use oral contraception and smoke have an increased risk of stroke and 10 times the risk of heart attack, compared with women who do neither.

Prescription Drugs

Women disproportionately use both prescribed and nonprescribed over-the-counter medications, including highly addictive antianxiety medications, tranquilizers, and sleeping medications, pain killers, antidepressants, and diet pills (Poole & Dell, 2005). Consequently, addiction and withdrawal symptoms are both significant concerns attendant on this higher level of use.

Illicit Drugs

Of reports about variations in drug effects that are due primarily to gender differences, it appears that Ecstacy causes more intense perceptual changes in women, along with impaired decision making and more long-term effects such as depression, mood swings, paranoia, and anxiety (Poole & Dell, 2005).

It should also be noted that women are at an increased risk of experiencing physical health complications from injection drug use (IDU), particularly blood-borne diseases. There is an ominous trend both in AIDS cases and HIV diagnoses among adolescent girls. For 2001, data show that of AIDS cases diagnosed in 13- to 19-year-olds, 48% were female; of new HIV diagnoses among 13- to 19-year-olds, 56% were female. While the majority of these cases were contracted through risky heterosexual contact, IDU was the second cause (Stewart, 2004).

The Trauma Connection

A strong connection between substance abuse and trauma for both ado-lescent girls and women is well established (Kendler et al., 2000; Najavits et al., 1997; Wilsnack, Vogeltanz, Klassen, & Harris, 1997). Recent brain research on women with histories of sexual abuse provides interesting neurodevelopmental support for this clinical finding, implicating injury to the part of the brain that regulates emotion: the cerebellar vermis. Damage to the cerebellar vermis makes people particularly irritable, and may cause them to seek external means—drugs and alcohol—to quell this irritability (Anderson, Teicher, Polcari, & Renshaw, 2002).

The relationship between trauma and substance use is complex but it can also follow a fairly direct path whereby girls self-medicate to han-dle the trauma or its attendant damage (e.g., anxiety, depression, poor self-esteem, stress). Substance use problems, mental health symptoms, and compromised physical health also interact in indirect, mutually reinforc-ing ways for girls with trauma histories (Logan, 2003; Poole & Dell, 2005; Ullman & Brecklin, 2003). Good assessment and treatment of substance use in adolescent girls therefore explores the presence and impact of a traumatic past on coping.

Harm Reduction

The most promising model for addressing adolescent drug use to date is harm reduction. This new paradigm emerged in the late 1980s, shifting focus away from the highly unsuccessful strategy of abuse prevention, and transforming traditional purposes and methods of drug education.

Harm reduction is a policy of preventing the potential harms related to drug use rather than trying to prevent the drug use itself. Harm reduc-tion accepts as a fact that drug use has persisted despite all efforts to pre-vent it and will continue to do so. Further, it recognizes that measures intended to prevent drug use have often had the unintended effect of in-creasing the harms associated with drug use (Duncan et al., 1994). Harm reduction supports the adage that the best should not be the enemy of the good.

At the conceptual level, harm reduction maintains a value-neutral and humanistic view of drug use and the user, neither insisting on nor objecting to abstinence, and acknowledging the active role of the user in harm reduction programs (Cheung, 2000). At the practical level, the aim of harm reduction is to reduce the more immediate harmful consequences of drug use through pragmatic, realistic, and low-threshold programs. At the policy level, harm reduction generates an array of measures that match more sensitively the full spectrum of use ranging from, for example, the availability of nicotine gum for adolescents attempting to quit smoking, to needle-exchange programs for addicts.

The primary aim of harm reduction programs is to reduce harmful consumption and associated problems. They typically meld concepts and techniques of motivational interviewing, cognitive behavioral skills training, and relapse prevention. This approach has several key assumptions: Adolescent-chosen goals are more powerful than goals set by the clinician or required by others; the factors that maintain heavy use for adolescents are different from those that sustain it for adults; and, successful experiences in the direction of achieving goals are more important (and possible) than immediate and complete elimination of risk.

The harm reduction paradigm stands in marked contrast to traditional disease models that focus exclusively on the negative outcomes of illicit drug use, and feature instead prohibition and abstinence. Harm reduction is also more in tune with broader strengths-based practices that explore patterns of adaptation and competence in adolescence.

Strengths-Based Substance Abuse Treatment

Strengths-based practitioners work from the premise that adolescents have resources that can help them overcome adversity. The focus of the work becomes "finding, enhancing, and encouraging the utilizations of coping skills with which to navigate troubled waters" (Norman, 1997, p. 74). The strengths perspective seeks to offer a more fruitful position from which to describe the reasons why adolescents get involved with drugs and alcohol; it points clinicians in the direction of finding opportunities, hope, and solutions (Laursen & Brasler, 2002). Rather than channeling efforts toward correcting deficits of adolescent substance use, strengths-based clinicians work to provide girls with opportunities for belonging, mastery, independence, and generosity (Brendtro, Brokenleg, & Van Bockern, 2002). Harm reduction and strengths-based approaches go hand in hand; as we work to help girls make better choices about their substance use, we are also building up their problem-solving, interpersonal, and self-soothing strategies, thereby giving them new ways to cope and succeed.

Interventions

Within a harm reduction and strengths based focus, there are some specific considerations for assessing and treating adolescent girls as outpatients. Of course, a good evaluation will help determine if outpatient treatment will be sufficient; girls who are seriously abusing substances and not managing their lives at all may require inpatient or residential care to get back on track.

Confidentiality

One of the first sticky wickets of substance abuse treatment is what to do about pledges of confidentiality. Beyond the provisos about breaking confidence for imminent danger and court-ordered evaluations, there is more of a gray area here than most clinicians like to concede. States typically have strict requirements on this subject, specifying that without an adolescent's consent not much can be shared at all, including, for example, information about buying and selling drugs, peer behaviors, or worrisome use. And most practice guidelines recommend that we observe "appropriate levels" of confidentiality for the adolescent during assessment and treatment (American Academy of Child and Adolescent Psychiatry, 2004) though such directives can feel vague in the moment.

It is, of course, good practice to encourage and support the adolescent's disclosure of substance involvement to parents. However, if girls are reluctant, we are often in a tough spot because we have information that we may feel strongly parents should also have, but we are not legally able to share it. Our bind is unintentionally reinforced by our usual introductions that establish the complete privacy of the therapy space except in cases of immediate danger.

As discussed in Chapter 5, Ron Taffel's (2005) strategy for managing confidentiality sets the stage for more latitude in disclosure to parents. Instead of promising more privacy than you may be able to provide, just let girls know that they should tell you up front if they are discussing information they do not want their parents to have. Explain that you'll never violate their confidentiality without first talking it over with them and working with them. With substance abuse issues, we struggle to find a balance between helping adolescents in individual treatment and potentially increasing their parents' involvement and efficacy at the same time. When we get that feeling in our gut that tells us a girl is not safe, even if her behavior doesn't clearly cross the confidentiality-rules line, we still may need to have some flexibility to act.

Opening Questions

To get discussions going, begin with very general kinds of inquiry, but be direct:

- "Generally speaking, what are the substances that kids in your group are trying?"
- "You and I both know that kids your age are using alcohol, and drugs, and smoking so I was naturally wondering about your involvement with these things?"
- "I'm interested in your health and how you take care of yourself, so I'd like to know about your recreational use of drugs and alcohol, and how you feel about it."
- "How would you describe your alcohol or drug use?" Do you think it has become a problem for you, or dangerous to your health?"
- "I'm curious about what drugs/alcohol do for you? Tell me about how you think and feel about them? How come they are in your life right now?
- "It seems to me that most drug experimentation has risks and benefits to it. Can you tell me what you think the risks and benefits of this are for you?"
- "What's the best and worst thing that's happened to you with drugs/ alcohol?"
- "How much do your parents know about your substance use? How much do you think they should know? What would happen if they did?" "What's the impact of your using on your relationship with them?"

If you have greater concern (or more information up front) and want to ask even more specific questions, you can try some of these screening procedures:

Screening for Substance Use Problems

Two or more yes responses suggest the need for a more extensive evaluation:

_____ Have you ever ridden in a car driven by someone (including yourself) who was high or had been using alcohol or drugs?

_____ Do you drink or use drugs to relax, feel better about yourself, or to fit in?

_____ Do you ever drink alcohol or use drugs when you are alone?

_____ Do you or any of your closest friends drink or use drugs at least every week?

_____ Does a close family member have a problem with alcohol or drug use?

_____ Have you ever gotten into trouble from drinking or drug use (e.g., skipping school, bad grades, trouble with the law or with your parents?)

_____ Does your alcohol or drug use ever make you do something that you would not normally do, like breaking rules, missing curfew, breaking the law, or having sex with someone?

_____ Is anyone you know (including you) worrying that you might be headed into a serious problem here?

Assessing Problem Severity

_____ Age at onset, and progression of use for specific substances (When did you start, what happened next?)

_____ Drinking frequency (About how often? Every day? How many times a week?)

_____ Drinking quantity (How much did you drink the last time you got drunk? How much do you usually drink? Do you ever drink to pass out? How often do you get drunk?)

_____ Drinking activity (What do you do when you are drunk. How do you act? How do others around you behave? Was this what happened last time? What happened next?)

_____ Drug use frequency (How often do you use drugs. Every day? How many times a day? How many times a week? Tell me about the past week so I can get a sense of what it's been like for you recently.)

_____ Settings of use (Where do you drink/take drugs? Parties? With friends in school, in cars, at home, on the street, in the woods? By yourself? Where?)

____ Dependence (Do your social activities usually involve alcohol or drugs? What would happen if you couldn't have any alcohol or drugs? Tell me about the last time you didn't have any and what happened.)

____ Social consequences (What kinds of trouble have you gotten into because of alcohol/drugs? What is the impact on your relationships with family members? With school/work? Your feelings about yourself? Your health?)

____ Other problems that may be interacting with substance use (trauma, family, school, or social stressors?)

Once you have a sense that a girl may have a substance abuse problem, you will have to work with her on it and share your concern with her based on the information you have collected from her, her family, school, and anyone else who has weighed in on the matter. In order to be effective, though, you'll need her to buy in at least enough to discuss it. Often, the harm reduction approach is a relief to adolescents who might be willing to become more responsible with their use, but unwilling to consider abstinence.

Sometimes though, our ability to make change on an outpatient basis seems quite limited in face of the power of the substances and the culture that sustains them. In these cases, you will need to reconsider whether you can be effective without some kind of inpatient detoxification and rehabilitation first. Your assessment and the quality of a girl's engagement with you will help determine whether outpatient treatment will work.

Therapy

Within the broad frame of a harm reduction paradigm, there are several individual and family-based approaches to substance abuse treatment that appear to have some efficacy in reducing the harmful impact. With particular reference to adolescent girls, the most effective strategies attend to the unique motivations for use and the accelerated consequences of use. They are also "trauma informed," strengths based, and grounded by the critical importance of the therapeutic relationship.

Individual Therapy

Optimal treatment plans include the following:

- Engagement in the whole life of the adolescent and solid therapeutic alliance.

- Family involvement including improved supervision, monitoring, and communication between parents and adolescents.
- Improving problem solving, social skills, competencies, and self-soothing strategies.
- Addressing other individual and family issues (trauma, anxiety, depression, learning problems, marital conflict, parent substance issues).
- Increasing prosocial behaviors, positive peer relationships, academic support. Girls who are competent, have interests and plans, and develop a larger array of self soothing strategies will use fewer drugs and disengage more readily from the drug culture.
- Adequate duration of treatment and follow-up care so that the supportive relationship lasts long enough to accomplish these goals.

Family Therapy

Family treatment approaches to adolescent substance abuse have some clear promise (Waldron, 1997) since a number of family-related factors—such as parental substance use or abuse, poor parent-child relationships, low perceived parental support, poor communication, and poor parent supervision and management of the adolescent's behavior—have been identified as risk factors for the development of substance abuse among adolescents (American Academy of Child and Adolescent Psychiatry, 2004). These strategies are largely the same as family therapy for girls diagnosed with conduct disorder; girls often (though not always) have other conduct problems when they are overinvolved with substances.

Prevention

Prevention programs have a range of success. They seem to be particularly promising when they can be offered in the schools over an extended time, reaching students through graduation, or in other places frequented by adolescents (Durlak, 1997). To be effective, however, programs must be offered early enough, often enough, long enough, and in ways that engage the prosocial yearnings of adolescent girls (Callan, 1999). Good prevention (and intervention programs) provide comprehensive services in other domains, too—addressing, for example, vocational counseling, recreational activities, medical services, family intervention, academic support, peer skills, and mentoring.

AA/NA

Twelve-step approaches using AA and NA are widely used in the United States and are often helpful in conjunction with therapy (Williams & Chang, 2000). These groups provide ongoing support from a (theoretically) nonusing peer group, available sponsors, and an opportunity to work on personal goals, including the possibility of abstinence. While other forms of group treatment may place substance-abusing adolescents at more risk with substantial negative effects on outcome (Dishion, Poulin, & Burraston, 2001), the structure and premises of AA/NA groups have a long history of benefit to participants.

Out-of-Home Alternatives

As with CD, some substance abuse problems are not amenable to outpatient treatment. Even short of a full blown addiction, some girls become too engaged with the culture of substances—peers and community—and parents and therapists are impotent to stop it. Here, too, we have a broad range of substance abuse treatments that get girls away from home and neighborhood for a time—into the woods, foster care, group homes, residential treatment centers, therapeutic schools, halfway houses, and hospitals. All of these alternatives are discussed in detail in Chapter 13.

When girls behave in troubled and troubling ways, we hold a systemic frame of mind. Biology, family, relationships, environment, and culture are invariably operating in complex interaction as girls make bad choices or end up in situations that are harmful to them and others. In the preceding chapters, interventions have focused largely on the psychological, interpersonal, and societal changes that will help girls feel and act better. The following chapter, written by a child psychiatrist, Robert J. Racusin, MD, explores the role of medications, used adjunctively (or sometimes as the treatment itself), in treating symptomatic adolescent girls.

CHAPTER TWELVE

PSYCHOTROPIC MEDICATION IN THE TREATMENT OF ADOLESCENT GIRLS

Robert J. Racusin, MD

The use of medication for the treatment of adolescents with psychiatric disorders has increased dramatically since the mid-1980s (Martin, 2003), a phenomenon parallel to the use of medication in the field of psychiatry as a whole. Medications with FDA approval only for adult use are frequently used to treat adolescents, based upon adult study data and clinical experience. This use of medication with younger patients is often termed "off label," viz., for a purpose beyond that approved by the FDA for labeling and advertising by the manufacturer.

It is important to understand that off label is not synonymous with unsafe, ineffective, experimental, or inappropriate. In the United States, the regulatory process for FDA approval of a medication requires that the manufacturer demonstrate that a medication is both safe and effective for a particular disorder. This is accomplished when at least two randomized clinical trials involving several hundred patients for two to three months show that treatment with a new medication is statistically superior to placebo, and that the benefits significantly outweigh any adverse drug reactions (side effects). Once a medication has received FDA approval it can be marketed by the manufacturer only for the approved "indication"; however, physicians can legally and ethically prescribe a medication for the treatment of other conditions based upon clinical judgment and reasonable standards of care. This off-label use of pharmaceuticals is common practice not just in psychiatry. In fact, many pediatric medications are used off-label (e.g., pain medications, antibiotics, anticonvulsants).

Both the federal government and academic medical centers have begun to make efforts to conduct the necessary studies of the use of psychiatric medications with younger people. For example, The Best Pharmaceuticals for Children Act (2002) and The Pediatric Research Equity Act (2003) require that manufacturers study pediatric uses when new medicines are developed, as well as pay increased attention to drug side-effects in children. To spur more research in this area, in the year 1996–1997 the National Institute of Mental Health (NIMH) developed a network of Research Units on Pediatric Psychopharmacology (RUPP) to study the safety and efficacy of psychiatric medications in children. This effort coordinates research at multiple academic centers with specialized expertise in these types of studies.

The results of these efforts, although preliminary, have been promising. For example, in a large study of depressed adolescents called The Treatment for Adolescents with Depression Study (TADS), March and colleagues (2004) demonstrated the superiority of antidepressant medication alone or in combination with cognitive-behavioral treatment (CBT) compared to CBT alone or placebo. Many other studies are underway to determine the effects of longer-term use of medications in children and adolescents with a variety of psychiatric disorders. Thus, there is reason for optimism that doctors and families will increasingly be able to make more informed decisions about the benefits and risks of using specific medications for particular illnesses.

In the meantime, the judicious use of pharmacological treatment, both for FDA-approved and off-label conditions, is justified on the grounds that the risks of not treating psychiatric illness, in terms of mortality and personal suffering, outweigh the risks associated with treatment, and depression in adolescents is a good example of this. Left untreated, major depression in teenagers carries a substantial risk of significantly interfering with normal psychological development, as well as a significantly increased risk of death by suicide. While there is an apparent small increase in the risk of suicidal ideation (as opposed to suicidal behavior) at the outset of treatment with antidepressants, with continued treatment there tends to be a substantial overall decrease in suicidal thinking and behavior. Where a psychosocial intervention (e.g., cognitive-behavioral therapy), also has demonstrated efficacy, it should be considered the first line of treatment for most teenagers. However, when combined psychosocial and medication treatment is known to be more effective, or when psychosocial treatments are not available, the carefully monitored use of medication often presents far less risk to adolescents than no treatment or ineffective treatment.

General Principles of Medication Treatment for Adolescents

Medication Treatment Should Generally Be Adjunctive to Psychosocial Treatment

While there is little doubt that medications are important to relieve suffering and improve functional outcomes for many psychiatric conditions seen in adolescents, medications rarely "cure" these illnesses. In addition, all medications expose those who take them to the possibility of side effects. Their use also may represent a significant financial burden for families and the effort required to adhere to a regular dosing schedule can negatively affect the quality of life for both teenagers and their parents who must supervise treatment. At the same time, a number of evidence-based, time-limited, nonmedication interventions (e.g., cognitive-behavioral therapy, certain types of family therapy), have been developed for a range of psychiatric disorders such as depression, anxiety, posttraumatic stress disorder, and eating disorders.

Therefore, a rational approach to deciding about whether to use medication should include consideration of nonmedication treatments either before starting medications or, if the clinical situation is sufficiently serious, using combined medication and psychosocial treatment, rather than relying upon medication treatment alone.

Match Treatment to Specific Symptoms That Have Been Prioritized

There are few psychiatric conditions (ADHD, depression, and schizophrenia are among the notable exceptions) for which the diagnosis can be reliably matched with a specific type of medication treatment. It is the rule, rather than the exception, that psychiatric disorders in adolescents present complex clinical pictures with symptoms presenting from more than one condition simultaneously. For example, anxiety symptoms frequently accompany disorders ranging from ADHD, to depression, to eating disorders. As a result, it is important to prioritize symptoms in terms of the amount of suffering they cause, the risk to the safety to self and others, and the degree to which they impair functioning. Thus, for an individual experiencing problems with both poor attention and disabling anxiety, it may be more important to start by attempting to relieve anxiety before using medication for inattention.

Use Broad-Based Agents Before Polypharmacy

Because adolescents typically experience multiple symptoms of different disorders simultaneously, effective medication control of the most significant symptom(s) often results in the need to address remaining symptoms, possibly with a second (or even third) medication. While this may be clinically necessary, it also increases the likelihood of encountering adverse drug effects. Sometimes this is a result of the additive effect of combining medications with similar side-effect profiles. For example, when two medications are given, each of which causes mild but tolerable sedation, the combined effect may be sedation that interferes with daily functioning.

It is also important to recognize that one medication can have important effects on how the body handles other medications. Typically, this involves the enzymes in the liver that are engaged in the process by which the body breaks down anything that is ingested so that it can then be eliminated (metabolism). Many medications have the ability to interfere with specific enzymes important in the breakdown of other medications taken simultaneously. The result can be a decreased rate of elimination of the second medication, leading to an abnormally high concentration in the body that, in turn, may cause side effects that would not occur if the medications were not taken in combination. Many of these drug-drug interactions have been sufficiently described for physicians to make the necessary dose adjustments; however, many of these interactions have yet to be discovered and they may differ between adults, children, and adolescents in important ways that have also yet to be fully defined.

As the number of medications increases, the possibility of drug–drug interactions also increases significantly. Thus, the benefit and importance of controlling symptoms must be carefully weighed against the potential risks of using multiple medications (polypharmacy). A prudent approach in nonemergency situations is to start with only one medication, at the lowest reasonable dose, and to increase the dose slowly with frequent observations for possible side-effects. It is also important to use a medication for a sufficient period of time (e.g., 6–8 weeks for antidepressants), at a dose expected to be therapeutic before deciding to change to or add a new medication. When additional medication is added, the same process should be followed.

Once adequate symptom control is achieved, it is also important to periodically consider whether maintenance treatment is necessary. Often, a positive response to combined medication and psychosocial treatment will persist even after one or all medications are tapered and stopped. Reassessing medications in this manner is good clinical practice and serves to counteract the tendency of medication treatment to continue longer than is necessary to control clinically important symptoms.

Classification of Medications

A wide variety of medications have been used for both adult and adolescent psychiatric disorders. Historically, some of the most important discoveries of medical treatments in psychiatry were the result of serendipity. For example, the beneficial effect of lithium for mania in bipolar disorder was discovered when Dr. John Cade in Australia in the 1940s was investigating the effects of a different compound. Similarly, reserpine, an antihypertensive isolated in the 1950s, was also noted to have benefits for psychosis and depression. One reason for these "accidental" discoveries is that neurotransmitters, the chemical systems in the body that regulate nervous system activity, are involved in many bodily functions unrelated to the brain or nervous system. For example, the neurotransmitter norepinephrine, which is the target of some blood pressure lowering medications, is also involved in the symptoms of attention deficit/hyperactivity disorder.

This overlap in how medicines act in the body has led to a rather confusing system of how they are categorized. Medications are sometimes grouped based upon their chemical characteristics or structure. For example, the benzodiazepines, a large group of medications used for anxiety and sleep problems, are classified based upon similarities of chemical structure (benzodiazepine refers to a specific arrangement of carbon and other atoms in a 3-ring configuration). Alternatively, medications are frequently linked based upon the primary symptom or diseases for which their use was first discovered or developed. For example, there is a large, heterogeneous group of medications often referred to as antidepressants. Many of these medicines are as, or even more effective, for problems other than depression, such as panic attacks, obsessive–compulsive symptoms, or posttraumatic stress disorder. This can lead to confusion when a medication widely known as an "antidepressant" is prescribed for a person who is not depressed. Finally, medications are frequently classified on the basis of their primary chemical effect in the body. For example, serotonin-reuptake inhibitors (SRI's) are a widely used group of medications that all have in common the property of blocking a specific chemical process that takes place at the junction between adjacent nerve cells, resulting in an increase in the concentration of the neurotransmitter serotonin. To make matters even more complicated, the SRIs are also included in the group of medicines referred to above as antidepressants! Thus, it is not surprising that families are often at a loss to understand why a certain medication has been chosen and might understandably wonder whether the physician is making an appropriate recommendation.

As a result of these inconsistencies in how medications are classified there is no "right" or best way to review them. In order to provide as much clarity as possible, therefore, this chapter will discuss the topic from two perspectives. First, medications will be reviewed based upon how they are mostly commonly referred to in the professional and lay literature because this is how they are most widely known. This creates the unavoidable necessity of combining the three different categories mentioned above: chemical characteristics, psychiatric condition for which the medication was first used, and mechanism of action in the body. Second, these same medications will be organized according to the different conditions for which they are most frequently used in teenagers, viz., by clinical diagnosis. This "cross-referencing" will allow readers to access information in a manner that is most useful for their particular needs.

Most medications can be referred to either by a generic (chemical) name or by a proprietary (brand) name. This can also be the source of confusion. In this chapter, medications will be referred to by generic names, with brand names given in parentheses the first time the generic name is used.

Specific Medications Used for Adolescents

Stimulants

Stimulants are among the safest and most widely used medicines in child and adolescent psychiatry. They have been in use in this country since 1937 when Bradley discovered that amphetamine helped hyperactive children perform better in school. The term *stimulant* comes from the observation that amphetamines were known to increase certain bodily functions (e.g., alertness, heart rate). This has led to confusion at times because a primary benefit of these medications is to help children become more focused and less hyperactive (i.e., calmer rather than more wound up, or stimulated).

This group of medications includes two primary types of compounds. First, as noted above, are different variations of the drug amphetamine (Dexedrine) and mixed amphetamine salts (Adderall). The second·is different forms and preparations of methylphenidate (e.g., Ritalin, Metadate, Ritalin-LA, Focalin). Both types of stimulants are available in both short-acting and long-acting forms. The exact mechanism of action of these medications in unknown; however, it appears that they primarily affect the activity of the neurotransmitters dopamine and norepinephrine in a manner that enhances the functioning of the prefrontal cortex, the part of the brain involved in inhibition and working memory.

Stimulant medications are primarily used in adolescents for the treatment of attention deficit/hyperactivity disorder (ADHD), including both the symptoms of hyperactivity/impulsivity and inattention. There have been numerous studies that demonstrate the safety and efficacy of these medications, including a large study sponsored by the National Institute of Mental Health, the Multimodal Treatment Study of ADHD (MTA) study. This study demonstrated that for children with ADHD (and without other psychiatric or learning problems), stimulants alone were more effective than placebo or medication combined with psychosocial interventions, as long as the medications was taken regularly and in adequate doses (MTA Cooperative Group, 1999).

The dose of stimulant medication will vary depending upon which type is being prescribed and whether it is a short- or long-acting form. There is no precise formula available to determine the correct dose for a particular child. Therefore, medication should be started at a low dose and then increased gradually on the basis of improvement of symptoms while monitoring for side-effects. The side-effects of stimulants are generally minor but may include decreased appetite, difficulty falling asleep, stomachache, a small increase in heart rate and/or blood pressure, headache, and shakiness. While long-term use of stimulants appears to be quite safe for most children, recent evidence suggests that some children will fall slightly short of the height they would have achieved if not on medication. Of more concern is the rare possibility of sudden cardiac death that may be a risk for children with underlying heart problems. For this reason, it is important to know if there is a family history of cardiac problems or if the child has been having symptoms of cardiac problems (e.g., palpitations, irregular heartbeat, dizziness). One concern often expressed by parents is the risk that the use of stimulant medications, which are controlled substances under federal law, will increase the likelihood that a child will use illegal drugs in adolescence.

In fact, the opposite seems to the case. Studies have demonstrated that, compared to children who are not treated with medication, children with properly treated ADHD are less likely to abuse substances, including their medication, when they become teenagers. Of course, parents should ensure that stimulants, as with all medications, are kept in a secure place and should appropriately supervise their use by children and teenagers.

As with all medications discussed in this chapter, stimulants can potentially interact with other medications (and possibly some ingredients found in food or herbal supplements, such as caffeine) in ways that can be dangerous. While addressing this in depth is beyond the scope of this chapter, it is essential that the prescribing physician be aware of *all* medications being taken, whether prescription or over-the-counter, as well as any herbal supplements or alternative medications.

Adrenergic Agents

The two medications in this category are clonidine (Catepres) and guanfacine (Tenex). They are also sometimes called "alpha agonists." The term *adrenergic* refers to their effect on the neurotransmitter norepinephrine, which is related to the neurotransmitter epinephrine, also know as adrenalin. These medications were originally developed for use in hypertension which is partially regulated by norepinephrine.

There are four primary psychiatric uses of these medications in children and adolescents: to help reduce tics (e.g., in Tourette's disorder); to reduce hyperactivity in ADHD; to help with difficulty falling asleep; and to help with aggression. There are relatively few published studies on the safety and efficacy of the adrenergic agents, and there are other medications that are frequently more effective for each of these problems. Therefore they are most often used as a "second line" treatment for children who either do not respond to a more established treatment or are sensitive to the side-effects of a first line agent.

Clonidine and guanfacine are quite similar in their actions and side-effects. Clonidine is shorter-acting and frequently requires three to four doses per day, whereas guanfacine can usually be given just twice a day. The most frequent side effects of the adrenergic agents are sedation, fatigue, and dizziness. A much smaller number of children experience agitation, nervousness, or sleep problems. The most medically important side-effects involve blood pressure and heart rhythm. As antihypertensives, these medications lower blood pressure, usually less than 10% in healthy children, which does not generally cause clinical problems. For children with preexisting blood pressure abnormalities, or who have a lowering greater than 10%, however, these medicines should be avoided.

Also, it is very important not to stop an adrenergic agent suddenly because it could result in potentially dangerous rebound hypertension; rather, the medication dose should be tapered. Adrenergic agents can also affect heart rhythm, typically by slowing heart rate. While this is rarely a problem in healthy children, it is important to assess the presence of underlying cardiac disease. An EKG is often recommended before starting an adrenergic agent and again when the dose has been stabilized.

Antipsychotics

As the name suggests, this group of medicines was originally discovered to be effective in the treatment of the most severe symptoms of mental illness. The first such medication to be used was chlorpromazine (Thorazine) which was found to reduce symptoms such as hallucinations in patients with schizophrenia. Eventually almost a dozen such medications were discovered; for example, haloperidol (Haldol), mesoridazine (Mellaril), and perphenazine (Trilafon). All of these medications have a couple of functions in common. First is their ability to block the neurotransmitter dopamine at a particular receptor site in the brain. Second is their tendency to cause side-effects called extrapyramidal side-effects, which involve muscle stiffness, restlessness, and abnormal movements (some of which can be permanent). Based upon these common features, this group of medications became know as the "typical antipsychotics."

More recently, a group of medications that, in addition to blocking dopamine, also have a significant effect on the neurotransmitter serotonin, were discovered to have certain advantages over the "typical antipsychotics." These "atypical antipsychotics" are much less likely to cause extrapyramidal side-effects and may be more effective with the "negative" symptoms of schizophrenia (e.g., apathy). The first of these medications to be discovered was clozaril (Clozapine). Its use is limited by the need for frequent blood tests because of a potentially dangerous side-effect involving bone marrow suppression. Subsequently, a number of other atypical antipsychotics have become available and are in use with adolescents. These include olanzapine (Zyprexa), risperidone (Risperdal), quetiapine (Seroquel), ziprasidone (Geodon), and aripiprazole (Abilify).

Primarily as a result of the lower risk for extrapyramidal symptoms, the atypical antipsychotics have largely replaced their older counterparts, although the typical antipsychotics are still frequently used and are generally much less expensive because of their availability in generic form. While the atypical antipsychotics have an important advantage with respect to extrapyramidal symptoms, they are not without significant side effects of their own. First, while less likely to occur, extrapyramidal problems have been observed, even with the newer medications. All of these medications can result in sedation, dry mouth, constipation, urinary retention, and blurred vision. Depending upon the specific medication there can also be sexual, skin, cardiac, endocrine, and eye-related problems. Of particular concern is the possibility of developing a "metabolic syndrome" characterized by obesity, diabetes, and elevated lipid levels (which are a risk factor for later cardiovascular disease). Aripiprazole and ziprasidone appear to present the least risk of metabolic syndrome, while olanzapine and clozapine carry the greatest risk, with risperidone and quetiapine somewhere in between. It is important that adolescents be monitored carefully for side-effects when taking any antipsychotic medication including assessments for weight gain, abnormal movements, metabolic and endocrine problems, and cardiac problems (with specific typical and atypical antipsychotics).

As noted above, the antipsychotic medications were first found to be helpful with the symptoms of schizophrenia; however, they are also valuable in the treatment of other psychotic disorders including psychotic depression and bipolar disorder. The atypical antipsychotics used in bipolar disorder have been shown in adults to be effective as mood stabilizers, often in conjunction with a second mood stabilizing medication (see below). Preliminary studies have suggested this is also true for adolescents. Several well-designed studies have shown that the atypical antipsychotics are effective for the treatment of aggression in children with developmental disorders such as mental retardation and autistic spectrum disorders. Additional studies have shown their effectiveness in treating Tourette's disorder. While there are fewer studies supporting their use in other conditions, the atypical antipsychotics may have promise in treating aggression, agitation, extreme anxiety, and psychotic symptoms in a variety of disorders (e.g., conduct disorder, posttraumatic stress disorder, certain anxiety disorders).

None of the atypical antipsychotic medications has been approved by the FDA for use with children and adolescents. Of the older (typical) antipsychotics, only two medications have FDA indications for pediatric use: haloperidol for treatment of tics (Tourette's disorder), and both haloperidol and thioridazine for severe behavioral problems associated with conduct disorder.

Antidepressants

The group of medications commonly referred to as antidepressants is typically divided into three categories: an older group referred to as the tricyclic antidepressants (based upon a feature of their chemical structure); a new group called the serotonin reuptake inhibitors (reflecting their action in the body); and a mixed group of both older and newer medications that are neither tricyclic in structure nor primarily involved with serotonin reuptake.

The tricyclic antidepressants were first discovered to be effective in treating adult depression in the 1950s; however, no studies have demonstrated their efficacy in adolescent depression despite their widespread use until the arrival of the serotonin reuptake inhibitors (SRIs) in the late 1980s. There are five medications in this group, but only two have FDA approval for use in children: clomipramine (Anafranil) for obsessive–compulsive disorder (OCD), and imipramine (Tofranil) for nighttime bedwetting (enuresis). An important characteristic of these medications is that they affect multiple neurotransmitters throughout the body, which increases the likelihood of side-effects, the most serious of which are cardiac arrhythmias, particularly if taken in overdose. As a result of their combined lack of effectiveness for depression and overdose risk, tricyclics, except clomipramine, are no longer routinely used for adolescents.

Unlike the tricyclic antidepressants, the SRIs are widely used with adolescents for depression as well as other disorders. This group includes five medications available in the United States: fluoxetine (Prozac), fluvoxamine (Luvox), citalopram (Celexa), paroxetine (Paxil), and sertraline (Zoloft). Only one (fluoxetine) is FDA-approved for depression in adolescents, while fluvoxamine and sertraline are approved for OCD. Recent studies with different SRIs in the treatment of adolescent depression have shown mixed results. There is evidence to suggest that all of the SRIs, with the possible exception of paroxetine, may be safe and effective for teenagers with depression; however, fluoxetine remains the SRI with the most scientific support, including a large study which showed the superiority of fluoxetine to both cognitive–behavioral therapy (CBT) and placebo (March et al., 2004).

In addition to the treatment of depression, SRI's have been widely used with adolescents because of their ability to decrease anxiety in conditions such as social phobia and generalized anxiety disorder; help relieve symptoms of OCD and PTSD; diminish the irritability that often accompanies symptoms of depression and anxiety; and lower the frequency of binge eating in teenagers with bulimia. Most studies have shown that SRIs are most effective when used in combination with a psychosocial treatment such as cognitive–behavioral therapy (e.g., for depression, OCD, PTSD).

The SRIs are widely used because of their high level of safety, even when taken in overdose, in addition to their ability to help reduce symptoms in a variety of important psychiatric illnesses. The most frequently seen side-effects with SRIs are sexual dysfunction, nausea, drowsiness, constipation, nervousness (including agitation and anxiety), and fatigue. Other problems include dizziness, dry mouth, headache, insomnia, abdominal pain, and tremor (A. Martin, 2003). With the exception of sexual dysfunction and drowsiness, the frequency of side-effects is typically quite low.

Research on adolescents taking SRIs has raised some concerns within the past several years. A small percentage of adolescents being studied who began taking SRIs (approximately 2%) showed either new or increased levels of suicidal thinking or self-harm behavior, a rate significantly greater than the placebo group in the study. As a result, the FDA has placed a "black box" warning on the labeling of all antidepressants highlighting the need to carefully weigh the risks and benefits of treatment as well as the need for careful monitoring for safety when these medications are being started.

It is important to note, however, that, to date, there have been no reports of death by suicide in any teenager being studied. At the same time, adolescents with untreated major depression are known to have a risk of death by suicide of up to 8% over a 10-year period. In addition, the overall adolescent suicide rate since the mid-1990s has decreased by 25% as the frequency of the use of SRIs has increased dramatically. As a result, there is an emerging consensus that the risks associated with untreated major depression far outweigh the risk of self-harm associated with medication treatment when careful monitoring is in place.

In addition to the SRIs, there is a diverse group of other medications that fall into the antidepressant category including the monoamine oxidase inhibitors (MAOIs), nefazadone (Serzone), trazodone (Desyrel), mirtazapine (Remeron), bupropion (Wellbutrin), and atomoxetine (Strattera). As with many of the medications in the antidepressant class, there are a lack of data concerning the safety and efficacy of these medications for the treatment of adolescent depression. Bupropion, which affects primarily the neurotransmitters dopamine and norepinephrine, is the most widely used for depression in teenagers. Atomoxetine, which effects primarily norepinephrine, has been approved as a nonstimulant alternative for the treatment of ADHD. It has not been widely used for the treatment of depression. Some of the others (e.g., mirtazapine, trazodone) are used for their sedating effects to help with sleep. For the MAOIs and nefazadone, side-effects, including some medically severe risks involving liver function and blood pressure, greatly limit their use.

Antianxiety Agents

Symptoms of anxiety are frequently seen in adolescents both as primary symptoms of a psychiatric disorder (e.g., panic disorder), or in conjunction with another underlying problem (e.g., depression). One of the most effective medication treatments for anxiety (known as an anxiolytic effect) is the SRI class of medications (see above under "Antidepressants"). In addition, there are two other often-used medication approaches for anxiety: a class of medications, the benzodiazepines, and a medication, buspirone.

The benzodiazepines (BZDs) were first discovered in the late 1950s. They have in common a characteristic molecular structure that permits them to affect the receptors for a particular neurotransmitter called gamma-aminobuteric acid (GABA). As a class, the BZDs have effects in the body as muscle relaxants, anticonvulsants, and anxiolytics. The BZDs have been shown to be both effective and safe in treating adult anxiety for up to several months; however, they are FDA-approved in children only for their use in anesthesia. There are upwards of 10 different BZDs available in the United States which differ primarily in terms of their duration of action. The one with the shortest duration (1–3 hours) is alprazolam (Xanax). Intermediate duration BZDs (4–10 hours) include oxazepam (Serax), lorazepman (Ativan), and clonazepam (Klonipin), while others, including diazepam (Valium) and chlordiazepoxide (Librium), can stay active in the body for more than 24 hours.

There have been few studies in children and adolescents using BZDs to treat anxiety, most of which have involved alprazolam. In practice, the short-acting BZDs are not frequently used because they require frequent doses and often result in "rebound anxiety" when they wear off. Most commonly used are the intermediate-duration preparations (e.g., lorazepam, clonazepam), which can help both with daytime anxiety and difficulty falling asleep secondary to anxiety (although they do not improve the quality of sleep and may interfere with normal sleep patterns). The most common side-effect of the BZDs is sedation; however, loss of coordination and cognitive dulling have also been seen. Some children, particularly preadolescents, may be vulnerable to a "paradoxical" response to BZDs where they become agitated and disinhibited, sometimes appearing as if intoxicated. The primary concern with long-term use of these medications is the risk of physiological dependency resulting in a withdrawal syndrome that may require careful medical management to avoid the risk of seizures (A. Martin, 2003).

Buspirone (BuSpar) is a novel medication, unrelated to other anxiolytics, whose mechanism of action involves the neurotransmitters serotonin and dopamine. There is only anecdotal evidence supporting the benefits of buspirone in adolescents and it is FDA-approved only for adults. Buspirone typically requires several weeks to have its full effect and it is generally not considered useful when rapid symptom relief is required, unlike the BZDs whose effect can be observed within a matter of hours or less. The most frequently seen side effects with buspirone include headaches, nausea, fatigue, and dizziness. Unlike with the BZDs, there does not appear to be any risk of physiological dependency or withdrawal.

Mood Stabilizers

This group of medications originally included only lithium carbonate which, as noted earlier in this chapter, was serendipitously found in the 1940s to "stabilize" symptoms of mania in adult patients with bipolar, hence the general name of this class of drugs. Subsequently, two other groups of medications have come to be included in this group: some of the atypical antipsychotics described previously (e.g., olanzapine), which is FDA-approved for the acute treatment of adult mania, and the anticonvulsants.

Lithium is a relatively simple compound that is unlike many other psychiatric medications in that its effects are not based on blocking or activating a specific neurotransmitter; rather, it apparently works by affecting a complex series of intracellular chemical processes in a manner that reduces the excitability of nerve cells. It has been shown to be effective both in reducing the acute symptoms of mania, as well as in reducing the frequency and intensity of subsequent manic episodes. It is FDA-approved for the treatment of bipolar disorder in children over the age of 12, although there are relatively few randomized controlled trials in adolescents.

Lithium is a medication that must be monitored carefully, especially at the outset of treatment, with blood level measurements and frequent appointments to assess for side-effects. This is because there is a narrow "window" between a blood level necessary for therapeutic response and one that is associated with side effects which can be severe, and even life-threatening. The most commonly seen immediate side effects are gastrointestinal, neurological, and cardiac. Diarrhea, nausea, abdominal pain, and decreased appetite are frequently seen, but are usually mild or can be controlled by dividing the dose. Tremor is the most frequently seen neurological side-effect, although loss of coordination and slurred speech are often seen at higher doses and may be the first signs of toxicity. Reversible EKG changes are frequently seen when taking lithium; however, these are usually not clinically significant in patients without underlying cardiac disease.

Acute intoxications can result in coma and death, making lithium an extremely dangerous drug when taken in overdose. Longer-term side effects include suppression of thyroid function (which can usually be corrected with supplemental hormone replacement therapy) and a decrease in the kidney's ability to concentrate urine, which may result in increased urine output and frequency. In rare instances, lithium has been associated with irreversible changes in kidney function, although this problem has not been studied in children and adolescents. Thus, in addition to careful monitoring at the outset of treatment, patients taking lithium on an ongoing basis should have regular (3–6-month) periodic blood tests to measure thyroid and kidney functioning.

There are also several anticonvulsants that have been shown to have benefits as mood stabilizers. These include carbamazepine (CBZ; Tegretol), divalproex (DVP; Depakote), lamotragine (Lamictal), gabapentin (Neurontin), and topiramate (Topamax). None of the anticonvulsants has been FDA-approved for the treatment of psychiatric disorders in children or adolescents; however, they have approval for a variety of seizure-related neurological illnesses. Of this group, DVP has the most data to support its effectiveness for bipolar disorder in adolescents, although there is a lack of controlled trials. As with lithium, treatment with DVP and CBZ requires periodic blood tests which are more frequent at the outset of treatment and when the dose is changed. Lamotragine has been shown in adults to be of unique potential benefit in the depressed phase of bipolar disorder, and there is some limited evidence to suggest that this may be true also for adolescents. There are essentially no data concerning the benefits of gabapentin or topiramate in adolescent bipolar disorder.

All of the anticonvulsants are associated with a variety of side effects, some of which can make taking the medications intolerable for some patients. Readers are advised to review a comprehensive resource for a complete description (e.g., *Physicians' Desk Reference*). Some of the most medically significant side effects will be mentioned here. CBZ is associated with birth defects when taken by pregnant women and is therefore potentially dangerous for adolescent girls. It is also associated with white blood cell suppression in some individuals and therefore requires regular blood tests for monitoring. DVP has also been implicated in birth defects. It also can be responsible for considerable weight gain, liver function abnormalities, lowered levels of blood platelets (important for clotting), and, in adolescent girls, may be associated with a syndrome of multiple ovarian cysts (polycystic ovary syndrome). Further, lamotragine has been associated with a potentially fatal skin condition in children. The risk appears to decrease with age and to be lessened if the medication is started at a very low dose and increased slowly (e.g., every 2–3 weeks). Topiramate has been associated with weight loss and cognitive dulling.

In addition to the treatment of bipolar disorder, mood stabilizers have been used for aggression and other problems of mood regulation and impulse control in adolescents. While there are case reports suggesting clinical benefits for these symptoms, there are even fewer studies in adolescents using mood stabilizers for these purposes than there are for their use in bipolar disorder.

Frequently Treated Conditions

Attention Deficit Hyperactivity Disorder (ADHD)

ADHD is a highly prevalent disorder that affects between 5 and 8% of children. It is characterized by three symptom clusters: inattention, hyperactivity, and impulsivity. When a child has symptoms in all three areas, it is referred to as the "combined type" of the disorder. Alternatively, a child could have either the "inattentive" or "hyperactive/impulsive type" reflecting symptoms limited to a specific cluster or clusters.

ADHD is now recognized as a chronic neurobiological condition that affects multiple areas of the brain, particularly those involved with working memory, inhibition, and problem solving (also referred to as "executive functions"). Because the more prominent problems of motor activity tend to diminish as children get older, it was long thought that most adolescents "outgrew" ADHD as they reached adulthood. It is now clear, however, that the majority of teenagers with ADHD have continued difficulty with inattention, distractibility, memory, and organization that can significantly interfere with academic and interpersonal functioning. Hence, treatment often has to extend into adulthood as well.

Medications have been shown to be the most effective single treatment, as noted in the MTA study previously described. Of the medications currently available, the long-acting stimulants are the most useful for most adolescents. Because of differences in the duration and mechanisms of action of the various medications, if an individual does not respond well to an initial medication (or has intolerable side-effects) it is worthwhile trying either a different preparation from the same class (e.g., amphetamine or methylphenidate) or a medication from the other class. If a stimulant medication is not effective, alternative medications that may be useful include atomoxetine, bupropion, clonidine, and guan-facine. Another medication not mentioned earlier in this chapter, modafinil (to be marketed as Sparlon), may become available in the near future as an alternative unrelated to any of the currently available medication treatments for ADHD.

Anxiety Disorders

As noted above, anxiety is frequently seen concomitantly with many psychiatric conditions in adolescence (e.g., depression, ADHD). In addition, there is a group of overlapping disorders that have anxiety as a core symptom. These disorders include specific phobias, separation anxiety, social phobia, obsessive–compulsive disorder, panic disorder, and generalized anxiety disorder. As a group, anxiety disorders can be disabling and they are highly prevalent. Numerous well-conducted studies have demonstrated that the first line treatment for most anxiety disorders is a psychosocial intervention (e.g., cognitive–behavioral therapy), with medications helpful as an adjunctive treatment.

Among the medications available in this country, none has FDA approval for the treatment of anxiety disorders in children. The exception is that sertraline and fluvoxamine are approved for the treatment of OCD. Based upon treatment studies in adults, however, the SRIs are frequently used with adolescents for anxiety associated with each of the diagnoses mentioned above. Benzodiazepines are also used, although less frequently because of problems with sedation and the risk of dependency. Buspirone has also been used, although there are few data supporting its efficacy.

Depression

Major depression, while infrequent in young children, approaches the adult level of frequency during adolescence. As a result, teenagers have an almost 20% chance of experiencing a major depressive episode by the age of 18. For many people, depression is a chronic, recurring illness that results in significant impairment in multiple areas of life functioning (e.g., academic success, interpersonal relationships). Left untreated, approximately 8 to 10% of people with major depression will die by suicide over a 10-year period. Thus, depression is a serious medical condition that requires active treatment as early as possible. As described previously, the FDA has required a warning that treatment with antidepressants, for any condition, is associated with a small increase in the rate of suicidal thinking and self-harm behaviors, particularly at the outset of treatment. The consensus of professional opinion, however, is that the risk of not treating major depression far outweighs the risks of using medication if treatment is properly monitored.

The Treatment of Adolescents with Depression (TADS) Study described previously, has demonstrated the efficacy of medication treatment alone and when combined with cognitive–behavioral treatment. While other psychosocial treatments (e.g., IPT-A) also have proven empirical benefit, these have not been studied in conjunction with medication. Further, of the medications available in the United States, only fluoxetine, one of the SRIs, has been approved by the FDA for the treatment of depression in adolescents. Approximately 30% of depressed teenagers, however, will not respond to this medication. An ongoing study in adults (STAR-D) has suggested that patients who do not achieve remission with an antidepressant will still have a good response if given a different antidepressant or if given a combination of two antidepressants.

Due to the serious potential consequences of not adequately treating major depression in adolescents, if a patient does not respond well to fluoxetine or psychotherapy, many psychiatrists will try a different SRI. If treatment is still unsuccessful, the treatment strategy will often include a trial of an alternative antidepressant (e.g., bupropion), a combination of two antidepressants (e.g., fluoxetine and bupriopion), or augmentation of an antidepressant with a nonantidepressant (e.g., fluoxetine and lithium).

Posttraumatic Stress Disorder (PTSD)

PTSD, as the name implies, is a disorder associated with exposure to a traumatic event. It is estimated that 6 to 8% of children will develop PTSD by age 18 as a result of experiencing a wide range of traumas including abuse, neglect, medical procedures, injuries, witnessing violence, and being involved with natural and human caused disasters. As discussed in Chapter 9, the symptoms of PTSD are divided into three major areas: reexperiencing (e.g., intrusive memories, nightmares, flashbacks, responding to environmental "triggers"); numbing (e.g., avoidance of feelings, situations, and people); and, hyperarousal (e.g., irritability, anger, aggression, increased startle response, insomnia).

As with the other anxiety disorders (PTSD is technically classified as an anxiety disorder by the American Psychiatric Association), psychosocial interventions (e.g., CBT, IPT-A) are considered first line treatments. Many teenagers, with PTSD, however, have symptoms of such severity, including depression, anxiety, aggression, and suicidal thinking, that medications are an important adjunct. And as with the other anxiety disorders, the SRIs are generally the safest and most useful "broad spectrum" medications; that is, they are helpful with a wide range of symptoms including anxiety, depression, sleep, and irritability. Other medications that may of use include stimulants (attention problems), alternate antidepressants, adrenergic agents (hyperarousal), and atypical antipsychotics or mood stabilizers (self-injurious behavior, aggression).

Bipolar Disorder

The characteristics of bipolar disorder in children and adolescents have been the subject of much professional controversy and debate over the past decade. A consensus seems to be emerging that bipolar disorder does occur in young people, although only a minority develop the "classic" clinical course described in adults; that is, discrete episodes of depression and mania, each lasting weeks to months and interspersed with periods of normal mood (euthymia).

Children and adolescents appear more likely to have an illness characterized by a simultaneous mixture of manic and depressive symptoms ("mixed state") that switch with great rapidity, even within the same day, and which tend to persist without euthymic intervals. Mood symptoms in pediatric bipolar disorder may also be predominantly those of anger and irritability, with a corresponding predominance of angry, defiant, aggressive, and explosive behaviors. As with depression, bipolar disorder is a serious disorder associated both with a high level of functional impairment as well as a high risk of suicidal behavior. As a result, hospitalization is frequently necessary for safety and mood stabilization with a combination of medication and psychosocial treatment.

Lithium is the only FDA-approved treatment for bipolar mania in adolescents (older than 12). There is a relative paucity of controlled data concerning the efficacy and safety in teenagers for any of the medication treatments used in bipolar disorder in adults. Some studies have suggested that divalproex (DVP) may be more effective for rapid cycling states. In addition, some of the other anticonvulsants (e.g., carbamazepine, lamotragine) have also shown some promise, while others (e.g., oxcarbazepine) have had negative results in controlled studies.

Atypical antipsychotics have also emerged as potentially useful treatments, particularly in combination with either lithium or DVP. In fact, it has begun to appear that a significant percentage of young people with bipolar disorder will require such a combination therapy for adequate symptom control. As described above, all of the mood stabilizers are associated with significant potential medical risks and require careful monitoring by an experienced physician familiar with the treatment of this complex and disabling disorder.

Aggression

While not a diagnosis, excessive irritability and aggressive behavior are symptoms associated with a large number of psychiatric conditions in adolescents, including ADHD, conduct disorder, mood disorders (e.g., depression and bipolar disorder), anxiety disorders, PTSD, schizophrenia, and developmental disorders. In addition, certain neurological conditions (e.g., Tourette's syndrome) are associated with aggressive outbursts. This heterogeneity of causes of aggression leads to several important principles of treatment. First, treatment must be preceded by a comprehensive and thorough diagnostic assessment, including neurological, intellectual, developmental, and neuropsychological evaluations where indicated. Second, treatment should be directed to the underlying disorder where one can be clearly identified. This will potentially ameliorate the causal factors associated with aggression (e.g., the treatment of depression), which in turn may decrease irritability.

The implications for the treatment of aggression with medications flow from these principles of treatment. Depending upon the underlying condition(s), a wide variety of medication treatments have been used successfully for aggressive symptoms; for example, stimulants for ADHD, antidepressants for depression, and mood stabilizers for bipolar disorder. For teenagers with developmental disorders, such as mental retardation or autistic spectrum disorders, low-dose treatment with an atypical antipsychotic (e.g., risperidone) has been found helpful in a number of controlled trials in controlling aggression.

Schizophrenia

Schizophrenia is a serious and complex disorder characterized primarily by disturbances of thinking, emotions, cognition, and social interactions.

Symptoms are sometimes described in two clusters: "positive" symptoms include perceptual disturbances, such as hallucinations, and disordered thinking, such as, loss of reality testing, delusions, illogical speech; "negative" symptoms include loss of motivation, apathy, social withdrawal, and a highly constricted range of emotional expression. Schizophrenia is considered a rare disorder in children and young adolescents; however, it becomes more prevalent in older adolescents and young adults, eventually affecting approximately 1% of the population. In the past, schizophrenia typically was associated with a deteriorating course with a very poor prognosis. Recent advances in both medication and psychosocial treatments have improved the outlook considerably for many patients, particularly in the absence of serious coexisting problems such as substance abuse.

The mainstay of the pharmacological treatment for schizophrenia in people of all ages is the antipsychotic medications described earlier in this chapter. As noted above, the FDA has not approved the use of any of these medications for the treatment of schizophrenia in children or adolescents; however, because of the devastating effects of not treating this disorder, these agents are widely used when the disorder is present.

Most psychiatrists prefer to treat initially with one of the atypical antipsychotics because of the decreased risk of extrapyramidal symptoms to which adolescents appear to be more vulnerable than adults. Adolescents, however, are also vulnerable to the adverse metabolic effects associated with many of the atypical antipsychotics. Recent studies in adults have suggested that the typical and atypical antipsychotics are quite comparable both with regard to effectiveness and tolerability of side-effects, with some studies suggesting that typical antipsychotics may be more effective; however, this has not been adequately studied in adolescents.

Given the increased concern about extrapyramidal symptoms with typical antipsychotics in teenagers, a rational approach to treatment would be to consider the initial use of an atypical agent associated with a lower risk of metabolic problems (e.g., aripiprazole, ziprasidone). An alternative strategy would be to use one of the more well-studied atypical antipsychotics such as risperidone or quetiapine, with careful monitoring of metabolic parameters. A switch to ziprasidone or aripiprazole can be considered if metabolic problems arise. A third rational approach would be to start with one of the less-sedating typical antipsychotics, such as haloperidol or perphenazine, and monitor carefully for extrapyramidal and metabolic side-effects. If problems arise, or the response is poor, an atypical antipsychotic would be substituted.

Eating Disorders

The two most frequently encountered eating disorders in adolescents are anorexia nervosa and bulimia nervosa. While both occur more frequently in girls, boys can also be affected. Both involve distorted beliefs and perceptions about body image: a dread of gaining weight and an inability to correctly perceive one's body image. Adolescents with anorexia behave primarily to prevent weight gain or to lose weight through a combination of dietary restriction, excessive physical activities, and a rigid, ritualistic approach to eating. Individuals with bulimia are characterized by eating large quantities of food compulsively and intermittently (binge eating) followed by compensatory actions to "purge" the body of the unwanted calories by self-induced vomiting or the use of laxatives. Both conditions tend to be chronic and can be life threatening because of starvation (anorexia) or metabolic or electrolyte problems that can lead to fatal cardiac complications (anorexia and bulimia).

Both conditions require careful assessment, medical monitoring, and integrated individual, family, and behavioral treatment. Both are also frequently associated with coexisting psychiatric conditions (e.g., depression, anxiety, or obsessive–compulsive disorder). There is little scientific evidence to support the use of medication as a primary treatment for anorexia, particularly in the absence of weight restoration. For adolescents whose anorexia is accompanied by another psychiatric disorder, it may be helpful to treat the coexisting condition with medication (e.g., an antidepressant). In contrast to anorexia, the FDA has approved fluoxetine for the treatment of bulimia in adults, specifically to reduce the frequency of binge eating. Dose requirements are often higher than those used for depression. Medication treatment for bulimia should be used in conjunction with psychosocial intervention (e.g., cognitive–behavioral or interpersonal therapy).

The use of medications in the treatment of adolescents with psychiatric disorder has increased significantly over the past several decades. While some view this trend with alarm, there is increasing evidence that, when used carefully and in conjunction with other treatments, medications can significantly decrease suffering, protect lives, and improve the functional outcome in a number of psychiatric conditions. It is of concern that some children and adolescents are being treated with medications without adequate assessment, follow-up, and in the absence of other needed services. It also is of concern that large numbers of children and adolescents, whose lives could be significantly improved, or even saved, do not have access to high-quality psychiatric or other medical care.

Complicating the situation is the relative dearth of good studies about the safety and efficacy of medications in children and adolescents. This "knowledge gap" is being closed; however, there are still many more questions than answers, and this is likely to remain the case for quite some time. Nevertheless, based upon what we *do* know, there is a rational way that specific medications can be usefully brought into treatment for particular symptoms and disorders. Families have an essential role to play in this process by asking questions of physicians about the rationale for treatment, the nature of the evidence about both risks and benefits, and the alternatives to treatment with a particular medication. Parents and teenagers are encouraged to become active collaborators in their own care. They need to equip themselves with information so that they can ask the right questions and to help them understand the information given by health care providers. In the context of the uncertainty and complexity that characterizes current psychopharmacology, good health care providers should welcome adolescents and families in this joint decision-making process.

CHAPTER THIRTEEN

HOSPITALIZATION AND
OUT-OF-HOME INTERVENTIONS

The outpatient care discussed in the preceding chapters describes one point on a continuum of treatment options, and is the least restrictive way to treat adolescent girls. Since the mid-1980s, alternatives to home-based treatment for troubled and troubling adolescents have burgeoned, and are now a multibillion dollar major growth industry (Kearns, 1998; Press & Washburn, 2002; Szalavitz, 2006). The rapid increase in number and variety of out-of-home options raises interesting questions about changes in the culture that presume so many girls need to be treated away from their families. It seems unlikely that, evolutionarily speaking, girls themselves are so dramatically more impaired than 20 years ago.

Indeed, as the previous chapters have noted, statistics show that teenagers aren't acting up or out more than they have in the past. Instead we may be more likely to be in a sorry time in history when a crisis of parenthood has met up with a cultural willingness to marginalize and stigmatize adolescents with behavior problems. These forces together appear to have germinated a lucrative new economic niche for specialty schools and educational consultants (Chen, 2005; Ollivier, 2000). The emergence of an "at-risk youth industry" (Press & Washburn, 2002) may reflect more of a problem of parenting and perception driven by the marketplace than a rise in the number of "bad kids." As adolescent psychiatrist, Lynn Ponton notes:

> There is no evidence that risk taking among teens is any worse today, quite the contrary. But there is a shift among parents. Baby boomer parents look at their own past risk taking, exaggerate it, and then project it onto their kids. . . . There is also a mistaken notion that peers create high-risk behavior. In fact, it's parenting that

creates high-risk behavior and there are many studies to prove it. Some kids are quite seriously dysfunctional and some of these schools are quite good. But what frequently happens is that kids are shipped off to these schools, come back better, but the parents are still pathological. (Ollivier, 2000)

So the marketplace has fed voraciously on parental inadequacy, fear, confusion, and desperation, resulting in an array of programs ranging from remarkable and innovative vision quests to bizarre and cruel "tough love" facilities that have produced lasting injuries, dozens of deaths, and numerous lawsuits (Szalavitz, 2006). Most alternative programs operate outside of the constraints that might be imposed if there were some state or federal regulation prescribing a clinically based standard of care for the children who attend them. Some of these more marginal programs even appear to derive profits from their own failure through, for example, making internal referrals, creating or allowing a breach of contract, allowing or keeping adolescents who fail to thrive or benefit, and creating contracts that eliminate parental rights and legal recourse (Conner, 2006).

Yet, legal restraints are only one part of a problem that is defined more broadly by an inadequate youth behavioral health system. Parents who enroll their adolescents in private facilities typically lack insurance coverage for complex therapies. And even those who could afford more intensive outpatient treatment may not know about it, or may not have access to interventions, like multisystemic family therapy (MFT), that could prevent placement and have empirically-proven success rates.

Families finance out-of-home placements and programs in a variety of ways, depending upon the nature of their adolescent's problems, the type of alternative intervention, their ability to pay, and state mental health funding options. Parents may pay for programs out-of-pocket by taking out tax-deductible loans or second mortgages, or piling up credit card debt. They may also relinquish custody of their adolescent to force the state to step up. One study conducted by the U.S. General Accounting Office (2003) estimated that in 2001, more than 12,000 children were placed in eitheir child welfare or in the juvenile justice system by parents desperate to get costly mental health treatment for their severely emotionally disturbed child or adolescent.

Adolescents already involved with child welfare services, juvenile justice, or special education may have some or all of their treatment paid for by these systems. For example, sometimes the school system will pay for the residential placement, or they may only cover the educational component of a program and share the residential costs with state child welfare or mental health agencies. In some instances, private insurance will foot the bill. Medicaid and school systems, operating under the Individuals with Disabilities Education Act (IDEA), have also worked together in recent years to fund out-of-home placements (Bazelon Center for Mental Health Law, 2003). In many instances, a lack of local options for a troubled adolescent influences the placement decision. Ironically, in many parts of the country, the more costly and distant alternative may be more feasible than finding suitable community services.

Insufficient numbers of therapists skilled in working with families in crisis is the norm in most communities. Recent research concludes that 79% of insured 6- to 17-year-olds do not receive the mental health services they need; the unmet needs of uninsured children are even greater (Kataoka, Zhang, & Wells, 2002). The growth of the alternative youth treatment industry indicates at very least that there is a dire need in the United States for better services and supports closer to home so that families can get the help they need without sending adolescents away.

In the meantime, researchers have estimated that there are more than 280,000 at-risk students in alternative programs in the United States (Conley, 2002). Indeed, the range of options for schools and other types of facilities (particularly for those with the means to pay) is a veritable smorgasbord of interventions. These programs include: outdoor programs (adventure programs, wilderness therapy programs, vision quests); school programs (boarding schools, emotional growth/therapeutic boarding schools); transition programs (foster homes, group homes, therapeutic communities, halfway houses); treatment programs (day treatment programs, residential treatment centers, psychiatric hospitals); and juvenile justice programs (detention/incarceration, boot camps).

A fascinating side-industry, that has emerged in conjunction with some of these programs is the adolescent "escort" or "transport" service; there are dozens of these agencies advertising on the web. For a substantial fee, parents who do not feel they can safely get their girls to the woods or to residential treatment, hire "escorts" to come secretly in the middle of the night, rouse their adolescent in the wee hours of the morning, and take her by road and plane to the wilderness for them. During the time of this staged abduction, parents are not even supposed to be in the house, lowering the adolescent's resistance by virtue of the disorienting time of day and unfamiliarity of transporters. The network of educational consultants, escort services, wilderness programs, and emotional growth schools is tightly formed, with groups recommending one another to parents who have little way of assessing information independently.

In the absence of adequate community services, and the sense of urgency for many adolescents and parents, these programs do have a place in our toolboxes to help girls in crisis. Thus it is useful to know a bit about the programs, how they are supposed to operate, and how to guide families (particularly those who have sufficient means to have real options) in thinking through the possibilities. For less privileged families, our work as advocates within educational, social service, legal, and mental health systems can also facilitate needed out-of-home placement funded by local, state, and federal agencies. When it comes time to consider removal of an adolescent girl from her home, this role of advocate may accompany or even supersede our position as therapist.

Outdoor Behavior Programs

Outdoor behavior programs include adventure, wilderness, and vision quests. These programs share in common a belief that adolescents benefit from leaving behind their complex social and cultural contexts to grapple instead with the raw simplicity of nature. Stripped of familiarity and artifice, teens may then come to know themselves and others more authentically.

Adventure Programs

The general purpose of adventure programs is to provide adolescents with experiential learning activities in the wilderness. These programs offer girls an array of adventure activities including, for example, outdoor education, outdoor leadership training, mountaineering, rock climbing, whitewater rafting, kayaking, and backpacking expeditions (Conner, 2006). Through participation, girls have the potential to develop skills includes leadership, communication, awareness, cooperation, self-confidence, and strategic planning abilities.

Adventure programs began to grow in popularity and number in the 1960s as hospitals and detention programs started experimenting with adventure therapy as an adjunct to treatment of a variety of psychiatric and offender populations (Cason & Gillis, 1994). There are now over 500 wilderness experience programs (WEPs) in the United States (Russell & Hendee, 1999) most of which can be described as adventure programs. Among them, Outward Bound and National Outdoor Leadership School (NOLS) are perhaps the best known. These programs do not offer therapy for participants per se, but rather hold that nature serves as the ultimate teacher and guide.

Adolescent participation in adventure programs is voluntary, and adolescents who do not follow the rules will be asked to leave. Still, if a girl is willing to give it a try, she may develop a sense of the larger world that she would not otherwise have discovered. Perhaps she will learn about natural limits; that she cannot manipulate the wilderness. Girls may also discover that they can function competently as part of a larger community. For girls who need some help, but not necessarily a more intensive therapeutic environment, adventure programs can be hugely transformative. Participants learn directly through experience. Through facing natural and technical challenges, they may grow emotionally and interpersonally since trust, cooperation, and feedback are necessary for group and individual success.

Indeed, research suggests that adventure programs may have greater advantages for girls than institutional alternatives (Berman & Anton, 1988; Levitt, 1994; Williams, 2000). Many researchers also describe the many ways that adventure programs serve a therapeutic purpose for girls, with personal, social, emotional, and cognitive benefits (Levitt, 1994). In the United States today, the vast majority of adolescents are deprived by seldom being out in the natural world (Louv, 2005). Thus, wilderness camping appears to have a therapeutic impact in and of itself for many adolescents— being outside, camping with a group of peers, and learning through natural challenges all appear to be valuable aspects of it.

Wilderness Treatment Programs

Wilderness therapy programs can be distinguished from adventure programs in a few important ways. Adventure programs are voluntary; most teens end up in wilderness treatment against their will. While the wilderness is a "therapist" for both, only wilderness treatment programs have actual clinical individual and group therapy and additional specific therapeutic goals. The kinds of interventions and structured activities further distinguish the programs; oppositional behavior that would not be tolerated in an adventure program is handled as an expected part of wilderness therapy. Adolescents in adventure programs are stepping up to new challenges; those in wilderness treatment often arrive there in acute crisis, as a last-ditch effort to keep them from self-destructing. The length of time in the wilderness for adventure programs is dictated by the nature of the activity; an adolescent's defiant behavior may keep her longer in a wilderness treatment program or land her back there.

Of the 500 WEPs in the United States, fewer than 40 are specifically wilderness therapy programs for adolescents. All of these programs make money; wilderness therapy programs are particularly lucrative, costing about $400 a day. In 1998 over 12,000 adolescents went into a wilderness therapy program, generating over $148 million in revenues for the management (Russell & Hendee, 1999).

The basic premise of these programs is that the wilderness is a most powerful teacher of teenagers who have been rebellious and defiant, and who are prone to rule breaking. Through the use of positive peer pressure, introspective group discussions, and the building of primitive skills, adolescents begin to understand, via metaphor, what they will need to live more productively and meaningfully in society.

Optimally, adolescents in wilderness treatment programs will quickly learn how cooperation, responsibility for behaviors, and a strong work ethic can create a positive group environment through which they can develop self-esteem and obtain greater self-knowledge. By being away from their home environment and all the influences of modern culture—parties, iPods, malls, television, videos, e-mail—adolescents may have a unique opportunity to explore their motives, behaviors, and attitudes that have gotten them into trouble and have been self-defeating. In the dislocation of the wilderness, they can begin to explore their relationships with others and their issues with authority, peers, and family members. Here too, positive peer influence is supposed to replace negative peer pressure.

Many wilderness programs have a structured system of levels that also operate as metaphors for life in the real world. These metaphors relate to time-honored systems of initiation for young people, and are often taken from Native American rituals. An adolescent may progress from coyote to eagle level, for example (Davis-Berman & Berman, 1994). This level system stands in for the absence of such rites of passage that could better move adolescents along developmentally in contemporary culture.

Wilderness therapy programs provide two types of interventions. *Contained system* wilderness therapy programs are usually up to three weeks long, operating in a wilderness expedition model in which clients and leaders stay together for the duration of the trip. *Continuous flow system* programs are longer, up to eight weeks in length, and have clients continually admitted to ongoing groups, with leaders rotating in and out of the field (Russell & Hendee, 1999).

In both contained and continuous flow wilderness therapy systems, the therapeutic process includes the careful selection of appropriate clients, based on a clinical assessment, and the creation of an individual treatment plan for each participant (Russell & Hendee, 1999). Individual and group therapy techniques are applied in the wilderness setting, and facilitated by qualified professionals, with formal evaluative procedures used to assess the clients' progress.

Wilderness therapy uses expedition-based outdoor pursuits (hiking, backpacking), educational curricula (cooking outdoors, setting up camp, fire making), and individual and group therapy strategies. In addition, it provides for extended periods of solitary introspection time. Wilderness self-care and group safety are facilitated by natural consequences, thereby teaching personal and social responsibility. Programs typically have three phases:

1. *Cleansing phase:* The initial goal of wilderness treatment is to rid clients of chemical dependencies by removing them from the destructive environments that perpetuated their addictions. The cleansing is accomplished with a minimal but healthy diet, intense physical exercise, and the teaching of basic survival and self-care skills. Adolescents are also removed from the trappings of their former environment including the numerous distractions of adolescent culture and their families. The cleansing process is in itself therapeutic and prepares adolescents for more in-depth work later in the program.

2. *Personal and social responsibility phase:* After the initial cleansing phase, natural consequences and peer interaction are strong therapeutic influences helping adolescents to learn and accept personal and social responsibility. Self-care and personal responsibility are facilitated by natural consequences in the wilderness, not by authority figures, whom troubled adolescents are apt to resist. For example, if they refuse to set up a tarp and it rains, they'll get wet and have no one to blame but themselves. Wilderness therapists have the task of helping the adolescents generalize these metaphors of self-care and natural consequences to their lives back home (Russell & Hendee, 1999).

In this second phase also, adolescent social skill deficits are also addressed by intense social involvement with the group. Girls learn, in vivo, better ways to manage anger, share emotions, tell the truth, and process interpersonal conflicts. Under the guidance of the leaders, new behaviors are modeled and practiced all day long. This hands-on instruction in personal and social responsibility is reinforced by the logical and natural consequences provided by the condition of living in the wilderness.

3. *Transition and aftercare phase:* Upon completion of the wilderness therapy program, most adolescents (80% in one study) head next to another residential program—an emotional growth boarding school, an alcohol and drug treatment center, or a residential mental health facility (Russell & Hendee, 1999). Seldom do the skills attained in the woods generalize on their own without significant therapeutic aftercare.

Most wilderness therapy programs insist on some parent involvement. This represents a departure from "hoods-in-the-woods" programs that just focus on modifying adolescent behavior. Parents are expected to be in their own treatment, and to continue to be involved in the work their daughters are doing in the wilderness. Although they will not speak to each other during the time the adolescent is away, parents do have telephone contact with the field therapists on a regular basis to learn of progress and issues.

Well-run wilderness therapy programs appear to have many interesting advantages for adolescents, including therapeutic use of small-group interactions, natural risks, supportive adults, and concrete problem-solving opportunities. B. Williams (2000) surmises further that wilderness programs have three clear advantages over inpatient groups: the transference issues between counselors and adolescents are worked on around the clock; the group dynamics are more intensive and rapidly create a social microcosm, whereby the group benefits or suffers more immediately from individual behavior; and group activities are usually physical, mental, and verbal—adolescents are more fully engaged in the experience. Additionally, outdoor adventure "can be intense, physical and emotional just like teens" (Marx, 1988, p. 517). Being outside, as opposed to being inside, may further provide some adolescents with a feeling of freedom and hope in not being locked up or institutionalized.

Vision Quests

A Vision Quest is a wilderness experience for adolescents that is more expressly a rite of passage into adulthood, based on initiation rituals from some Native American cultures. There are a variety of Vision Quest experiences available throughout the United States for adolescents who have sufficient internal resources to withstand a solo experience lasting two or three days in the wild, with no food or scheduled activities. Vision Quest is appropriate for adolescents who are capable of taking sufficient care of themselves and seek a meaningful challenge to test themselves as they grow toward adulthood. It is not a substitute for psychotherapy or substance abuse treatment.

Vision Quests have emerged in response to an time-honored yearning in adolescents to undertake rites of passage. In our contemporary culture there are few such positive initiatory experiences available. Filling this void, adolescent peer culture creates its own risky rituals. These usually fail miserably at bringing increased self-awareness, responsibility, or maturity. Since the early 1980s, a variety of programs have evolved with the goal of providing adolescents with a very different and deeper kind of challenge than they typically face. Vision Quest programs typically have three phases: beginning with a group experience where both safety issues and personal development are addressed, the solo experience, and then time back with the group so new learning can be shared and witnessed.

All types of experiences in the wilderness for adolescents address a growing cultural imperative of removing girls far away from the destructive social forces and expectations of their everyday lives. To varying degrees these programs also prepare girls for managing reentry into reality so that gains made in the wilderness can be sustained back in the face of old pressures and stressors.

School Programs

School programs include boarding schools, and emotional growth/therapeutic boarding schools. For some adolescents, living away from the stresses of home and community offers a compelling alternative. Both regular and therapeutic boarding schools are structured to emphasize academic progress. They afford a new set of challenges for girls who have become accustomed to the patterns and problems of living in families and attending local schools. Privileged teens have gone to boarding schools in this country for many centuries; more recently it has become an option for a broader range of adolescents, crossing lines of race, class, and emotional distress.

Boarding Schools

There are 370 boarding schools in the United States serving a broad range of students, with significant financial aid available for those who need it. The Milton Hershey School, in Hershey, PA, is entirely free of cost. Although most of these schools do not seek out adolescents with major emotional problems, to varying degrees they are all equipped to handle girls with some psychological and learning difficulties. Boarding schools offering significant financial aid and low-interest loans may be more of a placement resource than we generally consider them to be. For girls who are not getting their needs met in their homes or community schools, but who might thrive with a little more structure and challenge, boarding schools may offer a less-stigmatizing and more enriching alternative to other residential programs.

Emotional Growth Schools/Therapeutic Boarding Schools

Emotional growth boarding schools integrate therapeutic programs with academics to provide for students whose emotional, psychological, and behavioral issues prevent them from learning effectively in a traditional day or boarding school environment. Therapeutic components of these schools include daily and weekly group and individual therapy, highly structured behaviorally oriented learning, and living environments, experiential learning, and individualized academic programming. As with wilderness treatment programs, many emotional growth programs have level systems, with defined rituals and changes in privileges marking progress; some of these are also derived from Native American traditions.

Because the root of many emotional and behavioral problems is low self-esteem and negative perception of others, emotional growth programs tend to focus on helping students permanently change negative self-perceptions, discover and heal emotional trauma, and identify and change negative behaviors. Foremost they are supposed to provide newfound safety, stability, and structure.

Emotional growth boarding schools usually offer rolling admission; that is students are accepted year-round and academics are available year-round, too. Adolescents usually stay in these programs from 9 to 18 months. Families requiring emergency placement can send their adolescents to emotional growth programs if their adolescents meet the criteria for admission. It is most common that adolescents head to these programs directly from a therapeutic wilderness experience (and back to the woods if they act out while in the emotional growth program). Some schools accept students after psychological and educational testing and interviews, to determine therapeutic need, academic level, and fit between the adolescent and the program (Conley, 2002).

Emotional growth/therapeutic boarding schools in the United States represent a relatively new billion-dollar industry. In the mid-1990s, there were only about 40 schools in the country devoted to "troubled teens." One year after the Columbine tragedy, the number rose to 250; there are now over 500 such schools (Tarrant, 2005). These programs deal with roughly 10,000 to 20,000 adolescents a year (Chen, 2005; Szalavitz, 2006), and typically charge in the range of $4,500 to $9,000 per month (Tarrant, 2005).

Family members usually also sign onto a big commitment beyond the money. Most emotional growth programs have an intensive therapy requirement for parents as well. They may be expected to take weeks off at a time to participate in family events at the school, and to engage in their own therapy. Most emotional growth schools also have parent support networks. There is no research documenting whether these programs are superior to intensive home-based treatments. However, one outcome study reports that more than 85% of students completing such programs have improved family and peer relationships, attend college or find a job, and remain free from substance use (Sisk, 2006).

Transition Programs

Transition programs include therapeutic foster care, group homes, and therapeutic communities. These programs have developed to serve adolescents, who, at least for a while, are not fully safe at home, but still do not require more restrictive settings. Girls may wind up in transitional settings heading in both directions—on the way from home into a residential placement, or as a needed step-down on the way back to family and community.

Therapeutic Foster Care

Therapeutic foster care is the least restrictive form of out-of-home therapeutic placement, but it typically requires the involvement of child welfare agencies to procure. Adolescents in therapeutic foster care live in private homes with specially trained foster parents. The combination of family-based care with specialized treatment interventions creates "a therapeutic environment in the context of a nurturant family home" (Stroul & Friedman, 1996). Therapeutic foster care is often funded jointly by child welfare and mental health agencies; they are responsible for arranging for foster parent training and oversight.

Although the research base is modest compared with other widely used interventions, some studies have reported positive outcomes, mostly related to behavioral improvements and movement to even less restrictive living environments, such as traditional foster care or placement back home. In several studies, adolescents in therapeutic foster care made significant gains in adjustment, self-esteem, sense of identity, and reducing aggressive behavior. In addition, these gains were sustained for some time after leaving the therapeutic foster home (U.S. Department of Health and Human Services, 1999).

While therapeutic foster care programs vary considerably, they have some features in common. Adolescents are placed with foster parents who are trained to work with adolescents with special needs. They receive extensive preservice training and inservice supervision and support. Usually, each foster home takes one adolescent at a time, and caseloads of supervisors in agencies overseeing the program remain small. In addition, therapeutic foster parents are given a higher stipend than that given to traditional foster parents. Frequent contact between case managers or care coordinators and the treatment family is expected, and additional resources and traditional mental health services may be provided to adolescents as needed.

It is clear from some studies that therapeutic foster care can produce better outcomes at lower costs than more restrictive types of placement. Furthermore, with the fairly recent development of standards for therapeutic foster care, as well as a standards review instrument (Foster Family-Based Treatment Association, 1995), services can be monitored for quality and fidelity to the therapeutic approach. Thus, this out-of-home strategy is worth considering if the resource is available and girls meet criteria for eligibility.

Therapeutic Group Homes

For adolescents with serious emotional disturbances, the therapeutic group home provides another type of alternative environment that can help with social skills and psychological growth. As with therapeutic foster care, girls gain access to this resource if they act out or are otherwise unsafe in their homes, and thus involve local child protection, legal, or social service agencies that may then help pay for placement in these homes.

In therapeutic group homes, specially trained staff live and work with the adolescents in the community, so girls can continue to attend local schools. Each home typically serves 5 to 10 girls and provides an array of therapeutic interventions. Although the types and combinations of treatment vary, individual psychotherapy, group therapy, and behavior modification are usually included.

Research on the efficacy of therapeutic group homes is limited. Some research suggests that therapeutic group home programs produce positive gains for adolescents while they are in the home, but the limited research available reveals that these changes are seldom maintained after discharge (Pottick, Warner, & Yoder, 2005). The conclusion may be similar to that for residential treatment center placement: long-term outcomes appear to be related to the extent of services and support after discharge.

Adolescents who have been placed in therapeutic group homes because of emotional problems frequently have histories of multiple prior placements (particularly in foster homes), a situation that is already associated with a poor prognosis. Still, it makes sense that any program worth considering has thought through the thorny issues of aftercare, especially if adolescents are supposed to return home to families that struggled with parenting in the first place.

Therapeutic Communities

A therapeutic community (TC) is a drug-free residential program that provides a highly structured, prosocial environment for the treatment of drug abuse and addiction, and seriously impaired social functioning. TCs are for older adolescents who stay in the residence typically for around 6 to 12 months. TCs differ from other treatment approaches by using the community as the key agent of change.

Treatment staff and recovering clientele interact in both structured and unstructured ways to influence attitudes, perceptions, and behaviors associated with drug use. In addition, TCs use a staged, hierarchical model in which treatment stages are related to increased levels of individual and social responsibility. The sense of a strong, structured hierarchical environment—in which all participants and staff have specific tasks, responsibilities, and rights—is crucial to the success of most TC programs (Mello, Pechansky, Inciardi, & Surratt, 1997). The ultimate focus of the TC is on the resocialization of the adolescent to a drug-free, crime-free life.

Peer influence is also an important component of TC programs. Residents learn and assimilate social norms and develop more effective social skills through daily community meetings, work assignments, and the peer group process. Daily interactions are used to cultivate a sense of community mission and mutual self-help. Under the mutual self-help concept, individuals assume responsibility for the recovery, personal growth, and right living of their peers in order to maintain their own recovery. And although the adolescent may have a substance abuse problem, the therapeutic community is designed to treat the whole person, not just the disordered drinking or drug use (Messina, Wishe, & Nemes, 2000).

Treating adolescents in a residential TC has its own unique challenges, most notably the difficulty of engaging the entire family in treatment, especially when the adolescent is placed at a distance from home. By the time the adolescent enters a TC, family communication has usually eroded. As with other alternative programs, it is crucial that a TC program engages and treats the adolescent alongside her family, from assessment through continuing care.

For the family, treatment should include individual-family and multifamily counseling, parent support groups, and chemical dependency education. In addition, family members should be integrated into a variety of activities and social events that will aid in communication and to reinforce the family's ongoing commitment to recovery.

Meta-analyses of TC programs in the general population have consistently supported the efficacy of TC treatment protocols for substance abusers, especially when treatment has been continued over long periods of time, and families are involved in a comprehensive aftercare program. This is imperative because research indicates that juvenile substance abusers are most likely to experience relapse within the first six months after treatment and reentry (DeLeon, 2000; Sealock, Gottfredson, & Gallagher, 1997).

Halfway Houses

Adolescent girls who have been treated for substance abuse problems, but are not sufficiently resolute to return home, can live for a few months in a community-based halfway house. A halfway house is a kind of therapeutic community, but typically a step closer to the adolescent's hometown. Halfway houses are drug-free facilities in which individuals recovering from drug or alcohol problems can live with others in a similar level of abstinence. These homes get the name *halfway* because people with substance abuse problems who use them are halfway between requiring full supervision and being able to live independently.

A halfway house provides the former substance user with a safe, supportive environment in which to practice living drug-free in a world filled with the temptations of drugs (Baumohl & Jaffe, 2002). These residences are located in regular neighborhoods within communities. Halfway houses vary in terms of their size, sources of financial support, and kinds of treatment they offer. Some specialize in alcohol abusers or drug abusers, while some serve both; some focus on adolescents. Most halfway houses do not offer much family involvement; thus aftercare for adolescents who will be returning home is still a serious concern.

Treatment Programs

Treatment programs include: day treatment, residential, and psychiatric hospitals. These programs share an expressly therapeutic intent within a medical model of psychiatric care. They are designed to serve adolescents whose emotional distress exceeds the resources of outpatient facilities. Intensive treatment programs for adolescents have burgeoned in recent years, and have proven to be quite profitable for private companies and the insurance industry. They are most effective when they include families in the treatment plan, and assist with the adolescent's ultimate re-entry into the community.

Day Treatment Programs

Although day treatment (also known as partial hospitalization) is not, strictly speaking, an alternative placement, it defines a level of care exceeding outpatient and home-based services, so merits some description. Indeed, many adolescent day treatment programs are so intensive—five days a week, for at least four or five hours a day—that girls just sleep at home. Adolescents referred to day treatment have behavior that can be managed by their parents; that is, they do not require 24/7 residential services. Before sending a girl to a residential program, or hospitalizing her, this is a worthwhile option to explore. Day treatment is also often a helpful step-down option following hospitalization for girls who still need a little more external structure and support than can be provided by outpatient therapy and life in the community.

Although there is great variability among programs, girls (and their families) who participate in day treatment can expect to receive: special education, individual, family, multifamily, and group counseling, skill building, parent training, vocational training, and crisis intervention. Most day treatment programs are behaviorally based using positive reinforcement to promote success, with recreational, art and music therapy to further aid in emotional and social development (Stroul & Friedman, 1996). Some adolescent "day" treatment programs are not really offered during the day; girls arrive after school and stay into the evening. Insurance companies typically pay for at least a portion of a day treatment program. Families and schools may also have to contribute depending on the program. Additionally, some insurance companies will allocate inpatient funds for this less costly intervention strategy.

The available data on overall effectiveness of day treatment suggest mixed results, although it is clearly more cost-effective than residential treatments, and does not suffer from the problems associated with reintegrating an adolescent back into home and community (Kutash & Rivera, 1995). Interestingly, even with some demonstrable benefits, these services have not developed as rapidly as the residential alternatives.

The marketplace appears to be dictating here as well. Insurance companies tend to reimburse for day treatment at a lower rate because it is usually considered to be an outpatient treatment. Patients then opt for inpatient care because, ironically, they cannot afford the cost of day-treatment (Grizenko & Papineau, 1992). But if local resources are available, good day treatment that involves the outpatient therapist, school, and family in the treatment plan can be a worthy step to pursue ahead of other alternatives.

Residential Treatment Centers

Residential treatment centers (RTCs) typically offer a combination of substance abuse and mental health treatment programs and 24-hour supervision in a highly structured (often staff-secure) environment. They usually house adolescents with significant psychiatric or substance abuse problems who have proved too emotionally handicapped or unruly to be treated in foster care, day treatment programs, and other nonsecure environments, but who do not yet merit commitment to a psychiatric hospital or secure corrections facility. RTCs also serve as transitional programs for students coming from even more restrictive settings like the wilderness, locked hospital wards, or drug treatment centers.

Although RTCs must be licensed by the state, they are frequently run by private, for-profit, and nonprofit institutions, and the treatment approaches and admissions criteria used by RTCs vary widely from state to state and institution to institution. Residential treatment is, like many of the other intervention strategies described in this chapter, big business. There were over 43,000 admissions to RTCs in 1997 according to a report by the U.S. Surgeon General (Satcher, 1999). They can cost more than a year in college, and they do not guarantee results. RTCs are used by a relatively small number (8%) of treated children and adolescents but nearly a quarter of the national outlay on child mental health is spent on care in these settings (Burns, Hoagwood, & Maultsby, 1998). This is so despite variable evidence, at best, for their effectiveness (U.S. Department of Health and Human Services, 1999).

As with most treatment options where there is enormous diversity in the type and quality of services being offered, the literature regarding RTCs demonstrates concern about its efficacy. A summary of research findings prepared by the U.S. Surgeon General reports that "in the past, admission to an RTC has been justified on the basis of community protection, child protection, and the benefits of residential treatment." (U.S. Department of Health and Human Services, 1999). However, numerous studies have demonstrated that equally efficacious results can be achieved in less restrictive, community-based settings (Joshi and Rosenberg, 1997). Mental health and substance abuse professionals have also repeatedly called for clearer admission criteria for RTCs, to avoid incarcerating youth in inappropriate settings or with inappropriate and potentially dangerous peer groups.

Types of treatment offered in RTCs may include psychoanalytic and interpersonal therapy, psychoeducation, behavioral management, group therapy, and medication management. However, some of these programs also feature a "tough love" behavioral approach that has come under justifiable scrutiny and outrage in recent years. In such interventions, the primary approach to treating adolescent problems is intense humiliation and confrontation, and very strict discipline. This treatment strategy operates within a behavioral point system favoring punishment over rewards, in which consequences, ranging from loss of privileges, to solitary confinement, and even physical punishment in some RTCs, are doled out for misbehavior.

These "tough love" RTCs tend to be on physically isolated campuses with extremely limited governmental oversight. In summarizing an extensive review of the data from a range of RTCs, Szalavitz (2006) concludes that the RTC industry is dominated by the idea that harsh rules and even brutal confrontation are necessary to help troubled teenagers, even though there is little empirical evidence to support such an approach to adolescents, and much evidence against it.

The lack of regulation of programs is of extreme concern. Several of the larger private RTCs have had numerous complaints and hundreds of lawsuits against them. This review is not to condemn all RTCs out of hand, though careful selection is imperative. But we have ample data now to suggest that these "get tough" behavioral strategies ultimately do not work, and may even cause increased distress and dysfunction for many adolescents (National Institutes of Health, 2004).

There are RTCs that offer more in the way of nurture and compassion (Moses, 2000). These alternatives to "tough love" approaches hold greater appeal and potential for helping girls who need it. Recent research (widely reported by the RTCs themselves, and funded by the industry) suggests that licensed facilities are indeed beneficial in reducing symptoms in severely disturbed adolescents (Behrens, 2006).

RTCs also often have a problem with adequate aftercare. Without follow-up, and if they return to an unchanged home environment, adolescents who have been engaged in even highly therapeutic RTCs are likely to regress. Inadequate aftercare can be an impediment to sustained progress for adolescent girls from all socioeconomic classes referred into the system in every possible manner. Thus, before supporting the decision to place an adolescent girl in an RTC, ample thought and legwork needs to precede the plan, and strategies for her return home have to be explicit.

Psychiatric Hospitals

Inpatient hospitalization is considered the most restrictive type of care in the continuum of mental health services for children and adolescents. It is sometimes necessary for safety—if a girl is in imminent danger of harming herself or others and she cannot be contained adequately at home. It is also advised when serious mental disorders are significantly impairing functioning and a thorough evaluation is warranted. But girls are on psychiatric units for many other problems, too. They're inpatients for substance abuse, disordered thinking, and acute anxiety, mania, self-mutilation, and depression, all problems for which a hospital stay may, at least in some cases, be beneficial. And they're also admitted for more complex systemic issues like ODD and CD (stealing, truancy, running away), and for more transient adjustment difficulties as well with no obvious advantage at all.

In recent years fewer than one-third of adolescents admitted for inpatient mental health treatment were diagnosed with a severe or acute mental disorder such as psychosis, or serious depression—diagnoses usually associated with the need for psychiatric hospitalization. Neither did the behavior of these adolescents require an inpatient setting to protect them or others from their dangerous behaviors. The majority of these hospitalized adolescents were found to be reacting to troubled or inadequate family situations: they were rebellious, disruptive, and noncompliant (Eamon, 1994; Pottick, Warner & Yoder, 2005; Weithorn, 1988; Weller, Cook, Hendren, Woolston, et al., 1995). Thus some girls are hospitalized for serious mental disorders but these cases make up the minority of referrals.

Most hospital stays are quite brief, a few days or a couple of weeks, particularly for those with private insurance; Medicaid patients stay a bit longer (Pottick, McAlpine, & Andelman, 2000). Stays aren't long enough to get better regulated on most medications or to make dramatic intervention into a troubled home life. The hope for hospitalization in the postmanaged care era is generally to get a girl out of imminent danger, perhaps get a closer evaluation of the situation, and begin to head toward some eventual stabilization through therapy, and initiation or adjustment of medication.

While girls are usually sent to hospitals with loftier goals of transformation, the reality is that they aren't all that effective in ameliorating most problems for which girls are admitted (Curry, 1991; Grizenko & Papineau, 1992; Mason & Gibbs, 1992). Indeed, both theory and empirical research stress that most of the problems for which adolescents are hospitalized should be handled within a variety of community-based settings that have demonstrable economic and psychological benefits over inpatient treatment.

Still the trend toward greater psychiatric commitment for adolescents (particularly those who are Caucasian and have insurance) in the past two decades has continued unabated even in the absence of increased social or clinical need for such treatment (Weller et al., 1995). According to the National Association of Psychiatric Health Systems annual survey (2005), occupancy rates for inpatient adolescent programs increased 33% just between 1997 and 2001, and are now at an all-time high. From an empirical standpoint, we don't know how the different forces—dynamics of insurance type, hospital ownership, characteristics of adolescents, and their changing environments—play into these trends (Pottick et al., 2000). Notably, paralleling the increase in other forms of teen residential treatment, the private psychiatric hospital industry has also burgeoned, and is competing intensively for adolescents via outreach and advertising in order to fill their beds (H. Metz, 1991).

One skeptical review of private psychiatric admissions from the 1980s concluded that the admission criteria were not based on need or behavior but on insurance coverage or other ability to pay (Select Committee on Children, Youth and Families, 1989). Similarly, a study of 2,000 psychiatric admissions in California showed that youth with insurance were held in treatment twice as long as their uninsured peers (H. Metz, 1991). Further, youth in general were held in private psychiatric facilities twice as long as adults with similar disorders, despite the lack of clinical evidence showing that, "juveniles are twice as sick or that it takes twice as long to cure them" (Select Committee on Children, Youth and Families). Yet inpatient care continues to consume about half of child mental health resources, but it is the clinical intervention with the weakest research support (National Association of Psychiatric Health Systems, 2005; U.S. Department of Health and Human Services, 1999).

High occupancy rates probably don't reflect the critical need for these services or the limited availability of beds for adolescents in crisis. It is easy to surmise cynically that other factors, including the marketplace, are also operating. And in the managed care world, inpatient treatment can be disappointingly brief, rushed, and inadequate. So any referral for inpatient psychiatric services should be based on the adolescent's acute need, a clear understanding of what benefits (and costs) might be incurred by the adolescent and family from the choice, and the lack of compelling or realistic outpatient alternatives. And as with all of these out of home options, a plan for involving the family during the hospitalization and through aftercare is also essential.

Juvenile Justice Programs

Juvenile Justice programs include boot camps or incarceration/detention. While boot camps tend to be much more oriented toward boys, the rest of the juvenile justice system is bursting at the seams with adolescent girls. Girls are being detained and incarcerated in unprecedented numbers; however, discrimination abounds and few juvenile justice programs are meeting their special needs.

Juvenile Boot Camps

There are two types of boot camps: privately funded and state run. Private boot camps are short-term and designed to help "troubled teens get back to the basics" (Teens in Crisis, 2001). State boot camps are mainly used for boys (though there are a few programs for girls, too) who would otherwise be placed in a state correctional facility for juveniles, or are considered high risk. For example, some of these camps are "preadjudication" volunteer camps for at-risk teenagers (i.e., unemployed high-school dropouts) which receive a combination of federal and state funding. Many others have developed in response to "parents desperate to ship their troubled teens to a military-style camp for a dose of discipline" (Krajicek, 1999, p. 37).

Boot camps are designed to emulate the Army's basic training, and typically last around two- to six-weeks in duration. The environment is highly confrontational and adversarial. The intervention is comprised of a series of challenges and activities designed to "break down, break through, and then build back up" (Parenting Teens, 2003). Adolescents sleep on cots in tents, get up at 6:00 A.M. and are treated to a high-intensity, in-your-face methodology that is intended to scare them into behaving better.

Boot camps were more prevalent a decade ago (Congress allocated $45 million for new boot camp initiatives in 1994 and 1995—total beds: 4,500; total designated for females: 200; Krajicek, 1999), and appear to be losing some of their appeal. Research has demonstrated very limited effectiveness over the longer term in this sort of approach (Krajicek, 1999). High recidivism rates for adolescents who have attended boot camps suggest that the key to rehabilitation is in quality aftercare, not uniforms, push-ups, or marching.

Additionally, because so many girls adjudicated delinquent have significant trauma histories, it is quite likely that these strategies are worse than ineffective; they're retraumatizing, too. However, boot camps continue to have some popular appeal despite the research suggesting they don't work. Politicians see benefits in the lower cost, shorter duration, and evidence of toughness in the approach. While it is worth knowing about them, boot camps would not be a first choice intervention for girls under any circumstances, and, if need be, we should find a way, as part of our jobs to say so.

Detention/Incarceration

Juvenile detention is meant to be a temporary secure placement for adolescents who are due to appear in court, but have not yet had a hearing. It was created to serve two purposes: to assure that adolescents would appear in court at the proper time, and to protect the community by minimizing delinquent acts while their cases are being processed. In recent years, a number of utilization changes have affected the length of time and manner in which detention is used. These changes include increased use of pretrial facilities for short punitive incarceration sentences. They also include the detention of children charged as adults who are often held in detention for long periods of time—in some cases up to two years—while their cases are handled by much slower adult courts.

Between 1988 and 1997 the national rate of female involvement in the juvenile justice system increased by 83% as compared with a 30% increase for boys, with data showing these increases in all racial groups (American Bar Association & National Bar Association, 2001). There has been an exponential increase in the number of girls arrested, in detention, and in jails and prisons. The rate of arrests for girls (in almost all offense categories) has outstripped that of boys (although of course there are still many more boys who are committing these same crimes). Law enforcement agencies reported 670,800 arrests of girls under the age of 18 in 1999—which accounted for 27% of the total number of juvenile arrests made that year (American Bar Association & National Bar Association, 2001).

These arrest rates translate into increased pressure on detention centers. On any given day, approximately 25,000 adolescents are held in around 500 secure detention facilities nationwide (Annie E. Casey Foundation, 1997). Even with 75 new facilities, there has been a sixfold increase in overcrowding in the past decade. Indeed, almost 600,000 children and adolescents are admitted to secure detention annually (Annie E. Casey Foundation, 1997).

Along with increased detention for girls, there is ample evidence that girls are being detained for less serious offenses than boys. Girls are more likely to be detained for minor offenses (e.g. public disorder, status offenses, traffic offenses) that do not actually warrant detention according to the principle of "the least restrictive alternative," and for technical violation of probation in the absence of new offenses (American Bar Association & National Bar Association, 2001). And girls are more likely than boys to be returned to detention after being released.

In other words, once girls are in the system, they often stay in the system due to a violation of a court order, probation violations, or contempt charges. This practice is called "bootstrapping" and often results in female offenders remaining in the system without having committed new offenses (American Bar Association & National Bar Association, 2001). The gender biases described are even more marked for minority girls. This increase in the use of detention for girls has resulted in overcrowding, poor conditions of confinement, and a reduction of appropriate services, further straining the already limited educational, physical, and mental health services available to meet the girls' needs. It has also led to girls being held in detention centers employing intervention strategies designed for boys, and alongside of boys—both developmentally harmful strategies.

Boys and girls are both also incarcerated in alarming numbers. Amnesty International (1998) reports that the United States puts more children behind bars than any other nation in the world. Among their stunning findings: 200,000 children are prosecuted annually in criminal courts, with an estimated 7,000 of them held in adult jails before trial. Over 11,000 children are currently being held in U.S. prisons and other adult correction facilities. Nearly 89,000 cases included the use of solitary confinement for more than 24 hours. Contrary to expectation, more than half of the children who were transferred out of juvenile courts to be tried as adults were charged with nonviolent offenses. These sobering statistics are also of concern because children who are incarcerated, even in juvenile facilities, are more likely to reoffend and have worse future economic prospects than those who receive alternative sentences—and remain in the community.

Moreover, the growth in the number of girls in detention and incarcerated in the United States is clearly due to a number of factors, and not just an increase in girls' aggressive and violent behavior that might put them behind bars. Rather, preliminary research suggests that the relabeling of girls' conflict with their families as violent offenses; the changes in police arrest practices and procedures regarding domestic violence and aggressive behavior; the gender bias in processing misdemeanor and status offense cases; and a systemic failure to understand the unique developmental issues facing girls have all contributed to the increase in the number of girls entering the juvenile justice system (American Bar Association and National Bar Association, 2001). While the exact nature of justice system bias against girls is a subject of ongoing debate, both gender and race are causes of significant disparity in how cases move through the juvenile justice system.

And it is well documented that, in addition to the different reasons girls enter the system, the problems that got them there also make them more vulnerable than their male peers. One national study found that 54% of girls incarcerated in U.S. juvenile correction settings had been sexually abused; 61% had been physically abused, and the majority of these girls had been abused multiple times. Over 80% had run away from home, and over half had attempted suicide (American Civil Liberties Union, 2006). Other studies report even higher abuse and victimization rates (Acoca & Dedel, 1998). Female offenders also demonstrate very high rates of depression and anxiety, and significant substance abuse problems.

Girls in the juvenile justice system also have more extreme family fragmentation and dysfunction than do their male peers, compounded by poverty, the incarceration of their parents, and their own early parenting (Acoca & Dedel, 1998; Child Welfare League of America, 2004). They similarly share a history of school struggle and failure leading to truancy, suspension, and expulsion, with rates of school difficulty even greater for minority girls.

There are insufficient numbers of gender-competent programs at all levels of the juvenile justice system, from arrest to detention to incarceration (and through diversion and probation as well). Gender competent programs (e.g., the PACE Center for Girls; Schaible, 2001) address the relationship between victimization and juvenile crime involvement by girls, focus on strengths, and provide gender specific counseling, education, training, and advocacy. These programs are also heavily relational, emphasizing staff–girl relationships as well as strengthening connections with family and peers.

When we are working with girls who become involved with the juvenile justice system, our advocacy with court and social service personnel can help direct outcomes. If we have a good sense of a girl's special needs (e.g., trauma, special education, pregnancy) and talents, we can offer our expert opinions about the intervention strategies that would best help them. In a legal system with so much bias against girls, especially poor and minority girls, we need to speak up on their behalf all the more.

Advocacy and Referral Considerations

With so many possible placement options, it can be difficult for an outpatient provider to guide families in making sound decisions for their adolescent girl in crisis. Following are some thoughts and questions that are important to consider as different alternatives are weighed:

- Help parents address their own embarrassment, humiliation, fear, and despair that might be interfering with exploration of options closer to home.
- Help parents get a "reality check" from school officials, teachers, family, and friends to assess the seriousness of the behavior problems.
- Explore local options first, and offer or look for a therapy program that works with the whole family, not just the adolescent.
- Recommend or conduct thorough assessments that will define the problem and point more clearly to specific remedies.
- Know enough about what the family and adolescent need to know in order to proceed intelligently.

- If considering an RTC, and it is possible, have the families investigate the RTC in person or online with the parent watchdog groups to learn more about their procedures and avoid the worst offenders (e.g., www.nospank.net/boot.htm).
  - Ask how long the program, or the company that owns the program, has been in operation, who licenses it, how many children it can serve and is serving, what the admission criteria are.
  - Ask about the admissions process: testing, interviewing, collateral materials reviewed, and what kind of ongoing assessment will be conducted.
  - Find out about how the program communicates with families, outside therapists, how progress is measured and reported. Who determines the treatment goals?
  - Find out if there are any lawsuits outstanding, any allegations of misconduct by staff in any of the programs run by the company.
  - Find out how often the family is allowed to be in contact with their child, and what kinds of parent and family support services they offer.
  - Find out about the behavioral system being used. You can help families assess whether it is an appropriate level system with significant emphasis on success and rewards, or too harsh and punitive in structure.
  - Find out about physical searches and other civil rights matters.
  - Ask about the food, the special education services, the medical team.
  - Ask very specifically about the therapy that will be provided. Again, you can assist families in determining whether these strategies will be helpful for their child, or involve too much "tough love."
- Encourage parents to show the enrollment contract to a lawyer before signing it.
- Help parents hire an independent educational consultant who works only for the family. Be sure this is a consultant who specializes in placing adolescents in treatment facilities. Questions to ask of the educational consultant include:
  - Do you take compensation from any of the schools or treatment centers that you may refer families to?

— How long have you been consulting?
— Do you travel to see programs?
— How many do you visit a year?
— Do you specialize in placing adolescents in alternative programs (as opposed to college consulting)?
— How many adolescents have you placed?
— Two websites that may help families find educational consultants: National Association of Therapeutic Schools and Programs (www.natsap.org) and Independent Education Consultants Organization (www.iecaonline.org)

• Make sure both you and the family stay in contact with the adolescent and the RTC throughout the placement so that safety and progress can be monitored.
• In Wilderness Treatment Programs: Find out about how they ensure safety in the field.
— Ask about the kinds of adventures the adolescent will be undertaking,
— Ask what other therapeutic and social activities are available,
— How are staff trained?
— How are danger (e.g., severe weather, changes of temperature) and injury handled?
• In Inpatient Psychiatric Programs: Find out what the program will offer the adolescent.
— Are there home-based alternatives that would still keep the adolescent safe?
— Is there aftercare? Day treatment? Other supports? How will the family be involved during and after the hospitalization?
— What is the schedule/program offered by the unit?
— Will the adolescent be able to keep up with her schoolwork?
— How will payment work—how long will it last, how much will it cost?
— What happens when the insurance runs out if the adolescent is not ready to be discharged?
— Ask the intake worker to describe the members and functions of the treatment team.

— How does the decision to discharge get made?
— How will the inpatient team work with school, outside therapist, other community agencies to ensure optimal care?
— How will medication be prescribed and managed?
- For Juvenile Justice Programs
  — Know the names and addresses of those involved with the case — judges, probation officers, social worker, lawyers.
  — Make sure you understand the legal options in how the case is being adjudicated and can discuss these with the adolescent and her family.
  — Make yourself a part of the team, respectfully offering suggestions and opinions as the case progresses through the system
  — Find out about diversion, home-based alternatives, and gender competent programs in your area.
  — Work with families to stay involved, to advocate, and to make changes that will help the adolescent with reentry if she is placed.

With so many different kinds of diagnoses, treatments, theories, programs, *and* girls, even the most seasoned and confident therapist is likely to have dark and doubtful moments about how to proceed. It is invariably reassuring to know that our willingness to learn and to try again matters a lot to the girls we treat. We make mistakes, figure out a new plan, and keep on going. And we are all growing and changing—the girls, their families, the world, and us. There is much to be hopeful about. In the following chapter, I suggest 10 reasons for such optimism.

CHAPTER FOURTEEN

TEN REASONS FOR HOPE

Hope is the thing with feathers—
That perches in the soul—
And sings the tune without the words—
And never stops—at all
                    —*Emily Dickinson*

It is unarguably challenging and frightening to take on the responsibility of helping adolescent girls in crisis. Yet it is also true that we get up in the morning to try again because we have trust and hope that we can make a difference, even so. Our faith in girls (and in ourselves) sometimes feels blind and crazy, but we persevere nonetheless.

And it's exciting and inspiring, too. We are in the middle of important changes in how we understand girls, adolescence, the life course, and the culture we live in. This flux is in itself hopeful because it suggests that there is room for opportunity alongside of the uncertainty. Following, then, are 10 reasons why we should remain invested in girls and hopeful about our work with them as we look ahead to the future:

Demographics

There are more adolescents and more of us to help them than ever before. The demographic profile of the adolescent population has changed dramatically during the past few decades and these changes are expected to continue well into the 21st century. The number of adolescents in the United States began to grow in the 1990s; by 1993 there were close to 36 million adolescents between 10 and 19 years of age (more than half were girls), representing about 14% of the population. This number will continue to increase up to the year 2050, and beyond (Kipke, 1999). Still, compared to the 77 million baby boomers also alive today these numbers remain relatively small; the demographic pyramid will be inverted for a long time to come.

These demographics instill hope for two reasons. First, it will become harder to ignore adolescents—their problems and what they can contribute. Those of us who are devoting our lives to making theirs better will have time to get the work done. Further, our advocacy will have an enduring base; needed policy changes will have a bigger impact on a growing population. And, much as those of us born in the last large cohort made a mark on the world with our strong voices, the sheer numbers of adolescents in this big group have the potential to be comparably heard should they decide to organize.

The second reason for hope here is that there are so many older adults in the general population, too. As boomers age, we have the chance to invest in this next generation, to give back and to increase "social capital" by reaching out (Center for Health Communication, Harvard School of Public Health, 2004). As we become grandparents to teenagers, or we have more time if we work less, volunteer, work alongside of adolescents, or otherwise find new meaningful ways to have contact with them, our numbers can support theirs. Adolescent girls need more adults in their lives; the boomer cohort indicates this shouldn't be such a problem.

Diversity

Those of us who have the will and the curiosity to live in a more diverse world will thrive. It's going to get interesting here in the United States. Increasing proportions of adolescents will belong to a larger variety of racial and ethnic minority groups; this can offer a richer multicultural experience for us all. In 1980, 74% of children in this country were white; this percentage has decreased steadily since that time and is expected to continue to shrink through 2050 (Kipke, 1999). By 2001, the Census reported that the percentage of white children had decreased to 63%. In 1993, more than one-third of the population of adolescents ages 10 to 19 were Hispanic or nonwhite. Black children were the largest minority population prior to 1997, but now their census numbers lag slightly behind Hispanic children (each making up about 15% of the total child population). The U.S. Bureau of Census is estimating that by the year 2020, more than one in five U.S. children will be Hispanic. Immigrants from the Pacific Rim will also make up a bigger percentage of the population as well; the Asian minority is expected to continue its rapid increase, from 4 to 6% by the year 2020 (Kipke, 1999). This rapid rise in racial and ethnic diversity is expected to continue through the coming decades.

Added to this growing ethnic diversity is linguistic diversity. According to the U.S. Department of Education, the number of youth who do not speak English fluently has doubled in the last decade to 5 million (Zhao, 2002). In addition, gay and lesbian youth are becoming aware of their sexual orientation at an earlier age and both boys and girls are "coming out" and making their orientation public by age 16 (Ryan & Futterman, 2002). Youth are also likely to have classmates who are differently-abled thanks to the Individuals with Disabilities Education Improvement Act that promotes mainstreaming disabled youth into regular school classes and activities (Wright & Wright, 2004). The future holds vast forms of diversity for us all.

Thus, more than ever, the country (and world) will benefit from adults who are culturally competent. Those of us with training in cultural diversity, interest, and compassion will be needed increasingly in years to come. We can work to have sufficient understanding, acceptance, and ability to honor the unique contributions of all people, regardless of ability, age, disability, ethnicity, gender, gender identity, geographic region, health, language, mental health, race, religion, sexual orientation, socioeconomic status, and spirituality. Living with so much diversity poses new challenges ahead for everyone. Our willingness to engage competently and empathically with diverse girls will not only enrich our own lives, but will also aid them in creating the compassionate kind of world we all want to live in.

Feminism's Enduring Legacy of Choices

Girls coming of age in the new Millennium will get to live in a world with many possibilities and opportunities. Adolescent girls have a new level of "girl power" where they are admired for being sassy, confident, Alpha, and sometimes dangerous (MacRobbie, 2000). Indeed some girls are feeling the strains along with these advantages. We face, for the first time, "the supergirl dilemma," where the expectations bar for girls seems to have gone up, maybe too rapidly. In one recent large-scale study, for example, a significant percentage of girls gave voice to the pressure they feel to be perfect, thin, accomplished, and accommodating (Girls Inc., 2006).

This version of girls stands to trump the sagging and factually incorrect counterstory of endangered girls, featuring exclusive focus on risk taking—drugs, sex, crime, resulting in popular reports of girls on the edge—and more elaborate girl-directed "regimes of youth regulation" (Griffin, 1997). The debate that continues to rage on is argued within a framework which constructs young women as either "having everything" or being in serious trouble (Harris, 2001).

As has been argued throughout the book, however, this dichotomous way of understanding the complex experience of girls is too limiting, even on the face of it. We are slowly and steadily moving past it. Regardless of whether today's girls are cognizant of it or not, the women's movement of the 1960s and 1970s created a sustaining legacy for adolescent girls today that endures for them, and still has the potential to move beyond the constricting discourse.

This inheritance, which has not reached all races and classes as much as it must, is still encouraging. Feminism has given girls (and those of us who work with and love them) some real choices: in education and sports, in contraception and abortion, in relationships and caregiving, in health and work, and in pleasure and power over their own lives. Many of these changes have resulted in increased equality, opportunity, and quality of life for girls. While there are forces operating on the other side of self-determination and new pressures to endure, to be sure, the opportunities that girls have now give them the possibility of a voice in their lives that they would not have had a couple of generations ago.

Girls Are Making Better Choices

Counter to those who cavil about "kids today," (and in juxtaposition to the girl-at-risk scenario) there are many spheres in which girls are managing their lives *better* than even a decade or two ago. They're less likely to murder than in the 1960s and 1970s, less likely to die from suicide, homicide, drug abuse, guns, and other violent causes. They're also less likely to be mothers, drop out of school, smoke, binge drink, or drive drunk. They're much more likely to use contraception, to do well in school at all levels of education, to be in good health, and find gainful employment. This is not the whole picture, of course, but it is certainly a part that generates hope.

It is interesting how difficult it is to get this news out there. When we hear about girls' success in school, for example, it is mostly in conjunction with concern that boys are somehow being shortchanged by education if girls are doing better. It's not a zero sum game. (Indeed, upper- and middle-class boys are doing quite well in school). The real problems (and they're a concern for girls, too) are poverty and racism. Sure, girls are struggling in some areas of their lives, but in others, they're making good choices and doing well.

And even the girls who are struggling are in the minority. As has been discussed earlier, most epidemiological studies consistently note that about 25 to 30% of girls are at high risk. This means that 70 to 75% of them are doing reasonably well by a variety of measures. When girls are in significant distress, it is not normal at all. Thus we need to get the good word out, and interrupt the bad hype when we hear it. Girls, by and large, are doing better than they have in the past in a variety of ways, and many are doing quite well.

The Emergence of Emerging Adulthood

Girls get longer to grow up. Adolescence—as a distinct stage of preparation for adulthood—is expanding in length in virtually all parts of the world, as a product of earlier puberty, later age of marriage, longer schooling, more engagement in peer worlds, economic instability, and a variety of other social factors. Some suggest (Arnett, 2000) that this developmental period extends all the way through the 20s as emerging adults try out different possibilities in love and work.

There are a couple of reasons why emerging adulthood is a boon to adolescent girls (and their therapists). First, many girls are overwhelmed by the number of choices they have, and by the pressure to decide that accompanies these options. The idea of emerging adulthood is hugely reassuring to them, letting them know that it is quite normal not to fully know who you are and what you want when you're just 18 or 20 years old. Further, many girls who suffer mightily during adolescence begin to even out a bit during their 20s. They benefit from some time to "catch up" with their peers who were not primarily focused on managing their distress so had more opportunities for exploration. The concept of emerging adulthood suggests that many people benefit from a transitional period after adolescence, too.

It's also true that emerging adulthood coincides with the time span required for remodeling and development of the prefrontal cortex. Adolescent brains continue to grow through the 20s; indeed, we do not have fully adult brains until the end of that decade. Thus it makes sense, developmentally, that the important adult decisions are postponed until more of an adult brain is making them.

Additionally, the world is a more difficult and complex place to navigate now. Many girls (and boys) need the support of family and community for a longer time to begin to take hold of their own economic and social lives. Staying closer to home, or returning home after some school or work, gives emerging adults that extra booster of financial, instrumental, and emotional help. The stable base of home may offer the additional structure, support, and regulation that can help them launch with greater confidence at a later time.

The Limbic System and Enduring Attachments

We have brains that, no matter what else they do, allow us to connect profoundly to one another. One of the greatest gifts that evolution has bestowed upon us is the length of time that humans (among other mammals) require and benefit from nurture and connection. Our capacity to form and sustain attachments is the cornerstone of all that follows developmentally. We ascribe great significance to early attachments (as well we should) but then devalue their importance in development. In Western culture, we tend instead to value separation and individuation as the real goals of adolescence.

This also becomes another of those false dichotomies. An adolescent's capacity for developing deeper and more varied intimacy with peers, parents, and other adults is vital to her survival, self-esteem, and well-being. In fact, there is no such thing as separation without attachment as an underpinning for it. Anything we do, that anyone does, to give girls the skills, opportunities, and relationships that foster attachment, is a gift.

The emotional control center of the brain—the limbic system—works overtime in adolescence as the prefrontal cortex is being remodeled. This occasionally creates a challenge with too many overwhelming feelings and too little capacity to handle and make sense of them. But in all this limbic activity girls also have a greater capacity to feel, and to feel felt by someone who cares about them. This newly expanded capacity for bonding and for love in adolescence creates the possibility for both great hope and joy.

Model Programs That Make a Difference

There are some great strategies for reaching girls all across the United States, and these interventions are helping girls. All of the research and program development since the mid-1980s has led to some wonderful innovations. Many of these are gender-specific and strength-based projects that are culturally and developmentally sensitive. They are diverse, like the girls they serve, and can be found in schools, community health, and mental health settings, social services and law enforcement, communities, and homes, reaching and teaching girls with knowledge acquired from empirical and clinical research.

These interventions include mentorship programs (e.g., Big Brother/Big Sister, Across Ages), school-based community service efforts (e.g., Girl Power), school-to-work transition programs (e.g., YouthBuild), teen pregnancy (e.g., Girls Incorporated), substance abuse (e.g., Early Risers), violence prevention programs (e.g., Project LEAP), and others (Dryfoos, 1998). Model programs provide services to girls and their families, and expect girls to contribute to their communities, too. The cutting-edge projects do not focus on deficits (delinquency, drug use, pregnancy, violence) but on helping girls become more resilient, and reconfiguring assets within the community in an effort to promote positive youth development (Blum, 1998). Although many of these projects may lack sustained funding, and are still just scattered across the country, they suggest that we do have the know-how (if not sufficient resolve) to reach out to girls in their communities and really make a difference in their lives.

Repair

One of the most encouraging aspects of clinical practice with adolescent girls (and pretty much all relationships for that matter) is the human capacity to mend ruptures and heal more deeply as a consequence. The possibility for rupture in the therapeutic alliance is one of the great challenges in working with adolescent girls. We risk such disconnection when we give advice (or don't), when we have to share information with parents and others, when we listen inadequately or too well. We might well live in constant fear of the fragility of our connection with a girl in crisis.

But when our usual attunement is disrupted, as it inevitably will be, only then will we have the opportunity to repair the rupture. Repair doesn't just reestablish a connection, but it heals and deepens it, too. When we apologize, strategize for how to do better, try harder, and try again, we provide a lesson, too; one that can't be taught any other way. We show a girl, in real time, that life is filled with inevitable moments of misunderstandings and missed connections that we can actually identify, and then we can become more deeply reattuned to one another. Through our efforts to reconnect, girls learn about how we think about ourselves, about them, and our relationship. For many girls that we work with, our willingness to try to repair things may be a unique experience for them. They will have the chance to feel what consistent, predictable, reflective, intentional, and mindful caregiving feels like. Most girls are surprisingly forgiving, too. The growth engendered by such repair is a tremendous source of hope.

The Human Ability to Survive

Despite so many environmental and developmental obstacles, and the greater demands placed on them, many adolescents are rising to the challenge. Reports from the United States (and even around the world) suggest that most adolescents, even in disadvantaged situations, are optimistic about their futures. Harris polls conducted in the United States post-9/11 provide affirmation of this: youth are extremely optimistic about their futures, believing they will reach their personal goals, live a long life, and earn a living to do the things they want despite the terrorist attacks. Eight in 10 (83%) believe they will reach their personal goals. Girls are more likely than boys to believe this (86% vs. 79%). (Harris Interactive, 2002).

Girls are resilient, and even in the face of great adversity many show astonishing reserves of courage and determination. They make valuable contributions to their families and communities. It is important to keep in our minds their tenacity, their hope, and faith that their lives will be better. Especially in the face of so much cultural pessimism, even girls who are fighting are letting us know that they think they're worth fighting for.

You

The final and most important source of hope I can imagine is the willingness of people like us to show up over a period, and get to know a girl well. We sometimes underestimate the value of what we do, minimize the importance of what we have to offer, and generally dismiss the amount of help we can provide to girls with so much adversity in their lives.

In our self-doubt we lose sight of the most vital contribution we have to make: a willingness to be fully and empathically present with a girl who needs us. We must always remember that through the relationships we have with adolescent girls in crisis, the nurturing connections we form and sustain are ultimately the most therapeutic interventions of all.

References

Achenbach, T., & Howell, C. (1993). Are American children's problems getting worse? A thirteen year comparison. *Journal of the American Academy of Child and Adolescent Psychiatry, 32*(6), 1145–1154.

Ackard, D., & Neumark-Sztainer, D. (2003). Multiple sexual victimizations among adolescent boys and girls. *Journal of Child Sexual Abuse, 12*(1), 17–37.

Acoca, L. (1999). Investing in girls: A 21st century strategy. *Juvenile Justice, 6*(1), 3–13.

Acoca, L., & Dedel, K. (1998). *No place to hide: Understanding and meeting the needs of girls in the California juvenile justice system.* San Francisco: National Council on Crime and Delinquency.

Afterschool Alliance (2004, October). *Afterschool fact sheet.* Washington, DC: Author.

Alan Guttmacher Institute. (1994). *Sex and America's teenagers.* New York: Author.

Alan Guttmacher Institute. (2004). *U.S. teenage pregnancy statistics.* New York: Author.

Allen, R. (2002). Class size, school size. *Educational Leadership, 59*(5), 36–41.

Allgood-Merton, B., Lewinsohn, P., & Hops, H. (1990). Sex differences and adolescent depression. *Journal of Abnormal Psychology, 99*(1), 55–63.

Amato, P. R., & Keith, B. (1991). Parental divorce and the well-being of children: A meta-analysis. *Psychological Bulletin, 110,* 26–46.

American Academy of Child and Adolescent Psychiatry. (1999). *Your adolescent.* New York: HarperCollins.

American Academy of Child and Adolescent Psychiatry. (2004). *Practice parameters for the assessment and treatment of children and adolescents with substance use disorders.* Retrieved May 5, 2006, from www.aacap.org/galleries/PracticeParameters/substanceUseDisorder.pdf

American Association of University Women. (1993). *Hallowed hallways: AAUW survey on sexual harassment in American schools.* Washington, DC: AAUW Education Foundation.

American Association of University Women. (1995). *Growing smart: What's working for girls in school.* Washington, DC: AAUW Education Foundation.

American Association of University Women. (1998). *Girls in the middle: Working to succeed in school.* Washington, DC: AAUW Education Foundation.

American Bar Association and National Bar Association. (2001, May). *Justice by gender: The lack of appropriate prevention, diversion, and treatment alternatives for girls in the justice system.* Washington, DC: Author.

American Civil Liberties Union. (2006). *Words from prison: Did you know . . .?* Retrieved October 29, 2006, from www.aclu.org/womens rights/violence/25829res20060612.html

American Psychiatric Association. (2002). *Diagnostic and statistical manual of mental disorders (4th ed., Text Revision).* Washington, DC: Author.

Amnesty International. (1998, November). *"The best interests of the child:" Human rights and the juvenile justice system.* Retrieved December 5, 2005, from www.amnesty.org/ailib/intcam/juvenile/

Anderson, C., Teicher, M., Polcari, A., & Renshaw, P. (2002). Abnormal T2 relaxation time in the cerebellar vermis of adults sexually abused in childhood: Potential role of the vermis in stress-enhanced risk for drug abuse. *Psychoneuroendocrinology, 27,* 231–244.

Annie E. Casey Foundation. (1997). *The juvenile detention alternatives initiative: Progress report.* Baltimore, MD: Author.

Annie E. Casey Foundation. (2006). 2006 *Kidscount data book.* Retrieved November 15, 2006, from www.aecf.org/kidscount

Apter, T. (1990). *Altered loves: Mothers and daughters during adolescence.* New York: St. Martin's Press.

Apter, T. (1993). *Altered views: Father's closeness to teenage daughters.* London: Sage.

Apter, T. (2001). *The myth of maturity: What teenagers need from parents to become adults.* New York: W. W. Norton.

Archer, L. (2005). Girls, gangs, and crime: Profile of the young female offender. *Social Work Today, 5*(2), 38–45.

Armistead, L., McCombs, A., Forehand, R., Wierson, M., Long, N., & Fauber, R. (1990). Coping with divorce: A study of young adolescents. *Journal of Clinical Child Psychology, 19*(1), 79–85.

Arnett, J. (2000). Emerging adulthood: A theory of development from the late teens through the twenties. *American Psychologist, 55*(5), 469–480.

Arnett, J. (2004). *Emerging adulthood: The winding road from late teens through the twenties.* New York: Oxford University Press.

Arnold, L. E. (1996). Sex differences in AD/HD: Conference summary. *Journal of Abnormal Child Psychology, 24,* 555–569.

Artz, S. (1998). *Sex, power, and the violent schoolgirl.* Toronto: Trifolium Books.

Aunola, K., Stattin, H., & Nurmi, J. (2000). Parenting styles and adolescents' achievement strategies. *Journal of Adolescence, 23,* 205–222.

Ballou, M. (1995). Naming the issue. In E. J. Rave & C. C. Larsen (Eds.), *Ethical decision making in therapy: Feminist perspectives* (pp. 42–56). New York: Guilford.

Barber, B. L., & Eccles, J. S. (1992). Long-term influence of divorce and single parenting on adolescent family- and work-related values, behaviors, and aspirations. *Psychological Bulletin, 111,* 108–126.

Bardone, A., Moffitt, T., Caspi, A., & Dickson, N. (1996). Adult mental health and social outcomes of adolescent girls with depression and conduct disorder. *Development and Psychopathology, 8,* 811–829.

Basow, S., & Rubin, L. (1999) Gender influences on adolescent development. In N. Johnson, M. Roberts, & J. Worrell (Eds.), *Beyond appearance: A new look at adolescent girls* (pp. 25–52). Washington, DC: American Psychological Association.

Baumohl, J., & Jaffe, J. (2002). Halfway houses. *BookRags.* Retrieved February 3, 2006, from www.bookrags.com/other/drugs/halfway-houses-edaa-02.html

Bazelon Center for Mental Health Law. (2003). *Teaming up: Using the IDEA and Medicaid to secure comprehensive mental health services for children and youth.* Retrieved March 30, 2007, from www.bazelon.org/issues/children/publications/teamingup/report.pdf

Beck, K., Shattuck, T., Haynie, D., Crump, A., & Simons-Morton, B. (1999). The association between parent awareness, monitoring, enforcement, and adolescent involvement with alcohol. *Health Education Research, 14*(6), 765–775.

Behrens, E. (2006). *Beyond "Brat Camp:" Does private residential treatment for teens really work?* Paper presented at the American Psychological Association Annual Meeting, August 10, 2006, New Orleans, LA.

Bem, S. L. (1993). *The lenses of gender: Transforming the debate on sexual inequality.* New Haven, CT: Yale University Press.

Benson, P. (2004). The scientific foundations of youth development. In *New directions for youth development* (pp. 20–32). Philadelphia: Public/Private Ventures.

Berman, D., & Anton, M. (1988). A wilderness therapy program as an alternative to adolescent psychiatric hospitalization. *Residential Treatment for Children and Youth, 5,* 41–53.

Berndt, T., & Savin-Williams, R. (1993). Peer relationships and friendships. In P. Tolan & B. Cohler (Eds.), *Handbook of clinical research and practice with adolescents* (pp. 203–220). New York: John Wiley.

Bernstein, R. M. (1980). The development of the self-system during adolescence. *Journal of Genetic Psychology, 136,* 231–245.

Best Pharmaceutical for Children Act, Pub. L. No. 107–109, 115 Stat. 1789 (2002).

Biederman, J., Faraone, S., Mick, E., & Williamson, S. (1999). Clinical correlates of ADHD in females: Findings from a large group of girls ascertained from pediatric and psychiatric referral sources. *Journal of the American Academy of Child and Adolescent Psychiatry, 38,* 966–975.

Biederman, J., Kwon, A., Aleardi, M., & Chouinard, V. (2005). Absence of gender effects on attention deficit hyperactivity disorder: Findings in nonreferred subjects. *The American Journal of Psychiatry, 162*(6), 1083–1089.

Biederman, J., Mick, E., Faraone, S., & Braaten, E. (2002). Influence of gender on attention deficit hyperactivity disorder in children referred to a psychiatric clinic. *The American Journal of Psychiatry, 159*(1), 36–43.

Bierman, K., Bruschi, C., Domitrovich, C., Yan Fang, G., Miller-Johnson, S., & Conduct Problems Prevention Research Group. (2004). Early disruptive behaviors associated with emerging antisocial behavior among girls. In M. Putallaz & K. Bierman (Eds.), *Aggression, antisocial behavior, and violence among girls* (pp. 137–161). New York: Guilford.

Bjorkqvist, K., Lagerspetz, K., & Kaukiainen, A. (1992). Do girls manipulate and boys fight? Developmental trends in regard to direct and indirect aggression. *Aggressive Behavior, 18,* 117–127.

Bloomquist, M. (1996). *Skills training for children with behavior disorders: A parent and therapist guidebook.* New York: Guilford.

Blum, R. (1998). Healthy youth development as a model for youth health promotion: A review. *Journal of Adolescent Health, 22,* 368–375.

Bogolub, E. (1995). *Helping families through divorce: An eclectic approach.* New York: Springer.

Bourne, E. (2005). *The anxiety and phobia workbook.* Oakland, CA: New Harbinger.

Breggin, P., & Breggin, G. (1995). The hazards of treating ADHD with methylphenidate. *The Journal of College Student Psychotherapy, 10*(2), 55–72.

Brendtro, L., Brokenleg, M., & Van Bockern, S. (2002). *Reclaiming youth at risk: Our hope for the future.* Bloomington, TN: National Education Service.

Briere, J. (1992). *Child abuse trauma.* Newbury Park, CA: Sage.

Brisch, K. H. (2004). *Treating attachment disorders.* New York: Guilford.

British Medical Association. (2004). *Smoking and reproductive life: The impact of smoking on sexual, reproductive, and child health.* Retrieved June 27, 2005, from www.globalink.org/

Brooks, R. (1994). Children at risk: Fostering resilience and hope. *Journal of Orthopsychiatry, 64,* 545–553.

Brooks-Gunn, J. (1991). How stressful is the transition to adolescence for girls? In M. Colten & S. Gore (Eds.), *Adolescent stress: Causes and consequences* (pp. 131–149). Hawthorne, NY: Aldine de Gruyter.

Brown, L. M. (1995). Lesbian identities: Concepts and issues. In A. R. D'Augelli & C. J. Patterson (Eds.), *Lesbian, gay, and bisexual identities over the lifespan: Psychological perspectives* (pp. 3–23). New York: Oxford University Press.

Brown, L. M. (1998). *Raising their voices: The politics of girls' anger.* Cambridge, MA: Harvard University Press.

Brown, L. M. (2003). *Girlfighting.* New York: New York University Press.

Brown, L. M., & Gilligan, C. (1992). *Meeting at the crossroads: Women's psychology and girls' development.* New York: Ballantine Books.

Brown, L. M., Way, N., & Duff, J. (1999). The others in my I: Adolescent girls' friendships and peer relationships. In N. Johnson, M. Roberts, & J. Worrell (Eds.), *Beyond appearance: A new look at adolescent girls* (pp. 205–225). Washington, DC: American Psychological Association.

Brumberg, J. (1997). *The body project.* New York: Random House.

Buelow, G., & Range, L. (2001). No-suicide contracts among college students. *Death Studies, 25*, 583–592.

Burns, B., Hoagwood, K., & Maultsby, L. (1998). Improving outcomes for children and adolescents with serious emotional and behavioral disorders: Current and future directions. In M. H. Epstein, K. Kutash, & A. Duhnowski (Eds.), *Outcomes for children and youth with emotional and behavioral disorders and their families: Programs and evaluation best practices* (pp. 686–707). Austin, TX: Pro-Ed.

Cain, L. (1999, Winter). Are girls still playing catch-up in education? *Outlook, 92*, 12–13.

Callan, J. (1999). Practice and education issues related to adolescent girls. In N. Johnson, M. Roberts, & J. Worrell (Eds.), *Beyond appearance: A new look at adolescent girls* (pp. 355–375). Washington, DC: American Psychological Association.

Carlson, E., Sampson, M., & Sroufe, L. (2003). Attachment theory and pediatric practice. *Journal of Development and Behavior Pediatrics, 24*(5), 364–379.

Carnegie Council on Adolescent Development. (1992). *What young adolescents want and need from out-of-school programs.* Washington, DC: Author.

Carnegie Council on Adolescent Development. (1995). *Great transitions: Preparing adolescents for a new century.* New York: Author.

Cason, D., & Gillis, H. (1994). A meta-analysis of outdoor adventure programming with adolescents. *Journal of Experiential Education, 17*(1), 40–47.

Center for Health Communication, Harvard School of Public Health. (2004). *Reinventing aging: Baby boomers and civic engagement.* Boston, MA: Author.

Centers for Disease Control. (1991). Attempted suicide among high school students—United States, 1990. *Morbidity and Mortality Weekly Report, 40,* 633–635.

Centers for Disease Control. (1994). Prevalence of overweight among adolescents—United States, 1988–1991. *Morbidity and Mortality Weekly Report, 41,* 818–821.

Centers for Disease Control. (2005). *HIV/AIDS Surveillance Report, 17,* 1–46. Atlanta: U.S. Department of Health and Human Services.

Chambers, R. A., Taylor, J. R., & Potenza, M. N. (2003). Developmental neurocircuitry of motivation in adolescence: A critical period of addiction vulnerability. *American Journal of Psychiatry, 160,* 1041–1052.

Chamberlain, P., & Reid, J. (1998). Comparison of two community alternatives to incarceration for chronic juvenile offenders. *Journal of Consulting and Clinical Psychology, 6,* 624–633.

Chen, M. (2005, November 21). At some youth "treatment" facilities, "Tough Love" takes brutal forms. *The New Standard.* Retrieved March 21, 2006, from www.newstandardnews.net/content/index.cfm/items/2619

Chesney-Lind, M. (1998). *What to do about girls? Promising perspectives and effective strategies* (Executive summary). Manoa, HI: University of Hawaii Press.

Chesney-Lind, M., & Belknap, J. (2004). Trends in delinquent girls' aggression and violent behavior. In M. Putallaz & K. Bierman (Eds.), *Aggression, antisocial behavior, and violence among girls* (pp. 203–220). New York: Guilford.

Chesney-Lind, M., & Shelden, R. (1998). *Girls, delinquency, and juvenile justice.* Belmont, CA: Wadsworth.

Child Welfare League of America. (2004). *Girls in the juvenile justice system: The need for more gender responsive services.* Retrieved November 19, 2005, from www.cwla.org/programs/juvenilejustice/jjgirls.htm

Cheung, Y. (2000). Substance abuse and developments in harm reduction. *Canadian Medical Association Journal, 162*(12), 1697–1700.

Cicchetti, D., & Rogosh, F. A. (2002). A developmental psychopathology perspective on adolescence. *Journal of Consulting and Clinical Psychology, 70*(1), 6–20.

Clark, M. L., & Ayers, M. (1991). Friendship similarity during early adolescence: Gender and racial patterns. *Journal of Psychology, 126,* 393–405.

Claussen, A. H., & Crittenden, P. M. (1991). Physical and psychological maltreatment: Relations among different types of maltreatment. *Child Abuse and Neglect, 15,* 5–18.

Clifford, P., Edmundson, E., Koch, W., & Dodd, B. (1991). Drug use and life satisfaction among college students. *International Journal of the Addictions, 26,* 45–53.

Cohen, P., Cohen, J., Kasen, S., Velez, C., Hartmark, C., Johnson, J., et al. (1993). An epidemiological study of disorders in late childhood and adolescence: I. Age and gender specific prevalence. *Journal of Child Psychology and Psychiatry, 34,* 851–867.

Cohen-Sandler, R. (2005). *Stressed-out girls: Helping them thrive in the age of pressure.* New York: Viking.

Colder, C., & Stice, E. (1998). A longitudinal study of the interactive effects of impulsivity and anger on adolescent problem behavior. *Journal of Youth and Adolescence, 27,* 255–275.

Cole, P., Michel, M., & O'Donnell, L. (1994). The development of emotion regulation and dysregulation: A clinical perspective. In N. Fox (Ed.), *Monographs of the society for research on child development, 59,* 73–100.

Commission on Adolescent Anxiety Disorders. (2005). Anxiety disorders. In D. Evans, E. Foa, R. Gur, et al. (Eds.), *Treating and preventing adolescent mental health disorders* (pp. 162–253). New York: Oxford University Press.

Commission on Adolescent Depression and Bipolar Disorder. (2005). Depression and bipolar disorder. In D. Evans, E. Foa, R. Gur, et al. (Eds.), *Treating and preventing adolescent mental health disorders* (pp. 4–74). New York: Oxford University Press.

Commission on Adolescent Suicide Prevention. (2005). Youth suicide. In D. Evans, E. Foa, R. Gur, et al. (Eds.), *Treating and preventing adolescent mental health disorders* (pp. 445–496). New York: Oxford University Press.

Commission on Positive Youth Development. (2005). The positive perspective on youth development. In D. Evans, E. Foa, R. Gur, et al. (Eds.), *Treating and preventing adolescent mental health disorders* (pp. 498–527). New York: Oxford University Press.

The Commonwealth Fund. (1999). *Improving the health of adolescent girls.* New York: Author.

Compas, B., Grant, K., & Ey, S. (1994). Psychosocial stress and child and adolescent depression: Can we be more specific? In W. M. Reynolds & H. F. Johnston (Eds.), *Handbook of depression in children and adolescents* (pp. 509–523). New York: Plenum Press.

Conger, R. D., & Chao, W. (1996). Adolescent depressed mood. In R. L. Simon (Ed.), *Understanding differences between divorced and intact families: Stress, interaction, and child outcome* (pp. 157–174). Thousand Oaks, CA: Sage.

Conger, K., Reuter, M., & Conger, R. (2000). The role of economic pressure in the lives of parents and their adolescents: The family stress model. In L. J. Crockett & R. Silbereisen (Eds.), *Negotiating adolescence in times of social change* (pp. 201–223). New York: Cambridge University Press.

Conley, B. (2002). *Alternative schools: A reference handbook.* Santa Barbara, CA: ABC-CLIO.

Conlin, M. (2003, May 26). The new gender gap. *Businessweek, 3834,* 74–82.

Conner, M. (2006, October 12). *Crisis intervention for teenagers: A family guide.* Retrieved December 1, 2006, from www.crisiscounseling.com/Crisis/CrisisInterventionTeens.htm

Conway, A. M. (2005). Girls, aggression, and emotional regulation. *American Journal of Orthopsychiatry, 75*(2), 33–339.

Cook, A., Blaustein, M., Spinazzola, J., & van der Kolk, B. (Eds.) (2003). *Complex trauma in children and adolescents.* National Child Traumatic Stress Network. Retrieved March 5, 2005, from www.NCTSNet.org.

Costello, E., Mustillo, S., Erkanli, A., Keeler, G., & Angold, A. (2003). Prevalence and development of psychiatric disorders in childhood and adolescence. *Archives of General Psychiatry, 60,* 837–844.

Cottrell, L., Li, X., Harris, C., D'Allesandri, D., Atkins, M., Richardson, B., et al. (2003). Parent and adolescent perceptions of parental monitoring and adolescent risk involvement. *Parenting: Science and Practice, 3*(3), 179–195.

Courtois, C. (1999). *Recollections of sexual abuse: Treatment principles and guidelines.* New York: W. W. Norton.

Crain, R. (1997). Who knows what ad lurks in the heart of consumers? The mind knows. *Advertising Age, 68*(23), 25.

Crick, N. R. (1995). Relational aggression: The role of intent attributions, feelings of distress, and provocation type. *Development and Psychopathology, 7,* 313–322.

Crick, N. R., & Nelson, D. (2002). Relational and physical victimization within friendships: Nobody told me there'd be friends like these. *Journal of Abnormal Child Psychology, 30,* 599–607.

Crick, N. R., & Rose, A. J. (2000). Toward a gender-balanced approach to the study of social-emotional development: A look at relational aggression. In P. H. Miller (Ed.), *Toward a feminist developmental psychology* (pp. 153–168). New York: Taylor & Francis/Routledge.

Csikszmentmihalyi, M. (1997). *Finding flow: The psychology of engagement with everyday life.* New York: Basic Books.

Curry, J. (1991). Outcome research on residential treatment: Implications and suggested directions. *American Journal of Orthopsychiatry, 61*(3), 348–357.

Dahl, R. E. (2001). Affect regulation, brain development, and behavioral/emotional health in adolescence. *CNS Spectrum, 6*(1), 60–72.

Daley, A., & Ryan, J. (2000). Academic performance and participation in physical activity by secondary school adolescents. *Perceptual and Motor Skills, 91*(2), 531–534.

Davis, L., & Tolan, P. (1993). Alternative and preventive interventions. In P. Tolan & B. Cohler (Eds.), *Handbook of clinical research and practice with adolescents* (pp. 427–451). New York: Wiley.

Davis-Berman, J., & Berman, D. (1994). *Wilderness therapy: Foundations, theories, and research*. Dubuque, IA: Hunt.

Day, J. C. (1996). Population projections of the United States by age, race, and Hispanic origin: 1995–2050. In *Current Population Reports*. Washington, DC: U.S. Government Printing Office.

Debold, E., Brown, L., Weseen, S., & Brookins, G. (1999). Cultivating hardiness zones for girls: A reconceptualization of resilience in relationships with caring adults. In N. Johnson, M. Roberts, & J. Worrell (Eds.), *Beyond appearance: A new look at adolescent girls* (pp. 181–204). Washington, DC: American Psychological Association.

DeLeon, G. (2000). *The therapeutic community: Theory, model, and method*. New York: Springer.

Delligatti, N., Akin-Little, A., & Little, S. (2003). Conduct disorder in girls: Diagnostic and intervention issues. *Psychology in the Schools, 40*(2), 183–192.

Demo, D. H., & Acock, A. C. (1996). Family structure, family process, and adolescent well-being. *Journal of Research on Adolescence, 6*, 457–488.

Denmark, F. L. (1999). Enhancing the development of adolescent girls. In N. Johnson, M. Roberts, & J. Worell (Eds.), *Beyond appearance: A new look at adolescent girls* (pp. 377–404). Washington, DC: American Psychological Association.

DeZolt, D., & Henning-Stout, M. (1999). Adolescent girls' experiences in school and community settings. In N. Johnson, M. Roberts, & J. Worell (Eds.), *Beyond appearance: A new look at adolescent girls* (pp. 253–275). Washington, DC: American Psychological Association.

DiFranza, J. R., Savageau, J. A., Rigotti, N. A., Fletcher, K., Ockene, J. K., McNeill, A. D., et al. (2002). Development of symptoms of tobacco dependence in youths: 30-month follow-up data from the DANDY study. *Tobacco Control, 11*(3), 228–235.

Dishion, T. (2000). Cross-setting consistency in early adolescent psychopathology: Deviant friendships and problem behavior sequelae. *Journal of Personality, 68*(6), 1109–1126.

Dishion, T., Poulin, F., & Burraston, B. (2001). Peer group dynamics associated with iatrogenic effects in group interventions with high-risk young adolescents. In D. W. Nangle & C. A. Erdley (Eds.), *The role of friendship in psychological adjustment: New directions for child and adolescent development* (pp. 79–92). San Francisco: Jossey-Bass.

Dodge, K. (1993). The future of research on the treatment of conduct disorder. *Development and Psychopathology, 6*, 43–55.

Doherty, W. J. (2002). *Take back your kids.* Notre Dame, IN: Sorin Books.

Doherty, W. J., & Carlson, B. Z. (2002). *Putting family first.* New York: Henry Holt.

Doll, B. (1996). Children without friends: Implications for practice and policy. *School Psychology Review, 25*, 165–183.

Draut, T. (2006). *Strapped: Why America's 20- and 30-somethings can't get ahead.* New York: Random House.

Draut, T., & Silva, J. (2004, October 13). *Generation broke: The growth of debt among young Americans. Borrowing to make ends meet.* Retrieved June 15, 2006, from www.demos.org/pubs/Generation_Broke.pdf

Drew, B. (2001). Self-harm and no-suicide contracting in psychiatric inpatient settings. *Archives of Psychiatric Nursing, 15*(3), 99–106.

Drug Policy Alliance. (2007). *Drug policy around the world.* Retrieved March 30, 2007, from www.drugpolicy.org/global/

Dryfoos, J. (1990). *Adolescents at risk.* New York: Oxford University Press.

Dryfoos, J. (1998). *Making it through adolescence in a risky society: What parents, schools and communities can do.* New York: Oxford University Press.

Dubois, D. L., & Hirsch, B. J. (1990). School and neighborhood friendship patterns of blacks and whites in early adolescence. *Child Development, 61*, 524–536.

Duff, J. L. (1996). *The best of friends: Exploring the moral domain of adolescent friendships.* Unpublished doctoral dissertation, Stanford University, CA.

Duncan, D., Nicholson, T., Clifford, P., Hawkins, W., & Petosa, R. (1994). Harm reduction: An emerging new paradigm for drug education. *Journal of Drug Education, 24*(4), 281–290.

Durlak, J. (1997). Primary prevention programs in schools. *Advances in Clinical Child Psychology, 19*, 283–318.

Eamon, M. (1994). Institutionalizing children and adolescents in private psychiatric hospitals. *Social Work, 39*(5), 588–594.

Eccles, J. S., & Appleton, G. J. (Eds.) (2002). *Community programs to promote youth development.* Washington, DC: National Academy Press.

Eccles, J. S., Barber, B., Jozefowicz, D., Malenchuk, O., & Vida, M. (1999). Self-evaluations of competence, task values, and self-esteem. In N. Johnson, M. Roberts, & J. Worell (Eds.), *Beyond appearance: A new look at adolescent girls* (pp. 53–84). Washington, DC: American Psychological Association.

Eder, D. (1990). Serious and playful disputes: Variation in conflict talk among female adolescents. In A. D. Grimshaw (Ed.), *Conflict talk: Sociolinguistic investigations of arguments in conversations* (pp. 242–287). Cambridge, UK: Cambridge University Press.

Egan, J. (1997, July 27). The thin red line. *New York Times Magazine,* 21–35, 40, 43–44.

Ehrhardt, A, (1996). Editorial: Our view of adolescent sexuality—A focus on risk behavior without the developmental context. *American Journal of Public Health, 86,* 1523–1525.

Elder, G. H., & Russell, S. T. (1996). Academic performance and future aspirations. In R. L. Simon (Ed.), *Understanding differences between divorced and intact families: Stress, interaction, and child outcome* (pp. 176–192). Thousand Oaks, CA: Sage.

Elkind, D. (1967). Egocentrism in adolescence. *Child Development, 38,* 1025–1034.

Elkind, D. (2001). *The hurried child* (3rd ed.). Cambridge, MA: Da Capo Books.

Elmen, J., & Offer, D. (1993). Normality, turmoil, and adolescence. In P. Tolan & B. Cohler (Eds.), *Handbook of clinical research and practice with adolescents* (pp. 3–20). New York: Wiley.

Emanuele, M., Wezeman, F., & Emanuele, N. (2003). Alcohol's effects on female reproductive function. *Alcohol Research and Health, 26*(4), 274–281.

Eng, T., & Butler, W. (1996). *The hidden epidemic: Confronting sexually transmitted diseases.* Washington, DC: National Academy Press.

Erickson, P., Riley, D., Cheung, Y., & O'Hare, P. (Eds.) (1997). *Harm reduction: A new direction for drug policies and programs.* Toronto: University of Toronto Press.

Erlandson, G. (1997). Restoring the ritual of the family meal. *The Family Therapy Networker, 21*(3), 34–35.

Evans, C., & Eder, D. (1993). "No exit:" Processes of social isolation in the middle school. *Journal of Contemporary Ethnography*, 22, 139–170.

Fairburn, C. (1997). Interpersonal psychotherapy for bulimia nervosa. In D. M. Garner & P. E. Garfinkel (Eds.), *Handbook of treatment for eating disorders* (pp. 278–294). New York: Guilford.

Falbo, T., Lein, L., & Amador, N. (2001). Parent involvement during the transition to high school. *Journal of Adolescent Research*, 16(5), 511–529.

Favazza, A. (1998). The coming of age of self-mutilation. *Journal of Nervous and Mental Disease*, 186(5), 259–268.

Fine, M. (1988). Sexuality, schooling, and adolescent females: The missing discourse of desire. *Harvard Educational Review*, 58(1), 29–53.

Fine, M. (1992). *Disruptive voices: The possibilities of feminist research.* Ann Arbor, MI: University of Michigan Press.

Finkelhor, D., & Dziuba-Leatherman, J. (1994). Children as victims of violence: A national survey. *Pediatrics*, 94, 413–420.

Fishel, A. (1999). *Treating the adolescent in family therapy.* Northvale, NJ: Jason Aronson.

Flouri, E., & Buchanan, A. (2002). The protective role of parental involvement in adolescent suicide. *Crisis*, 23(1), 17–22.

Forehand, R., Wierson, M., Thomas, A., Fauber, R., Armistead, L., Kempton, T., et al. (1991). A short-term longitudinal examination of young adolescent functioning following divorce: The role of family factors. *Journal of Abnormal Child Psychology*, 19, 97–111.

Foster Family Based Treatment Association. (1995). *Program standards for treatment foster care.* New York: Author.

Frankel, L. P. (1992). *Women, anger, and depression.* Deerfield Beach, FL: Health Communications.

French, D., Jansen, E., & Pidada, S. (2002). US and Indonesian children's and adolescent's reports of relational aggression by disliked peers. *Child Development*, 73, 1143–1150.

Gaines, D. (1991). *Teenage wasteland: Suburbia's dead-end kids.* New York: Pantheon.

Galambos, N. L., Almeida, D. M., & Petersen, A. C. (1990). Masculinity, femininity, and sex-role attitudes in early adolescence: Exploring gender intensification. *Child Development*, 61, 1905–1914.

Garbarino, J. (2006). *See Jane hit: Why girls are growing more violent and what we can do about it.* New York: Penguin.

Garrison, C., Addy, C., McKeown, R., & Cuffe, S. (1993). Nonsuicidal physically self-damaging acts in adolescence. *Journal of Child and Family Studies*, 2(4), 339–352.

Geller, B., & Luby, J. (1997). Child and adolescent bipolar disorder: A review of the past 10 years. *Journal of the American Academy of Child and Adolescent Psychiatry*, 36, 1168–1176.

Gelles, R., & Straus M. A. (1990). The medical and psychological costs of family violence. In M. A. Straus & R. J. Gelles (Eds.), *Physical violence in American families* (pp. 425–430). New Brunswick, NJ: Transaction.

Gil, E. (1996). *Treating abused adolescents*. New York: Guilford.

Gilbert, S., & Thompson, J. (1996). Feminist explanations of the development of eating disorders: Common themes, research findings, and methodological issues. *Clinical Psychology: Science and Practice*, 3, 183–202.

Gilligan, C. (1982). *In a different voice*. Cambridge, MA: Harvard University Press.

Gilligan, C., Rogers, A., & Tolman, D. (1991). *Women, girls, and psychotherapy: Reframing resistance*. New York: Haworth Press.

Girls Incorporated. (2006). *The supergirl dilemma: Girls feel the pressure to be perfect, accomplished, thin, and accommodating*. New York: Author.

Gluckman, R. (2002). *The scapegoating of America's youth*. Retrieved March 12, 2005, from www.zmag.org/content/Youth/gluckman_scape goating.cfm

Gore, S., & Colten, M. E. (2004). Gender, stress, and distress. In. J. Eckenrode (Ed.), *The social context of coping* (pp. 139–163). New York: Springer.

Gortmaker, S. L., Must, A., Sobel, A. M., Peterson, K., Colditz, G. A., & Dietz, W. H. (1996). Television viewing as a cause of increasing obesity among children in the United States: 1986–1990. *Archives of Pediatrics and Adolescent Medicine*, 150(4), 356–362.

Gotlib, I., & Hammen, C. (1992). *Psychological aspects of depression: Toward a cognitive-interpersonal integration*. New York: Wiley.

Greene, R. (1998). The *explosive child*. New York: HarperCollins.

Greenwald, R. (2000). The trauma orientation and child therapy. In K. Dwivedi (Ed.), *Posttraumatic stress disorder in children and adolescents* (pp. 7–24). London: Whurr.

Griffin, C. (1997) Troubled teens: Managing disorders of transition and consumption. *Feminist Review*, 55, 4–21.

Grizenko, N., & Papineau, D. (1992). A comparison of the cost-effectiveness of day treatment and residential treatment for children with severe behavior problems. *Canadian Journal of Psychiatry, 37,* 393–400.

Gustafson, S. (1997). Female underachievement and overachievement: Parental contributions and long-term consequences. *International Journal of Behavior Development, 18*(3), 469–484.

Hallowell, E. (1996). *When you worry about the child you love.* New York: Simon & Schuster.

Hammer, H., Finkelhor, D., & Sedlak, A. (2002, October). *Runaway/ Thrownaway children: National estimates and characteristics.* Washington, DC: U.S. Department of Justice.

Hanna, F., Hanna, C., & Keys, S. (1999). Fifty strategies for counseling defiant aggressive adolescents: Reaching, accepting, and relating. *Journal of Counseling and Development, 77,* 395–404.

Hanna, F., & Hunt, W. (1999). Techniques for psychotherapy with defiant, aggressive adolescents. *Psychotherapy, 36*(1), 56–68.

Harris, A, (2001, May). Not waving or drowning: Young women, feminism, and the limits of the next wave debate. *Outskirts, 8.* Retrieved May 5, 2006, from www.chloe.uwa.edu.au/page/79607

Harris Interactive. (2002). *One year after 9–11 attacks, America's youth say "individual rights and freedoms" is top social concern.* Retrieved October 27, 2005, from www.harrisinteractive.com

Harter, S. (1990). Causes, correlates, and the functional role of global self-worth: A life-span perspective. In J. Kolligian & R. Sternberg (Eds.), *Perceptions of competence and incompetence across the life-span* (pp. 67–98). New Haven, CT: Yale University Press.

Hartwig, H., & Myers, J. (2003). A different approach: Applying a wellness paradigm to adolescent female delinquents and offenders. *Journal of Mental Health Counseling, 25*(1), 57–75.

Haste, H. (1994). *The sexual metaphor.* Cambridge, MA: Harvard University Press.

Hayward, C., & Collier, J. (1996). Anxiety disorders. In H. Steiner (Ed.), *Treating Adolescents* (pp. 187–222). San Francisco, CA: Jossey-Bass.

Heinberg, L. (1996). Theories of body image: Perceptual, developmental, and sociocultural factors. In J. K. Thompson (Ed.), *Body image, eating disorders, and obesity: An integrative guide to assessment and treatment* (pp. 27–48). Washington, DC: American Psychological Association.

Henry. B., Moffitt, T., Robins, L., Earls, F., & Silva, P. (1993). Early family predictors of child and adolescent antisocial behaviour: Who are the mothers of delinquents? *Criminal Behaviour and Mental Health*, 3, 97–118.

Herman, J. (1992). *Trauma and recovery*. New York: HarperCollins.

Hernandez, D. (1993). *America's children: Resources from family, government, and the economy*. New York: Russell Sage Foundation.

Hetherington, E. M., Bridges, M., & Insabella, G. M. (1998). What matters? What does not? Five perspectives on the association between marital transactions and children's adjustment. *American Psychologist*, 53(2), 167–184.

Hetherington, E. M., & Kelly, J. (2002). *For better or worse: Divorce reconsidered*. New York: Norton.

Hinshaw, S., & Anderson, C. (1996). Conduct and oppositional defiant disorders. In E. J. Mash (Ed.), *Child psychopathology* (pp. 113–149). New York: Guilford.

Hoek, H. W. (1991). The incidence and prevalence of anorexia nervosa and bulimia nervosa in primary care. *Psychological Medicine*, 21, 455–460.

Hofferth, S. (2001). How American children spend their time. *Journal of Marriage and the Family*, 63, 295–308.

Hogan, R., Mankin, D., Conway, J., & Fox, S. (1970). Personality correlates of undergraduate marijuana use. *Journal of Consulting and Clinical Psychology*, 35, 58–63.

Hughes, D. (1998). *Building the bonds of attachment*. Northvale, NJ: Jason Aronson.

Hussong, A. M. (2000). Perceived peer context and adolescent adjustment. *Journal of Research on Adolescence*, 10(4), 391–415.

Impett, E., & Peplau, L. (2003). Sexual compliance: Gender, motivational, and relationship perspectives. *Journal of Sex Research*, 40(1), 87–100.

Jackson, D., & King, A. (2004). Gender differences in the effects of oppositional behavior on teacher ratings of ADHD symptoms. *Journal of Abnormal Child Psychology*, 32(2), 215–223.

James, B. (1989). *Treating traumatized children*. New York: Free Press.

Johnson, K. (1998). *Trauma in the lives of children*. Alameda, CA: Hunter House.

Johnson, J., Cohen, P., Gould, M., Kasen, S., Brown, J., & Brook, J. (2002). Childhood adversities, interpersonal difficulties, and risk for suicide attempts during late adolescence and early adulthood. *Archives of General Psychiatry, 59,* 741–749.

Johnston, J., Kline, M., & Tschann, J. (1989). Ongoing post-divorce conflict: Effects on children of joint custody and frequent access. *American Journal of Orthopsychiatry, 59*(4), 576–592.

Johnston, L., O'Malley, P., & Bachman, J. (2003). *National survey results on drug use from the Monitoring of the Future study, 1975–2002. Volume 1: Secondary school students (NIH publication no. 03-5375).* Bethesda, MD: National Institute on Drug Abuse.

Johnston, L., O'Malley, P. Bachman, J., & Schulenberg, J. (2005, December 19). *Teen drug use is down but progress halts among youngest teens.* Ann Arbor, MI: University of Michigan News and Information Services.

Joshi, P. K., & Rosenberg, L. A. (1997). Children's behavioral response to residential treatment. *Journal of Clinical Psychology, 53,* 567–573.

Juang, L., & Silbereisen, R, (2002). The relationship between adolescent academic capability beliefs, parenting, and school grades. *Journal of Adolescence, 25*(1), 3–18.

Kagan, R. (2004). Rebuilding attachments with traumatized children. New York: Haworth.

Kalter, N. (1990). *Growing up with divorce.* New York: Free Press.

Kann, R., & Hanna, F. (2000). Disruptive behavior disorders in children and adolescents: How do girls differ from boys? *Journal of Counseling and Development, 78*(3), 267–276.

Kaplowitz, P., & Oberfield, S. (1999). Re-examination of the age limit for defining when puberty is precocious in girls in the United States: Implications for evaluation and treatment. *Pediatrics, 104*(4), 936–941.

Kataoka, S., Zhang, L., & Wells, K. (2002). Unmet need for mental health care among U.S. children: Variation by ethnicity and insurance status. *American Journal of Psychiatry, 159*(9), 1548–1555.

Katz, R. (2000). Explaining girls' and women's crime and resistance in the context of their victimization experiences. *Violence Against Women, 6,* 633–660.

Kazdin, A. (1995). *Conduct disorders in childhood and adolescence* (2nd ed). Thousand Oaks, CA: Sage.

Kazdin, A. (1998). Conduct disorders. In R. J. Morris & T. R. Kratochwill (Eds.), *The practice of child psychotherapy* (pp. 199–230). Boston: Allyn and Bacon.

Kearns, R. (1998, May). Finding the profit in at-risk kids. *Youth Today, 1,* 10–11.

Keenan, K., & Shaw, D. (1997). Developmental and social influences on young girls' early problem behavior. *Psychological Bulletin, 121,* 95–113.

Keiley, M. (2002). Attachment and affect regulation: A framework for family treatment of conduct disorder. *Family Process, 41*(3), 447–493.

Kendler, K., Bulik, C., Silberg, J. Hettema, J., Myers, J., & Prescott, C. (2000). Childhood sexual abuse and adult psychiatric and substance use disorders in women: An epidemiological and co-twin control analysis. *Archives of General Psychiatry, 57,* 953–959.

Kernberg, P., & Chazan, S. (1991). *Children with conduct disorders: A psychotherapy manual.* New York: Basic Books.

Kilbourne, J. (1999). *Deadly persuasion: Why women and girls must fight the addictive power of advertising.* New York: Free Press.

Kindlon, D. (2006). *Alpha girls: Understanding the new American girl and how she is changing the world.* New York: Rodale.

King, N., Hamilton, D., & Ollendick, T. (1994). *Children's phobias: A behavioural perspective.* Oxford, UK: Wiley.

Kipke, M. (Ed.) (1999). *Risks and opportunities: Synthesis of studies on adolescence.* Washington, DC: National Research Council and Institute of Medicine.

Klein, R., & Pine, D. (2001). Anxiety disorders. In M. Rutter, E. Taylor, & M. Hersov (Eds.), *Child and adolescent psychiatry* (3rd ed) (pp. 160–182). New York: Blackwell Scientific.

Koplewicz, H. (2002). *More than moody.* New York: Putnam.

Krajicek, D. (1999, November). Boot camps lose early swagger. *Youth Today, 8*(10), 1.

Kruesi, M., Hibbs, E., Zahn, T., Keysor, C., Hamburger, S., Bartko, J. et al. (1992). A 2-year prospective follow-up study of children with disruptive behavior disorders. *Archives of General Psychiatry, 49,* 429–435.

Kutash, K., & Rivera, V. (1995). Effectiveness of children's mental health services: A review of the literature. *Education and Treatment of Children, 18*(4), 443–488.

Laursen, B. (Ed.) (1993). New directions for child development. *Close friendships in adolescence.* San Francisco: Jossey-Bass.

Laursen, B., & Brasler, P. (2002). Is harm reduction a viable choice for kids enchanted with drugs? *Reclaiming Children and Youth, 11*(3) 181–183.

Laursen, B., & Mooney, K. (2005). Why do friends matter? *Human Development*, 48(5), 323–326.

Lee, V., Croninger, R., Linn, E., & Chen, X. (1996). The culture of sexual harassment in secondary schools. *American Educational Research Journal*, 33, 383–417.

Lee, V., & Smith, J. (1995). Effects of school restructuring and size on early gains in achievement and engagement. *Sociology of Education*, 68(4), 241–270.

Levine, M. (2005). *Ready or not, here life comes.* New York: Simon & Schuster.

Levitt, L. (1994). What is the therapeutic value of camping for emotionally disturbed girls? *Women and Therapy*, 15(3), 129–142.

Lewinsohn, P. M., Hops, H., Roberts, R. E., Seeley, J. R., & Andrews, J. A. (1993). Adolescent psychopathology: 1. Prevalence and incidence of depression and other DSM-III-R disorders in high school students. *Journal of Abnormal Psychology*, 102, 133–144.

Lewinsohn, P. M., Rohde, P., & Seeley, J. R. (1996). Adolescent suicidal ideation and attempts: Prevalence, risk factors, and clinical implications. *Clinical Psychology Science and Practice*, 3, 25–46.

Linehan, M. (1993). *Cognitive behavioral treatment of borderline personality disorder.* New York: Guilford.

Litt, I. F. (1997). *The Commonwealth Fund Commission on Women's Health.* NY: The Commonwealth Fund.

Lloyd, E. (1998). Self-mutilation in a community sample of adolescents. *Dissertation Abstracts International*, 58(9-B).

Loeber, R., Burke, J., Lahey, B., Winters, A., & Zera, M. (2000). Oppositional defiant and conduct disorder: A review of the past 10 years, part I. *Journal of the American Academy of Child and Adolescent Psychiatry*, 39, 1468–1484.

Logan, T. (2003). Victimization and substance abuse among women: Contributing factors, interventions, and implications. *Review of General Psychology*, 6(4), 325–397.

Loredo, C., Reid, A., & Deaux, K. (1995). Judgments and definitions of sexual harassment by high school students. *Sex Roles*, 32, 29–45.

Louv, R. (2005). *Last child in the woods: Saving our children from nature deficit disorder.* New York: Workman.

Maccoby, E. (1998). *The two sexes: Growing up apart, coming together.* Cambridge, MA: Harvard University Press.

Machoian, L. (2001). Cutting voices. *Journal of Psychosocial Nursing,* 39(11), 22–29.

MacRobbie, A. (2000). *Feminism and youth culture.* London: Macmillan.

Maerlander, A., Isquith, P., Racusin, R., Sengupta, A., & Straus, M. (2004). Self-regulation, behavior, and emotional function in children in foster care. *Proceedings of the Annual INS Conference.* Baltimore, MD.

Maine, M. (2000). *Body wars: Making peace with women's bodies.* Carlsbad, CA: Gürze Books.

Males, M. (1996). *The scapegoat generation: America's war on adolescents.* Monroe, ME: Common Courage Press.

Males, M. (1999). *Framing youth: 10 myths about the next generation.* Monroe, ME: Common Courage Press.

Males, M. (2006). And now . . . superpredatrixes?: More fact-bending hype about the alleged spike in girl violence. *Youth Today, 15*(5), 34.

March, J., Silva, S., Petrycki, S., Curry, J., Wells, K., Fairbank, J., et al. (2004). Fluoxetine, cognitive-behavioral therapy, and their combination for adolescents with depression: Treatment for Adolescents with Depression Study (TADS) randomized control trial. *Journal of the American Medical Association, 292*(7), 807–820.

Martin, A. (Ed.) (2003). *Pediatric psychopharmacology: Principles and practice.* New York: Oxford University Press.

Martin, K. (1994). *Puberty, sexuality, and the self: Gender differences at adolescence.* University of California Dissertation Services.

Martin, C., & Winters, K. (1998). Diagnosis and assessment of alcohol use disorders among adolescents. *Alcohol Health and Research World, 22,* 95–105.

Marx, J. (1988). An outdoor adventure counseling program for adolescents. *Social Work, 33*(6), 517–520.

Mason, M., & Gibbs, J. (1992). Patterns of adolescent psychiatric hospitalization: Implications for social policy. *American Journal of Orthopsychiatry, 62*(3), 447–457.

McArney, E., Kreipe, R., Orr, D., & Comerci, G. (Eds.) (1992). *Textbook of adolescent medicine.* Philadelphia: W. B. Saunders.

McBride-Murray, V. (1996). Inner city girls of color: Unmarried, sexually active nonmothers. In B. J. Ross Leadbeater & N. Way (Eds.), *Urban girls: Resisting stereotypes, creating identities* (pp. 272–290). New York: New York University Press.

McDaniel, J., Purcell, D., & D'Augelli, A. (2001). The relationship between sexual orientation and risk for suicide: Research findings and future directions for research and preventions. *Suicide and Life-Threatening Behavior, 31,* 84–105.

McEwin, C., Dickenson, T., & Jenkins, D. (1996). *America's middle schools: Practices and progress—a 25-year perspective.* Columbus, OH: National Middle School Association.

McHale, S., Kim, J., Whiteman, S., & Crouter, A. (2004). Links between sex-typed time use in middle childhood and gender development in early adolescence. *Developmental Psychology, 40,* 861–881.

McKnight, L., & Loper, A. (2002). The effect of risk and resilience factors in the prediction of delinquency in adolescent girls. *School Psychology International, 23*(2), 186–198.

McLanahan, S., & Sandefur, G. (1994). *Growing up with a single parent: What hurts, what helps?* Cambridge, MA: Harvard University Press.

McMahon, R., & Wells, K. (1998). Conduct problems. In E. J. Mash & R. A. Barkley (Eds.), *Treatment of childhood disorders* (pp. 111–207). New York: Guilford.

McNeill, P. (2000, April 14). *Smaller schools and learning communities: The wave of the future?* Paper presented at the 2000 American Youth Policy Forum, Washington, DC. Retrieved September 10, 2005, from www.aypf.org/forum-briefs/2000/fb04100.htm

Mello, D., Pechansky, F., Inciardi, J., & Surratt, H. (1997). Participant observation of a therapeutic community model for offenders in drug treatment. *Journal of Drug Issues, 27*(2), 299–314.

Merten, D. (1997). The meaning of meanness: Popularity, competition, and conflict among junior high school girls. *Sociology of Education, 70,* 175–191.

Messina, M., Wishe, E., & Nemes, S. (2000). Predictors of treatment outcomes of men and women admitted to a therapeutic community. *American Journal of Drug and Alcohol Abuse, 26,* 207–227.

Metz, H. (1991). Kids in the cuckoo's nest. *Progressive, 62,* 22–25.

Miller, D. (1994). *Women who hurt themselves: A book of hope and understanding.* New York: Basic Books.

Miller, J. B. (1976). *Toward a new psychology of women.* Boston: Beacon Press.

Moffitt, T., Caspi, A., Rutter, M., & Silva, P. (2001). *Sex differences in antisocial behavior.* Cambridge, UK: Cambridge University Press.

Molina, J., & Duarte, R. (2006). Risk determinants of suicide attempts among adolescents. *American Journal of Economics and Sociology 65*(2), 407–434.

Moore, D., & Saunders, B. (1991). Youth drug use and the prevention of problems. *International Journal on Drug Policy, 2*(5), 13–15.

Moses, T. (2000). Attachment theory and residential treatment: A study of staff-client relationships. *American Journal of Orthopsychiatry, 70*(4), 474–490.

Mosher, W., Chandra, A., & Jones, J. (2005). *Sexual behavior and selected health measures: Men and women 15–44 years of age, United States, 2002.* Washington, DC: U.S. Department of Health and Human Services, National Center for Health Statistics.

Mott, F. L. (1994). Sons, daughters, and fathers' absence: Differentials in father-leaving probabilities and in home environments. *Journal of Family Issues, 15*, 97–128.

MTA Cooperative Group. (1999). A 14-month randomized clinical trial of treatment strategies for attention deficit/hyperactivity disorder. *Archives of General Psychiatry, 56*(12), 1073–1086.

Muehlenhard, C., & Peterson, Z. (2005). Wanting and not wanting sex: The missing discourse of ambivalence. *Feminism & Psychology, 15*(1), 15–20.

Mufson, L., Weissman, M., Moreau, D., & Garfinkel, R. (1999). Efficacy of interpersonal psychotherapy for depressed adolescents. *Archives of General Psychiatry, 56*, 573–579.

Myers, J., Sweeney, T., & Witmer, J. (2000). The Wheel of Wellness counseling for wellness: A holistic model for treatment planning. *Journal of Counseling and Development, 78*, 251–266.

Nadeau, K. (2005). *Is your daughter a daydreamer, tomboy, or "chatty Kathy?"* Retrieved October 13, 2006, from www.addvance.com/help/women/daydreamer.html

Nadeau, K., Littman, E., & Quinn, P. (1999). *Understanding girls with AD/HD.* Washington, DC: Advantage Books.

Najavits, L., Weiss, R., & Shaw, S. (1997). The link between substance abuse and posttraumatic stress disorder in women: A research review. *American Journal of Addictions, 6*, 273–283.

National Association of Psychiatric Health Systems. (2005). *Annual survey report.* Washington, DC: Author.

National Center on Addiction and Substance Abuse. (2003). *The National survey of American attitudes on substance abuse VIII: Teens and parents.* New York: The National Center on Addiction and Substance Abuse at Columbia University.

National Council for Research on Women. (2002). *Girls report: Executive summary*. Washington, DC: Author.

National Institutes of Health. (2004). *Preventing violence and related health-risking social behaviors in adolescents*. Washington, DC: Author.

Newes-Adeyi, G., Chen, C., Williams, G., & Faden, V. (2005, October). *Surveillance report #74: Trends in underage drinking in the United States, 1991–2003*. Washington, DC: National Institute on Alcohol Abuse and Alcoholism.

Newman, S., Fox, J. A., Flynn, E., & Christeson, W. (2000). *America's after-school choice: The prime time for juvenile crime, or youth enrichment and achievement*. Retrieved March 5, 2005, from www.fight crime.org/reports/as2000.pdf

Nolen-Hoeksema, S. (1994). An interactive model for the emergence of gender differences in depression in adolescence. *Journal of Research on Adolescence, 4*, 519–534.

Norman, E. (1997). New directions: Looking at psychological dimensions in resiliency enhancement. In E. Norman (Ed.), *Drug-free youth* (pp. 73–93). New York: Garland-O'Neil.

O'Dea, J. (2006). Self concept, self esteem, and body weight in adolescent females. *Journal of Health Psychology, 11*(4), 599–611.

Odgers, C., & Moretti, M. (2002). Aggressive and antisocial girls: Research update and challenges. *International Journal of Forensic Mental Health, 1*(2), 103–119.

Office of Justice Programs. (1998). *Women in criminal justice: A twenty-year update*. Retrieved October 15, 2005, from www.ojp.usdoj.gov/reports/98/Guides/wcjs98/

Office of Juvenile Justice and Delinquency Prevention. (1999, July). *Report to Congress on juvenile violence research*. Washington, DC: U.S. Department of Justice.

Ollivier, D. (2000, August 30). *Whose crisis is this, anyway?* Retrieved September 21, 2005, from www.archive.salon.com/mwt/feature/2000/08/30/parent_crisis/index2.html

Orenstein, P. (1994). *Schoolgirls: Young women, self-esteem, and the confidence gap*. New York: Doubleday.

Owens, L., Slee, P., & Shute, R. (2001). Victimization among teenage girls: What can be done about indirect harassment? In J. Juvonen & S. Graham (Eds.), *Peer harassment in school: The plight of the vulnerable and the victimized* (pp. 215–241). New York: Guilford.

Pakaslahti, L., Karjalainen, A., & Keltikangas-Jaervinen, L. (2002). Relationships between adolescent prosocial problem-solving strategies, prosocial behaviour, and social acceptance. *International Journal of Behavioral Development, 26*, 137–144.

Palladino, G. (1996). *Teenagers: An American history.* New York: Basic Books.

Paquette J., & Underwood, M. (1999). Young adolescents' experiences of peer victimization: Gender differences in accounts of social and physical aggression. *Merrill Palmer Quarterly, 45*, 233–258.

Parenting Teens. (2003). *Options for troubled teens and at-risk youth.* Retrieved November 5, 2006, from www.parentteen.com/troubled_teen_options.html

Pate, R., Trost, S., Lenn, S., & Dowda, M. (2000). Sports participation and health-related behaviors among U.S. youth. *Archives of Pediatrics and Adolescent Medicine, 154*(9), 904–911.

Patten, P. (1999). Divorce and children. Part I: An interview with Robert Hughes, Jr., Ph.D. *ParentNews, 5*(5), 1–5.

Patterson, G., Reid, J., & Dishion, T. (1992). *Antisocial boys.* Eugene, OR: Castalia Press.

Pearce, J., & Pezzot-Pearce, T. (1997). *Psychotherapy of abused and neglected children.* New York: Guilford.

Pediatric Research Equity Act of 2003, Pub. L. No. 108–155, Stat. 650 (2003).

Pennington, B. F., Bennetto, L., McAleer, O. K., & Roberts, R. J., Jr. (1995). Executive functions and working memory: Theoretical and measurement issues. In G. R. Lyon & N. A. Krasnegor (Eds.), *Attention, memory, and executive function* (pp. 327–348). Baltimore, MD: Paul H. Brookes.

Peterson, M., Ellenberg, D., & Crossan, S., (2003). Body-image perceptions: Reliability of a BMI-based Silhouette Matching Test. *American Journal of Health Behavior, 27*(4), 355–363.

Phelps, J., Belsky, J., & Crnic, K. (1998). Earned security, daily stress, and parenting: A comparison of five alternative models. *Development and Psychopathology, 10*, 21–38.

Philip, K., & Hendry, L. (1996). Young people and mentoring: Towards a typology. *Journal of Adolescence, 19*, 189–207.

Piaget, J. (1954). *The construction of reality in the child.* New York: Basic Books.

Pike, K. (1995). Bulemic symptomatology in high school girls: Toward a model of cumulative risk. *Psychology of Women Quarterly, 19*, 373–396.

Pipher, M. (1994). *Reviving Ophelia.* New York: Putnam.

Poole, N., & Dell, C. (2005). *Girls, women, and substance use.* Ottawa, ON: Canadian Centre on Substance Abuse.

Porter, N. (2005) Mental health diagnosis and the rights of children. *Child and Family Policy and Practice Review, 1*(1), 1–5.

Pottick, K., McAlpine, D., & Andelman, R. (2000). Changing patterns of psychiatric inpatient care for children and adolescents in general hospitals: 1988–1995. *American Journal of Psychiatry, 157*(8), 1267–1273.

Pottick, K., Warner, L., & Yoder, K. (2005). Youths living away from families in the U.S. mental health system. *Journal of Behavioral Health Services and Research, 32*(3), 264–281.

Press, E., & Washburn, J. (2002, December). The at-risk youth industry. *The Atlantic Monthly, 290*(5), 38–41.

Putallaz, M., & Bierman, K. (2004). *Aggression, antisocial behavior, and violence among girls: A developmental perspective.* New York: Guilford.

Putnam, F. (2003). Ten-year research update review: Child sexual abuse. *Journal of the American Academy of Child and Adolescent Psychiatry, 42,* 269–278.

Putnam, R. (2000). *Bowling alone: The collapse and revival of American community.* New York: Simon and Schuster.

Racusin, R., Maerlender, A., Sengupta, A., Isquith, P., & Straus, M. (2005). Psychosocial treatment of children in foster care: A review. *Community Mental Health Journal, 41*(2), 199–221.

Range, L., Campbell, C., Kovac, S., Marion-Jones, M., Aldridge, H., Kogos, S. et al. (2002). No-suicide contracts: An overview and recommendations. *Death Studies, 26,* 51–74.

Reid, L., & Krasnegor, N. (1996). *Attention, memory, and executive function.* Baltimore, MD: Paul H. Brookes.

Remafedi, G., Resnick, M., Blum, R., & Harris, L. (1992). Demography of sexual orientation in adolescents. *Pediatrics, 89*(4), 714–721.

Remillard, A., & Lamb, S. (2005). Adolescent girls' coping with relational aggression. *Sex Roles: A Journal of Research, 53*(3), 221–229.

Rhee, S., & Waldman, I. (2002). Genetic and environmental influences on antisocial behavior: A meta-analysis of twin and adoption studies. *Psychological Bulletin, 128,* 490–529.

Rice, P. (1996). *The adolescent.* Boston: Allyn and Bacon.

Rinaldi, R., Steindler, E., Wilford, B., & Goodwin, D. (1988). Clarification and standardization of substance abuse terminology. *Journal of the American Medical Association, 259,* 555–557.

Robins, L., & Regier, D. (1991). *Psychiatric disorders in America: The epidemiological catchment area study.* New York: Free Press.

Rodham, K., Hawton, K., & Evans, E. (2005). Deliberate self harm in adolescents: The importance of gender. *Psychiatric Times, 22*(1), 36.

Rodin, J. (1992, January/February). Body mania: Insights of body image. *Psychology Today, 25*(1), 56–61.

Rogers, A. (1993). Voice, play, and a practice of ordinary courage in women's lives. *Harvard Educational Review, 63,* 3.

Rogers, L., Resnick, M. D., Mitchell, J. E., & Blum, R. W. (1997). The relationship between socioeconomic status and eating-disordered behavior in a community sample of adolescent girls. *International Journal of Eating Disorders, 22,* 15–23.

Roisman, G., Padron, E., Sroufe, L., & Egeland, B. (2002). Earned-secure attachment status in retrospect and prospect. *Child Development, 73*(4), 1204–1219.

Rosario, M., Meyer-Bahlburg, H., Hunter, J., Exner, T., et al. (1996). The psychosexual development of urban lesbian, gay, and bisexual youths. *The Journal of Sex Research, 33*(2), 113–126.

Rosenfeld, A., & Wise, N. (2000). *The over-scheduled child.* New York: St. Martin's Press.

Rossello, J., & Bernal, G. (1999). The efficacy of cognitive-behavioral and interpersonal treatments for depression in Puerto Rican adolescents. *Journal of Consulting and Clinical Psychology, 67,* 734–745.

Russell, K., & Hendee, J. (1999). Wilderness therapy as an intervention and treatment for adolescents with behavioral problems. In A. Watson, G. Aplet, & J. Hendee (Eds.), *Personal, societal, and ecological values of wilderness: 6th World Wilderness Congress Proceedings on Research Management and Allocation* (Vol. 2). Ogden, UT: USDA Forest Service, Rocky Mountain Research Station.

Rutter, M. (2001). Psychosocial adversity: Risk, resilience, and recovery. In J. M. Richman & M. W. Fraser (Eds.), *The contexts of youth violence: Risk, resilience, and recovery* (pp. 13–41). Westport, CT: Praeger.

Ryan, C., & Futtermann, D. (2002). Lesbian and gay adolescents: Identity development. *The Prevention Researcher, 8,* 1.

Rys, G., & Bear, G. G. (1997). Relational aggression and peer relations: Gender and developmental issues. *Merrill-Palmer Quarterly, 43*(1), 87–106.

Sadker, M., & Sadker, D. (1994). *Failing at fairness: How America's schools cheat girls.* New York: Scribner.

Sartor, C., & Youniss, J. (2002). The relationship between positive parental involvement and identity achievement during adolescence. *Adolescence, 37*(146), 221–234.

Satcher, D. (1999). *Mental health: A report of the surgeon general.* Washington, DC: U.S. Public Health Service.

Savin-Williams, R. C. (1995). Lesbian, gay male, and bisexual adolescents. In A. R. D'Augelli & C. J. Patterson (Eds.), *Lesbian, gay, and bisexual identities over the lifespan: Psychological perspectives* (pp. 167–189). New York: Oxford University Press.

Schaible, N. (2001). PACE Center for Girls: Gender-specific prevention. *The Link, Child Welfare League of America, 1*(3), 1–7.

Schneider, B., & Stevenson, D. (1999). *The ambitious generation: America's teenagers, motivated but directionless.* New Haven, CT: Yale University Press.

Schonert-Reichl, K., & Mullen, J. (1996). Correlates of help-seeking in adolescence. *Journal of Youth and Adolescence, 25,* 705–731.

Schor, J. (2004). *Born to buy.* New York: Simon and Schuster.

Sealock, M., Gottfredson, D., & Gallagher, C. (1997). Drug treatment for juvenile offenders: Some good and bad news. *Journal of Research in Crime and Delinquency, 34*(2), 210–236.

Select Committee on Children, Youth, and Families. (1989). *U.S. children and their families: Current conditions and recent trends.* Washington, DC: U.S. House of Representatives.

Seltzer, J. A., & Brandreth, Y. (1994). What fathers say about involvement with children after separation. *Journal of Family Issues, 15,* 49–77.

Shedler, J., & Block, J. (1990). Adolescent drug use and psychological health: A longitudinal study. *American Psychologist, 45,* 612–630.

Sherwood, N., Neumark-Sztainer, D., Story, M., Bevhring, T., & Resnick, M. (2002). Weight-related sports involvement in girls: Who is at risk for disordered eating? *American Journal of Health Promotion, 16,* 341–344.

Shirk, S., & Russell, R. (1996). *Change processes in child psychotherapy.* New York: Guilford.

Shroff, H., & Thompson, J. (2006). Peer influences, body image dissatisfaction, eating dysfunction, and self-esteem in adolescent girls. *Journal of Health Psychology, 11*(4), 533–551.

Shumow, L., & Lomax, R. (2002). Parental efficacy: Predictor of parenting behavior and adolescent outcomes. *Parenting: Science and practice, 2*(2), 127–150.

Siegel, D. (1999). *The developing mind*. New York: Guilford.

Siegel, D., & Hartzell, M. (2003). *Parenting from the inside out*. New York: Tarcher.

Silverthorn, P., & Frick, P. (1999). Developmental pathways to antisocial behavior: The delayed onset pathway in girls. *Development and Psychopathology, 11*, 101–126.

Simeon, D., Stanley, B., Frances, A., Mann, J., Winchel, R., & Stanley, M. (1992). Self mutilation in personality disorders: Psychological and biological correlates. *American Journal of Psychiatry, 149*, 221–226.

Simmons, R. (2002). *Odd girl out: The hidden culture of aggression in girls*. New York: Harcourt.

Simons, R. L. (Ed.) (1996). *Understanding differences between divorced and intact families: Stress, interaction, and child outcome*. Thousand Oaks, CA: Sage.

Sisk, J. (2006). *Encyclopedia of children's health: Alternative schools*. Retrieved December 1, 2006, from www.eNotes.com/childrens-health-encyclopedia

Smith, G., Cox, D., & Saradjian, J. (1999). *Women and self-harm: Understanding, coping, and healing from self-mutilation*. New York: Routledge.

Snarey, J. (1993). *How fathers care for the next generation*. Cambridge, MA: Harvard University Press.

Snyder, H., & Sickmund, M. (1999, September). *Juvenile offenders and victims: 1999 national report*. Washington, DC: National Center for Juvenile Justice.

Solomon, Y., & Farrand, J. (1996). "Why don't you do it properly?": Young women who self injure. *Journal of Adolescence, 19*, 111–119.

Sommers, C. H. (2000). *The war against boys: How misguided feminism is harming our young men*. New York: Simon & Schuster.

Spear, L. P. (2000). The adolescent brain and age-related behavioral manifestations. *Neuroscience and Biobehavioral Reviews, 24*, 417–463.

Sroufe, L., Egland, B., Carlson, E., & Collins, W. A. (2005). *The development of the person: The Minnesota study of risk and adaptation from birth to adulthood*. New York: Guilford.

Stanhope, R., Wilks, Z., & Hamill, G. (1994). Failure to grow: Lack of food or lack of love? *Professional Care of Mother and Child, 4*, 234–237.

Stanton-Salazar, R. (1997). A social capital framework for understanding the socialization of racial minority children and youths. *Harvard Educational Review, 65*, 145–162.

Stark, K., Dempsey, M., & Christopher, J. (1993). Depressive disorders. In R. T. Ammerman, C. Last, & M. Hersen (Eds.), *Handbook of prescriptive treatments for children and adolescents* (pp. 115–143). Boston: Allyn & Bacon.

Steinberg, L., Brown, B., & Dornbusch, S. (1997). *Beyond the classroom.* New York: Simon and Schuster.

Stepp, L. S. (1999, July 8). Unsettling new fad alarms parents: Middle school oral sex. *The Washington Post,* p. A1.

Stern, D. (1985). *The interpersonal world of the infant.* New York: Basic Books.

Stewart, S. (2004). *HIV/AIDS in women.* Retrieved February 27, 2006, from www.thedoctorwillseeyounow.com/articles/womens_health/aids.14/

Strauch, B. (2003). *The primal teen: What the new discoveries about the teenage brain tell us about our kids.* New York: Doubleday.

Straus, M. B. (1988). *Abuse and victimization across the lifespan.* Baltimore, MD: Johns Hopkins University Press.

Straus, M. B. (1994). *Violence in the lives of adolescents.* New York: Norton.

Straus, M. B. (1999). *No-talk therapy for children and adolescents.* New York: Norton.

Stroul, B. A., & Friedman, R. M. (1996). *A system of care for children and adolescents with severe emotional disturbance* (Rev. ed.). Washington, DC: National Technical Assistance Center for Child Mental Health, Georgetown University Child Development Center.

Substance Abuse and Mental Health Services Administration. (2006). *Results from the 2005 National Survey on Drug Use and Health: National Findings.* Rockville, MD: Office of Applied Studies, NSDUH Series H-30, DHHS Publication No. SMA 06-4194.

Suyemoto, K. L., & Kountz, X. (2000). Self-mutilation. *The Prevention Researcher,* 7(4), 1–4.

Suyemoto, K. L., & Macdonald, M. L. (1995). Self-cutting in female adolescents. *Psychotherapy,* 32, 162–171.

Szalavitz, M. (2006). *Help at any cost: How the troubled teen industry cons parents and hurts kids.* New York: Riverhead Books.

Taffel, R. (2001). *The second family.* New York: St. Martin's Press.

Taffel, R. (2005). *Breaking through to teens.* New York: Guilford.

Tarrant, D. (2005, May 11). Seclusion at therapeutic boarding schools unlocks hope for troubled kids. *The Dallas Morning News,* p. A10.

Teens in Crisis. (2001). *Is your teen on the wrong track?* Retrieved March 15, 2006, from www.troubledteens.org/34%20Warning%20Signs.htm

Terr, L. (1991). Childhood traumas: An outline and an overview. *American Journal of Psychiatry, 148*, 10–20.

Thomas, J., & Daubman, K. (2001). The relationship between friendship quality and self-esteem in adolescent boys and girl. *Sex Roles, 45*(1), 53–65.

Thompson, J., Heinberg, L., Altabe, M., & Tantleff-Dunn, S. (1999). *Exacting beauty*. Washington, DC: American Psychological Association.

Thorne, B. (1993). *Gender play: Girls and boys in school*. New Brunswick, NJ: Rutgers University Press.

Timmons-Mitchell, J., Brown, C., Schulz, C., Webster, S., Underwood, L., & Semple, W. (1997). Comparing the mental health needs of female and male incarcerated juvenile delinquents. *Behavioral Science Law, 15*, 195–202.

Tolman, D. (1994). Doing desire: Adolescent girls' struggle for/with sexuality. *Gender and Society, 8*(3), 324–342.

Tolman, D., & Debold, E. (1994). Conflicts of body and image: Female adolescents, desire, and the no-body body. In P. Fallon, M. Katzman, & S. Wooley (Eds.), *Feminist perspectives on eating disorders* (pp. 301–317). New York: Guilford.

Tolman, D. (2001). Female adolescent sexuality: An argument for a developmental perspective on the new view of women's sexual problems. *Women & Therapy, 24*(1/2), 195–209.

Tomm, K. (1988). Intensive interviewing: Part III: Intending to ask linear, circular, strategic, or reflexive questions? *Family Process, 27*(1), 1–15.

Topping, A. (2007, March 9). *Government drugs policy does not work, says report*. Retrieved March 30, 2007, from www.guardian.co.uk/drugs/Story/0,,2029756,00.html

Twenge, J. M. (2000). The age of anxiety? Birth cohort changes in anxiety and neuroticism, 1952–1993. *Journal of Personality and Social Psychology, 79*(6), 1007–1021.

Ullman, S., & Brecklin, L. (2003). Sexual assault history and health related outcomes in a national sample of women. *Psychology of Women Quarterly, 27*(1), 46–57.

Underwood, M. (2003). *Social aggression among girls*. New York: Guilford.

Updegraff, K., McHale, S., Crouter, A., & Kupanoff, K. (2001). Parents' involvement in adolescents' peer relationships: A comparison of mothers' and fathers' roles. *Journal of Marriage and the Family, 63*(3), 655–668.

U.S. Bureau of the Census. (1997). *Statistical abstracts of the United States: 1997.* Washington, DC: Author.

U.S. Centers for Disease Control and Prevention. (2006). Youth risk behavior surveillance—United States, 2005. *Morbidity and Mortality Weekly Report, 55,* 1–112.

U.S. Department of Education. (n.d.). Individuals with Disabilities Education Act (IDEA), 1997. Retrieved March 1, 2006, from www.ed.gov/offices/OSERS/Policy/IDEA/index.html

U.S. Department of Health and Human Services. (1999). *Mental Health: A report of the Surgeon General—Executive Summary.* Rockville, MD: U.S. Department of Health and Human Services, Substance Abuse and Mental Health Services Administration, Center for Mental Heath Services, National Institutes of Health, National Institute of Mental Health.

U.S. General Accounting Office. (2003). *Child welfare and juvenile justice: Federal agencies could play a stronger role in helping states reduce the number of children placed solely to obtain mental health services* (GAO-03-397). Washington, DC: Author.

van der Kolk, B. (1989). The compulsion to repeat the trauma: Re-enactment, revictimization, and masochism. *Psychiatric Clinics of North America, 12,* 389–411.

van der Kolk, B., Perry, C., & Herman, J. (1991). Childhood origins of self-destructive behavior. *American Journal of Psychiatry, 148,* 1665–1671.

van der Kolk, B. (2005). Developmental trauma disorder: Toward rational diagnosis for children with complex trauma histories. *Psychiatric Annals, 35*(5), 401–408.

Vasquez, M., & de las Fuentes, C. (1999). American-born, Asian, African, Latina, and American Indian adolescent girls: Challenges and strengths. In N. Johnson, M. Roberts, & J. Worrell (Eds.), *Beyond appearance: A new look at adolescent girls.* (pp. 151–174). Washington, DC: American Psychological Association.

Vissing, Y. M., Straus, M. A., Gelles, R. J., & Harrop, J. W. (1991). Verbal aggression by parents and psychosocial problems of children. *Child Abuse and Neglect, 15,* 223–238.

Wagner, B., Silverman, M., & Martin, C. (2003). Family factors in youth suicidal behaviors. *American Behavioral Scientist, 46,* 1171–1191.

Waldron, H. (1997). Adolescent substance abuse and family therapy outcome: A review of randomized trials. In T. Ollendick & R. Prinz (Eds.), *Advances in Clinical Child Psychology, 19*, 199–234. New York: Plenum Press.

Walker, G. (1999). The policy climate for early adolescent initiatives. *When School Is Out*, 9(2), 147–150.

Waller, M., Hallfors, D., Halpern, C., Iritani, B., Ford, C., & Guo, G. (2006). Gender differences in associations between depressive symptoms and patterns of substance use and risky sexual behavior among a nationally representative sample of U.S. adolescents. *Archives of Women's Mental Health*, 9(3), 139–150.

Wallerstein, J., Lewis, J., & Blakeslee, S. (2000). *The unexpected legacy of divorce: A 25-year landmark study*. New York: Hyperion.

Way, N. (1996). Between experiences of betrayal and desire: Close friendships among urban adolescents. In B. Leadbeater & N. Way (Eds.), *Urban girls: Resisting stereotypes, creating identities*. New York: New York University Press.

Way, N., & Robinson, M. (2003). A longitudinal study of the effects of family, friends, and school experiences on the psychological adjustment of ethnic minority, low-SES adolescents. *Journal of Adolescent Research*, 18(4), 324–346.

Weinberger, D. (2001, March 10). A brain too young for good judgment [Op-ed]. *New York Times*, 13A.

Weinberger, D., Elevaq, B., & Gredd, J. (2005). *The adolescent brain: A work in progress*. Washington, DC: National Campaign to Prevent Teen Pregnancy.

Weissberg, R., Caplan, M., & Harwood, R. (1991). Promoting competent young people in competence-enhancing environments: A systems-based perspective on primary prevention. *Journal of Consulting and Clinical Psychology*, 59(6), 830–841.

Weithorn, L. (1988). Mental hospitalization of troublesome youth: An analysis of skyrocketing admission rates. *Stanford Law Review, 40*, 773–838.

Weller, E., Cook, S., Hendren, R., & Woolston, J. (1995). *On the use of mental health services by minors: Report to the American Psychiatric Association Task Force to Study the Use of Psychiatric Hospitalization of Minors: A review of statistical data on the use of mental health services by minors*. Washington, DC: American Psychiatric Association.

Werner, E. (1988). Individual differences, universal needs: A 30-year study of resilient, high-risk infants. *Birth to Three, 8*(4), 1–5.

White, M. (1986). Anorexia nervosa: A cybernetic perspective. In J. Elka-Harkaway (Ed.), *Eating disorders* (pp. 117–129). New York: Aspen.

White, M., & Epston, D. (1990). *Narrative means to therapeutic ends.* New York: Norton.

White House Conference on Teenagers. (2000, May 2). *Raising responsible and resourceful youth.* Washington, DC: Author.

Wilcox, B. (1999). Sexual obsessions: Public policy and adolescent girls. In N. Johnson, M. Roberts, & J. Worrell (Eds.), *Beyond appearance: A new look at adolescent girls* (pp. 333–354). Washington, DC: American Psychological Association.

Wilens, T. E., Biederman, J., Brown, S., Tanguay, S., Monuteaux, M., Blake, M. C., et al. (2002). Psychiatric comorbidity and functioning in clinically referred preschoolers and school aged youth with ADHD. *Journal of the American Academy of Child and Adolescent Psychiatry, 41,* 262–268.

Williams, B. (2000). The treatment of adolescent populations: An institutional vs. a wilderness setting. *Journal of Child and Adolescent Group Therapy, 10*(1), 47–56.

Williams, R., & Chang, S. (2000). A comprehensive and comparative review of adolescent substance abuse treatment outcome. *Clinical Psychology, 7,* 38–166.

Wilsnack, S., Vogeltanz, N., Klassen, A., & Harris, T. (1997). Childhood sexual abuse and women's substance abuse: National survey findings. *Journal of the Study of Alcohol, 58,* 264–271.

Wilson, J., Peebles, R., Hardy, K., & Litt, I. (2006). Surfing for thinness: A pilot study of pro-eating disorder site usage in adolescents with eating disorders. *Pediatrics, 118*(6), 1635–1643.

Wilson, R. (2006). Facing our worst fears. *Psychotherapy Networker, 30*(6), 54–59, 68.

Wiseman, R. (2002). *Queen bees and wannabes: Helping your daughter survive cliques, gossip, boyfriends, and other realities of adolescence.* New York: Random House.

Wolf, A. (1992). *Get out of my life but first could you drive me and Cheryl to the mall: A parent's guide to the new teenager.* New York: Farrar, Straus & Giroux.

Wolf, N. (1991). *The beauty myth.* New York: Morrow.

Wolf, N. (1994). Hunger. In. P. Fallon, M. Katzman, & S. Wooley (Eds.), *Feminist perspectives on eating disorders* (pp. 94–111). New York: Guilford.

Wozniak, J., Biederman, J., Kiely, K., Ablon, J., Faraone, S., Mundy, E. et al. (1995). Mania-like symptoms suggestive of childhood-onset bipolar disorder in clinically referred children. *Journal of the American Academy of Child and Adolescent Psychiatry, 34*, 1577–1583.

Wright, P. W., & Wright, P. D. (2004). *IDEA 2004.* Hartfield, VA: Harbor House Law Press.

Wylie, M. (1997). Food angst: Our trip to bountiful. *The Family Therapy Networker, 21*(3), 23–33.

Yip, K. (2005). A multi-dimensional perspective of adolescents' self-cutting. *Child and Adolescent Mental Health, 10*(2), 80–86.

Yurgelun-Todd, D. (1998). Adolescent brains. *American Psychological Association Monitor, 29*(8), 12.

Zahn-Waxler, C. (1993). Warriors and worriers: Gender and psychopathology. *Development and Psychopathology, 5*, 79–89.

Zahn-Waxler, C., Klimes-Dougan, B., & Slattery, M. (2000). Internalizing problems of childhood and adolescence: Prospects, pitfalls, and progress in understanding the development of anxiety and depression. *Development and Psychopathology, 12*, 443–466.

Zhao, Y. (2002, August 5). Wave of pupils lacking English strains schools. *New York Times.* Retrieved January 10, 2006, from www.nytimes.com.

Zoccolillo, M. (1993). Gender issues in conduct disorder. *Development and Psychopathology, 5*, 65–78.

Zoccolillo, M., Paquette, D., Azar, R., Cote, S., & Tremblay, R. (2004). Parenting as an important outcome of conduct disorder in girls. In M. Putallaz & K. Bierman (Eds.), *Aggression, antisocial behavior, and violence among girls: A developmental perspective* (pp. 242–261). New York: Guilford.

Zoccolillo, M., & Rogers, K. (1991). Characteristics and outcomes of hospitalized adolescent girls with conduct disorder. *Journal of the American Academy of Child and Adolescent Psychiatry, 30*, 973–981.

Zuckerman, D. (1999). Research watch. *Youth Today, 8*(10), 24.

INDEX